THE LOST WORLD
OF JAMES SMITHSON

THE LOST WORLD
OF JAMES SMITHSON

Science, Revolution,
and the Birth of the Smithsonian

Heather Ewing

BLOOMSBURY

First published in Great Britain 2007

Copyright © by Heather Ewing 2007

Maps by Reginald Piggott

Geneology chart by Leslie Robinson

Bloomsbury Publishing Plc
36 Soho Square
London W1D 3QY

www.bloomsbury.com

Bloomsbury Publishing, London, New York and Berlin

A CIP catalogue record for this book is available from the British Library

ISBN 9780747576532

10 9 8 7 6 5 4 3 2 1

Typeset by Hewer Text UK Ltd, Edinburgh.
Printed by in the United States of America by
Quebecor World Fairfield

for Chico
and
to the memory of Gene R. White
in token of gratitude

"Has Mr. what's his Name? been with you at Money hill? Mr Macie or Masy, originally written (I suspect) Mazy—a noun adjective from the Verb to amaze or make wonder!"

— Dr. William Drew to Lady Webster, 1797

CONTENTS

The Grand Tour
1791–1797

DENMARK Copenhagen

Baltic Sea

Tönning
Heligoland Kiel

PRUSSIA

Hamburg R. Elbe BRANDENBURG

HANOVER Berlin

Harz Mountains SAXONY

Kassel Meissen
Freiberg Dresden

Frankfurt BOHEMIA

Warsaw

POLAND

SILESIA

RUSSIA

Karlsruhe

Strasbourg BAVARIA R. Danube Vienna
AUSTRIA

Schemnitz

HUNGARY

Zurich
SWISS
CONFEDERATION

Bleiburg

Milan CISALPINE REPUBLIC VENETIA
Venice

R. Danube

EDMONTI

LIGURIA Genoa
Pisa Florence
Livorno TUSCANY
Siena
Monte Amiata
Elba

Adriatic Sea

OTTOMAN

EMPIRE

PAPAL
Lago di Bolsena
STATES
Rome

CORSICA

NAPLES

Naples
Vesuvius

SARDINIA

ean Sea

Palermo
SICILY

1865

The best blood of England runs through my veins.
On my father's side I am a Northumberland, on my
mother's I am related to kings, but this avails me
not; my name will live on in the memory of men
when the titles of the Northumberlands and Percys
are extinct or forgotten.

—James Smithson, undated

THE MORNING OF January 24, 1865, dawned bitterly cold in Washington. Nearly four years into the Civil War, the nation's capital—encircled with forts and filled with makeshift hospitals—was also battling a brutal winter. Business in the stores and counting rooms of Georgetown had come to a virtual standstill, customers unable to navigate roads buried in a deep frozen slush. The Potomac River bristled with ice, wreaking havoc with the transport steamers and delaying the mail boats. Near Indian Head a steamer carrying a load of mules sank after being cut through; by Jones Lighthouse the steamer *Sewanee* had run aground, the tugs unable to rescue her; and down at the city wharf the U.S. Transport *Manhattan* lay taking water, badly damaged after its tussle with the river. At the new Smithsonian Institution, the water kept in buckets and barrels throughout the building as a precaution against fire was frozen solid.[1]

The crisp turreted silhouette of the Smithsonian's red sandstone castle had formed a part of Washington's cityscape for scarcely a decade in 1865. Sitting alone in the marshy bottomlands of the monument grounds, halfway between the Capitol and the forlorn stump of the unfinished Washington Monument, the Smithsonian was nevertheless rapidly becoming the pride of the city—and well on its way, too, to becoming a showcase of the nation. Since its founding it had quickly assumed a leading role in America's fledgling scientific community. Its scientists, fitted out with instruments and collecting instructions, were attached to government surveys and expeditions, and the specimens they amassed made their way by the thousands back to Washington. Already the museum was hailed as the "most complete of any in existence in several branches of the natural history of North America."[2] A cadre of volunteers across the United States, comprising one of the Smithsonian's first research programs, collected daily meteorological data, and the institution had enlisted the country's private telegraph companies to transmit these weather reports across their wires—resulting in the world's first system of storm warnings.[3] A steady stream of publications issued from the institution, including the aptly titled *Smithsonian Contributions to Knowledge*. These journals began to fill the shelves of the academies of Europe, and the Smithsonian, as host of the government collections and promoter of knowledge, became the voice of a new nation's progress, rapidly raising the profile of American science.

On this grey January day the Smithsonian, despite the cold, was alive with activity. Secretary Joseph Henry, the head of the institution and the man who had ordered the buckets of water stationed throughout the building, sat in his office dictating to his chief clerk the voluminous annual report of the institution. It was due at the printers in a week's time. His family, assailed more than occasionally by the stench of drying animal skins from the adjacent museum offices, were at home in their quarters in the east wing. The young bachelor naturalists who lived in the towers that rose over Henry's office were employed in the museum, packing specimens on the

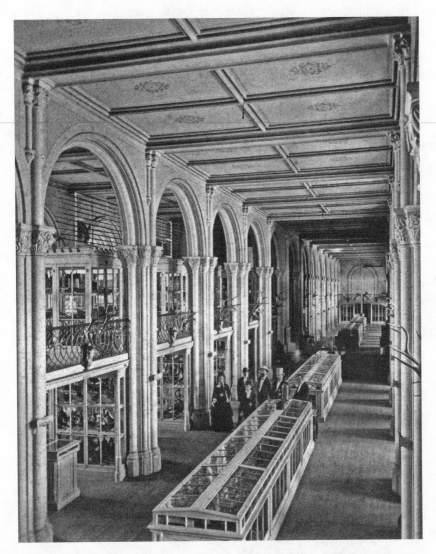

The great hall of the Smithsonian building, with the museum collections, c. 1867.

balconies overlooking the building's cavernous central hall. The low-vaulted basement, too, was humming with workmen wheeling out ashes and refuse and others busily crating the institution's publications for distribution.

A number of visitors had appeared that morning to see the new building. On the ground floor they admired the towering gothic cases of the museum, and they perused the contents of the chapel-like library. Upstairs they were shown the lecture hall, one of the finest in the country. A few even made the chilly climb to see the view from the top of the tall north tower, where President Lincoln had come earlier in the war to study the Confederate troops massing in Virginia. They also peeked into the regents' room, one of the most elegant spaces in the building. It was here that the institution's impressive governing board, consisting of the Vice President of the

REGENTS' ROOM.

The regents' room, where the Smithsonian's governing board met and where James Smithson's effects were kept.

United States, the Chief Justice of the Supreme Court, the mayor of Washington, six members of Congress and six appointed citizens, convened, sitting in muscular throne-like chairs under the soaring ribs of the gothic ceiling.

In the picture gallery two workmen were arranging the collection of Indian paintings by John Mix Stanley. At the beginning of the week, to brace themselves against the cold, the two men had brought a stove from the apparatus room at the other side of the lecture hall. All week the stove labored to keep the chill from the room as the men hung the paintings. The room was an immensely tall one, and the cold pushed across it between the enormous mullioned round-arched windows. Displayed on a pedestal in the center of the room was one lone statue, far from its classical siblings in the sculpture gallery downstairs. It was a marble copy of the antique figure *The Dying Gaul*—placed, apparently, to encourage visitors to draw an analogy between an ancient vanquished people and these "noble savages" now being extinguished across the West.[4]

Secretary Joseph Henry's office sat behind the great rose window between the two front towers of the building, on the third floor. A garrulous visitor had just settled down on the couch when a sharp crackling sound overhead startled them all. The chief clerk William Jones Rhees—the man who would pen the first biography of James Smithson—imagined it was simply a giant piece of ice sliding off the roof, but as the noise continued and grew louder, the men rushed to the door overlooking the lecture hall. All was gloomy and dark. Dense clouds of smoke billowing over the building could be seen through the oculus in the ceiling. "The house is on fire! Sound the alarm!" Henry cried, as he ran off down the stairs.[5]

All through the building men at their desks, working by natural light, noticed the sudden darkness that fell as the winter wind blew the black smoke over the building. There were rapid steps, doors opening, and everywhere the news being passed from one to another. Each man raced to the heart of the building, the giant shell-shaped lecture hall in the center of the second floor, to see for himself.

Just beneath the ceiling of the west wall, that which gave onto the picture gallery, the fire could be glimpsed gleaming through the ventilators. In the picture gallery itself a gaping hole in the ceiling where the plaster had fallen away showed the full extent of the blaze. The attic had been completely engulfed by roaring flames, and choking black smoke began to fill the tower offices.

Word of the fire spread rapidly through the city. The Senate adjourned at the news, as did the Supreme Court. Two steam fire engines responded immediately, but, impotent without water, they stood idly by. No water could be obtained for over an hour. Thousands of people moved south to the Smithsonian, crossing over the canal—that mephitic, sludgy stream Washington's founders had grandly named the Tiber—to reach the grounds of the institution. They stood in the snow, watching the conflagration, kept back by a large force of Union soldiers who had arrived on the scene. Stones from the top of the building began to rain down, and flames, brilliant and crimson, emitted a heat so intense the huge picture gallery windows exploded out of the building. High atop the main tower the institution's anemometer whirled furiously, recording the direction and force of the wind as it had always done. The crowd watched it, mesmerized, as a column of flames engulfed the tower; finally, it disappeared, swallowed up when the tower floors shuddered to the ground with a deafening crash.

Come dawn, the Smithsonian building stood like a ruined Norman abbey, its roof open clear to the sky. Secretary Henry's daughter Mary and a companion picked their way through the rubble of the upper floor. The apparatus room was completely destroyed, its prized collection of scientific instruments in ruins among the cinders and burnt bricks. In the offices the charred remains of paperwork lay a foot deep. And in the picture gallery the fragments of *The Dying Gaul*, scattered about the room, crumbled to dust in Mary's fingers.[6]

The ground floor housing the museum and the library had survived intact, though water coming down from the floor above had damaged some of the specimens. Some cases had been shattered and a few trays of birds' eggs smashed by overzealous rescuers. The Henry apartments in the east wing had emerged unscathed, but the great monument of Joseph Henry's work—the thirty-five thousand letters and reports, and the fifty thousand letters received by the institution—had been lost, and with it the record of the very founding of the Smithsonian. Mary Henry had watched the papers floating down when the fire finally took the upper room that had housed her father's office; "it was very hard," she wrote, ". . . to feel that in the space of an hour was thus destroyed the labor of years."[7]

In the days that followed an investigation was launched into the fire's origins, which quickly focused on the stove in the picture gallery. It had been inserted into a hole in the wall, one that appeared to be a flue but turned out in fact to be only part of the brick lining of the building. For nearly a week the ashes and embers and smoke had traveled up into the cockloft of the building before finally igniting. The suspicious flue-like hole had been used for a stove pipe before, without apparent mishap, for a meeting of the Mechanics' Institute around the time the building had first been completed, when the empty halls had filled with milling congregants and the jaunty strains of polka dancing. No one, in the end, was blamed for the fire.

Meanwhile, the men of the Smithsonian offered their testimonials. They recounted where they had been when they learned of the fire and how they'd spent their time in the face of disaster. Mostly the reports were keen averrals of valiant efforts, enumerations of which rooms they had raced between and what things they had saved—a Stanley Indian portrait, a stack of meteorological records, some books from the Secretary's office. But each also tallied the personal items lost: the linen collars, the woolen shirts and drawers, a partly worn frock coat and a pair of gum elastic overshoes, photographs and pictures, bedsteads, chairs, sofas, books and candelabras.[8] The towers stood still against the winter sky, charred and vacant. Everything within them had been consumed.

One of the losses, from the large square south tower, was quite distinct from all the others, reaching back across an ocean to the world of another century. The papers and personal effects of James Smithson, the Smithsonian's mysterious benefactor, had been kept in the regents' room. They had all been destroyed.

Smithson's trunks had been filled with some two hundred unpublished manuscripts, the record of countless experiments and investigations from the dawn of modern chemistry. They had also contained his correspondence, evidence of the extraordinarily sociable and international network of scientists in which he labored, and the diaries of his travels, which he had kept since adolescence. His extensive mineral collection, lauded as the finest in the United States in the 1840s, had been entirely consumed. Gone, too, were all the tools of his life's work—the thermometers, balances, and blowpipes; as well as his personal belongings, the trappings of his life as an aspiring aristocrat, a man accustomed to fine things: the sword and riding whip, the china service, his smoking pipes and candlesticks.[9] With these losses Smithson, along with the story of his life, seemed to have utterly vanished.

Joseph Henry had once ordered an inventory of Smithson's papers, but in the busy first years of the institution no one had ever found the time. Two or three people had given the papers and diaries a cursory examination. In one of the only lines that had been taken from Smithson's many unpublished manuscripts, Smithson had vowed, "my name will live on in the memory of men. . . ."[10] In the years that followed, Smithson's gift to the New World took root and flourished, eventually becoming the largest museum and research complex in the world. But a riddle remained at its very core—the mystery of a man who bequeathed his fortune to a country he had never seen. This undated phrase, plucked from some long-lost manuscript, seemed to be all there was to go on.

As an architectural historian at the Smithsonian in the early 1990s, I walked past Smithson's tomb at the entrance to the old Castle building almost daily. Like most of the tens of millions of visitors to the museums each year, however, I hardly cast a glance in his direction. So little was known of him, and so colorless were the existing biographical accounts, that he remained remote, imaginable only as a caricature: a periwigged effete with a handsome mineral cabinet and a penchant for gambling. More captivating were the quirky story of Smithson's posthumous arrival in Washington—the famed inventor Alexander Graham Bell and his wife exhumed the body from a condemned Genoa cemetery in a blinding snowstorm on the last day of 1903—and the ensuing debate over how best to memorialize him.

Smithson's few remaining effects are not kept enshrined, as might be imagined. With each generation's interpretation of Smithson's mandate, the Smithsonian has spread into new buildings up and down the Mall and beyond; the fragments of Smithson's life have scattered, too, to distant corners of the institution. Some portraits of Smithson are at the National Portrait Gallery, others at the Smithsonian American Art Museum. A medallion likeness has found its way to the numismatics collection in the National Museum of American History, and portraits of his brother and nephew are in yet another division of that museum. Smithson's personal collection of books, the only substantial material of his that survived the fire of 1865, sits in a state-of-the-art facility in the basement of the National Museum of Natural History. The library is at once full of interest and full of mystery, and embodies the challenges of recovering Smithson's life from his slender material legacy. The collection is evidently a working library, with many of the books annotated. Many are still in their original paper wrappers, indicating that Smithson never bothered to have them bound in leather after he bought them—which for an English gentleman, as one historian has noted, was the literary equivalent of serving milk in a carton at a fancy dinner party.[11] But the library is also surprisingly limited in size and scope, totaling only 115 volumes. It is missing many of the standard philosophical and scientific works one might expect of someone once described as "a gentleman of extensive acquirements and liberal views, derived from a long and intimate acquaintance with the world."[12]

The rest of the material is at the Smithsonian Archives: three original letters from Smithson, acquired since the fire, photocopies of about a dozen more from other repositories, and a handful of Smithson's notes, including a few draft catalogues of his mineral collection and some memoranda from experiments. There is a collection of calling cards and signatures of prominent scientists, dating from Smithson's days in Paris, as well as the diary of Smithson's brother and the passport of his nephew. Mostly, the archives contain a record of the search for Smithson, a long trail of dead-end inquiries made by various officials in the years since the fire. As long ago as 1880 the Smithsonian concluded that after "unusual exertions" they had collected "all the information likely to be obtained."[13]

In 1973 the Smithsonian exhumed Smithson a second time, in the hopes that the institution's forensic anthropologists might be able to glean some clues from his bones. The exhumation proved something of a comedy of errors, though, and narrowly missed destroying the last tangible evidence of the Smithsonian's benefactor. In the process of opening the tomb, the blowtorches used to unsolder Smithson's coffin ignited the casket's threadbare silk lining. The nearby fire extinguisher could not be used, as it would have ruined the bones for examination. Smithson was saved from absolute extinction only by the workmen racing down the hall to the water fountain, filling their mouths, and running back to put the fire out. The casket was covered with a tablecloth borrowed from the dining room, and Smithson was discreetly, if unceremoniously, carted across the Mall to the laboratory.[14] That night a disgruntled staff member put in a call to the local paper to report the tomb disturbance. The next day the Smithsonian found a journalist nosing around, hoping for an interview and a peep at the bones. Told the story of James

Smithson—a man with an insatiable curiosity, the illegitimate son of the Duke of Northumberland, elected at a mere twenty-two to England's oldest and most prestigious scientific society, who left his entire fortune to a country he had never visited—the reporter went away, satisfied. In the newspaper article that followed, the opening of the tomb was "a moment of high drama"—not, of course, because of the coffin fire (that would remain a secret), but because the Smithsonian had caught a glimpse of its enigmatic founder. It had been able to show its reverence for the generosity of one man, to cradle the skull that had once contained an imagination that hardly knew limits. The story was short and sweet, and ended, "Rest in peace, James Smithson." (Even this was not the end of the drama, however, as the newspaper article alerted D.C. government officials to the event, and they arrived with charges of illegal exhumation.) For all the mishaps, the forensic analysis did produce some interesting information. Smithson, it was learned, had not suffered from syphilis or any other common infectious diseases of the day, and he had a curious "extra flanging" of his right pinkie, perhaps the result of intense application to a musical instrument or some of his scientific apparatus. The report was shelved with the rest of the miscellanea in the archives, material that could not properly be called the makings of a biography.[15]

This book has come about through another kind of exhumation—an attempt to uncover Smithson's story, buried in the libraries and archives of Europe, Britain, and the United States. Biography aims to capture the essence of a life, painting a portrait with selective details, the turns of phrases, memorable routines, and vivid incidents. Smithson's forensic report conjured up a compelling physical picture: a relatively vigorous man in his sixties, about five foot seven inches in height, with a wide brow, wiry, strong hands, and a long torso, a man who smoked a pipe and was suffering from five abscessed teeth at the time of his death. But his humanity, his voice and his thoughts remained as inaccessible as if the tomb had never been opened. The lack of love letters and minimal evidence of friendships have led to conclusions that such intimacies must not have existed. In the absence of proof to the contrary, Smithson has been labeled an eccentric recluse; his science has been dismissed as dabbling and dilettantish, and the motivation behind his extraordinary bequest deemed ultimately unknowable. He lies now virtually forgotten, while his name, in the form of the Smithsonian, has become one of the most famous in the world. It seems a very long distance from the eighteenth-century English gentleman-scientist to the place known affectionately as the Nation's Attic, where America's iconic heritage is kept: the Star-Spangled Banner, the *Spirit of St. Louis*, Abraham Lincoln's top hat, and Dorothy's ruby slippers. I wondered if it might be possible to recover something of that lost world.

I set out to try to map Smithson's social and scientific networks, his web of cousins and colleagues, hoping to flesh out his life through the papers and diaries of others. I combed the registers of students at Oxford and the lists of guests at the Royal Society, and hunted through probate records and passport controls, amassing a cast of characters. I mined the faint, penciled marginalia in Smithson's books for indications of his taste and temperament, and tried to chart some of his travels through the people and places mentioned in his mineral catalogue notes. His bank records, still at Hoare's on Fleet Street— where the bayonets and muskets used to defend the bank during the Gordon Riots of 1780 line the entrance hall—offered a wealth of data and aided in constructing a chronology of his life. I was helped from the outset by Hugh Torrens, author of the *Oxford Dictionary of National Biography* entry on Smithson, who from his perch in the Potteries in Staffordshire—the heart of England's eighteenth-century industrial economy—has done remarkable work unearthing the forgotten figures of geology's early days, including Smithson and many of his friends.

The project was further complicated by the fact that Smithson had been known as James Louis Macie until he was thirty-five. Macie, his mother's name, is unusual, and in the haphazard world of eighteenth-century spelling it had near endless permutations, often

becoming Massey, Massie, Macey, or even, in the hands of one
French geologist-associate of Smithson's, the aristocratic de Mecies.
(I have for the most part referred to Smithson in the book as Smithson
not Macie.)

I followed hundreds of leads, from the astronomical observatory
in Krakow to the University of Åbo in Finland; I queried all the
regional academies of science in France and blanketed the Isle of
Jersey in search of the family papers of Smithson's Oxford tutor.
Most of these letters yielded nothing. For a long time it seemed likely
that Smithson would remain as inscrutable as ever, that my efforts
would join those in the Smithsonian Archives, a catalogue of one
more fruitless search. Slowly, however, letters from Smithson did
appear, and as my knowledge of his network grew, mentions of
Smithson emerged in the letters and diaries of his friends and
acquaintances. I began to be able to target where he had been, and
to guess whom he might have called on. I found him acting as a
kind of scientific cicerone for Lord Bristol, the profligate Earl-Bishop,
in Italy around the time of the great Siena meteorite fall of 1794,
and complaining of his health at a party in Paris with the German
explorer Alexander von Humboldt after the restoration of the
Bourbons in 1814. In the royal archives of Copenhagen I pored
through boxes of antique gothic script to find the records relating
to Smithson's arrest as a prisoner of war in 1807. And, in Paris
during the hallucinatory heatwave of August 2003, I found my
doppelgänger of two hundred years ago, someone who trailed
Smithson through the inns of the Rhine in 1805—a hapless French
policeman, as it turned out, convinced Smithson was a "vagabonde
d'intrigues." His dossier was filled with wild theories about Smithson's
nefarious exploits, and included Smithson's passport, which the
policeman had pinched from his hotel room.

As these finds piled up in my files and notebooks, a new portrait
began to emerge. The protean blur of Smithson came into better
focus, and a man of infectious exuberance and ambition replaced
the retiring loner. "How can a man of his ardour ever be idle?" one

friend wondered. "Macie is my delight!" crowed another. "His brain like my own is fruitful in whimsies."[16] His intensity brought with it new questions, and thoughts of the lacunae and silences that must be negotiated in the telling of lives. Smithson never married, and he had no children. Keepsake lockets of hair were found among his belongings after his death, and he gave two portraits of himself to one woman, but details of his intimate life remained elusive.

The discovery of a series of extraordinary lawsuits at the Public Record Office in Kew concerning Smithson's mother, Elizabeth Macie, shed light on the emotional forces that shaped his outlook, while giving some vivid, alarming color to the once blank expanse of his childhood. The documents were nearly the size of billboards, blackened by age and embossed with crumbling red wax seals; unfurled, they revealed yards of florid legal language recounting Elizabeth Macie's dogged pursuit of ancestral properties as well as the lurid saga of her rash second marriage to a lothario and fortune hunter named John Marshe Dickinson. She sued an extraordinary number of people in addition to this husband: her sister, her architect, multiple cousins, and even an illiterate farm tenant. Smithson's mother had long been completely obscure. "Nothing has been learned of her history," the Smithsonian's nineteenth-century biography of Smithson read. From the details in these suits she emerged all of a sudden as haughty and tempestuous, a domineering, emotionally erratic presence for her fatherless son.[17]

This vantage on the larger-than-life personality of Smithson's mother illuminated another facet of Smithson's story, too. It has often been argued that Smithson's fortune came from his mother. But these lawsuits exposed Elizabeth Macie's manic profligacy and made clear that she left her son much less than she might have. Her estate at probate was valued at less than £10,000; the gift that established the Smithsonian totaled more than ten times that. It is not possible to gain a complete picture of Smithson's finances from the official bank records that remain. In the volatile financial climate of the late eighteenth and early nineteenth centuries, when Britain was almost constantly at war, gentlemen did not confine their holdings to one place. Smithson's records at Hoare's Bank, and his subsequent account at Drummonds, reflect probably only a small portion of his dealings, but they do show a man with an avid interest in his portfolio. Smithson, it seems, made his own fortune; he took a small inheritance from his mother and, through a lifetime of shrewd management and investment, turned it into the largesse that was bequeathed to the United States.

I studied old maps and paintings as I traveled in Smithson's footsteps, walking the streets, visiting the museums and the mineral collections, looking as I might through his eyes. The hotel where he stayed in Paris during the Revolution was there in the shadow of the Abbey of St. Germain, its tall shuttered windows overlooking the same cobbled streets, his friend Bertrand Pelletier's pharmacy still open a few doors down. The marshy fenlands of Schleswig-Holstein in a cold late September still carried the damp salty chill that so haunted him when he was a prisoner of war. At the British Library I called up one of Smithson's publications, only to discover it had been inscribed by him to Sir Joseph Banks. The Muséum d'Histoire Naturelle in Paris contained four of his donations, single crystals mounted like obelisks on small ebonized slabs of wood, each enclosed in a miniature gilt-edged bell jar. In the sunlit studio of a chemist in western Massachusetts I took an antique blowpipe to my lips and discovered the thrill of transforming a simple candle flame into a blue jet worthy of a blowtorch, fierce enough to melt copper (at 2000 degrees F). These experiences brought Smithson's world a little closer, made it seem not so irretrievably mysterious.

In many ways it is Smithson's science that has contributed to the remoteness. His twenty-seven published papers, had he been a poet or a novelist, might have represented a means to interpret his story after the loss of his diaries and correspondence. But Smithson's writings on the subject to which he dedicated his life were for the most part written in an antique language now indecipherable but to a few specialists. In describing his calamine experiments, for example, he talked of a specimen which when "urged with the blue flame . . . became extremely friable . . . and entirely exhaled," and of others "being digested over a spirit-lamp with diluted vitriolic acid," and of observing at another moment "the apparent sublimation of the common flowers of zinc at the instant of their production."[18] His papers hardly convey the excitement that drove his investigations. His science nevertheless proved the crucial key to his story.

Chemistry was the cutting-edge field of Smithson's era, one that lay at the heart of the making of modern commercial society. Smithson's formative years unfolded in the midst of unprecedented discovery, much of it directly connected to chemical advances. He was eighteen when man broke the bounds of gravity and the Montgolfier brothers' balloon floated up over the heads of royalty, amazing thousands of spectators in the gardens of the Tuileries. Within the year Smithson was in a coach in the company of two aeronaut experts—Paolo Andreani, the first Italian balloonist, and the Frenchman Faujas de St. Fond, who penned the first book about the Montgolfiers—rumbling up to Scotland, on an expedition of geological discovery. In Edinburgh, he met and impressed James Hutton, who was on the verge of debuting his pioneering "theory of the earth," which would upend the biblical timeline. William Herschel was off discovering Uranus and distant galaxies with a telescope he built himself; Henry Cavendish, having identified myriad new gases within what was once known as the Aristotelian element of Air, was now leading the way to the discovery that Water was not an element either; and soon Humphry Davy's work exploring galvanism was to raise the idea that even the inanimate might be brought back to life. Smithson's contemporaries were extending the boundaries of the known world, plumbing the earth, reaching for the heavens, expanding time, even entering the realm of the invisible.

These developments brought with them an unshakeable optimism for modernity. "The present, beyond all former times," as one of Smithson's friends said, "teem[s] with wonders."[19] They also brought a belief that it was scientists who would dominate the hierarchy of the future. Many of the men leading the charge for modernity stood on the margins of society; in England they were the chemists and industrialists of the provinces, Protestant Dissenters for the most part, excluded from the Anglican and aristocratic Establishments. Science for them became the means of overthrowing the system as it existed, of replacing a corrupt order based on superstition and inherited privilege with one that rewarded talent and merit—a society that would bring prosperity and happiness to the many rather than the few. Smithson's friends formed a virtual who's who of European science between the 1780s and the 1820s. Even as the world they inhabited was convulsed by war, they proclaimed themselves citizens of the globe and pledged allegiance first of all to truth and reason. Their highest aspiration was to be a benefactor of all mankind.

Where a majority of the English reacted with fear and repression to the political and social upheavals of the late eighteenth century, Smithson was part of a small elite who looked at the factories sprouting up across England's green hills and saw not dark satanic mills, but rather the glow of industry and improvement. In the French Revolution, they found not a threat to Britain's security, but triumphant confirmation that even the most hierarchical of societies could be transformed. And in America's unprecedented system of government, founded upon the rights of man, where each person was to be valued for his contribution rather than his pedigree, they saw the future—the most promising foundation for the pursuit of knowledge and the advancement of society. America's cause, as Tom Paine had famously said, was "the cause of all mankind." In this light, Smithson's bequest of an "establishment for the increase and diffusion of knowledge among men," entrusted to the United States for its execution, shines from a new perspective.

The mapping of Smithson's world reveals the crucible that he passed through, and how profoundly affected he was by the culture of improvement in the late eighteenth century. Although it was

1846 before Congress passed the Act establishing the Smithsonian Institution, the ideals that gave rise to Smithson's gift were fashioned more than half a century earlier. It begins to seem as if inside Smithson the Smithsonian existed all along—a seed, germinating.

ONE

Descended from Kings

Families, like Empires, have their origin, decline, and fall, and such has been the fate of the Hungerfords.

—Sir Richard Colt Hoare, *Hungerfordiana*, 1823

I N MAY 1800, when his mother died, James Louis Macie was about thirty-five years old, a rising young scientist living the life of a fashionable London bachelor. Elizabeth Hungerford Keate Macie had been a dominating presence in her son's life, an intoxicatingly fiery woman—twice married, twice widowed, twice a single mother, and mistress to a duke. She had spent much of her turbulent life fighting for her right to ancestral landed estates in the west of England—lands with a feudal pedigree, fit to provide status and income for her brilliant firstborn. And yet he did not now inherit them from her. She had passed the last decade of her life practically hemorrhaging money. Battling various lawsuits, she had sold the family estate and poured money instead into elaborate building works at her house outside Bath, which was destined to pass out of the family at the time of her death.[1]

James Louis Macie was left prostrate by her death, overwhelmed by the chaos of her affairs and the parlous state of his inheritance. Even a year later he was still declining dinner invitations, telling a friend he was "considerably unwell, unsettled, and harried with business."[2] In the midst of this turmoil, however, there was one matter he tended to very promptly. Within a month of his mother's burial, he adopted a new name. The change was noted first in the ledgers of his account at Hoare's Bank, in London, in June 1800, and it was made official by Act of Parliament in February 1801.[3] For thirty-five years, more than half his life as it turned out, he had been known as Macie, the name of his mother's first husband. Now he wanted to be known as James Smithson, the name of his real father. He wanted the world to know that he was a son, albeit the illegitimate son, of Hugh Smithson, the late first Duke of Northumberland, one of the most powerful and charismatic figures of Georgian England.

It is a testament to how desperately Smithson hungered for this public identification with his father that he so readily abandoned the name Macie. As Macie he had already made a name for himself. In 1787 he had become the youngest member of the Royal Society, England's oldest and most prestigious scientific society. A few years later the society's journal had published his first paper, which had been extremely well received. He had been part of a pioneering expedition to explore the volcanic origins of Scotland when still in his teens; he had been to Paris to meet the famous Antoine Lavoisier in the months after the publication of Lavoisier's revolutionary chemical theory; and he had gained the friendship and admiration of many of the age's most prominent scientists, including even the reclusive Henry Cavendish.

In 1800 he had only recently returned to London after a long tour on the Continent. He bore all the airs of a Romantic, his handsome youthful face framed by a cascade of brown curls, his letters sealed with an image of Eros and Psyche embracing.[4] His Grand Tour, though, had been unlike most young English gentlemen's coming-of-age travels, focused as it was on meeting the great men of science in the capitals of Europe, and it had become exceptional for other reasons as well. He had enjoyed a front-row seat to the revolution that brought down the French monarchy and catapulted the Continent into war. He had dodged the French army in Switzerland, Italy, and Germany and was returning with tales of adventure at a time when few English had set foot on the Continent since Britain's entry into the war in 1793. He set up house on Clarges Street off Piccadilly, with laboratory and library, purchasing elegant mahogany furniture and extensive china services for entertaining.[5] Eager as he was to resume his life among the scientific elite of London—and he had just become a founding proprietor of the new Royal Institution—the tangled web of his mother's affairs consumed him entirely.

Weston House, the property outside Bath that she had recently so lavishly renovated, had been left her for her lifetime only, and Smithson was now forced to vacate in favor of a distant cousin. The genealogical relationship was so remote that the cousin left blank the space explaining it in the lawsuit they launched against Mrs. Macie, accusing her of defrauding them of their inheritance. And he was locked in a dispute with Lord Malmesbury, the new owner of Great Durnford Manor, the Hungerford estate that his mother, after years of litigation to establish her right to the property, had sold in 1791. Nevertheless, from the depths of his mourning, Smithson devoted himself to defending his profligate mother's reputation, fighting for her right "to receive, at least a posthumous, possession of her due." It was a role that he had probably taken on at a very early age. As a single woman of property, and one who had once been disastrously seduced by a fortune hunter, Elizabeth Macie had been a defiant and much embattled character. "Womens estates are so neglected & consequently incroached upon," she complained, "that y.e. [the] idea of their being even drove to dispose of them presents its-self to every one."[6] She lived her life convinced that everyone was trying to take advantage of her, and she evidently passed on this besieged outlook to her son. Smithson warned Malmesbury, "The man who feels does not sit down easy under the sense of being wronged, and nor my family, or myself, have been inured by habit to the sensation."[7]

Smithson seems to have felt a fierce loyalty to his beleaguered mother, but her feckless ways also left him greatly conflicted. Nowhere was this fraught and complicated attachment more fully exposed than in Smithson's decision to change his name. His adoption of the name Smithson immediately identified him as a son of the late duke, but it also publicly declared his illegitimacy. And even more problematically, especially for one as image-conscious as Smithson, it presented the appearance of disrespectfully abandoning his mother at the very moment in which her name should be most honored and remembered. He had apparently protected her reputation during her lifetime by tacitly obscuring his real paternity. "Since her death," however, he explained, "I make little mistery [sic] of my being brother to the present Duke of Northumberland."[8]

To most people in the beau monde, the name Smithson blatantly signaled illegitimacy. Smithson was the name that the Duke of Northumberland had carried when he was a mere baronet from Yorkshire—before he married the well-born Elizabeth Seymour, granddaughter of the sixth Duke of Somerset, and before the two of them, on account of her brother's premature death, fell by happy accident into the earldom of Northumberland and the great fortunes of the Percy family. The Smithsons in the not so distant past had been London haberdashers, and Sir Hugh Smithson before this windfall had been destined for life as a Member of Parliament, holder of some lands and a middling fortune. Through his intellect, good looks and magnetic personality he had carried off a bride much above his station and made himself in the process into one of the most formidable taste-setters of eighteenth-century England.

The Act of Parliament permitting Hugh Smithson to assume the name of Percy in 1750 barred him from passing the Percy name to any children other than those by his wife. This restriction was common knowledge in their circles; Horace Walpole, writing to a friend in 1775, noted: "Another of our number is dying, the Duchess of Northumberland. Her turtle will not be so impatient for a mate, as his patent does not enable him to beget Percys—a Master or Miss Smithson would sound like natural children."[9]

Smithson seems to have taken elaborate steps to ensure that the name change be made as discreetly as possible. In his plea to the

Crown he argued that this change had in fact been his mother's idea: "James Macie of Clarges Street . . . hath by his petition humbly represented unto us, that his mother . . . having during her lifetime, expressed her earnest desire that the Petitioner and his issue should take and use the surname of Smithson, instead of that of Macie."[10] In this narrative, which has been readily accepted by subsequent generations, Smithson became simply a dutiful and adoring son, intent on fulfilling his mother's deathbed wishes.

Yet there seems reason to question whether in fact Smithson invoked his mother as a means of masking what otherwise might have appeared disrespectful and grasping. His old Oxford friend Davies Giddy confided to his diary, "Macie had the bad taste (not to use any stronger expression) to obtain the Kings Authority for taking the name of Smithson (his putative father) he still continuing to usurp, & wrongfully hold, by his own admission, the property of the Macies."[11]

The freighted emotions carried in his dynamic with his mother, and the import of his father's place in his life, are encapsulated in a letter he wrote at this time to his friend the political hostess Lady Holland, in which he described his mother's death as that only of "a very near relative." Referring to his mother so obliquely enabled him in the same breath to convey the news he seems really to have wanted to announce—his new name—without any crisis of conscience. He concluded the letter: "Having entirely relinquished the name of Macie to resume that of my Paternal Family I have the honor to subscribe myself, Dear Madam, Yr. very ob. & most humble Serv.t, James Smithson." (He was, it is worth noting, proud to "resume" a name he had never actually owned in the first place.)

The difficult months following his mother's death bring into focus how much Smithson was concerned with the pursuit of legacy—of both name and property—as well as the pursuit of knowledge. Ironically, by 1800 Smithson had already succeeded in finding an arena in which to make a name on his own account, one based on his accomplishments and talents rather than on a troubled bloodline.

The science to which he had devoted himself—chemistry—was the most exciting of all the sciences at the end of the eighteenth century, boding great things for the future prosperity and happiness of man. Smithson had been singled out from an early age for his exceptional promise. He immersed himself in an extraordinary collective of individuals who were bent on unmasking the secrets of nature and harnessing those powers for the benefit of society. Smithson and his friends lived in a universe still full of unexplained mysteries, but they believed that through the careful accumulation of observation and facts they could divine a system of laws that ordered the natural world. For all his investigations into the composition of ancient Egyptian paint colors or the crystalline structure of ice, however, for all his efforts to identify the constituent parts of calamines and zeolites and ulmin, the greatest mystery Smithson faced, the conundrum that possessed his life, was the accident of his birth.

In eighteenth-century British society name meant everything. It signified one's source of wealth and prestige; it provided a palpable link to one's ancestors. Smithson was raised by a woman who kept her pedigree carefully groomed and displayed, and he learned the twists and turns of his family tree out to its most remote branches.[12] Smithson's childhood was fueled with stories of his ancestors—the charting of "the best blood of England" that ran through his veins— and his adult life was consumed with efforts to ensure his own name added some luster to the family pantheon.

His mother's family, the Keates, was a fashionable London family. Although they were not heirs to any great fortune, the eighteenth century's cult of ancestry ensured their easy entrée to polite society.[13] Through the paternal line they could lay claim to the arms and crest of an old family, once very powerful and numerous, but now practically extinct: the Hungerfords. Sir Thomas Hungerford was the first identified Speaker of the House of Commons in 1377, and the brocaded mantle he wore as Speaker became one of the family's most cherished heirlooms, used by subsequent generations as a christening gown.[14] Thomas' son Sir Walter brought fame and honor to the Hungerford name on the battlefields of France under three Lancastrian kings, Henry IV, V, and VI. Even the nefarious exploits of Hungerford ancestors carried claims to greatness; another Walter Hungerford in 1540 mounted the gallows after Thomas Cromwell, the powerful minister who oversaw the dissolution of the monasteries before he fell from Henry VIII's favor. Their severed heads leered down together from adjacent spikes on London Bridge. (It was surely omitted from the family's boasts of ancestral accomplishments that Hungerford was charged, in addition to his seditious work on Cromwell's behalf, with sodomy and incest and the use of "magic arts.")[15]

Vast swathes of Wiltshire and Berkshire once sat under the command of the Hungerfords, but before the end of the seventeenth century, the then reigning Sir Walter—later dubbed Spendthrift Hungerford—was forced by his extravagances to sell the principal family seat, the castle of Farleigh Hungerford, and to demolish their great London palace, which ran from the Strand to the River Thames (commemorated today by the Hungerford foot and railway bridges). Farleigh Hungerford was already in ruins by the time Smithson was a teenager, its crumbling, ivy-covered embattlements symbolic of faded grandeur and a family driven to extinction. It was, one guidebook advised, "a place curious to the antiquary, pleasing to the painter, and which might be rendered of great utility to the public at large, since I know of no spot whither we could send, with so much advantage, those unfortunate patients who are under the influence of *family pride*, or of that inflation which worldly greatness is so apt to inspire."[16]

For Smithson, as for his mother and the rest of his family, family pride was indeed something of a sickness. The Hungerford name remained all their lives a talisman of status and privilege. Elizabeth Hungerford Keate Macie and her brother Lumley Hungerford Keate had both been given Hungerford as part of their name; and Lumley eventually even took to calling himself simply Hungerford Keate.

Their other sibling, James Smithson's aunt Henrietta Maria Keate, officially adopted Hungerford as her surname in 1789. Smithson himself bankrolled the establishment of a Hungerford Hotel on the rue Caumartin in Paris in the 1820s. And around the same time he also requested that his nephew and heir, Henry James Dickenson, change his name to Hungerford.[17] The Hungerford name was the relic that remained to them, their sole link to a history of conquest and feudal power. It gave them a sense of self.

The Hungerford link was also the vehicle by which the family could claim its descent from royalty. Elizabeth's great-grandfather Sir George Hungerford had married Elizabeth Seymour, the daughter of Charles Seymour, second Baron Seymour of Trowbridge, and the half-sister of Charles Seymour, sixth Duke of Somerset, the notorious "Proud Duke"—so-called on account of his extraordinarily arrogant behavior.[18] Traveling higher up the family tree through this Seymour link, the Keate family could reach back to Henry VIII, one of whose wives had been Jane Seymour (sister of Elizabeth Seymour), and through him to additional kings: his son Edward VI, his father Henry VII, and his ancestors Edwards I, II, III, and VI. They could also claim Lady Jane Grey, Queen of England for nine days in 1553, who was the sister of Catherine, wife of Edward Seymour, the first Earl of Hertford, Elizabeth Macie's great-great-great-great-great-grandfather.

But the fruits of the family tree were not all illustrious long deceased. The most rewarding living connection Elizabeth Macie's genealogical caretaking brought her was the Proud Duke's granddaughter, Elizabeth Percy, Lady Northumberland—and by extension her husband Lord Northumberland. Northumberland was not made a duke until 1766, a year or so after James Smithson's birth, but he was already by the early 1760s a commanding figure in public life—a Knight of the Garter, Chamberlain of the Queen's Household, a member of the Privy Council, and one of "the King's Friends," the secret, intimate circle that met daily to advise the King.[19] In an age that celebrated celebrity, Lord Northumberland was one of the most magnificent men of England.

In Lady Northumberland, a prodigious keeper of her own family history, Elizabeth Macie and her sister Henrietta Maria found an amiable companion.[20] These women, the Keate sisters and Lady Northumberland, had only to reach back as far as their grandparents' and great-grandparents' generations to find their kinship. When one kept tabs on a web of relations that reached back centuries, to Charlemagne and King Alfred, these nearest generations collapsed as if they were one. Thus could Elizabeth Macie call herself a "niece of the Proud Duke," as James Smithson referred to her in his will, when in fact he was her great-grandmother's half-brother. And so too did Lady Northumberland embrace Elizabeth Macie and Henrietta Maria Keate as blood. "The Dutchess ha[s] done me the honor to call me 'a near Relation by Her Father,'" Henrietta Maria boasted to the Earl of Shelburne, "'one to be made much of having so few.'"[21]

Elizabeth Macie and her siblings latched onto this connection with all their energies. They lived in a world incumbent on patronage, a world in which everyone knew their place, just as they knew the extent of any financial package vaunted for a marriage arrangement. At balls and assemblies, everyone stood conscious of their position in the firmament of society, and they passed the evenings fixing the ranks of their neighbors and newcomers. In this world, every link to a constellation of greatness represented a possible perquisite in the way of a preferment or annuity. Lord Northumberland sat in the inner circles of power; he represented one of their best hopes for advancement. When Henrietta Maria eventually married a Barbados plantation owner named George Walker, she petitioned Northumberland to help her husband secure a baronetcy. Lumley, through Northumberland's efforts, became Commissioner of the Lottery.[22] And Elizabeth, it seems, sought nothing less than Northumberland himself.

When her affair with Northumberland began, Elizabeth Macie was in her early thirties, recently widowed and childless. Her husband John Macie had been a well-liked and upstanding pillar of the community in the countryside outside Bath, a lieutenant in the Sixth

Company of the Eastern Battalion of the Somerset Militia, a justice of the peace for the county of Somerset, and High Sheriff for the same in 1753. Elizabeth enjoyed an income of about £800 a year from her late husband's estate, and he had also left her "a very considerable personal Estate consisting principally of Mortgages and other Securities for Money Household Goods and Furniture Plate Linnen [sic] and China," which enabled her to live quite grandly.[23] She did not, of course, live in a manner remotely in the league of the Northumberlands, who were spending about £400 a year on candles alone, and whose annual expenditures often topped £50,000. The properties that Lord and Lady Northumberland commanded— in Northumberland, York, Cornwall, Devonshire, and Middlesex— comprised one-hundredth of all England.[24]

In the 1760s Lord and Lady Northumberland were busily overhauling their seats, bringing them into fashion and creating a platform suitably opulent for their politicking and entertainment. They transformed the outdated Jacobean pile of Syon House into a dazzling suite of neoclassical rooms, a progression of monumental state apartments modeled on ideals of Roman architecture and filled with references to the latest archeological discoveries of antique style. They restored Alnwick Castle in the north as the ancient seat of the Percys, papering the walls with colorful escutcheons and other heraldic ornaments celebrating their family pedigree. And at Northumberland House, their palatial London base at the foot of the Strand, they likewise rebuilt extravagantly, paneling an entire drawing room in costly plate-glass mirrors imported from France.[25]

The parties they held were legendary, with six hundred, one thousand, even twelve hundred guests in an evening, the courtyard a perpetual scrum of carriages and sedan chairs. The prolific diarist Horace Walpole described one "pompous *festino*" at Northumberland House, where "not only the whole house, but the garden, was illuminated, and was quite a fairy scene. Arches and pyramids of lights alternately surrounded the enclosure; a diamond necklace of lamps edged the rails and descent, with a spiral obelisk of candles on each hand; and dispersed

The town of Weston, near Bath, home to generations of the Macie family, 1789.

over the lawn were little bands of kettle-drums, clarionets, fifes &c., and the lovely moon, who came without a card."[26]

James Smithson's mother, the widowed Elizabeth Macie, aspired to a stately life of her own. She reigned as the lady of the manor at Weston House, the largest and most elegant house in the humble village of Weston, near Bath, where for generations Macies had been among the principal landholders. Weston's picturesque topography and its romantic Gothic church and graveyard made it an inviting destination for strollers out from Bath, but there was no local fashionable society. Many of the sturdy stone houses hugging the meandering high street were inhabited by laundresses who took in the clothes of the wealthy of Bath. As Jane Austen playfully told her sister, "We walked to Weston one evening last week and liked it very much. Liked *what* very much? Weston? No, *walking* to Weston, I have not expressed myself properly."[27]

Elizabeth Macie also commanded an impressive house in town on Queen Square, one of the first grand developments of neoclassical

Bath, a property she and her late husband had probably taken on to assuage her appetite for society.[28] Bath, at mid-century, was England's premiere pleasure resort, a gleaming city of fashion and frivolity half a mile down the road from Weston. In the course of a few decades the city had been transformed from a medieval backwater into the most elegant exemplar of Georgian design, a theatrical stage set inspired by classical Rome. Stately rows of new buff-colored stone houses swept up the hills, curving in ripples of columns around crescents and circles, terraces and squares. Its greatest excitement, though, came with the influx of the wealthy, landed clientele who visited in the season that stretched from September to June. Visitors came under the pretense of taking the waters, which were promoted for all sorts of ailments—gout, fevers, pustules, infertility—but the city was a pleasure ground for the wealthy, where ritualized encounters offered a guise for titillation. Against a backdrop of musical serenades, the fashionable promenaded from one ceremoniously programmed activity to the next. In the morning men and women in brown linen costumes and caps bobbed, sweated and teased one another in the sulphurous waters of the baths before being carried home in their sedan chairs. Others watched and gossiped while quaffing the mineral waters in the Pump Room overlooking the baths. Breakfast, taken at home by the ladies and in the coffeehouses by the men, was followed by daily service at the Abbey. The afternoon was idled away in shopping, calls at people's houses, and gambling. Twice a week in the evenings formal balls drew every level of society to the Assembly Rooms.[29]

Bath was a regular stop for the Northumberlands on their junket of the seasons in the early 1760s—down from Dublin Castle in Ireland, where he was Lord-Lieutenant, off to the races at Newmarket, in London for sessions of Parliament, some summer time at Alnwick. In the autumn, they often spent several weeks and sometimes even a month in Bath. Both Lord and Lady Northumberland suffered prodigiously from gout; recourse to the waters was a popular solution, but Bath was equally a place to continue the business of politics in a freer and more playful environment. It was also here most likely that the affair between Mrs. Macie and Northumberland began. Despite the strictures that the Master of Ceremonies Beau Nash had imposed, Bath exhaled an air of transgression. "Is there, or is there not any other large town," one writer asked, "where young women indiscriminately run, either alone or in groups, from one end to the other, without any servant or steady friend to accompany them; talking and laughing at the corners of streets, and walking sometimes with young men only? I do not happen to know of any similar instance: in London certainly these matters are differently regulated."[30]

Despite the entourage that surrounded the Northumberlands, it would not have been difficult for Elizabeth Macie and Lord Northumberland to see one another. Lord and Lady Northumberland lived fairly independent lives, often traveling apart; both engaged in numerous dalliances. Northumberland fathered two other illegimate children by a different mistress, as well as conducting a couple of other known affairs during these years. His wife at one point caught him kissing Lady Lauderdale, when that woman and her husband were visiting Alnwick. Lady Northumberland, for her part, believed that "There are women who have never had an Intrigue, scarce any who have had but one." She carried on her own flings and flirtations, coyly chronicling her escapades with her lovers, using numbers in her diary to mask their identities: "Had a very agreeable private party in the evening [including] 500 & 9. . . . 9 not so prudent as usual had like to have betray'd himself more than once . . ." She rode out with them, traipsed through Ranelagh Gardens with them, gambled, supped and enjoyed their company over breakfast. She was caught out with 500 "on the stairs" while on one of their rides, by Princess Augusta and her two brothers.[31] Nevertheless, the Northumberlands' marriage by all accounts was a strong and loving one. In Parliament in 1763, presumably around the height of his dalliance with Elizabeth Macie, Lord Northumberland inserted into one of his speeches a passionate tribute to his wife, a subject which "inspired him with a vast Ardour." Lady Northumberland, happily recording the event in her diary, reported that "Ld. Drogheda said he [the Earl of Northumberland] was the first Man yt [that] ever brought a Declaration of Love into a speech in Parliament." She comforted herself with the knowledge of his love, and with the maxims: "We forgive as long as we love," and "Men find it more difficult to overlook the least infidelity to themselves than the greatest to others."[32]

In December 1761, in perhaps the early days of the affair between Lord Northumberland and Elizabeth Macie, the Northumberlands passed a month in Bath, taking in the theatre and the balls, games of three-card love or quadrille at the Assembly Rooms, and a private concert by the Italian singer Passini. At the end Lord Northumberland found reason to stay on at Bath a further four days after his wife. She, in the closest thing to an admission of abandonment in a diary otherwise free of self-pity and open declarations of pain, confided: "Left Bath quite alone shocking Day . . ." In the autumn of 1762 Lord Northumberland made a two-week visit to Bath without his wife, a trip he repeated in February 1763.[33]

Northumberland's correspondence has been culled of nearly all personal letters—presumably by a subsequent generation concerned with tidying up the family reputation. There is no trace of any of his dalliances, nor even hardly anything of his relationship with his wife or children. What survives provides a vivid illustration of the barrage of requests a lord in a position of power received in the mid–late eighteenth century. Most of the pleas the duke declined or punted to others he felt could better afford to deliver. On the outer leaf of many of the letters he has scrawled, in his confidently lean, looping hand, "Answered. Impossible." A rare few he felt beholden to satisfy. One such favor was the job he arranged for Elizabeth Macie's brother in May 1763—and which he worked the system assiduously to maintain in subsequent years. It is an indication, most likely, that the affair that led to James Smithson was by then already flourishing.

Northumberland was once more alone in Bath for two weeks in September 1764, and it was perhaps not long thereafter that Elizabeth Macie found herself pregnant. The news must have come as quite a shock. While it was relatively common, according to the Countess of Sutherland, for English women to present their children as legitimate when in fact they were not, Elizabeth Macie was a widow, about thirty-six years old, and clearly unattached. For eleven years she had been married to John Macie, without ever having had a child, though they had fervently hoped for one. Now she was with child, and in this situation—"when in scrapes," as the Duchess of Devonshire called it—she did as countless other well-born women did, before and after. She headed for the Continent to have the child in secret.[34]

No record appears to survive documenting James Smithson's birth, which happened in 1764 or 1765, though the petition for naturalization lodged on his behalf in 1773 makes clear that he was born in Paris. The French birth certificates, even in the unlikely event one was recorded for Smithson, were mostly lost in the torching of Paris' city hall during the Commune of 1871; and he does not seem to have been baptized in a church in England upon his return. Smithson's birthday remains unknown. The few pieces of evidence uncovered are contradictory and as yet irreconcilable. In any event, even before the catastrophic loss of his papers and belongings in the Smithsonian fire of 1865, James Smithson's story was shrouded in mystery.[35]

Almost nothing is known of Smithson's childhood prior to the petition of naturalization of 1773. Since he was already nearly ten when applying for British citizenship, it has been assumed that "Jacques Louis" largely spent his formative years being kept discreetly in France. In the late 1830s one friend of Smithson's recalled that "Mrs. Macie lived much abroad and her Son was much with her."[36] There are indications, however, that Smithson may sometimes have been left behind by his mother for long stints, and this reminiscence— by someone who did not know Smithson before university—may be a gloss on the real nature of Smithson's childhood.

Furthermore, it seems likely that he was raised in England, not

France. Before Smithson was even a year or so old, he and his mother were almost certainly back home, on account of a family crisis. On March 26, 1766, Elizabeth's brother Lumley died, aged thirty-one, leaving no wife or children. His only survivors were his sisters, the widowed Elizabeth Macie and the still unmarried Henrietta Maria Keate. Critically, Lumley had written no will, and the fate of the Hungerford estates lay in the balance.

For a couple of years Lumley had been locked in a court battle with a Mrs. Hungerford, the second wife of his father's cousin George, over several estates, including Studley House, a handsome property that sat adjacent to the Earl of Shelburne's seat of Bowood House in north Wiltshire. Studley House had been the seat of the last great scion of Elizabeth's branch of the Hungerford family, Sir Walter Hungerford. When Sir Walter died childless in 1754, his will was a subject of fascination, its abundant clauses elaborating a "fee tail male" chain through the family across the path of his nephews— ensuring that the properties would stay in the family via the male descendants. Elizabeth's father had come into possession of Great Durnford Manor, and he and his heirs seemed primed to come into all the other Hungerford lands as well after the death of his older cousin George, who was also childless; George, however, had married a second time late in life, and his widow was now doing her best to thwart any claims on the properties.[37]

In November 1766, when James Smithson was presumably about eighteen months old, Elizabeth Macie and her sister Henrietta Maria, both then resident in Bath, took up the suit themselves.[38] In it they called themselves the co-heiresses of Studley—an epithet Smithson would ostentatiously use to define his mother some sixty years later in his will. Over the next few years the suit wound its way through Chancery Court, an expensive drain on the sisters' resources. At New Year 1769 there was still no resolution in sight. Henrietta Maria passed a heartbroken "Holydays within sight of the house [Studley], at Lord Shelborne's [sic], it was a place I once dearly loved."[39]

Elizabeth Macie, though equally vested in the stakes tied to gaining the ancestral homeland, seems to have been content to entrust her sister with the battle for ownership. In search of attention and affection, she left everything behind and headed for the Continent. In early 1768 she seems to have put Smithson in a school in Hammersmith, a leafy village west of London. By April she was in Amsterdam.[40] She was gone, in the end, for more than a year, and when she finally returned she brought back with her incalculable misery—a calamitous entanglement that greatly complicated the lives and fortunes of her entire family.

At the resort town of Spa in the late summer of 1768 she took up with a young Englishman named John Marshe Dickinson, the roguish son of a former Lord Mayor, whom she had met in Amsterdam.[41] Their flirtation rapidly somersaulted into a torrid affair. Within a month the two were married at Paris, in a hastily arranged ceremony in the state room of the Dutch ambassador—the English ambassador and his chaplain being out of town. Some of Dickinson's big-spending Paris friends were invited as witnesses, including Sir John Irwin, a well-mannered major general known for lavish entertaining, the foppish Clotworthy Skeffington, the second Earl of Massereene, still in his twenties and recognized already as "the most superlative coxcomb that Ireland ever bred," and Isaac Panchaud, an English banker resident at Paris.[42]

The cracks in this precipitous liaison quickly revealed themselves. Dickinson had a roving eye and recommenced his romancing soon after their marriage. Not long after the wedding he set off on a solo trip to England, intent on securing his rights to Elizabeth's wealth. He renewed the suit at the King's Bench for the claim to the Hungerford estates, making the case now in his name.[43] Dickinson had learned the family history well; he knew already the intricacies of the tangled web of Hungerford cousinage and the potential reward that it could bring to him.

His departure left a desperate Elizabeth alone in Paris, pregnant with the child that had evidently precipitated the hasty wedding. She wasted away, a roiling bundle of emotions, confined to her bed.

At one moment she was madly in love with her new husband, fearing for his safety as the winter months whipped up the Channel waters. In the next, she felt despondent, humiliated over his betrayals and resentful of his lack of attention. The doctor came and ordered her blood let. His ministrations, which left her weak and feverish, were futile. She wrote an extraordinary letter to Dickinson in London, to tell him of the loss of the baby:

> With the utmost difficulty am I supported in my Bed, exactly in the same spot you left me to tell you that I am alive but ill indeed! And the little creature w[hic]h I hoped w[oul]d have been the means of bringing you to love, &c me, for all y[ou]r further follies is now in spirits at the apothecary shop. I pity and forgive you any fault you may have had herein, Nay love you still enough to be in agonies from the weather. Do not cross I conjure you till it is safe & then you may be sure I ever stand in need of you.
>
> I am entirely y[ou]rs
Eliza: Dickinson[44]

One child was lost, pickled in a jar in the apothecary shop, presumably awaiting burial, but one remained. Three-year-old James was still in London. She seems to have charged Dickinson with paying the boy a visit and even bringing him back to France. She waited for word from Dickinson, word that he had made the journey to Dover safely, gossip of life in London, and news especially of this precious child of hers. She sent more letters to him, "full of sighs, complaints, & murmurs." In her last letter, sent to Calais in an attempt to intercept Dickinson on his return, she included a message especially for her son:

> I cannot conclude without a little word to y[ou]r young companion if w.th you & was you indeed to bestow a little kiss upon him I will repay you most faithfully when we meet. Pray heav'n it may be soon.[45]

No further mention, however oblique, was made of young James Smithson in the material that survives. It is not possible to know whether the callow Dickinson brought him to Paris. Soon after Dickinson's return Elizabeth again became pregnant. But their relationship, fragile from the start, deteriorated tremendously over the winter of 1768–9. Both were drawn to the glittering nightlife of Paris. They frequented the Monday night parties hosted by the debauched Prince de Conti in his sumptuous Salon des Quatres Glaces at the Temple, long evenings of music and food and gambling popular with the English aristocracy and certain radicals in the French court.[46] One habitué of these soirées, the Duc de Lauzun, captured the tenor of this society in his indiscreet and entertaining memoirs. Though he lost his head during the Revolution, his book found its way to publication in the 1820s, scandalizing French society. Smithson owned one of the precious copies (the book was suppressed by the government soon after publication), aware perhaps, maybe even proud and titillated, that his mother had been a peripheral part of this circle.[47]

Elizabeth steeled herself against the disappointments of her alliance with Dickinson. Where she had once signed her letters to him, "I am my dear Dickinson tenderly and affectionately yours," she now closed, "I am, to my misfortune, Eliza: Dickinson." She tried to maintain some sort of moral high ground, rebuking him, "Let your treatment of me be what it will I shall always carry towards you as it becomes your <u>Wife</u> to do." She did, however, have much to rue. The man she had married was grossly in debt. His estate at Gloucester was mortgaged for much more than its worth, compounding the burden of maintaining his main house at Dunstable. She had rashly promised him £20,000 from her estate in the early days of their relationship, and from the moment the marriage had been enacted he had pressured her to advance him some of this money.[48]

By March 1769 the situation was dire indeed. Elizabeth decided she had to return to England; Dickinson fought her, believing she should not travel till after she had been delivered of the baby.

Meanwhile he carried on his affairs out on the town, forcing her to send a note out after him:

> If you are wise Dickinson return to me this Evening without going to the Temple [to the Prince de Conti's party] for perhaps on your conduct this Evening depends the future peace of both our lifes & the life its-self of an Infant you acknowledge to believe your own![49]

As much as she painted herself the wronged wife, Elizabeth too knew how to play the game. The letter's stormy conclusion—"an Infant you acknowledge to believe your own!"—suggests that perhaps he accused her, too, of infidelity. The night before their departure— which could conceivably be the same tumultuous day that she sent this letter—Elizabeth went herself to the public supper at the Prince de Conti's and, ignoring her pregnancy, stayed on for the dancing and gambling late into the night. According to Dickinson, she "did not return home till long after [he] was Retired to rest." The journey from Paris to London, a passage typically lasting from three to five days depending on the wind and weather, took the pair more than a month. Whether the loss of the baby was caused by the "Extreem fury of her Temper" and her reckless partying (as he alleged) or his "cruelty" and violent behavior (as she testified), by the time the couple finally arrived back in London Elizabeth Dickinson was, for the second time since her marriage six months earlier, no longer pregnant.

They returned to a house at Leicester Fields (now Leicester Square), a tiny island of desirability in an area that had lost much of its aristocratic sheen. The year that followed was one of absolute chaos, an unending series of highly damaging, terrifying events. If Smithson was present for much or even any of it, he would have been witness to scenes of violence, thunderous rage, threats, and the rapid, ugly disintegration of his mother's economic and emotional wellbeing.

Upon her return to England Smithson's mother was in "a low and languishing state," shattered physically and mentally by the second miscarriage. Dr. Hunter, physician to the fashionable and accoucheur to the Queen, was briefly brought in to consult. She should "repose all day on a Couch," he instructed, confined to one floor of the house. It was a prescription that suited John Marshe Dickinson very well. With his wife's movements curbed, Dickinson immediately set upon her once more to sign over her property to him. His oily solicitor came to add further pressure, in the guise of a confidant, aware that she suffered Dickinson's infidelities: "The way to make John Marshe Dickinson a Good Husband," he assured her, "was by laying him under a real Obligation." In the meantime, Dickinson took what steps he could on his own, taking possession of the Macie house at Queen Square in Bath, which was soon on the rate books under his name rather than hers.[50]

Elizabeth defiantly announced she would make no deal without the counsel of her own family lawyer. The declaration incensed her husband. He became, in her words, "so outragious [sic] and violent that [Elizabeth] considered her Life to be in the utmost Danger." She fled the house, aided by a sympathetic servant, and she hid successfully for over a month before Dickinson located her. He arrived finally late one evening at the house where she was staying, armed with his solicitor and a posse of men he had hired to help him take possession once more of his intractable wife. Refused entry to the room where she was hiding, Dickinson banged and thundered, breaking down the door while a crowd of neighbors and passersby gathered, drawn by the commotion and its promise of explosive familial theatre. The hired men faltered in the face of such a censorious audience, and Dickinson was driven away. It was 3.00 a.m. when his carriage rolled off into the darkness, without Elizabeth (or James) inside it.

The very next day she went straight to Lord Mansfield, the Lord Chancellor, to charge Dickinson with disturbance of the peace, the beginning of an escalating series of court battles between the couple.

Cut off from her sources of income, Elizabeth was without most of her clothes or even any belongings. Dickinson, after she had fled, had taken possession of her plate, her linens, her clothing, and most especially, her jewelry—most of which, she learned later, he had immediately hocked to pay his mounting debts. He had raided Weston and the town house in Bath and carted off the furniture, silver, and other goods she had inherited from John Macie, removing them to his house at Dunstable. She in turn began once more to call herself Elizabeth Macie, widow, as if the marriage had never taken place. She launched a suit of jactitation in the Consistory Court of the Bishops of London; jactitation, from the Latin *jactitare* or "to boast," is an archaic legal term meaning to prohibit someone from publicly claiming to be your spouse; Elizabeth's suit was one of the last such cases ever pursued in England. She also launched a separate suit at the King's Bench to reassert the Hungerford suits in her own name.[51]

Pursuing multiple cases in multiple courts, Elizabeth Macie stood in danger of being isolated as a radical, fallen woman. Even the Wiltshire chattering classes were against her. General Irwin, a frequenter of the Bath social scene, testified against her, siding with her erstwhile husband. Mrs. Harris, the wife of the author "Hermes" Harris and Elizabeth's tenant at Great Durnford Manor, wrote of the news to her son (later Lord Malmesbury): "I hear there has been a Tryal at the Salisbury Assizes between Mrs. Macie as she calls herself and Mr. Dickenson, whom she married at Paris; and now she disowns the match; but, as I am informed, General Irwine [sic] swore in the Court he saw them married at Paris, so a verdict was given for Dickenson."[52] The acid tone of the aside—"Mrs Macie, as she calls herself"—suggests Elizabeth had made a spectacle of herself in the very place where she would most have hoped for support.

Elizabeth Macie's indignant, self-righteous outrage at those who crossed her drew her into a staggering number of lawsuits for a woman of her time. Smithson's childhood was dominated by these suits, which lasted years and involved countless testimonials from relatives, tenants, and others. The spins and eddies of these legal challenges—the elation of small triumphs, the dark cloud of setbacks, the tense wait for appeal or reversal—must have underscored the idea that family heritage was everything: money, security, identity. His mother and aunt did finally win some important battles over the Hungerford properties, and through arbitration they managed between them an equitable split of the estates, Elizabeth Macie ending up with Great Durnford Manor, Henrietta Maria with Studley House.[53]

But James Smithson was a keen observer, and his apprenticeship in life began at the knee of a high-strung, tempestuous woman, a mother unlikely to have sheltered her son from her rage at a system she believed was unfairly slanted against her. Her disillusionment as often turned to petulance, and she had a fearsome temper. According to Dickinson, "any Contradiction or Disappointment threw her . . . into very violent Agitations."[54] All the lawsuits entered against Elizabeth Macie over several decades accuse her of making threats. She allegedly terrorized her first husband's cousins, the Leirs, over the Weston estate, threatening to destroy their inheritance by scorching the land and selling off all the timber. Dickinson she threatened to run into debt and ruin. These accusations seem vivid, credible reports of the outbursts of a shrill and unstable woman.

Smithson's mother, though, was not simply a harridan or an ogre. She was sparkling and witty enough to have captivated the Duke of Northumberland as well as others, and she seems to have lavished a fierce love on those she protected. Her capacity for devotion is evident in her early letters to Dickinson. Smithson was her firstborn, and he was probably much in her thrall, a faithful companion to her in the trenches. In a portrait that possibly depicts the two of them, painted around 1770, a little boy sits upon his mother's lap. He wraps his arm around her neck in a gesture at once possessive and protective. But he is the one who seems already world-weary; she stares out at the viewer in her sumptuous dress, proud, defiant, and vulnerable. The two of them in the end seem very much alone.[55]

In these early years Smithson suffered a series of dramatic childhood illnesses, episodes severe enough to have registered as growth-arrest lines on his teeth. The precarious state of his health plagued him for the rest of his life. As an adult Smithson projected an aura of vulnerability and weakness, and he regularly made reference to his feeble constitution. He was almost invariably described as "delicate" by those who met him. When he was nineteen, on an expedition to Scotland, his companions attempted to leave him behind at one point, advising him to wait for their return, "as he was delicate." And when Smithson was in his early thirties, one dinner-party guest refrained from teasing him, deciding that it "would have been cruel, considering the delicate state of his health & penury of Vital power."[56]

Today it is impossible to diagnose exactly the nature of Smithson's illnesses. He complained of spitting up blood at one point, a near-complete loss of hearing at another, and "a terrible cold which has made me fearful of going out" in yet another instance. Forensic investigation of his bones in 1973 revealed no syphilis or other infectious disease, and virtually no arthritis. The conclusions drawn from this posthumous analysis, in fact, indicated that Smithson was, at the time of his death, around the age of sixty-four, a relatively strong and vigorous man—despite terrible teeth problems, like most of his contemporaries. The one other independent perspective on Smithson's constitution, from 1805, yields a similar portrait, depicting the forty-year-old Smithson as fairly well built ("assez fortement constitué"). Neither of these assessors was privy to Smithson's chronic complaints about his health. Their conclusions suggest that Smithson may have been something of a hypochondriac, or at least vigilant and voluble about the slightest sign of frailty; Sir Charles Blagden, for one, who saw Smithson at a dinner party in Paris in 1814, noted in his diary: "Smithson pleaded his bad health: is capricious, does not know when to go."[57]

Smithson lived in an age that placed a high value on the persona of the consumptive, a figure who lived a life of intense feeling and who through suffering had developed a refined and sensitive spirit;

he may well have enjoyed the exclusivity of that Romantic disposition and sought to cultivate it.[58] It is also more than likely that from childhood, with a narcissistic mother prone to abandoning him for months at a time, Smithson learned early on that being sick was a very good way of gaining attention.

Mysteriously, towards the end of 1770, in the midst of these lawsuits, Smithson's mother at the age of forty-two again found herself pregnant. The child when it was born in August 1771 was called Henry Louis Dickenson, and it was clearly intended that the child be perceived as a son of John Marshe Dickinson; Elizabeth Macie seems to have opted for a slight alteration in the spelling of the name, perhaps to distance herself and her child in some small way from the odious Dickinson. And yet in the very weeks when this child must have been conceived, Elizabeth Macie (as she insisted on calling herself) and John Marshe Dickinson were hurling accusations at one another in several different courts. Dickinson had also rewritten his will to exclude any mention of her whatsoever.[59] Relations between them could hardly have been more antagonistic. They had not been living under the same roof since the summer of 1769, and Elizabeth Macie claimed in court not even to know the whereabouts of Dickinson. She suggested that he had "fled the Kingdom" and accused him of laying claim to her as his wife and yet leaving her destitute and without support. All in all, it was hardly a promising premise for even an irrational moment of reunion.

The Dickenson name appears to have been used as a cover. A month before the birth of this unanticipated child in the summer of 1771, John Marshe Dickinson conveniently died. Out of the way, he could not contest the naming of the boy. Henry Dickenson was in all likelihood a full brother to James Smithson. Elizabeth Macie, it seems, had either kept or renewed her relationship with the Duke of Northumberland. Neither of these boys was ever publicly acknowledged by the duke; they lived their lives as bystanders to his gilded story and hankered after any association with him. Smithson and Dickenson both collected memorabilia with the ducal arms as well as other tokens of their father: a silver medal from 1766 commemorating the restoration of Alnwick Castle, with the duke's portrait on the reverse; silver plate with the family crest; and an engraving of the duke.[60]

But although Smithson and Dickenson were not publicly recognized, they may well have enjoyed a measure of secret, silent support from their famous father. Their mother was assertive and determined enough that it is possible to imagine her engineering some kind of encounter or audience for her sons with the duke. And her solicitors, Edward Woodcock and his son Elborough, may have served as a quiet go-between. There were several large deposits made into Woodcock's account by the duke, in the 1770s, at a time when it is not clear that Woodcock had any official relationship as solicitor

An engraving of the first Duke of Northumberland
that was owned by Smithson or his brother Henry
Louis Dickenson.

to Northumberland. And Woodcock likewise paid out significant sums to Elizabeth Macie, who at the time owed large amounts to Woodcock on account of the multiple lawsuits in which she was involved.[61]

The duke did support the two other illegitimate children that he fathered—two girls, born of another widow, Margaret Marriott, a demure-looking woman with large eyes and light colored hair, some fourteen years younger than Elizabeth Macie. These girls, unlike the children the duke had fathered with Elizabeth Macie, were called Percy and given the treasured first names of Dorothy and Philadelphia—respectively the names of a sister of the duke who had died quite young, and of the duke's mother. Mrs. Marriott, who was born on an indigo plantation in South Carolina, probably traveled in similar circles as Smithson's mother. Her daughters grew up very close to Smithson, and she too was an important figure in his life—though whether as surrogate mother, or lover, or simply "a most particular and intimate friend of mine," as Smithson himself described her, is unclear.[62]

Smithson's back-story—a noble, famous father, a wild, theatrical seductress of a mother, an illegitimate secret birth, disputed ancestral lands, and untold family lawsuits and countersuits, lasting years—eventually acquired the status of legend. Years later his Oxford friend Davies Giddy disdainfully recounted a very convoluted version of it in his diary:

> Macie afterwards Smithson was a Gent. Com. [a Gentleman Commoner, a high social rank of student] when I entered at Pembroke College. His Mother's Husband was a country gentleman to whose estate he has succeeded; but the first Duke of Northumberland was allowed on all sides to be his Father. At the time of his matriculation I have heard that a Blank was left for his surname, Mr Macie having at that period instituted suit to annul his marriage which the wife defended. The Duchess of N. then died, when Mrs Macie wished the

marriage dissolved with the hope of marrying the Duke of N.
but this the Husband from spite opposed. I have heard that a
suit was actually instituted in which the parties switched sides.[63]

Giddy was mistaken about a number of basic facts. Smithson never
succeeded to John Macie's estate, though he did presumably enjoy
some of Macie's money simply by virtue of his mother's legacy to
him. And it was not, of course, the Macie marriage that was the
subject of spiteful suits of annulment. But Elizabeth Macie's actions—
her long involvement with the duke, her tormented relationship
with Dickinson, and her vengeful pursuit of her property rights—
colored Smithson with a kind of notoriety.

When Smithson was about eight years old, around the time he
would have begun formal schooling, he appears to have been left
once more by his mother, deposited in London as the ward of one
of the family solicitors. His guardian was Joseph Gape, a docile,
avuncular bachelor from a prominent St. Albans family, who enjoyed
the high-ranking post of treasurer at the Middle Temple and had
also long served as a legal adviser to the family.[64]

Since Smithson had been born in Paris, it remained first of all to
make him English. An act of naturalization, however, did not confer
full rights of citizenship. Inserted at the end of all bills of naturalization
were the restrictions that tolled for Smithson: "that the said Jacques
otherwise James Louis shall not be hereby Enabled to be of the
Privy Council or a Member of either House of Parliament or to
take any Office or place of Trust either Civil or Military or to have
any Grant of Lands, Tenements or Hereditaments any inheritable
property from the Crown to him or to any Person or Persons In
trust for him Any thing herein contained to the Contrary
Notwithstanding."[65] Since the time of Edward III, when plague and
war had sent many English subjects abroad, the government had
attended to the rights foreign-born subjects should enjoy back at
home, but a succession of kings with foreign allegiances had curbed
these privileges; the restrictions cited in Smithson's case had been

established in the time of William and Mary, as protection against
claims by his Dutch followers, and been reenacted under George I,
targeted likewise against his Hanoverian followers.[66] For Smithson
then, here already, before even the age of ten, was laid the
groundwork for a lifelong sense of disenfranchisement. The ceiling
on the heights he could attain as an English gentleman was entirely
due to the circumstances of his birth. Had his mother not felt
compelled to hide her pregnancy, it is unlikely he would have been
born abroad. The stain of illegitimacy had been compounded by
the privations of limited citizenship.

It was Gape, not Smithson's mother, who presented the petition
to the House of Lords for his naturalization in June 1773. And it
was probably Gape who took charge of the boy's schooling. It is
not known where, if anywhere, Smithson attended.[67] He might have
been tutored privately. It is also quite possible that he attended
Charterhouse, the school occupying the site of an ancient Carthusian
monastery in the heart of the City of London. Smithson's brother
Henry Louis Dickenson attended in the early 1780s, lodging in the
boarding house on Charterhouse Square run by Master Henry
Berdmore. And Charterhouse, through its Holford scholarships, had
a long-standing relationship with Pembroke College, Oxford, where
Smithson matriculated in 1782.[68]

Wherever Smithson gained his early education, he does in any
case seem to have been raised in the tradition of the Whig aristocracy,
with a great love for all things French, a penchant for travel, and a
belief in progress. He gained a thorough knowledge of history, a
love of logic, a fluency in French, as well as Latin and presumably
ancient Greek. He must have mastered the polite acquirements of
riding, fencing, music and dancing. To the polish of a gentleman
Smithson married the rigor and questioning of a scientist. An utter
perfectionist, he corrected any error that he came across in his books,
even grammatical ones. He remained hungrily acquisitive of
knowledge all his life, gathering information and observations into
myriad notebooks and journals. True to his times, he organized the

disparate knowledge that he collected, encyclopedia-like, under themed headings; it covered a vast discursive palette—"history, the arts, language, rural pursuits, gardening, the construction of buildings, and kindred topics."[69]

If Smithson did attend Charterhouse it was probably there that his friendship with the future chemist William Hyde Wollaston, a fellow Charterhouse pupil one year younger than Smithson, who went on to Cambridge, was kindled.[70] No tradition of natural philosophy is known to have been taught at Charterhouse at this time; neither was it especially common at other schools—though the itinerant lecturer Adam Walker did teach astronomy at Eton and Christ's Hospital, where among his eager listeners was one Percy Bysshe Shelley.[71] But based on the expert knowledge Smithson displayed at Oxford, it is likely that, by the time he headed to Pembroke, he was already awake to the mounting excitement surrounding the investigation of the natural world. It was the arena that would become the dominant focus of his energies, that to which he would dedicate his life, and, eventually, his fortune.

Oxford: The Lure of Novelty, 1782–1784

Macie I sincerely esteem—& as a Gent[leman]. of
fortune, who dedicates his whole time to
Mineralogy, in a rational manner, I think him a
valuable character in this country. He is very young.

—William Thomson to Joseph Black, 1784

WHEN SMITHSON ENTERED Oxford, in early May
1782, Britain was reeling from its humiliating surrender
of the American colonies, a defeat that had forced the
resignation of Lord North, the prime minister, and was to drive the
King to consider abdication. North happened also to be the chancellor
of the university, and the Tory stronghold of Oxford bore the gloom
and shock that pervaded the government particularly heavily.
Smithson, however, likely saw things in a different light. His family
friend, Lord Shelburne, whose neighboring estate of Bowood had
served throughout Smithson's childhood as a great salon for scientific
and political radicals like Joseph Priestley, Richard Price, and Jeremy
Bentham, had all of a sudden become the only member of the
opposition with whom the King would negotiate. Shelburne was
elevated to a key position in the new ministry; as secretary of state
for home affairs, he was in charge of negotiating the peace with the

United States. Smithson's aunt Henrietta Maria wasted no time in sending a letter of congratulations and recommending her husband George Walker as one who could "speak to America."[1]

Smithson at seventeen, his hair powdered and his slight frame clad in the latest fashions, had connections to the very pinnacle of power. Shelburne was not popular, however, and though he was made prime minister a few months later in the summer of 1782 following the death of Lord Rockingham, his ministry was short-lived. Shelburne's precarious position mirrored Smithson's own fragile equilibrium at university. Oxford, as one of only two universities in England, was a rarefied rite of passage for the elite of the land. It was above all an experience shared between fathers and sons, and this was a bond that eluded Smithson entirely. Most boys were accompanied by their fathers on their momentous entrance to this honey-colored kingdom of domes and spires and pinnacled towers. "When my Father & myself came in site [sic] of Oxford from the Hill on the Burford Road," Smithson's friend Davies Giddy recalled, "I was curious to inquire about the several buildings. My Father pointed out every one of them, excepting two which he could not make out. These were the Observatory & the Hospital. The Observatory had been built since my Father's time."[2] Smithson, though no stranger to the privileges of the place—his mother's husband John Macie, his uncle Lumley, and his own father the Duke of Northumberland had all attended (at Queen's, St. Edmund Hall, and Christ Church, respectively)—was without a father at this important moment, an absence underscored by the age-old rituals of that first day.

Following a tradition that had been in place since the sixteenth century, each newly arrived student was presented by his tutor to the Vice Chancellor to be matriculated. Smithson's tutor was Edward Dupré, a Fellow at Pembroke who went on to become Dean of the Isle of Jersey (and was so loathed for his reactionary politics during the Napoleonic Wars that his parishioners tried to leave and set up a new church).[3] While Dupré and perhaps his mother looked on, Smithson—like all students sixteen and over—took the oath of supremacy and subscribed to the Thirty-Nine Articles, testifying his adherence to the Church of England. He then joined his name to the ancient rolls of the university.

Smithson's entry, in the requisite Latin, encapsulates the problems of legacy and legitimacy that so dogged him. He signed his name "Jacobus Ludovicus Macie," and his college, "Col. Pem. [Pembroke College]," and provided the details of his age and where he had come from—"17, de Civit. Londin."—before supplying his status: "Arm. Fil." *Arm. Fil.* was short for *Armigeri filius*, son of an esquire. It was a label indicating gentle birth, signaling that the person so called was probably entitled to bear heraldic arms. Smithson, however, despite being the son of a duke was not entitled to a coat of arms, and it was extraordinarily audacious of him to register himself this way. No illegitimate son could make such a claim, and because arms could only be conveyed through the paternal line he could not gain any rights to heraldry through his mother, no matter how aristocratic his Hungerford ancestry.[4]

It was expected, too, that each student would provide his father's name; the ledger entry before Smithson's, for example, read "Coll: Di. Jo. Bap. 4. Thomas Keck 17 Samuelis de Civitate London:— Gen: Fil:" [St. John's College, May 4, Thomas Keck, 17, son of Samuel, of London, Gentleman]. But Smithson may simply not have known how to address this particular question. What he did with this space was something that had not been done in nearly two decades. He left it empty. The blank next to Smithson's name was the only such void in the register during Smithson's entire tenure at Pembroke. One would have to go back all the way to 1764, close to the time of Smithson's birth, to find another student from his college missing a father. It was a glaring omission, and one that seems to have been known to Smithson's peers. Davies Giddy, who entered Pembroke nearly three years after Smithson—and whose position could not have been more opposite to Smithson's, as Giddy's father *matriculated with him* and moved into Giddy's rooms at Pembroke to finish his own degree at the same time as his son—

recalled the blank in Smithson's entry vividly in his diary: "What is very curious his Father's name is omitted and he is merely stated to be a son of an Esquire."[5] The blank never ceased to be a subject of fascination in regard to Smithson's biography. Sometime around 1837, well after Smithson's death and probably inspired by the initiation in Chancery Court of the United States' suit over the Smithson bequest, Giddy even made an extract of Smithson's college register entry at the behest of Lord Egremont, who was related to Smithson through their shared Seymour ancestry.[6]

Life at Oxford served up a constant reinforcement of social hierarchy, a rigid stratification that mirrored society at large. It was an order predicated on wealth and intimately tied to ancestry. Two things underscored this state of affairs on a daily basis: costume and privileges. Oxford's inescapable ladder of sartorial prestige dictated a particular gown to each rank of student, and the top rung far outshone the ones below. From far down the cobbled length of Broad Street one could see the noblemen shimmering in their bright silk robes—in whatever color the student and his tutor selected: celestial blue, emerald green, a rich burgundy or claret. The gold tufts or tassels on their black velvet caps were just as easily spotted, giving rise to the term "tuft-hunters" to denote those toadies who sought to befriend the wealthiest students.[7]

Smithson probably suffered acutely the knowledge that he was not destined to wear the sparkling colored silk gown and gold-tasseled cap that the other sons of dukes wore. Nor was he bound for Christ Church, Oxford's most aristocratic college, and where his father had attended. Instead, Smithson's home lay across the street from Christ Church's bravura Tom Tower, at Pembroke College. Tucked in the shadow of St. Aldate's Church, Pembroke was not a rich college. It nestled quietly into its narrow site abutting the old city wall. The neoclassical chapel, the college's newest addition, was fifty years old when Smithson arrived. The library was tucked under the eaves above the Hall, an improvement at least on its original location in a cramped tower room over the south aisle of St. Aldate's. Pembroke projected no bold statement, it laid no claim to prominence, and it suffered still from this lowly status in the 1830s, when John Keble referred to it as "the cellar and dusthole of the university."[8]

Nevertheless, Smithson's gown, the elegant black silk gown and black-tufted velvet cap of the gentleman-commoner, marked him as a member of the elite just the same—on the rung below the nobles and enjoying many of the same privileges. Only the uppermost ranks enjoyed privileges such as special seats at Chapel and Table, and the liberty of free time and few responsibilities. At Pembroke in the 1780s there were no noblemen; Smithson as a gentleman-commoner, one of less than a dozen at Pembroke, sat freewheeling at the top of the pile, above commoners, scholars, and exhibitioners, battelers and servitors. Their easy access to large allowances enabled them to devote their days to parties, drinking, and games, and they whiled away their hours in the little pagoda-like summerhouse in the college's walled gardens. Gambling was common, a habit Smithson seems to have picked up early and pursued with gusto his entire life. Outside Oxford's walls these wealthy young men enjoyed the manly pursuits of hunting, shooting, and fishing. They were a famously bad influence on the many commoners, away from home for first time, whose desire to follow suit led to duns entrapping them for debt and to severe punishments from tutors and masters. Gentlemen-commoners were given lavish suites of rooms, often three or four rooms in total. In Pembroke certainly, Smithson would have had the finest the college had to offer. And the records of Smithson's expenditures, lodged in Pembroke's unwieldy buttery or battels books, vault him consistently during his time in residence up among the top two or three spenders in the college—making it likely that his rooms were the locus of many gatherings and parties.[9]

In May 1782 Smithson was Pembroke's only new student that month, and the third since January. Admissions were in decline across Oxford. A culture of decadence had settled on the university, and little was expected or required of these largely unsupervised, privileged students. Some professors had not taught a course in years,

Doctor Johnson at Pembroke College, Oxford, 1784. A pencil sketch done for the
Master's daughter by John Roberts, the artist who painted Smithson's Oxford portrait.

and many nobles and gentlemen-commoners scarcely attended
lectures. "In no places of education are men more extravagant,"
declaimed Vicesimus Knox in 1781. "In none do they learn to drink
sooner; in none do they more effectively shake off the firm sensibilities
of shame and learn to glory in debauchery; in none do they learn
more extravagantly to dissipate their fortunes."[10] For those of wealth,
life in eighteenth-century Oxford was one long, lazy stumble towards
the role of gentleman in society.

Pembroke, though home to few elites and even fewer famous
alumni, could however boast of one colossus. Samuel Johnson, who
left Pembroke after only thirteen months, without settling his debts
and without graduating, was now the glory of the entire university.
The friendship he enjoyed with Pembroke's Master, William Adams,
brought the celebrated doctor over the Pembroke threshold several

times in those last years of his life, the very years that Smithson was most enmeshed in life at Oxford. At the Master's "blue-stocking Parties" for Johnson, the conversation bounded through a staggering litany of subjects, from Milton's sonnets to marriage to an argument over what happens to wine or cider when it is frozen. Much of the tenor of the exchange was due to the setting provided by Master William Adams.[11]

Pembroke's Master Adams was an exception to the status quo at the university: a well-respected divine who was nevertheless immersed in nontraditional alliances. He was a frequent correspondent with the likes of the radical Dissenting minister Richard Price, whose prominent defense of the American rebels was attracting widespread notoriety in England. In Price's eyes the American "revolution in favour of universal liberty" opened up "a new aera in the history of mankind," and he told Adams, "No people ever enjoy'd a better opportunity for establishing a plan favourable to an amendment in human affairs."[12] Pembroke under Master Adams was a place of intense philosophical debate, and students must have closely followed events across the Atlantic. Had Adams lived into the fraught years of the French Revolution, he would probably have come to grief in Tory Oxford. Instead, in the early 1780s, it appeared only that he had finally breathed some life into Pembroke after the interminable rule of his predecessor John Ratcliffe.

Significantly, Adams was known to be "considerably deep" in that most avant-garde of fields, chemistry.[13] Pembroke under Adams gathered beneath its roofs a remarkable stable of young men who, quite exceptional to the general rule in eighteenth-century Oxford, went on to dedicate their lives to an Enlightenment ideal of public science. Smithson, masquerading confidently through an elite social world that he felt remained just beyond his grasp, had found an unlikely home, the closest thing the eighteenth century had to a meritocracy—the flourishing underground realm of chemistry.

In the matter of the sciences, as in so much else, the university in the eighteenth century had sunk into a gouty complacency. Oxford's era as a midwife of the scientific revolution was long since past.

Well over a century had elapsed since members of the "Invisible Club," the precursor to the Royal Society, had congregated at the coffeehouses of Oxford, or since Robert Boyle haunted rooms over the city's apothecary shops, assisted in his experimental work at the air pump by the brilliant Robert Hooke. In the intervening decades the Museum's chemical laboratory, the first purpose-built laboratory in all of England and hailed at its inception in 1684 as "perchance one of the most beautiful and useful in the world," had fallen into disrepair. Outdated and filthy, it sat ignored, its rear yard overflowing with bones, broken crucibles, retorts and other detritus.[14] Medical studentships at Christ Church, the preeminent college for such study—and lone among the Oxford colleges in not losing numbers during the late eighteenth century—were vacant for much of the second half of the 1700s, and if not vacant then filled by a lawyer rather than a physician. The Church's stranglehold on matriculation kept the university in this stolid state. Oxford was impervious to the winds of change blowing from places on the Continent like Leiden, where experimental physics had been introduced to the curriculum as early as 1675—breezes that were welcomed up in Edinburgh and down in London. Edinburgh was hailed as "the Lyceum of Brittain," and its medical students came from all over Europe and America. Physicians who chose to train in London found a world of professional opportunities that Oxford simply could not offer. Cambridge, too, while suffering as well from the strictures of a Church-dominated curriculum, offered a much better education in medicine and mathematics than could be found at Oxford.[15]

When Smithson arrived in the spring of 1782, however, there were distinct signs that the torpor was beginning to lift. The Radcliffe Observatory, under construction since 1772, brought a replica of the classical Tower of the Winds from ancient Greece to the skyline of Oxford. Equipped with the finest scientific instruments available, including two eight-foot mural quadrants, a transit telescope, and a twelve-foot zenith sector, it formed an important center for astronomical and meteorological observations. The astronomer Thomas Hornsby oversaw it, while also teaching experimental philosophy at the Museum (the Old Ashmolean, today the Museum of the History of Science). And a new Anatomy School had been endowed at Christ Church in the 1760s, where courses were offered in anatomy, physic or botany. Housed in a stately stone building in a back courtyard behind the college kitchens, the place was known informally as Skeleton's Corner, on account of the bodies that were quietly brought to the college's back entrance, used in dissection lectures, and then interred in a deep hole in the basement of the school.[16]

In the matter of chemistry in particular, great stirrings were afoot. In 1781, the year before Smithson's arrival, Dr. Martin Wall, Oxford's first Reader in Chemistry and fresh from study in Edinburgh, had given his first course.[17] In conjunction with his appointment the old chemical laboratory in the cool, vaulted basement of the Museum was completely refurbished (its thick stone walls furnished budding chemists with "fresh crops of nitre every three or four months," according to one of Smithson's contemporaries).[18] Oxford seemed cognizant that it was falling behind, especially as regarded its historic competition with Cambridge. The creation of a chemical professorship and the fixing up of the laboratory to accommodate it "to the purposes of a chemical school" went a long way in trying to redress the imbalance between the two rivals.[19] It was another small step for scientific education in the wave that had been building since the creation of the Radcliffe Infirmary in 1770. It also coincided with the beginning of a general elevation in the status of chemistry as a discipline.

For most of the century, chemistry had not been adjudged a subject of much standing. It was seen instead, along with anatomy, as a useful—but lowly—element in the preparation for the practice of medicine. It existed as a supporting or practical subject, buttressing the more theoretical discipline of natural philosophy, which typically encompassed the mathematical sciences of astronomy, mechanics, and optics. In an age before the term "scientist" was coined, the pursuit of knowledge of the natural world was called natural philosophy, and scientists termed natural philosophers. The scientific revolution of the seventeenth century had banished a medieval conception of the universe, ejecting man from his comfortable place at the center of it all. Newton, in his *Philosophiae Naturalis Principia Mathematica* and *Opticks*, had articulated a series of laws that made sense of this new world view and explained the forces and phenomena of nature both on earth and in the heavens. His work had given man a picture of the universe as a gigantic timepiece, a vast but rational mechanical world subject to universal laws. It also ushered in an entirely new way of thinking and established a practice of discovery rooted in experiment and empiricism. By the time of Isaac Newton's death in 1727, natural philosophy was viewed as the "handmaiden" of theology and had become an appropriate, and almost essential, gentlemanly pursuit.[20]

Chemistry, on the other hand, was still shaking itself loose from its occult roots in alchemy and the search for the philosopher's stone, the elixir of eternal life. It was a science that required dirtying the hands—which hardly made it a subject for polite education. In these last decades of the eighteenth century, even as chemistry made tremendous advances, the general public continued in some ways to perceive the science as the work of wizards and diviners, men who worked furtively behind heavy stone walls making rank-smelling concoctions and risking dangerous explosions. As late as 1798 one of Smithson's society friends jokingly referred to him as "Rosicrucian Macie," and boasted that he wouldn't be surprised if Smithson "discovered a method to prepare the universal medicine to prolong Life & also the long wished for Art of making Gold, that summum bonum of all human desires & concerns."[21]

There was in fact a major alchemical scandal in 1782, during Smithson's first year at Oxford, one that reverberated alarmingly in the university's tiny chemistry community. James Higginbotham Price, a respected and well-liked twenty-seven-year-old alumnus, announced that he had successfully converted mercury into gold and silver. His claim was confirmed by the King's assayer, and Price began to receive serious popular attention. He dedicated the paper publishing this discovery to Oxford's chemistry professor Martin Wall. Oxford some months earlier had awarded Price an honorary degree in physic, which gave the mistaken appearance that the university supported his work; the Royal Society, likewise, had recently elected him a Fellow. When the scientific establishment started clamoring for proof, however, the hoax began to unravel. Price finally welcomed a panel of Royal Society examiners to his house for a demonstration, where in front of them all he committed suicide, downing a glass of distilled laurel water. Back at Oxford Martin Wall and others scrambled to distance themselves from the sordid event, fearful of endangering their own reputations and the credibility of the science they were trying so valiantly to bring into prominence.[22]

From the vantage point of the early twenty-first century, Smithson inhabited a remote and murky chemical universe, a world in which oxygen was understood as dephlogisticated air and heat was perceived as an "imponderable" or weightless fluid. Chemical processes were evident all around them—a nail rusting, copper flashing turning green, grapes fermenting—but the principles underlying these changes were still unknown. Scientists were only just beginning to relinquish an understanding of matter based on the ancient Aristotelian elements of earth, air, fire, and water. They organized the knowledge they had of chemical reactions in affinity tables; each column charted in descending order a substance's attraction for another. In these diagrams minerals, metals and other substances were represented by their old alchemical signs—a crescent moon for silver, the female sign for copper, an inverted triangle for water. Chemistry, as Joseph Black told his students in Edinburgh, was not yet a science. "We are very far from the knowledge of first principles."[23]

Chemistry needed to find its own Newton, who would uncover the laws that governed the processes of change. The accumulation of knowledge through experiment and observation was the way forward. "Experiment is the Thread that will lead us out of the labyrinth," Joseph Black assured his classes.[24] Smithson learned early on that the best contribution he could make to increase knowledge, and in turn to better the condition of mankind, was to amass facts. Virtually all his publications exemplify this urge—they are narratives describing species and making them identifiable by broadcasting the typical reactions a substance made under certain replicable conditions. "If molybdate of soda or potash, or, I apprehend, any other molybdate, is heated in a drop of sulphuric acid," he explained in one paper, "the mixture becomes of a most beautiful blue colour, either immediately, or on cooling."[25] Smithson's papers, obscure and obsolete today, were some of the many incremental, essential building blocks that helped bring chemistry into the modern age.

For some 150 years chemistry's practices had remained fairly constant—a standard repertoire of experiments and techniques, using the furnaces, crucibles, and retorts that had long been in service. But now, in the decades prior to Smithson's matriculation, a series of discoveries had rocked the foundations of the science as it had long stood. Pneumatic chemistry, the study of different "airs" or gases, opened up an entirely new field of inquiry, bringing with it major changes in laboratory practice. British scientists had unmasked the ancient Aristotelian element of air, revealing it to be not elemental at all but rather a multiplicity of airs, each with different chemical properties. Joseph Black in Scotland discovered fixed air (carbon dioxide), a vapor which extinguished a piece of burning paper put in it "as effectively as if it had been dipped in water."[26] Joseph Priestley, in the laboratory of his patron Lord Shelburne, identified and described numerous airs, including nitrous air (nitric oxide), marine acid air (hydrochloric acid), alkaline air (ammonia), phlogisticated air (nitrogen), and dephlogisticated air (oxygen). And Henry Cavendish in London investigated inflammable air (hydrogen), given off by metals dissolving in acids, finding it to be highly explosive and much less dense than common air.[27]

Pneumatic chemistry was structured around the concept of phlogiston. The German professor Georg Ernst Stahl had coined the theory at the beginning of the eighteenth century to explain the process of combustion. Phlogiston (from the Greek word meaning "to burn') was posited as the invisible substance inside all flammable bodies, like a spirit present in the heat or light released by burning bodies, and by metals in the process of calcination. When a candle burning in a closed vessel was extinguished after a time, it was understood that combustion had stopped because the air inside the bell jar had become completely saturated with phlogiston. Conversely, oxygen, when Priestley discovered it in 1774, enabled a candle to burn more brightly, and a little mouse enclosed in it to live twice as long as in common air, and thus Priestley decided that the air must be utterly void of phlogiston—so he called it dephlogisticated air.

Air, so difficult to capture, weigh, or analyze, had for the most part eluded chemists in the past. Priestley and Cavendish pioneered a number of new techniques for the collection and manipulation of gases. They developed new instruments as well; Priestley's nitrous air test led to the design of the eudiometer, used to analyze the purity of the air, and soon inspectors all over Europe were assessing the quality of the air at resorts and in cities and other spaces. His "Directions for impregnating water with fixed air" (a paper dedicated to the Duke of Northumberland) promoted the making of artificial soda water, bringing the supposed medicinal benefits previously available only at spas to a much wider audience.[28]

Chemistry, with these discoveries, began to move into the realm of the acceptable as an object of study. The natural philosophy lecturers who had already been traversing the country for much of the century, exhibiting the awe-inspiring secrets of the universe to genteel society, added chemistry experiments to their repertoires. And the inventions these discoveries soon engendered, the hot-air balloon most notably, captivated the public and greatly enhanced the allure of chemistry.

Chemistry's rising status in late eighteenth-century England derived most especially from a growing appreciation of its role in transforming modern life. As the first stirrings of the Industrial Revolution spread

over the country, men became increasingly aware of the power to
be commanded through the harnessing of the natural world. Martin
Wall, angling to make his case that chemistry was an appropriate
subject for Oxford's gentlemen of fortune, focused especially on the
utility of the science. Chemistry, he told his students, was intimately
connected with "all those arts, which have a most material influence
in human life." He touted the invention of gunpowder, and the
application of mercury in curing venereal disease. He noted
chemistry's contributions to the arts of dyeing, tanning, painting,
and even bread-making; he called forth the improvements seen in
making glass, porcelain, enamel, and cement—and explained how
these improvements had led to advances in instrument making and
optics and further scientific discoveries. He galloped through the
worlds of agriculture and medicine, enumerating the advances that
chemistry had brought to these fields. He even credited chemistry
with the spread of civilization that followed the birth of the printing
press, by stressing chemistry's role in the improvement of printing
techniques. He exhorted his students to devote their attention to
this branch of knowledge, which he reminded them was indirectly
responsible for some of the most singular events in history. All the
work naturalists were currently engaged in seemed to be leading
society to a moment in the near future where it could be possible
to claim that the Moderns were finally surpassing the Ancients. "I
cannot conclude," he finished, "without congratulating you on the
advantages, which we of this age enjoy."[29]

The pursuit of science, and chemistry in particular, duly became
something of a craze during Smithson's tenure at Oxford. From a
state of near dereliction in the years preceding Smithson's
matriculation, the study of chemistry became by the late 1780s the
most popular subject at Oxford. Martin Wall had fourteen or fifteen
students enrolled in his first course in 1781; in 1788 the new
chemistry reader, Thomas Beddoes, could boast that his chemistry
course had drawn "the largest class that has ever been seen at Oxford,
at least within the memory of man, in any department of

knowledge."[30] One student wrote to his father, "If you ask how I relish this new science [chemistry],—perhaps I have been too much attached to it. It has engrossed so much time, that I have hardly been able to spare an hour for anything else."[31] The poet Percy Bysshe Shelley was just one of many who went through a phase of being obsessed by chemistry while at university; one contemporary recalled that "his hands, his clothes, his books and his furniture were stained and corroded by mineral acids. More than one hole in the carpet could elucidate the ultimate phenomenon of combustion . . . It seemed but too probable that in the rash ardour of experiment he would some day set the College on fire or that he would poison himself . . ."[32]

Parents were not pleased with their sons' enthusiasm for the subject. Chemistry to them was a siren, luring their sons away from the trammeled routes to gentlemanhood—the trajectories to Parliament, to callings in divinity or law, to managing the family estate, to all those destinations for which the boys embarked when they first went up to Oxford. Mrs. Harris wrote to her son James, the future diplomat Lord Malmesbury, at Christ Church: "You are desired not to attend the anatomical lectures this year, as your father has no idea of bringing you up as a surgeon."[33] Charles Hatchett's father was said to have offered him £3,000 and a place in Parliament in an attempt to get him to abandon chemistry.[34] "It [chemistry] is new," another son tried to reassure his father, "and, like other new things, has prejudice to contend with."[35]

For the most part, in the end, however, parents had little to worry about; the men at Oxford talking science did so in a superficial, fashionable way. The school was primarily, as the Victorian-era professor Henry Acland later reflected, for the "recreation of amateurs."[36] Smithson, nevertheless, was already very serious about the subject. His pursuit of science appears to have been rigorous and profound, unlike the dilettantish enthusiasms of many of his Oxford contemporaries. Though still in his teens he seems to have readily surpassed what Oxford had to offer. According to Davies Giddy,

Smithson, "an undergraduate, had the reputation of excelling all other resident members of the University in the knowledge of chemistry."[37] The curiously precise wording of this praise—"resident members of the University"—could be construed as encompassing the professor Martin Wall as well, suggesting that Smithson the student had already eclipsed his master. (Smithson was made a Fellow of the Royal Society a year before Wall, and, notably, did not step forward to be one of Wall's sponsors when Wall was nominated.)[38]

Smithson pursued his scientific investigations to such a degree that he soon developed an expertise in an arena hardly being taught yet at Oxford: mineralogy. As early as 1784, when Smithson was still just nineteen, his proficiency in mineralogy was declared to be "already much beyond what I have been able to attain to" by the person preparing the university's first course in the subject.[39]

Minerals had long been a subject of gentlemanly fascination. For centuries they had been prominently displayed in the cabinets of curiosities of kings and courtiers, as objects of beauty and symbols of wealth. Up until the 1780s these aesthetic interests had dominated efforts to systematize the world of minerals. Mineralogy had been organized as part of natural history, with a classification system much as Linnaeus had recently accomplished for the plant and animal kingdoms, based primarily on visible, external characteristics such as hardness, color, luster, and beauty. But the mineral world, with its wild profusion of types, presented a vastly more complicated organizational challenge. The drive to create a system to order the mineral produce of the world was an Enlightenment undertaking that guided Smithson's entire career; and it was a project that remained an unresolved challenge throughout his lifetime. He and his contemporaries recognized that only with an effective classification system could the full potential utility of the mineral riches of the earth—for mining, medicine, agriculture, and manufacturing—be exploited.

By the mid-eighteenth century scientists had begun to lay out the path for a new understanding of stones, one based in chemistry.

Chemical mineralogy made its first real advances in the German states and in Scandinavia, where the rulers—eager to exploit the natural wealth of their dominions—had established Europe's first mining academies. Sweden, in particular, had pioneered the art of mineralogical chemistry. Its academy featured a well-equipped laboratory and sent its students all over Europe to study the latest mining developments. Its chemists had developed a system of classification, which grouped substances into six "principles" or basic forms of matter: salts, earths, metals, inflammables, airs, and water; stones were considered earths, and divided into varying numbers of "primary earths," such as vitrescible, calcareous, argillaceous, and chalky. This system was adopted by the renowned lecturers in the medical school at Edinburgh, and made its way in turn via the Scottish-trained Martin Wall to Oxford.[40]

Smithson was profoundly influenced by this school of thought, and Swedish mineralogists like Torbern Bergman and Axel Cronstedt became his heroes. Smithson extensively annotated his English translations of Cronstedt's *System of Mineralogy* (both those of 1770 and 1788). He subscribed wholeheartedly to Cronstedt's belief that the laboratory was but a microcosm of the forces in nature. "Mineral bodies being, in fact, *native chemical preparations*, perfectly analogous to those of the laboratory of art," Smithson argued in one of his papers, "it is only by chemical means, that their species can be ascertained with any degree of certainty." In 1811 he still referred to Cronstedt as "the greatest mineralogist who has yet appeared."[41]

Cronstedt's most important contribution to the laboratory was the blowpipe, an old assayer's tool that he refined for analytical work. The blowpipe, when placed in the flame of a candle or lamp, could direct an intense jet of heat onto a mineral sample the size of a few grains, mimicking in miniature—and with considerably more control—the effects of a large furnace. Simple and compact, it could be packed into a small carrying case, making on-site analysis during mineralogical fieldwork possible. But it was also a tool that demanded incredible technical skills. In order to maintain a steady, high flame, it was necessary to breathe in through the nose while blowing out through the mouth, something the Swedish chemist Jöns Jakob Berzelius likened to "that which a man experiences when he endeavours at the same to turn his right arm and his right leg in opposite directions."[42] One also needed to develop a familiarity with a wide range of diagnostic results, to know how substances reacted to the flame. Calcareous spar (calcite) expanded and broke apart violently when heated; arsenic yielded a garlic smell; zeolites frothed and foamed; and fluors like phosphorus emitted a light in the dark. Smithson became very expert at the blowpipe. His prowess was such that later in life well-known scientists came to observe his technique, and he also contributed a number of improvements to the instrument.[43]

Smithson evidently undertook a profound self-education while at Oxford—going well beyond the mineralogy that was covered in Wall's chemistry lectures. He must have read widely, probably conducted extensive fieldwork, and experimented at length in the laboratory. His library includes a 1775 book entitled *A Method of Making Useful Mineral Collections*, and he had most likely already begun to build his own mineral collection by this time. In order to familiarize himself with as many varieties as possible he probably also studied all the mineral cabinets he could access. On the top floor of the Museum in the old Ashmolean building lay the moldering collection of rarities and curiosities donated by the Museum's founder Elias Ashmole, a seventeenth-century astrologer and alchemist. The room was crowded with skeletons and skins and muskets and model ships, along with the thigh bone of the Hertfordshire Giant, a crocodile in brandy, and a depiction of the crucifixion minutely carved on a fruit stone. In one corner sat a large old wooden cabinet, where Smithson perhaps passed hours poring over the specimens inside. It was full of precious stones, fossils, and crystals, augmented in 1758 with William Borlase's collection of crystals, minerals, and metallic bodies from Cornwall.[44]

In addition to his studies, Smithson drew about him all the people he could find who were similarly passionate about chemical mineralogy. The friendships that Smithson cultivated at Oxford, the ones that he maintained in the years after university, were founded upon a kind of cult of Cronstedt. Smithson's friend Christopher Pegge, for example, came from a long line of distinguished antiquaries. His love of mineralogy and his devotion to a career in science represented a profound shift in the natural order of things. He should by all rights have passed through the crucible of old Oxford and left as a member of the clergy, to pick up the torch carried already for generations by his illustrious family line. As he wrote to Mark Noble, a Birmingham-based antiquary and author of a book on Oliver Cromwell: "Had not my attentions been twin'd to different studies from those of my Ancestors I might I dare say have heard of my friend [Noble] before this by his productions but I must confess myself rather an admirer of a Bergman & Cronstedst [sic] than of a Camden [antiquary William Camden, author of the popular *Britannia*]."[45] Pegge elected to practice medicine, but posterity deemed him a second-rate talent, and he is remembered now mostly for some amusing doggerel (Pegge, "like Death, that scythe-armed mower, will speedily make you a peg or two lower") and for pompously donning, at the tender age of twenty-five, the ancient costume of the physician—the full-bottomed wig, large turned-up cocked hat, and gold-headed cane.[46] His enthusiasms nevertheless mark him as a member, with Smithson, of this distinct breed of English Enlightenment gentleman: citizens of a new republic of science, dedicated to the cause of "improvement."

First among Smithson's friends at Oxford was William Thomson, the one who delivered the introductory mineralogy lectures at the university. About four or five years older than Smithson, Thomson was originally from Worcester, the son of a physician who had studied in Leiden. He received his MA from Oxford in 1783, studied for a year at Edinburgh under the great chemist Joseph Black, and was back at Oxford, appointed Dr. Lee's Lecturer in Anatomy at Christ Church, in 1785. He had numerous contacts in the medical and scientific establishment; he was also an active member or founder member of several specialized philosophical societies, such as the Natural History Society in Edinburgh, the Society for Promoting Natural History in London (to which he sponsored Smithson), and the Linnean Society. Thomson and Smithson stayed in touch all the rest of their lives, even after a scandal caused Thomson to leave England in 1790 for good. They were best friends forging ahead together, and Thomson was absolutely critical to Smithson's early success.[47]

Among Smithson's other philosophically minded friends were Davies Giddy (later Gilbert), who eventually went on to become president of the Royal Society; George Shaw, an MA from Magdalen who was teaching several courses of botany at the university and later became assistant to the curator of the natural history collections at the British Museum; and William Austin, a physician at Oxford's Radcliffe Infirmary some ten years older than Smithson who became a professor of chemistry in 1785.[48] Two men not known to be Smithson's friends but who must have been acquaintances in the tiny world of science at Oxford were James Sadler and Thomas Beddoes. Sadler worked as an assistant in the chemical laboratory, but he is best known as the first English aeronaut; his balloon flights were major public theatre, drawing thousands of spectators. Beddoes, who later fathered the Romantic poet Thomas Lovell Beddoes, studied medicine and became a Reader in Chemistry at Oxford. His ardent embrace of the French Revolution, however, ultimately forced his departure from the university in 1792. He went on to Bristol and established the Pneumatic Institution, which was dedicated to applying the latest scientific research in gases to the treatment of disease and became famed for launching the career of Humphry Davy.[49]

Smithson and his friends knew that they still operated in profound ignorance. The current state of chemical knowledge, as Smithson wrote, consisted "entirely of isolated points thinly scattered like lurid specks on a vast field of darkness . . ."[50] But the air was fragrant with possibility, and they felt themselves to be on the cusp of greatness. They had discovered a life imbued with purpose, founded upon a belief that chemistry could be an engine of improvement and prosperity. Smithson in particular stood out as exceptional; William Thomson proudly broadcast his belief that Smithson was "a valuable character in this country."[51] His friends recognized him as a promising member of this new order of philosophers who would lead England to the forefront of the future.

James Smithson's university career can be split into two distinct halves. During the first years, 1782 to 1784, he was regularly in attendance at Pembroke and presumably under the guiding force of divines such as his tutor Edward Dupré and Pembroke Master William Adams. However irreverent and decadent his life as a wealthy gentleman-commoner might have been, Smithson distinguished himself by acquiring an exceptional store of mineralogical and chemical knowledge and collecting about him the brightest scientific minds at the university, many of them friends he would carry with him as he exuberantly entered into the intellectual ferment of scientific London. For the second half of Smithson's Oxford career, 1785 to 1786, the scene of action moved to London. Smithson was scarcely up at Pembroke during the last two years of his degree. His gaze had turned already to the larger proscenium, to the scientific societies, the coffeehouses, the bookshops and the mineral dealers, the glassblowers, instrument makers, and traveling lecturers—to the spectacle of the most cosmopolitan city in the world.

The pivot dividing these two halves, the hinge which marked Smithson's entry into manhood and his precocious betrothal to a career in science, was a trip, a very important adventure. In late July 1784 he left Pembroke.

THREE

Staffa: The Cathedral of the Sea, 1784

You must know that the party consisted of 4—Mr. Massie [Smithson], a young English gentleman fond of chemistry at Oxford; Marquis _____ [Count Andreani], an Italian a good sort of man; St. Fonds; & Mr. Thornton, I believe an Irishman. They reached Inverary together, & Massie was advised to wait the return of the others, as he was delicate; but his object was Stafva.

—Charles Greville to his uncle Sir William
Hamilton, 1784

BY THE SUMMER of 1784, balloon mania had swept England. With the Montgolfier brothers' invention in France the previous year, flight—that immortal aspiration of man—had finally been achieved. Hardly a month went by without some new ascent. At Oxford a Mr. Rudge was exhibiting his red and white striped Persian silk balloon; a Frenchman had his Montgolfier model at the Anchor in Cornmarket, and James Sadler had raised enough of a subscription to build a highly decorated one seventy feet in circumference, and to send aloft a little "aerial traveler" (a dog). In London thousands crowded the artillery grounds and public parks to watch this miraculous new contraption rise into the clouds over the city's chimneypots and steeples. Ladies piled their powdered wigs high in balloon-like confections, trussed with swags of silk and tassels. There were parties and poems and even the first mention of a mile-high club—a dare of five guineas on 100 to "Lord C____y" to ascend with a "a female whom, if he is not positively to get with child, they are at least to be agitated into a delirium, and worked up and down among the clouds, till the senses are lost and then— Lord have mercy upon the balloon!"[1]

It was chemistry that had made all this possible. "Let Posterity know, and knowing be astonished," read the plaque erected near Hatfield in Hertfordshire to mark where Vincenzo Lunardi's blue silk balloon "Revisited the Earth" after the first manned flight in England, that this "Wondrous Enterprise" had been "successfully achieved by the Powers of Chemistry." Smithson's science was transforming the world. The heavens had been opened up for exploration, in large part thanks to the pioneering work on gases by Britain's own: Black, Cavendish, and Priestley. While the majority of English welcomed balloons as a source of wonder, for Smithson and his crowd they were the product of scientific research and the means to undertake further philosophical experiments—elegant floating laboratories. Scientists embarked on a whole range of new research problems: the best apparatus for making the gas, the quality of the air high in the atmosphere, its temperature and barometric pressure, and "whether the growling of thunder is owing to echoes, or to successive explosions."[2] For nineteen-year-old Smithson it was a time of unprecedented optimism. What further barriers could not be surmounted? The possibilities the future held seemed boundless.

In early August 1784, in a blaze of self-promotion, the French scientist Barthélemy Faujas de St. Fond, who had just published the first book on the Montgolfier brothers' balloon experiments, arrived in London. Traveling with him was a precocious twenty-one-year-old Milanese nobleman named Count Paolo Andreani, who had a

Fingal's Cave, Staffa, from Faujas' A Journey through England
and Scotland to the Hebrides in 1784.

few months earlier made the first balloon ascent in Italy, to the
approbation of 20,000 of his astonished countrymen. These balloon
experts had not come to London in pursuit of daring new aerial
exploits, however. Despite all the enthusiasm in the scientific
community surrounding this new frontier, Faujas was preparing for
a very different kind of voyage of discovery—one that presented an
opportunity for Smithson.

Faujas was mounting a geological expedition to the wilds of
western Scotland. He wanted to document a volcanic history of Britain,
a follow-up to his extensive tome on the extinct volcanoes of
France, the verdant conical mountains of the Massif Central, which
had only recently been recognized as volcanic. Faujas planned to
produce a lavish folio volume describing the natural wonders of
England and Scotland, with the third member of his party, a Quaker
doctor named William Thornton—an able draftsman who went on
to a second career as an architect in the United States—doing the
illustrations.[3]

The culmination of Faujas' trip was to be a visit to the remote Hebridean island of Staffa off the western coast of Scotland. Staffa was home to Fingal's Cave, a remarkable natural wonder that had only been "discovered" in the previous decade by Sir Joseph Banks. Fingal's Cave was a vast vaulted hall of sleek hexagonal columns of basalt, rising to meet in a majestic gothic arch—a more extraordinary sister to the Giant's Causeway in Ireland. When Banks came face to face with the cave for the first time, he exclaimed, "Compared to this what are the cathedrals or the palaces built by man! Mere models of playthings imitations as diminutive as his works will always be when compared to those of nature."[4]

A decade after Banks' visit, his account—published in Thomas Pennant's *Tour in Scotland* (of which Horace Walpole cuttingly said Banks' account was the only part worth reading)—remained the only natural history description of the island. A great debate over the origins of the earth was just beginning to be waged between two camps— the Neptunists and the Plutonists—and Staffa rapidly became a frontline in the controversy. The Neptunists, led by the German geologist Abraham Werner, believed that the earth had once been covered by a single universal ocean and that the crust of the earth had been formed by the sediment left when that chemical-rich body of water had receded. The Plutonists or Vulcanists, on the other hand, led by James Hutton in Edinburgh, saw the earth's formations as the work of an internal fire; they focused on volcanoes as evidence of the combustion inside the earth. Both sides grappled with the mysterious origin of crystalline rocks such as basalt, commonly found throughout the sandstones and limestones of northern Europe. Some, like Nicolas Desmarest in France, finding prismatic formations of basalt in the Auvergne, argued that basalt was in fact volcanic; Richard Kirwan, the Irish chemist soon to become one of Smithson's most important champions in London, believed that the extraordinary folds and forms of such rocks in the British Isles were caused by the great Flood; "Even the columnar basalts at Staffa and the Giant's Causeway, he claimed, were 'rent into pillars' by diluvial blows."[5]

As the eighteenth century progressed, extinct volcanoes had been discovered from Iceland to Italy. It became clear to scientists that volcanoes were not a modern phenomenon, and nor were they isolated formations. As Smithson, who became a strong proponent of volcanism, wrote, "volcanoes, and their ejections . . . cease to be local phenomena; they become principal elements in the history of our globe; they connect its present with its former condition; and we have good grounds for supposing, that in their flames are to be read its future destinies."[6] Such theories, however, were highly controversial. They challenged the centrality of the concept of the universal ocean and, by association, the biblical deluge. But they also implicitly argued that the globe was much older than had been supposed; the idea that volcanoes had once spewed and roared over the bucolic sites of present-day habitations, like the Habichtswald near Kassel in Hesse, was shocking. At Staffa, as at the Giant's Causeway, there was no visible crater or even volcano-shaped mountain. If basalt was volcanic, where had it come from? Faujas and others believed it to be the product of "a grand subterranean conflagration." William Whitehurst, a Derbyshire geologist, theorized that the volcano that must have existed there had sunk into the ocean; he even suggested that it might have formed part of the lost city of Atlantis.[7]

Staffa captivated the men of science, and it remained territory ripe for study. Smithson evidently saw this expedition to Staffa as an opportunity to make his mark. In 1784 his closest mineralogical friends were filled with talk of Staffa. Smithson's Oxford friend William Thomson had already made the hazardous trip on his 1782 tour of western Scotland after completing his studies in Edinburgh. And right at this moment, in the summer of 1784, the collector Charles Greville and his famous volcano-loving uncle Sir William Hamilton were en route for Staffa—though they never had weather good enough to permit them to visit. Greville, who was some fifteen years older than Smithson, seems already to have become fast friends with Smithson by this time, an acquaintance probably fostered through William Thomson. Smithson's family background would

have intrigued Greville, as Greville had been a good friend of
Smithson's half-brother Algernon Percy (the second son of the Duke
of Northumberland) when they were both at university in Edinburgh
around the time of Smithson's birth.[8]

At nineteen Smithson wanted to be at the forefront of some kind
of discovery, to join the community of science by making some
important contribution to knowledge. A voyage to study a part of
the world as yet untrammeled by European scientists was a bold,
classic way of doing so. Sir Joseph Banks had made his reputation in
his early twenties taking part in Captain Cook's *Endeavour* voyage of
1768. His name was forever entwined with the Transit of Venus (and,
less decorously, with the conquest of the South Seas women). His
triumph had brought him the patronage of George III, the directorship
of the botanical gardens at Kew, and eventually a baronetcy and the
presidency of the Royal Society. Staffa, while not so very far from
civilization, was nevertheless still at the forefront of the unknown; it
had yet to be fully documented and described, and its very caves and
cliffs seemed to hold a key to the mystery of the origin of the earth.

First, though, Smithson had to get himself attached to Faujas de
St. Fond's expedition, something he managed with the help of
William Thomson. On August 12, 1784, Faujas, Count Andreani,
and William Thornton, a few weeks before their departure for
Scotland, were guests at the Royal Society, England's oldest and
most prestigious scientific society. In the hours prior to the meeting,
they had been feted at the dinner of the Royal Society Club, held
in the Crown and Anchor tavern on the Strand. These convivial
dinners were open to an elite group from the Royal Society and
their guests. Toasts of port, Madeira, and claret, over mountains of
steaming beef, were followed by post-prandial glasses of brandy,
rum, and other liqueurs. By the end of this August dinner the men
were "all pretty much enlivened," according to Faujas, and they
had tripped along past the steeples of St. Clements Danes and St.
Mary-le-Strand to the white stone arches of the impressive new
Somerset House, just in time for the meeting.

The meetings of the Royal Society, in contrast, were anything but lively. Under the painted ceiling of the ornately decorated room, the latest scientific work was delivered as if from on high, without the possibility for debate or discussion. Members with their guests sat ranged like school children along narrow straight-backed benches, looking up at the mahogany throne where Sir Joseph Banks in his heavy tricorn hat presided, the secretaries on either side below him. One of the secretaries monotonously read out the papers reporting the latest scientific research; there were no demonstrations or illustrations. Count Andreani nevertheless confided to his diary that it was impossible to find the meetings boring, because the room was overflowing with the most celebrated men of science; he was awestruck scanning the faces of the assembled. Other visitors had much the same impression. The Swedish chemist Berzelius felt "a kind of intoxication" at seeing so many famous personalities gathered under one roof. And the Swiss botanist Augustin-Pyramus de Candolle likewise confessed that although the seances could not have been more lifeless, he was riveted by the opportunity to stargaze.[9] Most thrillingly, in this august company it was the guests who were especially honored. Banks' first order of business was to read out the names of the strangers in their midst, followed by the members who had presented them.

One of the names read out that evening was that of a young man who, like Andreani, would have been wide-eyedly taking in the proceedings for the first time: James Louis Macie. Smithson and Thomson (who was not yet a Fellow either) had succeeded in getting themselves invited.[10] At some point, Thomson—whom Faujas later lauded as "a very good naturalist"—managed to present Smithson to Faujas. Faujas readily accepted Smithson, whom he called "a studious young man, who was much attached to mineralogy," as a member of his expedition. They probably conversed in French. Thomson's respect for Smithson's standing as a wealthy gentleman, or perhaps Smithson's projection of himself as such, led Faujas to render Smithson's name Macie as the aristocratic Monsieur de

Mecies.[11] One imagines it was a mistake that Smithson did not readily correct.

Smithson surely passed the last days before departure excitedly packing his equipment and collecting information on the personages he might encounter on his travels. He had been based over the summer of 1784 out in West Haugh, in Surrey—in all probability at a place his mother had taken (she rented a series of elegant summer residences along the Thames, most of which were conveniently located across the Thames from the Duke of Northumberland's Syon House).[12] William Thomson in those final days busily wrote letters of introduction for Smithson to various acquaintances in Scotland. One such letter, to the distinguished professor of chemistry at Edinburgh, Joseph Black, commenced: "I send you my friend Mr. Macie, who is about to take the same tour that I did two years ago." Thomson went on to praise Smithson's skills in mineralogy; Smithson, he said, enjoyed a "proficiency . . . already much beyond what I have been able to attain to."[13] In addition to all his encouragement and support for the Scotland trip, Thomson also put Smithson forward at this time for membership in a new philosophical club: the Society for Promoting Natural History.

The Society for Promoting Natural History (SPNH), which met monthly at the Black Bear on Piccadilly, was one of a number of scientific clubs proliferating in the coffeehouses of London towards the end of the century; it offered a new and intensely egalitarian forum for science, with the possibility to congregate and debate, a kind of model of ideal civil society. The SPNH was the brainchild of James Edward Smith, who as a medical student in Edinburgh had started a similar society and who went on in 1788 to found the Linnean Society. It included members far from London, such as the potter and Lunar Society figure Josiah Wedgwood and honorary member John Wheelock, president of Dartmouth College in the United States. This wide-ranging corresponding network lent the effort an imprimatur of selflessness. The gathering became one of men interested in more than economic self-advancement; it became a group committed to the benefit of mankind through the exchange of scientific information. The order of business was quite formal; members had to be proposed and seconded. William Thomson, who had also been active in the natural history society in Edinburgh, had been unanimously elected in April 1784. At the end of August, as the sun went down on the first full day of Smithson's expedition to Scotland, Thomson nominated Smithson for membership. James Edward Smith seconded him. A month later, at the next meeting, while Smithson was just at that moment departing the Hebrides, he was admitted a member.[14]

On the evening of August 29, at six o'clock, Smithson set out on his first scientific tour. His travel was part of a new kind of Enlightenment age tourism, focused on studying the natural riches of the countryside and how these raw materials were being exploited. Whereas a typical traveler heading north might have sought out the minster at York or the picturesque ruins of Fountains Abbey, this group was fixated on geology and topography, and on the new manufactories taking advantage of these resources. England was pioneering the application of technology to industry, and Smithson and his fellow philosophers saw with rising excitement the future such developments could bring. As they passed up through the Midlands to eastern Scotland and then west across the Highlands to the Hebrides, they collected data on the weather, the lay of the land, and the local mineral productions. They took in the haze of smoke from the lime kilns, the clanging forges, and the giant roaring waterwheels powering the new mills and factories. They admired the wares and met with the men, like those who comprised the Lunar Society of Birmingham, who were transforming a region of wild and rocky hills filled with caves and underground streams into the heart of England's nascent industrial economy.[15]

Smithson was the youngest of the party, two years younger than Count Andreani, and he was, as William Thomson had noted, "very young" in general.[16] But he was hungry for new information and eager to establish himself. He was already diligently keeping a notebook of observations. As they left London in the bright summer evening light, the four men—Faujas, Count Andreani, William Thornton, and Smithson—were split between two carriages, with their servants together following in a third post-chaise. The roads outside London were so good—like "the avenue of a magnificent garden"—and the moonlight so fine, they continued until four in the morning before resting at Stevenage. There, Faujas noted—in remarks that typified the kind of observations the men made throughout their journey—that "the air [was] quite pure" and the mercury stood at "half a degree below the freezing point."[17]

Their first important stop was at Newcastle, where coal and lead were king, and which was already becoming an important center of heavy chemical manufacture. "Brick-fields, potteries, glass-houses, earthenware-works, and works for making white-lead, minium, and vitriol" crowded one bank of the River Tyne, facing an equally vigorous line-up on the other side of "manufactories of sheet-iron, of tin, of all kinds of utensils, brass-wire mills, flattening mills, &c." The men descended several coalmines, recording the strata that they passed through as they went down the pit, making notes on the steam engine pumping out water and the ventilator purifying the air, and regretting the twenty horses that "live in this profound abyss" hauling the coal through the underground passages—evidence to this group of the reliance still on some benighted age-old practices, despite so much progress.[18]

They devoted about five days to the study of Newcastle and its environs, and Faujas' extensive description of the region's commerce was indicative of the focus of the trip. Conversation was wide-ranging amongst these philosophers—all of them shared an interest in architecture, for example—but central to their thoughts were the concepts of utility, science as an engine of progress, and the role good government played in the wellbeing of society. Newcastle, to Faujas' eyes, represented "a magnificent picture, wherein so many useful men can be seen to find ease and happiness in work, while at the same time, they promote the well-being of others; and, as the last result, they contribute to the prosperity of the government, which watches over the safety of them all."[19]

In the evenings they drank toasts: "To liberty. To the happiness of mankind in general. To friendship." The newly minted government of the United States, triumphant following the signing of the Treaty of Paris the year before, supplied to these idealistic men a model for their musings. William Thornton was so enthusiastic about America that he emigrated to Philadelphia in 1786, became a citizen two years later, and a few years after that submitted the successful design for the new U.S. Capitol in Washington. Smithson was coming to this group from the stimulus of Pembroke under Master Adams, where America's unique political experiment was probably a topic of spirited discussion. Faujas, prior to his Scotland tour, had spent time in Paris at Benjamin Franklin's, where he met "several Americans of exceptional ability, who . . . have since played a distinguished part [in the founding of the United States]." His conversation with his travel companions seems to have been littered with references to Franklin's philosophies; in Newcastle, admiring the abundance of coal and the ingenious road system developed to bring it to the wharves, Faujas recalled the sage old Philadelphian's dictum that "those who assist in constructing them [roads and canals for the cheap transport of vital combustible materials] ought to be ranked among the benefactors of mankind."[20]

Just thirty miles north of Newcastle, directly on their route to Edinburgh, loomed Alnwick Castle, the sprawling crenellated seat of Smithson's father, the Duke of Northumberland. Virtually all of the land in the region lay under the control of the duke, whose wife's family had long been known as the Kings of the North for the tireless battles they had waged against the Scots on behalf of the Crown in centuries past. It would have been virtually impossible for Smithson not to have crossed his father's land, and equally unlikely that a stop at Alnwick was not at least discussed by this group.

Anyone in a position to obtain an invitation to the castle angled for entry. Samuel Johnson, on his way to meet Boswell for their Scottish tour in 1773, passed an afternoon at the castle, where he boasted of being "treated with great civility by the Duke"—a passage that, poignantly, Smithson marked in the copy of the *Works of Johnson* he acquired in the 1820s.[21] The duke, in resurrecting Alnwick as the Percy family seat after three hundred years of decay, had spared no expense to restore the castle's ancient splendor. Some 1,480 books of gold had been used to enrich the Gothic decorations in the chapel, and even the nails in the stables out in the courtyard had been gilded. He had hired the best, most fashionable architects and designers—Robert Adam in the castle and Capability Brown out in the gardens—and put hundreds of men to work. Thousands of trees had been added to the lush, rolling landscape, and the river had been dramatically widened to make it more picturesque.[22]

The duke, with his "enlightened" bearing, was exactly the kind of man that the people with whom Smithson was traveling would have admired and courted and generally esteemed. Even with his extravagant outlays—"expenditure unexampled in his time" according to one contemporary—Northumberland greatly augmented the Percy fortune, shrewdly exploiting the coal seams on the property to underwrite his many improvements to the land and the laborers' cottages.[23] He was a founding trustee of the British Museum, and vice president of the Royal Society of Arts, an organization founded to promote the prosperity and ingenuity of English manufactures. He was a commissioner of the first bridge of the eighteenth century over the Thames, the elegant engineering feat of Westminster Bridge— and he commissioned Canaletto to paint it for him. He was also a sponsor of the first successful balloon flight across the Channel, which took place shortly after Smithson's trip to Scotland; the story of the American adventurer John Jeffries desperately shedding the bunting, tassels, anchors, and even his own clothing as he and his mate tried to stay aloft long enough to reach the shores of France— they landed in a forest in France "almost as naked as the trees"— was trumpeted in a letter to the duke written while still in the air.[24]

The Duke of Northumberland was, in short, a great appreciator of beauty, a canny assessor of business, and a man utterly unafraid of the new. Smithson naturally wanted to claim him. But most of all, though, he must have wished to be claimed, to be acknowledged by his father and receive his approbation. Others were beginning to recognize Smithson for his scientific talents and enthusiasm; the duke of all people was a man capable of appreciating such qualities. If a stop at Alnwick Castle was discussed, or if the subject of Smithson's paternity came up in conversation, Faujas declined to write about it. In his account the party departed reluctantly from Newcastle, wishing for more time to study the area but conscious that as the season advanced the likelihood of reaching Staffa diminished.

Although Staffa was their much-anticipated destination, Edinburgh held equally tantalizing riches for the group. For Smithson in particular the visit to Edinburgh was a watershed; it was the place where he built the first of his many relationships with powerful, internationally respected figures in the world of science. Enlightenment thought in Britain had reached its fullest flowering here in Edinburgh. It was the seat of a famous university, the center of one of the most prestigious medical faculties in the world, and the playground of a group of philosophers renowned for their sociability. In clubs, pubs, and at each other's houses, these men immersed themselves in discussions on the moral progress of society, the role of the individual within it, and the great project of organizing human knowledge in all its many disciplines.

The group arrived in Edinburgh late in the evening towards the end of the first week in September, their carriages rolling up to an elegant inn fronting one of the expansive squares that anchored the neoclassical wonderland of the New Town. Across a ravine the medieval old city perched high on a forbidding outcropping, its ancient blackened castle towering over the scene, its narrow, dark streets vertiginously lined with tenement houses. Their first visit, the next morning, was to this crowded old part of the city, where the university was sited, to meet the chemist Joseph Black, a revered teacher then at the height of his renown. In his mid-fifties when Smithson met him, Black was tall and thin, with a low, clear voice and luminous dark eyes that danced out from his parchment-pale face.

Black, together with William Cullen before him, had moved chemistry beyond the province of artisans and medical men and into the realm of patronage and power. It was here in Scotland that chemistry had first become part of a gentleman's education, and here too that the aristocracy and landed gentry had embraced chemical innovation in agriculture and industry.[25] Black's research into the nature of heat had helped James Watt to see how to improve the steam engine, and his investigation of Henry Cavendish's work on the density of "inflammable air" (hydrogen), which had shown for the first time that the gas was lighter than air, had led to the idea of the balloon. He hardly published anything, however, and he was famed most of all for his teaching; many of the students he taught became professors themselves and spread their enthusiasm for chemistry to all the corners of the world. Black filled his lectures with clear, unshowy demonstrations. The Whig MP Henry Brougham years later would recall Black's "perfect philosophical calmness," and how he could "pour boiling water or boiling acid from a vessel that had no spout into a tube, holding it at such a distance as made the stream's diameter small, and so vertical that not a drop was spilt."[26] His emphasis on quantitative work and precise measurements, his dismissal of conjecture, and his reluctance to profit from any of his research were lessons that Smithson likely took to heart.

Joseph Black saw in Smithson a young man to encourage; Smithson in his turn saw an opportunity to cultivate a mentor. He began a correspondence, offering himself up as a conduit for news from London. "If I can do any thing for you in this part of the world I beg you will command me Sir," Smithson later wrote to Black, "as I shall be happy of any oportunity [sic] of testifying my grateful sence [sic] of the many civilities I received from you while at Edinburgh."[27] Smithson remained incredibly proud of this connection his whole life; in 1825, more than four decades after his first meeting with Black and already a quarter-century after the old man's death, Smithson resurrected a letter Black had written him and published it with annotations in the *Annals of Philosophy*.[28]

James Hutton, who at that moment was immersed in the writing of his *Theory of the Earth*, the publication that would later make him known as the father of modern geology, was equally impressed by the young Oxford student; he gave Smithson a plum assignment, a commission to collect some specimens for him from Stonesfield, an area near Oxford rich in slate where fossils had been discovered in the 1750s. Hutton had turned Edinburgh into his own geological laboratory; at the Salisbury Crags, below the twisted swirl of Arthur's Seat, he discovered evidence that the formation had once been molten rock, forced, he imagined, by the internal heat of the earth into a much older strata. His fieldwork led him to theorize an expansive new history for the earth, a world with "no vestige of a beginning, no prospect of an end." The idea of an endless cycle of geological change was a radical diversion from traditional biblical interpretations of the earth's short timeline. Hutton's theory offered a key to interpreting the geological evidence of the land that Smithson and some of his peers found feverishly exciting. "The mind seemed to grow giddy," John Playfair exclaimed, "looking so far into the abyss of time."[29]

Smithson's stopover in Edinburgh was not an extended one. "We took a rapid view of the town," Faujas noted. They planned instead to return after the Staffa expedition. Smarting from the gouging they received at the hands of their fancy Edinburgh hotel, they departed for Glasgow. (Faujas in his published account did not fail to mention the fee charged for the half-sheet of paper, "which one of us had called for, to save the trouble of opening his portfolio"— as much a barb at his travel companions as it was at the landlord, and evidence at this early stage of friction already in the party.) In

Edinburgh they hired a draftsman to accompany them, "to take such views as should appear to us the most important for the advancement of the natural history of volcanoes in the part of the Hebrides which we were going to visit."[30] For Smithson it was the beginning, finally, of the big adventure, the reason for the journey in the first place: the trip to Staffa.

They passed quickly through Glasgow, where "natural history is not so much cultivated . . . as it is at Edinburgh," explored Dumbarton for a day, and finally entered the outsized landscape of the Highlands at Loch Lomond. The rugged, unforgiving Highlands, full of melancholy mists, were only just becoming an object of touristic attention. An extensive network of roads had been built following the defeat of the Jacobite rebellion in 1746, making the area much safer and easier to access. There was a growing fascination too for raw and brutal scenes such as those the storm-tossed western coast of Scotland offered up; Edmund Burke's theory of the sublime had transformed how the English perceived beauty in nature, and travelers now sought out majesty in the fearsome rather than the picturesque.

And the Highlands were also the home of Ossian, the third-century warrior poet whose ancient Gaelic epics captivated Europe in the late eighteenth and early nineteenth centuries. The poems were eventually determined to be the fabrication of their discoverer and "translator," James MacPherson, but their popularity remained undimmed. William Hazlitt's list of the "four of the principal works of poetry in the world" featured Homer, the Bible, Dante, and Ossian. Napoleon would later carry his Italian translation onto the battlefields, and have scenes from Ossian painted on the ceiling of his study. The rage for Ossian spread even to America, where the city of Selma, Alabama, took its name from one of the poems, and Thomas Jefferson declared, "I think this rude bard of the North the greatest Poet that has ever existed." Smithson and his group were focused on Scotland's geology, but they were traveling through the landscape of Ossian, Scotland's own home-bred Homer, and the fascination was inescapable.[31]

It was 10.00 p.m. when they arrived at Luss, wet with the rain and weary with the road, only to be shooed away by the landlady. The circuit judge, Lord Braxfield, was fast asleep, his party occupying all the rooms. Off they trundled once more, the drenched postilions cursing in the darkness, and it was half past three in the morning before they came upon another lodging, further up the western edge of the loch, at Tarbet. Here too it was full, but there was room at least to stable the exhausted horses. They were saved from sleeping in their carriages by the landlady, who gave up the mattresses from her own bed. The lordly Count Andreani, who traveled with two servants, still chose to sleep in his carriage, Faujas reported, and "M. de Mecies kept one of the mattresses; Thornton and I shared the other. We slept three hours wrapped up in our cloaks, and our fatigue disappeared." When the morning dawned, the sun glinted off the silvery loch and the snowcapped Ben Lomond in the distance. Shepherds sheltered under the pines, their white sheep aglow against a verdant ground. The scene, sweetened with the perfume of fresh tea brought by their hostess, endeared Tarbet to all of the men. "I shall often dream of Tarbet," mused Faujas, "even in the midst of lovely Italy with its oranges, its myrtles, its laurels, and its jessamins."[32]

At Inveraray the group was again turned away at the only inn on account of the imminent arrival of the circuit judge. Faced with another night in their carriages, they sent a letter to the Duke of Argyll apologetically explaining their situation. An invitation to Inveraray Castle soon arrived, carried by a French painter employed at the castle, and they traipsed around the mirror-still waters of Loch Fyne to their regal new home. The duke was so delighted with his guests that he urged them to stay several weeks. Like a number of Scotland's aristocratic landowners, the duke had a personal interest in chemistry, especially as regarded its potential for agricultural improvements. Conversation at the castle was refined and learned, and often conducted in French for the benefit of Faujas and Andreani. The food was delicious and "prepared after the manner of an excellent French cook." Dinners lasted long into the evening, as the ladies retired to a separate room and the men continued to drink and talk, relieving themselves—as was the custom, to Faujas' astonishment—in the chamber pots in the corners without ever letting up their banter. Eager though they were to get to Staffa, the party nevertheless passed "three whole days in this delightful retreat, devoting the mornings to natural history, and the evenings to music or conversation."[33]

Already, however, relations in the traveling party were becoming problematic. Smithson, the youngest and the last to join the group, seems to have been the odd man out, though there was no love lost among any of them by the end of the journey. Here at Inveraray Castle the travelers apparently encouraged Smithson to remain behind with the duke's family while they continued on to Staffa, convinced he was too "delicate" for the treacherous sea voyage. Smithson was, unsurprisingly, angered by their plan to abandon him, and he probably nursed his wounded pride into a full-blown grudge. Throughout his life his behavior seems often to have been driven by a need for vindication and validation, a pattern that might well have been impressed upon him by his mother's behavior. In this case the affront seems only to have hardened Smithson's resolve to reach the pillared isle.[34]

As they left the castle and journeyed on towards the coast, tensions continued to simmer among the band of explorers. For eight long hours the group's three carriages jostled their way through a narrow, inhospitable pass, surrounded by "arid mountains of the most savage aspect," until they reached a little cluster of civilization called Dalmally, lying along a river in a pretty valley. There they were introduced to the village schoolteacher, an energetic twenty-eight-year-old named Patrick Fraser, whom the men hired as their guide in the Highland region. Fraser, an Ossian devotee, provided the group with an entertaining cultural detour from the route to Staffa. He ushered them into a humble stone cottage to meet MacNab the blacksmith, where they could hear "the sublime verses of this ancient poet" sung in the Hebridean singing tradition passed from generation to generation. The blacksmith, however, could not be found, and so the men never heard the Ossian poems, but the rest of MacNab's family gathered to honor the visitors nearby at MacNab's brother's house. Inside, clustered together by an open peat fire, and bathed in the light of an unusual iron shovel-like lamp, they all drank from a wooden bowl of milk ceremoniously passed around. The primitive smoky scene, at once intimate and sacred, struck Faujas as particularly memorable; he ordered the Edinburgh draftsman to sketch it. The resulting picture shows the four travelers together with Patrick Fraser at the left. Dressed in their long coats, hats and riding boots, they look on wryly as one of them—presumably Faujas—accepts the wooden cup from a barefoot woman in Highland dress. Two of Faujas' party stand apart, bemused, quietly talking. The other, small and focused, sits alone staring intently at the event; this one may well be Smithson.

The next morning, at the rather late hour of ten o'clock, the party set off for Oban, twenty-four miles distant on a terrible road. They were intent on completing the journey before nightfall, but this group of savants, preoccupied with observing the changing geological character of their surroundings, had never been one to pass quickly through a region. Busily making notes and collecting specimens as they advanced, they lost a further hour and a half studying an ancient "Druidical circle" they chanced upon. Darkness fell and brought with it a torrential thunderstorm, and the party became hopelessly lost. In complete blackness they stumbled on, the horses skittish and the road dropping off precipitously around them, the "frightful uproar" of the sea far down below. One of the carriages overturned in a stream; soaked and shivering, they finally found Oban completely by accident when an old man with long, white hair and "floating drapery of the same color" answered their cries for help. "It is Ossian!" cried out a giddy, exhausted Thornton. "Let us fall at his feet."[35]

When the bedraggled travelers awoke late the next morning, they discovered that the village's four fishing boats had already departed

Faujas' tour stops at a Druidical circle, 1784.

for the day's work, and only "two wretched boats" remained. Whatever tensions had been brewing exploded now as the men prepared to embark on the final leg of their journey. The passage to the island of Mull comprised at least thirty-three miles in treacherous reef-filled waters, according to Faujas, and he refused to make it in such a tiny boat, "with herring-fishers who did not understand a word of English."[36] Smithson and the others were nevertheless anxious to press on to Staffa and Fingal's Cave. In the end, a petulant Faujas alone among the men refused to get aboard. He promised to meet up with them within a few days, when he could catch a ride with a larger boat.

The arguments did not end with the loss of Faujas, however. Smithson, Andreani, and Thornton arrived on the island of Mull, but it is not at all clear that they stayed together thereafter. From Faujas' sunny account of their adventure, it would appear that the three men carried on together to Mr. Maclean's at Torloisk, set off eventually for Staffa, were forced by the weather to stay on there after a perilous sea voyage, were besieged by lice, had hardly any food, and returned to Mr. Maclean's for a jovial reunion with their

French friend. Smithson's own diary of the trip, which seems to have been very thorough, perished in the Smithsonian fire of 1865. The American scientist Walter Johnson, wishing to highlight Smithson's adventurous spirit, published a few excerpts pertaining to the Staffa trip in his 1844 article—and these are the only parts of Smithson's diary that survive today. Most importantly, Smithson sent a letter to London recounting what had happened. The letter itself no longer exists. Charles Greville, its likely recipient, however, excitedly transmitted the details amongst the London cognoscenti. He and his uncle Sir William Hamilton had made an unsuccessful stab at reaching Staffa just a few months earlier and had been humiliated by Faujas' taunting. With relish did he learn of Faujas' cowardice. "You remember," he told his uncle, "when we were at measuring of the base on Hounslow Heath, I was informed of Faujas de St. Fond's exultation over you that he should get to Staffa, which you could not do, & heard my lamentations on that occasion. I had the ill-nature to rejoice at the failure of his excursion; it convinces me he is a Gascon." Smithson's letter had apparently detailed the quarrels and breakdown of the rest of the party, too, such that Greville concluded: "these 4 philosophers, whose joint labours were to have been recorded in a folio volume, will return with the inclination of describing each other better than they will be able to do the country they have passed."[37]

According to the excerpts of Smithson's diary, Smithson landed at Aros on the east side of Mull and crossed overland to Torloisk, the closest point on Mull to Staffa. Torloisk was home to Lachlan Maclean, a member of the leading family on the island, and it seems that all the men ended up here eventually, despite their quarreling. From Maclean's austere stone house, high on a bluff over the sea, they gazed out on a breathtaking carpet of water dotted with rocky outcroppings and islands, including the one they had come all this way to visit: Staffa.[38] They probably waited for Faujas, eyeing the weather impatiently, until finally they decided they could wait no more. But the three—Smithson, Andreani, and Thornton—unable

to reconcile their differences, did not head off together. Smithson
set out on his own—in "a separate boat"—into the pitching waters:

> Mr. Turtusk [Torloisk] got me a separate boat,—set off about
> half-past eleven o'clock in the morning, on Friday, the 24th of
> September, for Staffa. Some wind, the sea a little rough,—wind
> increased, sea ran very high,—rowed round some part of the
> island, but found it impossible to go before Fingal's cave.[39]

The little boat, filled with Smithson, his servant, Mr. Maclean's
nephew, and the sailors, was tossed and smacked on the waves as
it made its way out towards the islands. Soon the men left the
relative shelter of the coast and emerged in the open gusting sea,
where they attempted to round Staffa. Reluctantly, Smithson was
forced to relinquish the idea of viewing Fingal's Cave, which was
located on the far side of the island, from its best vantage—out on
the open sea. They were "obliged to return," he confided to his
diary. Among the men, there can be little doubt that it was only
Smithson who wished to be out on the waters that day. Staffa
presented an almost unbroken line of cliffs, a forbidding prow of
rock that seemed eager to dash a boat to pieces. On the northeastern
corner of the island lay a small rocky beach, the only possible landing
place—and one usually only successful with the help of the few
island residents, who threw ropes to visitors and hauled them in.
They "landed on Staffa with difficulty," Smithson reported dryly.
Predictably, the "sailors press to go off again immediately." This
imperious nineteen-year-old, however, replied he was "unwilling
to depart without having thoroughly examined the island. Resolve
to stay all night."

The island was uninhabited, except for one family living in a
smoky stone cottage and eking out an existence on the land.
Inevitably, Smithson encountered Andreani and Thornton, who had
also landed on the island, but it seems at this point that the men
were barely on speaking terms. Smithson pointedly did not refer to

them by name in his diary, coldly noting only that "the other party which was there had already come to the very same determination" to spend the night. And so it happened that some fifteen people—the geologically minded visitors, their servants, and the family members—were "all crammed into one bad hut . . . [and] supped upon eggs, potatoes, and milk."

The ocean pounded the island so ferociously throughout the stormy night that no one could sleep. The little hut shook and the pot rattled on the fire as the waves concussed the land. As they listened to the roar and felt the sea thrashing against the rocky cliffs, the frightened visitors sensed the real brute force of nature. If the earth was the creation of a series of catastrophic events, or even if it was the result of a more gradual cycle of constant change, as James Hutton proposed, then might not such a raging ocean have the power to reshape the rocky cliffs or consume whole some section of the place? "The recollection of [Staffa's] ponderous masses of basalt, its confused heaps of bending pillars, its vast cavities, and all those signs which characterize it as the mere fragment of a mighty ruin," one visitor wrote in 1818, "would suggest the possibility of a similar visitation."[40] Geological change, so imperceptible to the human eye, seemed overwhelmingly visible here.

In the morning the unlucky sailors soon realized they were trapped for yet another day, for as Smithson recounted: "Got up early, sea ran very high, wind extremely strong—no boat could put off. Breakfasted on boiled potatoes and milk; dined upon the same; only got a few very bad fish; supped on potatoes and milk; lay in the barn, firmly expecting to stay there for a week, without even bread."

Interestingly, Smithson's diary entry as excerpted by Johnson includes no rapturous description of Fingal's Cave. Nor does it make any mention of the fieldwork Smithson must have undertaken on Staffa that blustery Saturday. Smithson sent an entire hogshead or barrel of material on to Edinburgh once he landed on the mainland; so there is little doubt that he did do some collecting on Staffa. Faujas complained on Mull of the difficulty of finding good cabinet specimens, on account of the "moss, lichens and heather" that covered everything. But while Faujas praised the "fine zeolites" that William Thornton brought back from Staffa, Smithson was not so lucky. Smithson evidently wrote to Charles Greville that he had been unable to find any good exemplars at all on the island. The swarm of naturalists who had descended on the island in the space of a few short years had practically denuded it of specimens. As Greville told his uncle, "The poor man I sent had been on Stafva, where he executed his orders so well that Massie could not find one piece of cubic Zeolithe, for which Stafva is most famed after the Collumns." When Smithson finally published his analysis of zeolite in 1810, he covered up this awkward fact and simply boasted of having collected his specimens on Staffa. By that time his friend Greville was dead, so there was no one left to dispute this little reference to the heroic adventures of his youth.[41]

On Sunday morning around 5.00 or 6.00 a.m. Smithson was awakened with the news that "the wind was dropped, and that it was a good day." His party, laden with all his finds, "set off in the small boat, which took water so fast that my servant was obliged to bail constantly—the sail, an old plaid—the ropes, old garters." Thornton and Andreani and the others had to wait the return of their two boats, which had pushed off to the safety of Iona after dropping them on Staffa.

Faujas had in the meantime arrived at Maclean's, and he spent the weekend anxiously scanning the raging seas with his telescope looking for his companions. He caught sight of them finally on Sunday afternoon around 1.00 p.m. If Smithson had left Staffa at dawn, he would surely have already have fetched up at Torloisk by mid-morning, hours before the others. Perhaps back at Mull Smithson did have one last final reckoning with his fellow tour members; it is here at Maclean's that Faujas reported "Monsieur de Mecies" left the party. However, in Greville's telling of it—which came from Smithson—Smithson "returned to another part of Mull" and carried on to the mainland, never turning back. No one's account seems wholly reliable; the squabbles amongst the party seem to have so poisoned relations that each had reason to inflate or gloss over certain events. Smithson, in any case, separated from the group.

He reached the mainland at Oban, where he stayed a night or two before leaving the town on September 29. Here at Oban he finally had an opportunity to lay out all his specimens, catalogue them, and wrap them carefully with hay or paper, before sending them on to Edinburgh. The innkeeper was horrified by the operation. "Mr. Stevenson charged half a crown a night for my rooms," Smithson grumbled to his diary, "because I had brought '*stones and dirt*,' as he said, into it." Smithson undoubtedly battled with recalcitrant innkeepers throughout his life; such encounters were a staple of the Englishman's Grand Tour. But this incident at Oban is more revealing as an example of how single-minded Smithson was about his collecting, and how incomprehensible that pursuit was to outsiders. He was like the young American explorer Ferdinand Vandiveer Hayden, caught up in the crossfire of the Sioux Indian wars of the 1850s, whose steadfast pursuit of specimens led the incredulous Indians to christen him, "He who picks up stones while running."[42] Smithson, too, remained doggedly bent on building a comprehensive mineral cabinet—despite his "delicate" constitution, and even as he found himself swept into what he called "the hurricane of war" during the turbulent years of Napoleon's domination of Europe.

Smithson spent more than a month making his way back down to London. He probably returned to Edinburgh—as the rest of the group later also did—to spend more time in the company of that city's philosophers. Anecdotal family history, passed down through the generations, has Smithson stopping to stay for a while with a schoolteacher living on the main street in Doune, near Stirling.[43] He also explored the rich mineral deposits in the mines at Leadhills, one of the most important ore deposits in Scotland, high up on the estate of the Earl of Hopetoun, where James Watt and Joseph Black and others had advised the operations.[44] By October 28, 1784, he had arrived in Northwich in Cheshire—the center of England's salt trade.

Rock salt occurs naturally in Cheshire, laid down some two hundred million years ago when the region was a wide, shallow sea. An "open pan" method of collecting salt by heating brine had been practiced in the region since before the arrival of the Romans. Mining for rock salt was, on the other hand, a much more recent development, the inadvertent discovery of coal prospectors in the late seventeenth century. Top-bed mines, lying approximately one hundred feet below the surface, had been worked for several decades by the time Smithson arrived in Northwich. He was most keen, however, to see the new bottom-bed mines, some three hundred feet below the surface, which had only been operational a few years. "They let me down in a bucket," he wrote in his diary, "in which I only put one foot, and I had a miner with me. I think the first shaft was about thirty yards, at the bottom of which was a pool of water, but on one side there was a horizontal opening, from which sunk a second shaft, which went to the bottom of the pit, and a man let us down in a bucket smaller than the first."[45] This primitive transport, by which one lurched precariously down into the dark airless pit, gave way within a few decades to a much more comfortable passage. The absence of the thick black dust found in coalmines and the spectacular effects of light on the lustrous, faceted, cathedral-like chambers below, with their giant supporting salt pillars, soon drew tourists from all over the world. In 1844 Tsar Nicholas was the guest of honor at a banquet in the bottom bed of Northwich's Marston mine, the crystalline vaults above illuminated by the sparkle of one thousand candles.[46]

By the time Smithson returned to London at the beginning of November, the scientific community had spent two weeks squawking with delight over the humiliating turn of events for Faujas' heavily promoted tour. Opinion on Faujas had universally turned. Scientific London had discovered that the Frenchman whom they had received so decorously a few months earlier had been playing many of them for the fool, borrowing indiscriminately to satisfy an unquenchable thirst for luxury. A wounded William Thornton complained that

Faujas "is entirely led by Interest and to it would sacrifice the dearest Friend—he is a total Stranger to delicacy . . . Nothing but treachery has marked his behaviour yet, and treachery of the most base kind."[47] The news that a cowardly Faujas had stayed behind on the mainland while the rest of his party forged ahead tickled the imagination of the cognoscenti in London.

It was Smithson's letter to Charles Greville that initiated all this talk. Greville's membership in the Dilettanti, the Royal Society, the Society of Antiquaries, and a number of gentlemen's clubs provided him with a variety of forums for the liberal exchange of gossip. The stories contained in Smithson's letter rapidly circulated in London. Sir Joseph Banks, as the one who had first brought Staffa to the scientific world's attention and who as the president of the Royal Society was patron and arbiter of discovery, was naturally the first person to whom everyone wanted to pass on the delicious tale. "Faujas de St. Fond has made a ridiculous figure in Scotland," Charles Blagden, secretary of the Royal Society, wrote to Banks, with some glee. To which Banks replied, "How Faujas is ever to shew his Face again I do not easily guess . . . those who see him will not easily forget his Conduct in his Scotch Tour."[48] A few days later Jonas Carlsson Dryander, Banks' librarian at Soho Square, also wrote to relay what he had heard: "Faujas, who is not yet come back, has not been to Staffa; but, when he came to the place where they were to cross over to Mull, he considered that the passage was dangerous and the vessel bad, and staid behind on the main: when the other three were come over to Mull they quarrelled; and Massey went by himself to Staffa. I don't know if Thornton and Andreani went to Staffa or not; but I heard from Mr. Greville to day that even they had quarrelled, and that Thornton was gone by himself to Glasgow. So much for the issue of this great company of travellers!"[49]

The form of both Blagden's and Dryander's stories was identical to Greville's. Blagden's letter confirmed that the source of the news was Smithson. He told Banks, "Luckily, Thornton, whose drawings will furnish a record, I have reason to believe, found courage enough to venture over [to Staffa]: the only person I am sure of having gone, however, is Mr. Massey, whose letters are come to town with this account."[50] The dissemination of this news marked Smithson's real initiation into the world of scientific London. Still only a nineteen-year-old student at Oxford, he was heralded, at least initially, as the only member of this famed party to have successfully ventured to Staffa.

In the half-century that followed, Fingal's Cave became one of the most important pilgrimage sites of the Romantic Age. It inspired countless poems and other works of art. Keats heralded the cave as "this Cathedral of the Sea," and Wordsworth called it the work of "the Sovereign Architect." Turner painted it dashed by great bursts of white water and blustery light, and Mendelssohn captured its shimmering beauty in his Hebrides Overture of 1832. It retained this mystique for years afterward; Queen Victoria felt compelled to make a visit in 1847, and the science-fiction writer Jules Verne chose the island as the setting for the dramatic finale of his romance *The Green Ray*.[51] Smithson's journey, one of scientific discovery, was among the earliest, presaging all the excitement to come.

Blagden, ever the wag, in writing to Sir Joseph Banks felt it necessary to add that other bit of intelligence he had been able to glean about this young explorer: "Mr. Massey is said to be a natural son of the Duke of Northumberlands [sic]: he is otherwise called Macey." The specter of Smithson's illegitimacy hovered over him, even as he made his debut among the scientific community he hoped to call home for the rest of his life.

FOUR

London: Science Like Fire, 1784–1788

Science like fire is put in motion by collision. Where
a number of such men have frequent opportunities
of meeting and conversing together, thought begets
thought, and every hint is turned to advantage. A
spirit of inquiry glows in every breast: each new
discovery relative to the natural, moral, or
intellectual world, leads to a farther investigation,
and each man pants to distinguish himself in the
interesting pursuit.

—*Account of the Literary and Philosophical Society
of Manchester*, quoted in the 1783 Oxford
chemistry syllabus

BACK IN LONDON fresh from his own successful journey
to the wilds of Scotland, Smithson returned to a city abuzz
with one of the biggest travel adventures of the time. The
captain of the *Antelope*, an East India Company packet that had been
wrecked off the shores of the Palau Islands (in modern-day
Micronesia), had recently arrived in town. Returned with the captain
was the beguiling young Prince Lee Boo, the son of the chief who
had welcomed the shipwrecked sailors.

*Prince Lee Boo, from a
portrait by Smithson's cousin
Georgiana Keate Henderson.*

Lee Boo was about nineteen or twenty, the same age as Smithson, and with "a countenance so strongly marked with sensibility and good-humour, that it instantly prejudiced every one in his favour."[1] London in 1784 was primed already for his arrival, still savoring a South Seas craze sparked by Captain Cook's journeys and the visit to the capital a decade earlier of the exotic Tahitian Omai. Lee Boo became London's own primitive, a Rousseau-esque creature set down amongst them, and through his reactions the *bon ton* delighted in their sophisticated society. Prints circulated, showing Lee Boo discovering himself in the mirror for the first time—arms (dressed in the latest English fashion) thrown up, eyes wide with astonishment. "In England there is a house for everything," he exclaimed, amazed at carriage transportation ("a little house, which was run away with by horses") and his four-poster curtained bed (a house for sleeping).

The English were captivated by the Prince's hunger for self-improvement, so in keeping with the spirit of the age, but it was his death that made his story an enduring one. Two days after Christmas, after five months in the capital, Lee Boo succumbed to smallpox. As befit the public's image of a noble savage, he passed without a groan, his mind clear to the end, far from his island home and tragically separated even from his beloved English father-figure, the captain of the *Antelope*, who could not attend Lee Boo's bedside because he had not been inoculated against the disease. Lee Boo's death became a milestone in the romantic imagination of Smithson's generation. Samuel Taylor Coleridge recalled weeping copiously at the death, a grief he memorialized later in one of his poems: "My soul amid the pensive twilight gloom, Mourn'd with the breeze, O LEE BOO! o'er thy tomb."[2]

The poignant story of Prince Lee Boo left its imprint on Smithson's contemporaries, even those like Coleridge who never met him, thanks to Smithson's cousin, the poet and man about town George Keate. Keate had been introduced to the young Prince within a week of his arrival in London. They became good friends and after Lee Boo's death it fell to Keate, as one acquaintance implored him, "not to let the memory of so much virtue pass unrecorded." Keate's *An Account of the Pelew Islands* (1787), which was based on Captain Wilson's diaries and log books and included a chapter on Lee Boo in London, became an instant best-seller. It ran through three editions within a year and was translated into French, German, and Spanish. A bowdlerized text, called *The Interesting and Affecting History of Prince Lee Boo*, became a standard primer for English schoolboys for much of the first half of the nineteenth century. After Cook's *Voyages*, Keate's *An Account of the Pelew Islands* was probably the most popular narrative of the Pacific in late eighteenth-century England, and it was more appealing in some ways than Cook's *Voyages* because of its optimistic, positive spin. Whereas Cook met his end amongst natives who were portrayed as cannibalistic savages, Keate's tract stressed the benevolence of the primitive—a reassuring message to the ever-exploring English.[3]

Smithson's great-uncle was something of a mini-celebrity in literary

London, a wealthy, gregarious dabbler in the arts. During a sojourn in Switzerland he had become friends with Voltaire, and he had remained the philosopher's closest English correspondent. Angelica Kauffmann was another of his many artistic friends. Fanny Burney, however, found him pompous and his "powers of conversation . . . not of a shining cast." Keate paraded his polish in the landscapes he frequently exhibited at the Royal Academy, in his memberships to numerous clubs and societies, and in his own museum—an old-style cabinet of curiosities, with shells, coins, medals, and minerals displayed in ormolu-encrusted mahogany cases. Keate's museum was housed in a special octagonal room decorated in the latest Etruscan style, designed by Robert Adam. (Not long after the museum was built the Etruscan ceiling collapsed and Keate sued Adam, unsuccessfully—a drama he played up in a poem called "The Distress'd Poet.")[4]

Keate shared his enthusiasms with Smithson, grandly bestowing books and minerals on his young relative.[5] The two had a number of interests in common. Like Smithson, Keate rarely neglected an opportunity to promote his illustrious Hungerford ancestry; he did not fail, for example, in the introduction to his poem "Netley Abbey, an Elegy" of 1764, to refer to his descent from Lady Jane Grey, Queen of England for nine days. On a personal level these two probably shared another profound connection. Keate, too, was haunted by the taint of illegitimacy. His father had married Rachel Kowalski, the daughter of Count Christian Kowalski, but questions swirled around Keate's parentage. One lampoon of Keate's work accused him of having been "Born of a spanking Polish Dam / Begot by God knows who—."[6]

And yet, despite this close family relationship, Keate in the end appears to have played no significant role in shepherding Smithson's entry into London circles. Although this lack of mentoring seems odd, there is an explanation. Smithson was not trying to become Keate. Even at the age of nineteen, he had no aspirations to a life as a gadfly or dilettante. He was not interested in pursuing knowledge solely in the tradition of the gentleman amateur.[7] His expedition to Staffa had taught him much about how to carry himself as an international man of science. He had begun already to cultivate prestigious contacts; he was keeping notebooks of careful observations; and he was reporting his findings, even if it was so far only in the casual form of a letter to his well-placed friend Charles Greville. Smithson was already seriously committed to a life in science, and he was, above all, ambitious.

In early 1786, for example, in the months before Smithson's graduation from Pembroke, George Keate put Smithson's Pembroke classmate Thomas Sandford forward for membership in the Royal Society. Fellowship of the Royal Society (F.R.S.) was Smithson's primary goal upon leaving university, as it was for most of his closest friends. "I never felt so interested about the attainment of an object in the whole course of my life as I did about being a Fellow of the Royal Society," Smithson's Pembroke friend Davies Giddy confided to his diary. After a scare on a boating trip, he wrote, "the wish came strongly to my mind that if it was my Fate to be drowned, the event might be postponed till after my election at the Royal Society, so that I might die F.R.S."[8]

Thomas Sandford, like Smithson, also had a London address, though he stayed up at Oxford for longer, taking his MA only in 1789. He was arguably better connected than Smithson. Among those others who seconded his nomination to the Royal Society were Horace Walpole and Charles Burney, father of Fanny and author of a vaunted multi-volume history of music. These men, like Keate, were not considered of the scientific faction; they represented the group the Royal Society was obliged to court, those whose patronage and funds helped keep the organization afloat. So Sandford was a candidate of the "non-useful" class, one of those who would most likely not be making material contributions to knowledge. Heir to the Sandford seat in Shropshire, Sandford was ordained like his father, and religion was to be his principal occupation, though he was "a Gentleman distinguished for his knowledge in many branches of Science and particularly in Natural History" according to his membership certificate. This tagline was common language on applications for the wellborn; a version of it can be found, for example, on the 1736 certificate of Smithson's father, back when he was the baronet Sir Hugh Smithson, "a Gentleman very well versed in all Polite Literature, and skill'd in Natural knowledge."[9] On April 6, 1786, Sandford was balloted for and rejected.[10]

The devastating rejection, for it was never less than that, must have made an immense impression on Smithson. The portentous presence of five black balls in the ballot box—the origin of the word blackballing—was a stain on a man's mind, and on his reputation. It happened rarely, making the event that much more shocking when it did occur. Smithson's swashbuckling Staffa companion Count Andreani described the infrequency of rejection in his diary of his 1784 visit to London, unaware that his own attempt to become F.R.S. in 1793 would end in blackballing on account of his republican sympathies.[11] Sandford's path no doubt stood as an example to Smithson; it was the way not to go. Smithson was already in 1786 establishing his own route to the summit of scientific London, but if his cousin George Keate stepped forward and offered to help, perhaps it was this episode that clinched a refusal.

In the weeks leading up to Sandford's blackballing, Smithson made two very significant strides regarding his own entry into the sacrosanct heart of scientific society in London. He was proposed, and elected, for membership in the Coffee House Philosophical Society, a coveted conversation group composed of chemists, medical practitioners, instrument makers, and political radicals, spearheaded by the Irish chemist and Royal Society member Richard Kirwan. And he was invited by Henry Cavendish, esteemed as the Newton of his age, to be Cavendish's dinner guest at the Royal Society Club. Both of these accomplishments indicated that Smithson was very close to achieving that ultimate goal, membership in the Royal

Society. But they also signaled his sense of himself as a serious scientist. Smithson had already distinguished himself from the gentleman amateurs who crowded his Oxford days; he had placed himself among those who were dedicating their lives to advancing the state of natural knowledge. It was the culmination of a campaign launched back in the summer of 1784, when Smithson had hitched himself onto Faujas de St. Fond's tour.

When Smithson returned from Scotland, two years remained of his education at Oxford. He had already pledged himself to the new fields of chemistry and mineralogy, though, and Oxford was not remotely a place at the cutting edge of scientific inquiry. There was little reason to stay, and as a gentleman-commoner he had few obligations to fulfill. Conveniently, his tutor—if Edward Dupré ever had any hold over his pupil to begin with—had been called away from Oxford to a living. While Smithson had been in Scotland, the Society for Promoting Natural History had elected him a member, his first entry into the scientific world of London. London was now his stage.

London in the 1780s was a vast, sprawling metropolis—the largest city in Europe. Its population was rapidly approaching one million, and one in every ten Englishmen lived in the capital. To accommodate this burgeoning society, the city was busily building. Capacious new squares were appearing ever westward, and rows of Georgian terraces marched northwards across the expanse of fields. Much of England was dedicated to supplying the hungry maw of the capital. Beyond London Bridge the Thames, the city's biggest commercial boulevard, flowed hardly visible under a thicket of masts and skiffs and coal barges carrying in the latest wares and fuel. But equally much of that consumed by Londoners was produced locally. Warehouses, factories, timber yards and wharves lined the riverbanks, and the chimneys of glass manufactories filled the sky. Brewers and distilleries blanketed the east end, churning out millions of barrels of ale and porter. Huguenot silk-weavers clustered in Spitalfields just outside the walls on the eastern end of town, their tall, narrow brick houses clattering with the sound of the looms in the clerestoried eaves. In the alleys around St. Paul's, printers, bookbinders, and engravers rubbed elbows with clockmakers and instrument makers. Two enormous shopping streets snaked across the city east to west, offering a theatre of plenty behind glass-fronted storefronts. London by the 1780s was its own revolution in living—a new urban existence, driven not by court or aristocratic tradition but rather by the marketplace.[12]

With its window displays, pleasure gardens, and street hawkers, London was a carnival of consumption. Across the city there was gambling and prostitution, bear-baiting, cock-fights, sideshows, and circuses. Spas like Sadler's Wells in Islington and Hockley-in-the-Hole in Clerkenwell offered sybaritic respite for those unable to venture out to Bath or Tunbridge Wells. Theatres at Covent Garden and Drury Lane, with their boxes close up to the stage, featured intimate encounters with the greatest celebrity actors of the age. Exhibitions at the Royal Academy showcased the latest art in a highly social environment, in the great sky-lit room atop the new Somerset House. The print publisher John Boydell opened his Shakespeare Gallery on Pall Mall in 1789. And in exhibition rooms over the Exeter Change on the Strand, the artist Philippe de Loutherburg introduced the public to the concept of moving pictures with his Eidophusikon; spectators watched a series of scenes—dawn over London as seen from Greenwich, an Italian sunset near Naples, Niagara Falls in America, a shipwreck, Pandemonium from Milton— made more dramatic with colored lighting and a full complement of sound effects. The scientific lecturer Adam Walker built an enormous orrery, a mechanical model of the planetary system; visitors entered the darkened interior of what he called his Eidouranion to watch the circling of luminous celestial orbs and learn about the elegant workings of the universe. The Lyceum showcased Diller's Philosophical Fireworks, a monstrous apparatus of whirling circles sprouting hundreds of multi-colored flames. The quack doctor James

Graham's Temple of Health and Hymen capitalized on the public's newfound curiosity for electrical experiments and their age-old interest in sex. Visitors willing to pay an exorbitant fee could allegedly cure their infertility with a night in the massive "Celestial Bed," in silk sheets perfumed "in oriental manner" atop mattresses stuffed with the "most springy hair, produced at vast expense from the tails of English stallions." The bed's domed canopy, supported by forty pillars of colored glass, contained a series of artificial lodestones or magnets, providing the participants with "the exhilarating force of electrical fire."[13]

Smithson was an avid consumer of these spectacles all his life. His library contained a booklet about two temples, each supported by fifteen jewel-encrusted elephants, made for the Emperor of China, which were put on display at Weeks' Mechanical Museum on Tichborne Street, Haymarket. He also owned the catalogue of an exhibit on ancient and modern Mexico, which the impresario and explorer William Bullock held at the fantastical Egyptian Hall in 1825. And he owned "Murder Most Foul," a pamphlet about the 1799 trial of Charles and Hannah Squire for the murder of their apprentice—though whether Smithson went to join the prurient crowds at Charles Squire's execution or whether he had some other more sober interest in this case, which documented a long history of cruelty and abuse against the apprentice child, is impossible to know.[14]

For someone like Smithson, so hungry for information, the city was a swirl of novel ideas and new acquaintances, of knowledge shared in convivial, social environs. Coffeehouses and newspapers brought new voices to the fore, giving rise to greater discussion and challenges to the status quo. Thousands of books were being published and new magazines established; circulating libraries and book clubs spread publications even further. New societies formed weekly to cater to every political whim or diverting hobby. There were clubs for gambling and drinking, but there were also clubs for lovers of theatre, literature, politics, wine tasting, natural history, and antiquities. Members came together to share their observations, report on recent travel, debate a philosophical question, and read the latest pamphlets. All over town men held *conversazioni* in their homes or their favorite coffeehouses.

Much of the discussion in the urban entrepot of the 1780s was tinged with a spirit of radicalism. Anticipating the centenary of the Glorious Revolution of 1688, the bloodless revolution that had marked the end of the Stuart reign, people began agitating for parliamentary reform. Questions of liberty and rights, brought on by the American War of Independence, reverberated as well in discussions of the new Irish legislative independence or the proposed repeal of the Test and Corporation Acts, which would have granted rights to Catholics and Dissenters. The world of nonconformism so absent from Oxford was thriving in London. Its most prominent advocates, such as Joseph Priestley and Richard Price, argued from their pulpits and in pamphlets for religious and educational freedoms unfettered by government or church interference. Dissenting academies like Newcombe's Academy in Hackney—where George Coleridge, Samuel Taylor's brother and a classmate of Smithson's from Pembroke, had just started teaching—encouraged such independent thinking. Their extensive curricula, encompassing language, history, and geography, were particularly rich in the experimental sciences. This cosmopolitan city was engaged in that great Enlightenment enterprise, the development of a public culture.

Beyond a brief few weeks up at Pembroke College around Christmas 1784—where he undoubtedly saw much of William Thomson, who was now teaching anatomy and preparing the university's first course on mineralogy (and where Smithson also seems to have thrown a huge party, as the buttery books show his expenditures to be vastly higher during the last week of the year than anyone else's at Pembroke)—Smithson was, as he wrote to James Hutton, "since my return from Scotland . . . very little at Oxford."[15] He opened his own bank account at Hoare's at the sign

of the Golden Bottle on Fleet Street, in the thrum of the city near
Temple Bar. The bank, which had strong ties to Wiltshire, was
where his mother—and also his father, the Duke of
Northumberland—transacted her business. Although it is difficult to
gain a full understanding of Smithson's finances, his income at this
early stage appears to have derived primarily from three sources:
investments (he had purchased a sizeable amount of the Bank of
England's consolidated 3 percents and 5 percents, stocks that operated
like today's bonds), regular income from various properties, and
unidentified cash deposits.[16] Smithson was already playing the lottery,
which in the unstable financial climate of the end of the eighteenth
century was practically as remunerative as investing in the Bank
stocks (twice in 1788 alone he won prizes).[17]

He moved into the city from Surrey and settled into apartments
in one of the grandest new developments in London, at No. 18
Portland Place.[18] The tradition of renting in town was very strong,
as most were in residence primarily for the frenetic season defined
by the rituals of Parliament; the recesses were passed in the country
and on visits to spa towns and the resorts of the Continent. Smithson
remained a renter his whole life, having—as one nineteenth-century
biographical dictionary noted—"the taste for travel, to the point
of not wanting to settle anywhere."[19] Portland Place, his first
home in London, was considered one of the finest avenues in all
Europe.

The choice of a residence was all-important. Each square conferred
its own reputation, and each street stood a measurable degree from
the epicenter of fashion. As one visitor explained, "The line of
demarcation, north and south, runs through Soho Square. Every
minute of longitude east is equal to as many degrees of gentility
minus, or towards west, plus."[20] Addresses were codes of status,
easily readable by contemporaries. They were more than an
indicator of wealth, though they were that, of course, first of all.
They implied connections and interests; they reflected the
reputations of one's neighbors. One's address was an integral part

of one's identity, a piece of information one could be expected to yield up for scrutiny. Set down in the rules and regulations of one of the first societies to which Smithson gained entry was the directive: "The proposer must give an account of the social, as well as the philosophical character of the candidate, together with the candidate's place of abode. A neglect of this last requisite renders the proposal void."[21]

Such concern was typical of the changing profile of clubs in London. By the 1780s clubs and societies were increasingly professional. They adopted official rules, followed a strict order of business, kept minutes and passed around printed by-laws.[22] Entry into the London club world—and for Smithson this would have applied especially for the Royal Society with its many aristocratic members—was also an initiation into philanthropy. Most societies drew their members from the upper and middling classes. These organizations were devoted to fostering a tradition of patronage from privilege.[23] Smithson was eager to assume his role as a patron. He engaged with his very first society, the Society for Promoting Natural History, by becoming a life member.[24] By bolstering the fledgling club with a more substantial financial commitment than that obligated by simple annual dues, Smithson asserted his support for the ideals of championing scientific discourse and disseminating knowledge. In so doing he also reinforced his position as a wealthy gentleman and gratified his sense of superiority. From the beginning of his public life, James Smithson identified himself as a benefactor.

At his very first attendance of the Society for Promoting Natural History, accompanied by Thomson who had come down from Oxford, Smithson was one of five members selected to head a mineralogy committee. He brought as show-and-tell a specimen of the highly prized "Terra Ponderosa combined with Gas (or Fix'd Air)," which he had learned about from Joseph Black in Edinburgh. Naturalists were at the time obsessed with this lustrous, milky-colored mineral, known also as heavy spar or barite (barium carbonate); the physician William Withering had only recently presented his findings on its composition to the Royal Society (it was later named witherite in his honor), and a few years later the doctor Adair Crawford developed a solution of *terra ponderosa* he believed could be used as a remedy for "cancerous & scrophulous diseases." Thomson must have been quite envious of Smithson's specimen; just a few weeks earlier he had written to Joseph Black, begging for some examples, saying, "I take the freedom of a pupil in requesting specimens of this curious mineral in its various forms— as I know nowhere else that it can be obtained . . ."[25]

The Society for Promoting Natural History's gatherings at the Black Bear immediately enlarged Smithson's community in London. Among his new friends was Johann Gottlieb Groschke, a German physician and professor visiting London. Groschke brought to one meeting his collection of volcanic productions from Weissenstein near Kassel in Hesse (a place where Smithson would spend a number of years during the Napoleonic Wars). He also gave Smithson a copy of his translation of Martin Klaproth's *Observations relative to the mineralogical and chemical history of the fossils of Cornwall*, printed by the radical bookseller Joseph Johnson.[26] David Pitcairn, the SPNH member who had nominated Groschke, became another of Smithson's acquaintances. Pitcairn was a doctor at St. Bartholomew's and served as physician extraordinary to the Prince of Wales. His father had been killed at Bunker Hill and his brother was the midshipman who had first spotted what became known as Pitcairn Island, later famous for hosting the lost colony of mutineers from the *Bounty*. Most importantly, Pitcairn was a Fellow of the Royal Society and would eventually become one of Smithson's sponsors.

Smithson's new life in London was dedicated to building his networks. He was already—at the tender age of twenty—corresponding with some of the most important scientific figures in Britain, such as the luminaries he'd met in Edinburgh: James Hutton, who had given him a commission, and Joseph Black. He shrewdly solidified this web of correspondents by offering himself up as a reporter, a reliable source on the news from London. At a time when travel was still difficult and time-consuming, the exchange of information via letters remained vital, and the role of correspondent was accordingly an invaluable one. Joseph Black told Smithson, "We have no chemical news. . . . Indistinct reports of new metals have reached us, but no particulars. Some further account of these things from you will, therefore, be very agreeable. Dr. Hutton joins me in compliments, and wishing you all good things."[27] Smithson also cultivated alliances by helping along friends who wanted to advance in the scientific world. In May 1785 he proposed his Oxford companion Christopher Pegge, now in London at St. Bartholomew's Hospital, for membership in the Society for Promoting Natural History.

Smithson was up at Oxford for all of the summer of 1785 through to early October, the only gentleman-commoner in residence at Pembroke during this period.[28] It was an eventful summer at the university, filled with James Sadler's balloon launches as well as a momentous visit by the King and Queen. On September 13 all the bells in Oxford rang and the city was illuminated at night to celebrate the first visit of the royal family to the university since Queen Anne at the beginning of the century.[29]

When Smithson returned to London he moved to rented quarters in John Street, Golden Square, in Soho. It was an area that had lost much of its cachet following the development of more fashionable squares to the west. Occupied now more by solicitors, doctors, chemists, and apothecaries, it would nevertheless have placed him right in the center of London's scientific bustle—a short walk from myriad places where Smithson could have carried on his program of chemical self-education. Bryan Higgins ran a pricey private chemical school out of his house on Greek Street, William Nicholson operated a "Scientific Establishment for Pupils" at No. 10 Soho Square, and, most importantly, Sir Joseph Banks hosted a stimulating extension of the Royal Society meetings in the open breakfasts and Sunday gatherings at his Soho Square house.[30] William

Thomson was also back in London for the winter of 1785–6, writing up lectures for his next course at Oxford. In the spring of 1785 Thomson had been appointed Reader in Anatomy. He was charged now with giving two courses each year and, more problematically, with obtaining at least one human body to dissect for each course. Cadavers were hard to come by; until the passing of the Anatomy Act in 1832, hanged criminals were the only legitimate source of bodies for dissection. Under Thomson the school began paying an annual subscription to the Association for Prosecuting Felons.[31]

As Smithson's circle expanded in London he made two acquaintances critical to his future. One was the brilliant and reclusive Henry Cavendish, one of the most respected men of science in any country by the 1780s. Cavendish was cousin to Georgiana, Duchess of Devonshire, and both his parents were children of dukes. His wealth and family connections offered avenues to a very different kind of existence. But Cavendish never married, dedicating his life to practical investigations of nearly all the physical sciences of his time: magnetism, electricity, chemistry, mathematics, mechanics, optics, and geology. Cavendish had few close friends and spoke rarely—though when he did talk, his words, as Humphry Davy later noted, were "luminous and profound."[32] Intensely discomfited in social situations, he went so far as to communicate with his servants by letter. In the world of science he found a small family-like community and some comfort; he almost never missed a Royal Society Club dinner, attending even up to the weeks before his death. The relish with which Smithson pursued knowledge and the exactitude of his chemical work probably appealed to Cavendish. Both were refugees from the traditional path of the gentleman, men of wealth who chose science above all else. Cavendish took Smithson to the Royal Society Club early on in their acquaintance, evidence that he would support him for membership.[33]

The other figure to whom Smithson was introduced was the gregarious Irish chemist Richard Kirwan. Kirwan had come to science relatively late—having embarked first, after college on the Continent at the University of Poitiers, on life as a Jesuit novice and latterly being called to the Irish bar. In London Kirwan energetically cultivated many correspondents; he knew most of the prominent European savants and literati and even received a portrait from Catherine the Great as a token of her esteem. He was elected F.R.S. in 1780 and around the same time helped to found the Coffee House Philosophical Society, a natural extension of the Wednesday evening scientific salons he held at his house off Oxford Street.[34]

These two highly regarded men—one a reclusive genius who offered a world of riches within his private library and laboratory, the other a networker who provided entrée to all of scientific Europe—provided Smithson with outstanding prospects. A week after Cavendish took Smithson to his first Royal Society Club dinner in March 1786, Kirwan nominated Smithson for membership in the Coffee House Philosophical Society.[35]

The Coffee House Philosophical Society epitomized the late eighteenth-century Enlightenment ideals of public science. Members came from different ranks of society, but they espoused an egalitarian approach to the society of knowledge. They believed fervently in creating a democratic participatory sphere in which to practice and communicate discovery. In true republican spirit they refused to give the group a proper name (it has come to be known by the coffeehouse in which it first met), insisted upon a rotating presidency for the group, and declined to stand when a newcomer appeared in the room. No specialist topics were permitted in their discussions, as it was imperative that conversation be open to all. Medical discourses were thus shunned, as were "mathematical disquisitions" and topics in astronomy. The conversation, according to the rules established, "must be general, and not between particular members, and commences with an enquiry on the part of the chairman." When so much was happening in natural philosophy, especially in the worlds of chemistry and mineralogy, meetings such as those in the Chapter Coffee House were vital. Discussion was expressly forbidden at the Royal Society, and London coffeehouse culture offered opportunities to debate the latest theories, many of which challenged long-held orthodoxies.[36]

Although discussions were kept to "philosophical" (i.e. scientific) matters, many of the participants identified strongly with the American cause. As the end of the century neared, these views lay increasingly at odds with those of England around them. No fewer than three members of the society—Joseph Priestley, Benjamin Vaughan, and Thomas Cooper—emigrated to the United States to escape persecution in England in the mid-1790s, when the reactionary backlash to the French Revolution reached its zenith.

Many of the members had correspondents among the fledgling American scientific community. A number of them—including Smithson's second sponsor, the well-connected Portuguese-born instrument maker John Hyacinthe de Magellan[37]—were fellows of the American Philosophical Society, the organization that Benjamin Franklin had founded to encourage scientific discussion and research in the U.S. Shortly before Smithson joined the Coffee House Philosophical Society, his second sponsor Magellan offered the American Philosophical Society 200 guineas to establish an annual scientific prize for the New World, a bequest enthusiastically accepted by Franklin. The Magellanic Premium rewarded the "best discovery or most useful invention" in the fields of natural philosophy or navigation (or astronomy, a category added by Franklin). The prize, still in existence today, was one of the earliest benefactions to the United States for the increase of knowledge. It could well have been a gift that resonated with Magellan's new protégé, a young and impressionable James Smithson.[38]

The first meetings of the Coffee House Philosophical Society that Smithson attended were typical of the feverish exchange of information among London's scientific cognoscenti in the late 1780s. The men, about a dozen of them in total, gathered each week at the Baptist's Head, an old coffeehouse on Chancery Lane popular with Masonic lodge members and the area's solicitors.[39] The group was intrigued by word from the United States that "at Albany [New York] & other places during the intense frost of Winter the fish which are caught are so immediately congealed as to be quite brittle, but that the vital powers are nevertheless so far from being destroyed that the fish resumes its life when thawed by means of cold water many weeks or even months after." William Babington reported that he found a "good Syrup of Violets" four times more effective than a turmeric solution as a test for alkalis. And Kirwan shared news of the Leipzig chemist Johann Friedrich Westrumb's new method of decomposing sea salt by melting it with "dryed Blood & lime."[40]

Entry to the Coffee House Philosophical Society and the Royal Society invitations from Kirwan and Cavendish brought some incremental gratification of Smithson's ambitions. He no longer seems to have needed the little natural history society that had been the first to welcome him. The April 1786 meeting of the Society for Promoting Natural History, which Smithson attended with his Oxford friend Christopher Pegge, was Smithson's last ever in that company. It is possible perhaps that he had some kind of falling out with members of the group—an early indicator of his easily wounded temperament—but this seems unlikely. There is no trace of any troubles in the minutes, and Smithson's name was never excised from the books. He was still hailed as a life member in 1791, with his then address of Orchard Street, Portman Square, current and up-to-date in their ledgers.[41] It seems simply that Smithson felt he had moved on to bigger and better things.

Smithson's life in London was going swimmingly. Flush with success and promise, he returned to Pembroke at the end of May for his degree, the awarding of an honorary Master of Arts, an event he enjoyed in the company of his young admiring friend Davies Giddy. They had not overlapped that much at Pembroke, as Smithson had spent much of his last year in London rather than at Oxford.[42] The relationship was not exactly one of equals. In Giddy's eyes, Smithson was the talented, worldly senior, the best chemist at Oxford.

Giddy was only two years younger, but Smithson had come to know him in the company of Giddy's omnipresent father, and a tone of superiority and condescension infused his dealings with Giddy: "whatever you bring me," Smithson wrote at one point, admonishing him over some forgotten mineral specimens, "shall be received king-like." For Giddy this graduation day became a moment impressed on the memory, the emblem of an entire friendship, a story he recounted in his diary some forty years later. At the ceremony in the Convocation House, Giddy remembered Smithson "being seated on the upper end of the Bench on the Floor on the Proctor's left hand." After the ceremony the two left the quadrangle together and walked back to Pembroke, where Smithson exchanged "his cap for a Hat," and then they strolled down the road past Tom Tower to wander in Christ Church meadows, the sun sparkling gold on the Cotswold stone, crisp against a blue sky.[43]

Graduation, while always a significant milestone, took on added importance for Smithson, as it possibly coincided with his literal coming of age, his twenty-first birthday. In England this landmark birthday had long been observed with extravagant festivities. Wealthy William Beckford, author of the popular Gothic novel *Vathek* and builder of Fonthill Abbey, famously held two parties. The first, the official celebration for relatives and all the locals, was a three-day affair for some ten thousand people, held under vast swags of tents and a specially erected triumphal arch in the grounds of the family estate; the second was a more intimate week-long house party at Christmas, which Beckford remembered as a "voluptuous festival." Davies Giddy recalled the bells ringing all day and "a great deal of Company" in Tredea, Cornwall, for his twenty-first birthday. Smithson, one imagines, at the very least had a party. He also had his portrait painted, by the artist James Roberts, who was then working in Oxford as a drawing master.[44]

In the painting a poised young man sits in a chair beneath a tree, gazing out confidently at the viewer. Under his cap his hair is fashionably curled and powdered to suggest a wig. The ruched sleeves of his gown loll nonchalantly off his shoulders, and the loosely draped collar about his neck signifies his attainment of a Master of Arts degree. A book perches on his crossed and stockinged knee, his finger in place as if he intends soon to return to its pages. It is a small, self-assured portrait, a representation emblematic of one young man's graceful entrance into the community of knowledge.

Coming of age was a momentous rite of passage in the life of a young gentleman. It was also a critical episode in the relationship between a father and son, being, as it was, intricately wrapped up in the matter of inheritance. Property in England was rarely owned outright; it operated instead under a system called strict settlement, in which the land was owned by the family in perpetuity, with each generation holding it in trust for the next. If the son was the tenant "in tail" on the family property, when he reached the age of twenty-one the father and son together could break the entail on the property and resettle the inheritance—usually transferring the entail to the son's typically as-yet-unborn first son.[45]

Smithson's passage to manhood, of course, involved no such connection between father and son, and no transfer of patrimony or legacy.[46] The Duke of Northumberland, absent in Smithson's college register at matriculation, was naturally not at Oxford to witness his illegitimate son's success. The duke, in fact, was on his deathbed. On June 6, 1786, at the age of seventy-four, he died at Syon House. For days afterwards he lay in state at Northumberland House, amidst hundreds of flickering candles and piles of roses as a steady stream of mourners came to pay their respects. On the 21st, following a vast procession of mourning coaches and men on horseback, the duke was buried in the family vault at Westminster Abbey, surrounded by the tombs of kings and queens and the nation's poets and heroes.[47]

The Duke of Northumberland's will was probated on July 4. Smithson was not mentioned in it. His father's death stood as an acute reminder that Smithson, never intended to inherit any mantle, would not ever even be recognized. In the long gallery at Syon, where the ceiling coffers undulated in a geometric pattern that babbled in synch with an equally busy carpet, small roundels peered out along the length of the decorated walls. Alongside portraits of Harry Hotspur, Henry VIII, and the first Earls of Northumberland, Smithson's half-brother Lord Warkworth ascended, his portrait as the new second Duke of Northumberland, along with that of his wife, joining those of his parents. The pageant of succession, the official line of the Percy family, continued.

When the season began again in London in the autumn, Smithson once more was taken under the wing of his scientific mentors, Henry Cavendish and Richard Kirwan. Cavendish took him again to the dinner of the Royal Society Club, and Kirwan took him as his guest to most of the weekly Royal Society meetings between December and January 18, 1787, when the certificate recommending "James Lewis [sic] Macie Esq. M.A. late of Pembroke College Oxford, & now of John Street, Golden Square a Gentleman well versed in various branches of Natural Philosophy & particularly in Chymistry & Mineralogy" was posted on the wall of the Royal Society's meeting room.[48]

During the requisite twelve weeks that the certificate hung on the wall at Somerset House, Smithson's sponsors came forward to vouch their support. Richard Kirwan, Charles Greville, and the Royal Society's secretary Charles Blagden had all signed the certificate prior to its posting. Blagden never became a good friend of Smithson's, but as Henry Cavendish's personal assistant he would have jealously noted that the elder statesman of science was grooming this young Oxford man as a protégé and duly gotten on board as a sponsor. Cavendish's name, in fact, soon followed under those of the first three sponsors. Last to join the list was Smithson's friend from the Society for Promoting Natural History, David Pitcairn.

When Smithson was balloted for and accepted into the Royal Society on April 18, 1787, he became at the age of twenty-two the group's youngest member.[49] This in itself was cause enough for

The meeting room of the Royal Society at Somerset House.

jubilation and pride, but Smithson's entry also placed him firmly in the bosom of the society's power structure; his backers were all men closely aligned with the president Sir Joseph Banks. In 1784 Banks had survived the "dissensions," a rancorous and lengthy debate over his maneuvers to influence the selection of members for the governing council. From this near putsch—a real referendum on Banks' leadership—the president of the Royal Society had emerged chastened but steadfast. A number of the allies who had rallied to him in the time of crisis were those who adopted the young Smithson.

The following week Smithson attended his first ever meeting as a member, signed the book and paid his dues. He immediately dove into the culture of the society, embracing its wide-ranging network and its connections to communities around Europe. On May 3, he brought the first of many of his own guests, Johan Gadolin, a Finnish chemist and mineralogist who had studied under the pioneering Torbern Bergman at Uppsala.[50] Smithson in those first years of membership brought a guest nearly every week—old friends from Oxford, instrument makers, literary friends, and, most especially, the foreign scientists like Gadolin, whom he was probably meeting at Sir Joseph Banks' breakfasts and at other scientific salons around town.

The Polish poet and mathematician Jan Sniadecki, in England on a study trip prior to the construction of the new astronomical observatory in Krakow, was another such guest of Smithson's. So was the German chemist Johann Friedrich August Göttling, author of *Description of a portable chest of chemistry*, and Johann Caspar Dollfuss, a Swiss pharmacy student in London for several years in the late 1780s. With these friendships Smithson began cultivating an international network of scientific correspondents before he even left London to explore the Continent.[51]

And through these foreign visitors Smithson seems to have reached out even further, to prominent scientific figures abroad he had not yet encountered personally. Lorenz von Crell, the founder of the first German chemistry journal, was eager for correspondents to supply him with the latest information from England; by 1790 two of his key contacts at the Royal Society seem to have been Sir Joseph Banks and Smithson, who was then still in his early twenties and unpublished.[52] Smithson, who had enjoyed something of the reputation of a prodigy ever since college, and perhaps even before, was clearly eager to make a success of himself and open to every opportunity.

Over the course of several months during the winter of 1787–8 Smithson was invited to form part of an exclusive committee at the Royal Society charged with verifying the accuracy of Henry Cavendish's latest experiment. Cavendish, using the same techniques and apparatus that had enabled him a few years earlier to make his groundbreaking observations on the composition of water, had managed to produce "nitrous acid" (nitric acid) from a mixture of dephlogisticated and phlogisticated air (the components, as Cavendish and his peers understood it, of common air: oxygen and nitrogen).

The replication of this labor-intensive experiment lasted through the winter, with Smithson attending along with a handful of others early in the day at the society rooms in Somerset House to witness the work.[53]

Public experiments such as these served a crucial role in the process of the verification of facts in the eighteenth century, at a time when many discoveries were completely upending long-held truths. Such experiments, often written up as publications— Cavendish reported this trial in the Royal Society's *Philosophical Transactions* of 1788—served as a kind of demonstration for the wider community of scientists. In this particular instance, many experimentalists—like Martinus van Marum in Holland, who owned the largest electrical machine then existing—had been unable, despite sophisticated equipment, to replicate Cavendish's results. Witnesses such as Smithson, then, were relied upon to serve as authenticators of the findings. Within the very first year of his membership Smithson, despite his youth, was clearly already part of an inner circle of the Royal Society's chemists.

Cavendish's experiments on air highlighted the confused state of chemical thought in the 1780s. Cavendish believed he had demonstrated with this experiment that the electric spark had deprived phlogisticated air of its phlogiston and left behind only nitrous acid (nitric acid); likewise, with his detonation of inflammable and dephlogisticated air (hydrogen and oxygen) he thought he had shown that dephlogisticated air was "in reality nothing but dephlogisticated water, or water deprived of its phlogiston." The theory of phlogiston had creakily served the chemical community for nearly one hundred years, being adapted and refined every so often to accommodate troubling inconsistencies or contradictory experiment results. In 1782 Kirwan claimed that he had finally fathomed the actual substance; he identified eight states of phlogiston and posited that at its most rarefied phlogiston was in fact inflammable air (hydrogen).[54] The French chemist Antoine Lavoisier, however, after years of research, soon launched a full-blown attack against the existence of phlogiston.

In his *Réflexions sur le phlogistique* Lavoisier proposed a radically different solution to the mystery of combustion. He claimed that metals and wood when burned did not release phlogiston; they did the opposite. They absorbed air—Priestley's dephlogisticated air (oxygen). It was Henry Cavendish's experiments, which had led Lavoisier to make his own investigations into the composition of water, that had ironically bolstered the case for this new theory.

The French chemists who were convinced by Lavoisier's experiments joined him in his efforts to convert public opinion. In 1787 Lavoisier together with Fourcroy, Berthollet, and Guyton de Morveau published a treatise, *Méthode de nomenclature chimique*, which laid out this new system of chemistry, using an entirely new vocabulary. Such a radical overhaul of traditional wisdom could not be expected to find easy acceptance; Cavendish condemned it as "very mischievous."[55] British suspicion of the French theory was compounded by a bias against the elitism of French laboratory practice; Lavoisier's instruments were extremely expensive, making them available only to a very exclusive circle.

In the meantime Smithson's old mentor Richard Kirwan penned a passionate defense of the phlogiston theory. The French school—and it did seem to English eyes to operate as a team, well-organized and with strong government backing—immediately began to form their rebuttal. Madame Lavoisier translated Kirwan's text into French, and within the year Lavoisier and his associates offered their response, refuting each of Kirwan's points. Lavoisier continued to lay out his theory in his *Traité Elémentaire de Chimie* of 1789. Here he listed the bodies he could not decompose further. These simple substances, or elements, replaced those of Aristotle. Lavoisier's list—which included light and heat, or caloric, as Lavoisier called it; the gases oxygen, azote (nitrogen), and hydrogen; carbon, sulfur, and phosphorus; and sixteen known metals—was not meant to be definitive. It was intended instead as a challenge to others: "As chemistry advances towards perfection, by dividing and subdividing, it is impossible to say where it is to end; and these things we at present suppose simple may soon be found quite otherwise," he explained. What were the exact compositions of acids and salts? The search for elementary bodies thus became a central focus of chemistry as it entered the nineteenth century.[56]

In these last decades of the eighteenth century the landscape of chemistry was changing so rapidly that the ground could hardly be found underfoot. The so-called French system—Lavoisier's radical proposition of a new nomenclature—threatened to obliterate the entire tradition on which English chemistry rested. What had long been known as "dephlogisticated air" was now to be called oxygen, "inflammable air" would be hydrogen, "fixed air" carbon dioxide, and so on. Lavoisier, however, was not only proposing to rename every substance and abandon a long-held common language. He was replacing the playing field altogether, enforcing his new ideas by making the actual terms dependent on his theory. He had constructed a new system in which all terms were now identified by their place in an antiphlogistic world. To the English it would come to seem as anarchic and abrupt an overthrow of tradition as the overthrow of the monarchy.

At the end of 1787, Kirwan—still steadfast in his embrace of phlogiston—moved back to Dublin on account of failing health. In 1789 he issued a defense of his essay, but finally in 1791 he relinquished his beliefs in favor of the French system. It was Joseph Priestley who remained phlogiston's most determined champion. Later on, from his new life in the United States, where he had escaped after the torching of his house and laboratory in the Birmingham riots on the second anniversary of the fall of the Bastille, Priestley would write, "There have been few, if any, revolutions in science so great, so sudden, and so general, as the prevalence of what is now usually termed the new system of chemistry, or that of the *Antiphlogistians*, over the doctrine of Stahl, which was at one time thought to have been the greatest discovery that had ever been made in the science."[57] Priestley when he penned this in 1796 still believed in phlogiston, though he acknowledged that he knew hardly a soul who hadn't been converted to the French school of thought. In the heat of those prime years of debate on the matter of one of the most pressing questions of chemical theory in his time, Smithson, it seems, wanted to see for himself.[58]

Science and Revolution, 1788–1791

Monsieur Macie qui aura l'honneur de vous remettre
cette lettre est membre de la Société Royale et
beaucoup plus versé dans la chymie philosophique
que des personnes de son age . . . comme il
ambitionne beaucoup votre connaissance, j'ai cru
vous la devoir demander pour lui. [Mr. Macie, who
has the honor to present this letter is a member of
the Royal Society and far exceeds his peers in his
knowledge of philosophical chemistry . . . as he
greatly desires to make your acquaintance, I thought
I should oblige him by asking you.]

—Sir Joseph Banks to Antoine Lavoisier, April 1788

O N APRIL 3, 1788, Antoine Laurent Lavoisier, who
had been nominated by Cavendish, Blagden, Greville, and
others, was elected to the new foreign list of the Royal
Society. On that same day another Frenchman was balloted for: the
vivacious and controversial Abbé Jean-Louis Soulavie. Soulavie was
the first person Smithson sponsored for membership in the Royal
Society, but it was not a successful debut. Soulavie was a bold, self-
taught geologist who had recently penned an enormous eight-volume

Histoire Naturelle de la France Meridionale. His theories about the extinction of species and the significance of volcanic activity in geological history drew plenty of skeptics, though he was awarded a prize for his book from France's Académie des Sciences.[1] He had the backing of a number of prominent Royal Society Fellows; Richard Kirwan, for example, had taken Soulavie as his guest to a meeting in 1787 during Soulavie's visit to London that year—which is probably when Smithson made his acquaintance. But Soulavie was a radical in politics, and when the votes were counted at Somerset House he was rejected.[2]

Smithson does not seem to have burdened himself with Soulavie's blackballing, having perhaps more important goals in his sights. He wasted no time after the election in soliciting a letter of introduction to Lavoisier from Sir Joseph Banks. He may even have hoped to be the one to carry news of the honor of membership across the Channel to the great man himself, but Banks ensured that would not be the case by entrusting the task, as he explained in the letter to Lavoisier, to another. This letter of introduction offers a window into Smithson at age twenty-three, seen through the eyes of the powerful president of the Royal Society. Banks did not speak French, and it is not too difficult to imagine him overflowing a great chair in his library at Soho Square, dictating in English how he wished to describe Smithson, his secretary scribbling furiously and running off to produce a translation. In the end the letter described a man not so different from Banks himself in years past—a precocious, talented young upstart, fearsomely ambitious but full of warmth and winning enthusiasm.[3] Banks, like Smithson, was an Oxford graduate who had become F.R.S. at a very early age (twenty-three). His explorer days, though, were now well behind him. As James Boswell explained, "Banks was an elephant, quite placid and gentle, allowing you to get upon his back or play with his proboscis."[4] Smithson seems to have tapped into this gentle giant, reminding the sedentary, gouty autocrat of his earlier self—the adventurer, the intrepid investigator.

It was July, as it turned out, before Smithson finally set foot in Paris. His companion for the trip was Charles Greville, who had recently disposed of his mistress Emma Hart by shipping her and her mother off to his widower uncle, the aged vulcanologist and collector Sir William Hamilton, head of the English community at the court in Naples—where she eventually met and famously took up with Lord Nelson. "A cleaner, sweeter bed-fellow did not exist," Greville said, but Emma could not bring him what he most needed: a handsome inheritance. Greville was on the lookout for a woman with at least £30,000—a quest that remained unfulfilled all his life; he died, like Smithson, a bachelor.[5]

The fascination Greville and Smithson had for each other was all-engrossing, and it was grounded in their pursuit of the latest, most spectacular mineral finds. Smithson's goals for his own collection seem to have changed dramatically as a result of this trip, but at the start, as these two finely appointed collectors set off for the Continent, they were very much of one mind. Greville was older than Smithson but probably not much wiser—he was legendarily short for cash even as he pursued his extravagant collecting of virtù. But he seems to have been devoted to his eager and intelligent young companion. Like Henry Cavendish, Greville clearly valued Smithson's powers of observation. Writing to Sir Joseph Banks during a controversy with the French over the process for melting platinum, Greville requested that Banks set up a public experiment and entreated him: "Do not let too many philosophers attend but good ones.—& I wish you would let Macie be of the party."[6] Smithson in his turn embraced a playful friendship with Greville, where he could write of bringing a specimen "some morning to pay its compliments to your specimens, to compare it with them."[7] For Smithson Charles Greville above all probably represented what he might have attained without the stigma of illegitimacy and the strictures of his status as a naturalized citizen. Greville was an MP for Warwick, a Lord of the Admiralty, and he had sat on the Privy Council with none other than Smithson's father, the Duke of Northumberland (Greville had hit a ceiling on how high he could rise, however, despite his being the brother of the Earl of Warwick, on account of his uncontained enthusiasm for the American cause during the Revolutionary War).[8]

Most young men heading off to the Continent on a warm July morning had mischief on their minds. The libertine ways of France permitted behavior that otherwise might have raised eyebrows in London society. "It is much to be regretted," intoned J. Andrews at the opening of his *Letters to a Young Gentleman on his setting out for France* (1784), "that the majority of our travelers run over to France from no other motives than those which lead them to Bath, Tonbridge, or Scarborough. Amusement and dissipation are their principal, and often their only, views."[9]

This jaunt to Paris was not, however, a dabbling, dissolute trip, or not wholly in any case. Smithson and Greville set forth with a collegial group of men, all of whom shared a thirst for knowledge; Smithson's journey was evidently to continue the heady brew of coffeehouse conversation that characterized his London life. Most appear to be friends from the Coffee House Philosophical Society. Major Valentine Gardiner, who had also been proposed for Coffee House Philosophical Society membership by Richard Kirwan, was a balloon enthusiast (he had ascended with James Sadler at Oxford) who had served with the 16th Regiment of Foot in America. Edward Gray, trained in medicine, was the keeper of Natural History and Antiquities at the British Museum; his membership in the Royal Society, like Smithson's, had been sponsored by Greville. Two of the other traveling companions might have been John Vinicombe, a Pembroke exhibitioner from Cornwall and friend to Davies Giddy, who was serving as tutor and chaperone for Thom Price, a rather wealthier Cornish son from Magdalen College. These last two had left Oxford in June 1788 and did not return there until three years later, bearing the signature gift from France at that time: the tricolor cockade. (The one they left with Davies Giddy at Pembroke in 1791 became "an object of much curiosity" in Tory Oxford, and the other students so clamored for a copy that Giddy engaged an attendant at the college to make some replicas, though he prudently decided against distributing them.[10])

Visitors to *ancien régime* Paris were welcomed first by the police for passport control. The tall, grey-roofed city on the Seine was newly contained within a high stone wall established by the *fermiers généraux* for collecting tax. Coming from the coast, travelers typically rode in past the royal sepulture at St. Denis and the windmills of Montmartre, through the classical customs barriers of the new wall, and down the old Roman road right through the city to the terminus at rue Notre Dame des Victoires. The police checked papers and inquired as to the nature of the journey, the places to be visited, and the establishment in Paris where the traveler was lodging. For most this was a routine exchange. The resulting notation—kept still today in the archives of the Ministère des Affaires Etrangères in Paris, the repository to which the police quickly handed over their information on foreigners in order to coordinate a more effective surveillance—was typically brief. If, however, the visitor hailed from a particularly illustrious family, pages were devoted to chronicling the heroic exploits of the traveler's ancestors. On the very day that Smithson, Greville, and the others passed into Paris, so too did the MP Dudley Ryder, Earl of Harrowby. Milords Greville, Macie, Gardiner et al. were duly noted. The ancestry of "Sir Dudley Rider" on the other hand was lauded for three pages in the ledger, the officer noting with especial flourish the family's valiant sacrifices made for kings long dead (Edwards II and IV). If Smithson witnessed this treatment, it would not have been lost on him the privileges the French accorded those of noble parentage. Smithson—descended from kings!—had none of his antecedents noted. He was, like his companions, simply a *Milord anglais*, intent apparently on spending only a few days in Paris before continuing on to partake of the pleasures of Spa, the fashionable watering hole in the Ardennes.[11]

The group descended on the Hôtel du Moscovie on the rue des Petits Augustins (today the rue Bonaparte), one of a number of hotels popular with the English in the warren of medieval streets by the Seine in the old aristocratic *quartier* of the Faubourg St. Germain. Paris' air was much cleaner and brighter than that of coal-fired London, but the French capital was a shock for visitors accustomed to London's decorous street life, with its crisp sidewalks of York stone flagging and roads wide enough for four carriages abreast. Here narrow, rutted streets, filled with mud and refuse and overshadowed by tall stone houses, were so crowded as to be almost impassable. Carriages backed and ground their wheels against each other; young men in cabrioles darted recklessly amongst the crowds. "Walking, which in London is so pleasant and so clean that ladies do it every day," remarked the English writer–agronomist Arthur Young, "is here a toil and a fatigue to a man, and an impossibility to a well-dressed woman."[12]

In July and August Smithson and Greville traveled out into the countryside. They might have carried on with their fellow English travelers to gamble and socialize at Spa, where years earlier Smithson's mother's ill-fated affair with John Marshe Dickinson had begun. At some point during that summer of 1788, though, Smithson and Greville ended up in the Alps, for when they returned to Paris on September 19 the passport control officer noted that they had been "running around Switzerland."[13]

Switzerland had long been a popular destination for the English. It was the homeland of Voltaire and Rousseau, a seat of liberty and learning, a place, as Smithson's cousin George Keate had said, where "philosophy is studied more than the sword."[14] Smithson's relative in fact had done much to promote a love of Switzerland; he had written a history of Geneva and its laws, and penned a number of poems as well, including "The Alps," one of the earliest poems in English to praise the beauty of the mountains. For many English visitors, Switzerland served primarily as a charming way station en route to and from Italy, experienced from the perspective of their sedan chair. Lady Webster, in fact, when heading home to England at the end of her Grand Tour, insisted on riding over the Alps backwards, so as to be able to continue to look at Italy.[15] As

"The Manner of Passing Mount Cenis," by Smithson's cousin George Keate.

the century wore on, though, and a taste grew for the sublime, Switzerland's outsized landscape—with its immense vistas, terrifying cold and ice, avalanches, abysses, and villages populated with people disfigured by goiter—became fascinating in its own right.

For scientists as well there was a dramatic shift in the perception of the mountains. Not so long ago the venerable French naturalist the Comte de Buffon had dismissed mountains as static, hideous deformations of nature, blighted features of the landscape. Smithson and his scientific peers now saw them in a wholly different light, as products of the earth's wrenching transformations. To these men the Alps offered themselves up as mineralogical cabinets of evidence—treasure chests in which to uncover a catalogue of the earth's development and clues to a theory of the earth. Smithson and Greville came to Switzerland with all the enthusiasm of the pioneer, eager to meet the men who were mapping the frontier and to see the mountains at first hand. Smithson armed himself with Jacob

Wyttenbach's *Instructions pour les voyageurs qui vont voir les glaciers et les Alpes du canton de Berne*, the first guide to studying the geology of the mountains, written by one of the pioneers of glaciology.[16]

Just the year before Smithson's arrival the Swiss scientist Horace Bénédict de Saussure had scaled Mont Blanc, the highest point in Europe, one of the first to do so. The research he conducted on this and other ascents—collecting samples, testing the temperature and conditions of streams and glaciers, making barometric readings, estimating the relative humidity of the atmosphere, and even measuring the pulses of all the members of his party as they made their way into the thin air of the summit—fueled his massive work-in-progress, a four-volume description of the Alps.[17] De Saussure was part of a vibrant community of savants in Geneva and Lausanne. Geneva boasted an excellent university, rich natural history collections, and the new and widely read journal founded by the Pictet brothers, the *Bibliothèque Britannique*.[18]

Smithson made several contacts in this thriving Enlightenment society that he kept for the rest of his life, including the mineralogist Henri Struve in Lausanne. But on this first trip to Switzerland he was introduced to this community by a man who was perceived first of all as a gentleman and a collector, rather than as a scientist—a fact that may well have colored perceptions of Smithson, and one that also serves to highlight some of the conflict inherent in Smithson's aspirations and desires. Charles Greville's passion for mineral collecting was driven by his aesthetic collector instincts rather than by any real desire to comprehend a larger system. De Saussure on first meeting him found him "ready to talk rocks: at first I was afraid he wanted to get the benefit of my observations, but I found with a pleasure which was perhaps ignoble that he was not a serious student and did not attempt to generalise. He was on the look-out for curious specimens for his collection, without any consideration for grouping them. I recognised that he was in no sense a formidable rival."[19] Greville's renown in Switzerland derived not from his pursuit of mineralogy but rather from his role as an unparalleled exemplar of the folly of English aristocratic extravagance. There was probably still talk in the monastery of St. Gotthard of the time some years earlier when he had insisted on crossing the narrow, treacherous pass in his carriage instead of on muleback—and of the poor donkeys that had struggled to ensure the wheels had not slipped off the vertiginous mountain track and the eighteen louis that had greased various palms to enable such a feat.[20] Was Smithson, at least initially, also dismissed by association as a wealthy dilettante?

Smithson wanted to be valued as a real contributor to knowledge. He was busily cultivating a network of collaborators and colleagues, he was building a comprehensive mineral cabinet, and he was working to the point of exhaustion in his laboratory. But, unable to relinquish his deep-seated need for recognition as the son of the Duke of Northumberland, he remained attentive first of all to presenting himself as a well-born gentleman and patron. On the Continent at least, freed from the stigma of his illegitimacy, Smithson seems to have been able to travel uncontested as a wealthy, educated foreigner, a fact that may have played a large role in his decision to settle in France later in life. This tension between his scientific ambitions and his aristocratic aspirations endured his entire life. His inclination for the world of patronage served him well in the clubbable, gentlemanly circles in which science was promulgated in the eighteenth century, but in the decades to come science itself was to leave the realm of the gentleman amateur and begin to enter the domain of the professional.

By late September 1788 Greville and Smithson were back in Paris, staying once more on the rue des Petits Augustins. Paris on the eve of the Revolution was already in a state of turmoil. The country was on the verge of financial collapse. Wild storms in July had devastated crops in the countryside, bread prices had rocketed, and famished peasants were streaming into Paris seeking relief. People rioted throughout the country, in Brittany, Burgundy, Béarn, and Provence. Near Grenoble there was fighting in the streets, an incident that came to be known as the Day of the Tiles after angry residents hurled their roofing materials at the soldiers who came to subdue them. In Paris police clashed with protestors amidst bonfires on the Pont Neuf; there were many casualties and arrests. Crowds cheered the burning in effigy of the new finance minister Loménie de Brienne, the Archbishop of Toulouse, who was forced a few weeks later to resign. The King announced finally that the Estates General would, for the first time since 1614, be summoned to Versailles in May the following year to address the nation's grievances.[21]

For one with money, though, Paris despite the chaos continued to be a city of delights. Smithson had a line of credit with Jean-Frédéric Perregaux, the well-connected Swiss banker whose thriving Paris banking house catered particularly to wealthy English tourists.[22] He probably passed a lot of time in the gambling houses tucked under the arcades in the Palais Royal, the epicenter of fashionable Paris. As the private property of the Duc d'Orléans, a cousin of the King, the Palais Royal existed as a law unto itself. "It is a city in the middle of Paris, where all breathe grandeur, ease, and liberty," proclaimed a 1788 guidebook.[23] At the Palais Royal all levels of society mixed together and the latest in every entertainment or luxury could be purchased. Pilâtre de Rozier, Paris' own Icarus, the very first balloonist (and the first to die, too, in a dramatic explosion over Boulogne), had established a museum nearby, where chemistry demonstrations and experiments of electrical effects were popular with the ladies.[24] In the waiterless Café Méchanique tables disappeared into the floor and reappeared resplendent with food. Ladies of the night promenaded as secure as duchesses, and pamphleteers cried out their causes. All enjoyed a freedom and looseness that provided the breeding ground for the fomenting of the Revolution.

Moreover, Paris was overflowing with scientific conversation. Charles Greville's brief, stimulating visit to Holland with Sir Joseph Banks in early 1773 can probably be taken as something of a model for this trip of Greville and Smithson's. In Holland Greville and Banks made many contacts with the scientific community; they hunted for rare books in dusty old shops and visited private cabinets and public collections. From the herbarium at the University of Leiden to the menagerie at Loo, they took in all the natural history wonders the country had to offer.[25] In Paris now with Smithson, instead of the discussions of botany that preoccupied Greville in Holland, mineralogy would have been the topic of choice, a passion that bound these two men together as ardently as botany did Banks and Greville.

Smithson presumably called upon Lavoisier in his apartments at the Arsenal, carrying the letter of introduction from Sir Joseph Banks. Lavoisier was actively seeking to convert members of the British scientific community to his new system, so he probably warmly welcomed his young visitor. Sir James Hall, a Scotsman who visited Paris in 1786, told his uncle that he had "received the greatest civilities from him [Lavoisier]—I have a standing invitation to dine with him every Monday."[26] And Arthur Young, who visited in 1787, recalled Lavoisier's talented young wife Marie-Anne serving a "*dejeuné Anglois*" of tea and coffee; he found her learned scientific conversation to be "the best repast," and much admired the "splendid" and "noble" machines of the laboratory.[27] Among the many other scientists Smithson met on this trip, he also befriended the chemist Comte Claude Berthollet, who was director of the Gobelins tapestry factory and inspector of dye-works for the government. Just as he had in Scotland, Smithson came away from this trip having met the most important figures in chemistry; and although there is no trace of the impression that Lavoisier made on the young Smithson, Berthollet became a friend and colleague for life.

Science in France, which enjoyed a long tradition of government support, was conducted very differently than in England. The Académie des Sciences had a fixed number of members, restricted solely—unlike in England—to scientists who had proven their worth, with each seat awarded a pension. In addition to the Académie des Sciences, which like its Royal Society counterpart had been in existence for over a century by the 1780s, the institutions of the

Paris Observatory, the Ecole des Mines, the Collège Royale, and the Jardin du Roi all employed scientists in positions of stature. Other military and technical government operations also required scientific advisers, and figures like Berthollet or Lavoisier could be found supervising the Sèvres porcelain manufactory, the Gobelins tapestry works, the Ponts et Chaussées, and the munitions factory at the Arsenal.[28]

Smithson and Greville would have met all the principal figures of French chemistry, attended public lectures and demonstrations, and studied the significant collections. Mineral cabinets seemed to lurk behind the elegant doors of nearly every sizeable *hôtel*. One guidebook listed upwards of fifty important collections, including that of the Duc de la Rochefoucauld—the honorary secretary of the Académie des Sciences and a passionate admirer of the United States, whose *hôtel* was just around the corner from where Smithson and Greville were staying.[29] Smithson and Greville probably visited the mineral collector Comte de Bournon, whom Greville later helped to escape Paris during the Revolution, and they surely studied the extensive mineral cabinet at the new Hôtel de la Monnaie (the Mint) along the river across from the Louvre, run by the jowly Balthazar-Georges Sage, who had been installed as the first director of France's new Ecole des Mines.

Paris in the 1780s was the scene of a critical new development in mineralogy, the science of crystallography. René-Just Haüy, professor of mineralogy at the Jardin du Roi and at the Faculté des Sciences of Paris and one of the principal architects of the new science, became a lifelong friend of Smithson's.[30] Haüy believed he had uncovered a series of fundamental rules that confirmed nature's simplicity and provided a mathematical means of determining species; he argued that each crystal had an underlying "primitive form," like a cube or a rhomboid, whose dimensions could be expressed as ratios of square roots, and he was convinced that these internal forms, once discerned, could provide a new system of mineral classification.[31] Smithson rapidly became expert at the techniques of this new science—like the use of the goniometer to determine the angles between the crystal's faces—adding these tools to his ever-increasing arsenal as an experimentalist. William Thomson was soon praising Smithson's talents, saying, "He is the best mineralogist I know—especially for crystallography."[32]

Crystallography, which offered the possibility of a systematic approach to mineral classification, proved hugely appealing to Smithson. While it ultimately never superseded his belief in chemical analysis as the best key to understanding the mineral kingdom, it had a radical impact on his collecting habits. At some point in the months following this trip to Paris Smithson entirely reorganized his system of collecting, to focus exclusively on the principles of crystallization. He was no longer interested in the large, impressive, and beautiful clusters sought after by gentleman connoisseurs like Charles Greville or his cousin George Keate. From this point forward, Smithson desired only perfect single crystal specimens. "The bodies I want are all kinds of crystals, and I value them in proportion as they show well their form," he later explained to one Italian colleague. "Hence I esteem first these which are isolated and quite complete, and after these, single crystals broken from groups. Amorphous minerals do not enter into the plan of my collection."[33]

When Smithson was still collecting large mineral specimens, he had commissioned a pair of elegant cabinets in which to display them. These "decently ornamental" cases, William Thomson told John Hawkins in 1789, Smithson had never had occasion to use, because he had "so completely changed his plan, f[ro]m oversized specimens, to minute single crystals."[34] After this Paris trip Smithson entirely abandoned the idea of a gentleman's collection. His collection when it came to the Smithsonian in the late 1830s had grown to number some ten thousand of these tiny, "extremely perfect" specimens, all systematically arranged, constituting "a very complete Geological and Mineralogical series" and carefully labeled with Smithson's notes.[35] Henceforth, it seems, Smithson dedicated himself to building a comprehensive study collection—the ultimate tool for that essential eighteenth-century project, the encyclopedic ordering and categorizing and controlling of nature.

Smithson was back in London by early November 1788, when the city was bedecked with lights to mark the centennial of the Glorious Revolution, and all over the country people celebrated England and her constitution. The anniversary was overshadowed, however, by alarming reports from the palace of the King's descent into madness; the crisis consumed Parliament and erupted into a full-blown struggle for control of the government, which was not resolved finally until the King's remarkable "recovery" three months later. Early November was also the opening of the Royal Society season, and Smithson dove right into the hubbub of activity, bringing guests, attending meetings, and putting prospective members forward. On November 6 he took Dr. George Shaw, an Oxford friend who was teaching a course of botany at the university, as his guest to the weekly meeting. Smithson was priming Shaw for election, the first of a number of people he successfully backed for fellowship.[36] Shaw became F.R.S. in early 1789. Two months later Smithson joined a number of prominent colleagues—including Cavendish, Blagden, Josiah Wedgwood, and John Hunter—in sponsoring Johann Karl Wilcke, the head of the Swedish Royal Academy of Sciences.[37] Soon after, he also supported his famous new acquaintance in Paris, Comte Berthollet, for membership.

By the summer of 1789 all eyes were on France. At a pace that could scarcely be believed, the strongest, most entrenched monarchy in Europe collapsed. In three dramatic months a new representative assembly was formed, a declaration of the rights of man drawn up, the privileges of the aristocracy reneged, and plans laid for the drafting of a constitution. The storming of the Bastille by the people, and the crumbling of those ancient walls, came to symbolize the destruction of the very foundations of the *ancien régime*. The French Revolution was initially greeted enthusiastically by many in England.

Even the Duke of Dorset, then ambassador to the court at Paris and a favorite of Marie Antoinette, wrote home: "The greatest revolution that we know anything of has been effected with, comparatively speaking—if the magnitude of the event is considered—the loss of very few lives. From this moment we may consider France as a free country, the King a very limited monarch, and the nobility as reduced to a level with the rest of the nation."[38]

Smithson was absolutely euphoric over the turn of events. For him and his coffeehouse society friends, the Revolution augured nothing less than the birth of an entirely new future. "Stupidity and guilt have had a long reign," Smithson believed, "and it begins, indeed, to be time for justice and common sense to have their turn." The French Revolution, as he saw it, was "consolidating the throne of justice and reason." The scientific breakthroughs of the previous decades made clear to Smithson and his like-minded contemporaries that massive improvement could be brought to society. Reason, a rational experimental approach, and education were the essential building blocks. "If the millions of money and the thousands of individuals which are at present sacrificed to war should be applied to the promotion of science and arts," Smithson believed, "what may not we expect even in our time!"[39] The human community could perhaps be perfected. At the very least, through the application of scientific method, it could be brought to a whole new level of existence. Smithson echoed the radical Priestley in arguing for a future in which science would serve as the crowning authority, rather than royalty or the Church.

It was America's example that had paved the way. The American war had awakened the slumbering nation of France "from the sleep of despotism in which they were sunk," as Thomas Jefferson observed in Paris in early 1789.[40] Priestley argued that the American and French revolutions had transformed the world "from darkness to light, from superstition to sound knowledge, and from a most debasing servitude to a state of the most exalted freedom."[41] They were now witnesses to nothing less than the beginning of a new age in the history of human development.

Smithson and his friends felt themselves to be at the center of this sea change. When Davies Giddy came to London in anticipation of becoming a Fellow of the Royal Society, the visit "formed an Epoch in [his] Life." In his diary the twenty-four-year-old breathlessly recorded every impression of his weeks in the big city, from having his hair done to the hour he went to bed after an evening of fireworks at Ranelagh Gardens (4.00 a.m.). His Cornish friend John Hawkins hosted him at his house in Chandos Street, Cavendish Square. Giddy called on Smithson, and Smithson later took him as his guest to the Royal Society meeting and introduced him to Sir Joseph Banks. He attended a "conversitione" [sic] at George Staunton's house, and Staunton took him another night to an evening meeting "at some Gentleman's House in one of the great Squares to meet those distinguished Personages, Tom Paine, Mr. Horne Tooke, & Mr. Mackintosh."[42] Giddy was the country mouse arrived in the big city, exposed to the exciting life Smithson and Hawkins were living in these revolutionary days. Science and politics were inextricably linked in this world, and it seemed that they lived on the verge of a revolution in every arena imaginable.

The Revolution had an unintended impact on the course of science, however. The widespread enthusiasm for the changes in France among natural philosophers, especially outside the Establishment Royal Society, in provincial clubs and among Dissenters and other Nonconformists, turned chemistry into a lightning rod for charges of radicalism. Edmund Burke made his famous condemnation of the French Revolution in terms that deliberately invoked the language of chemistry. He railed that "the wild *gas*, the fixed air is plainly broken loose." And in another tract he warned that "Churches, play-houses, coffee-houses, all alike, are destined to be mingled, and equalized . . . well sifted, and lixiviated, to crystallize into true democratic, explosive, insurrectionary nitre."[43] But chemistry was more than just a metaphor or a rich rhetoric to mine for descriptions of unsettling change and revolution. Burke, in identifying the threat to authority, specifically fingered the chemists,

Joseph Priestley
as the radical
"Dr. Phlogiston."
He stands on a book
that reads "BIBLE
explained away" while
waving burning
pamphlets labelled
"Political Sermon," his
pockets stuffed with
tracts on "Gunpowder."

who "bring from the soot of their furnaces dispositions that make them worse than indifferent about those feelings and habitudes which are the support of the moral world."[44] Chemists themselves, as personified by Joseph Priestley, were the real danger. In their pursuit of a world based in reason and science, they were advocating nothing less than the overthrow of English society. It was only a short time before chemistry in the minds of the general public no longer represented simply a source of wonder and popular entertainment. Chemistry in the light of the French Revolution underwent its own transmutation: it became a threat.

Smithson was away on the Continent for much of the 1790s, and thus escaped the very worst of this backlash. He missed the treason trials of 1794 and 1795, where a number of English radicals— what Burke called "the Frenchified faction"—were prosecuted in Parliament under the new sedition laws. Smithson also missed the fleeing of Joseph Priestley and Thomas Cooper and a host of other

English Jacobins to America. The ideals of public science articulated by Priestley, and so ardently embraced by Smithson, were dealt a very severe blow during these years. There were other setbacks, too. The ensuing decades of war greatly hampered scientific communications. Many governments no longer seemed supportive of or sympathetic to science. Lavoisier lost his head at the guillotine, and dozens of Smithson's colleagues were haplessly captured and imprisoned while trying to carry on with their work—including, eventually, even Smithson himself.

Towards the end of 1789 Smithson moved house again, to Orchard Street, Portman Square. He was still, in March 1790, according to Charles Blagden, "setting up his library and laboratory." (Smithson's arrival may well have frightened the neighbors—his fellow F.R.S. member Richard Chenevix had a hard time renting a house in Brook Street, on account of his wanting to set up a laboratory in the cellar; people "expected he would blow it up."[45]) He was juggling a number of projects simultaneously. With "extracts of spermaceti from liver," he was trying to replicate Antoine Fourcroy's study of the decomposition of animal matter, an experiment he had probably learned about in Paris, where Fourcroy, one of Lavoisier's collaborators, was an extremely popular public lecturer in chemistry.[46] And he was examining what he thought to be a specimen of Cumberland red ore of lead, but he became worried that it was factitious or manufactured; he asked Greville if he would check his cabinet's example and "see whether you can find any certain traces of the fingers of nature upon them, for my part I cannot, & begin to be apprehensive that they will turn-out to be products of art."[47]

Smithson's growing reputation for meticulous analysis garnered him an important new project at this time, one that led to his first publication. In the spring of 1790 "a remarkable substance called Tabasheer (Tabaxir in the Portuguese) much used in medicine by the oriental physicians" was presented to the Royal Society in a letter from Patrick Russell, an English physician in India. A renowned aphrodisiac, tabasheer was also employed as a poison antidote and an asthma and cough suppresser; Russell even wondered whether its extraordinary capacity for absorption might not make it a possible remedy for smallpox. Seven parcels were laid before the society, each containing a different specimen either collected or purchased by Russell from a variety of locations. Hard and opalescent, tabasheer appeared to form from the watery juice found inside the joints of bamboo. But only some pieces of bamboo contained these little seed-pearl-like concretions, and in some the tabasheer rattled around, while in others it adhered to the side of the cavity. Its use, as Russell recounted in his letter, was extensive throughout Asian cultures, but it was completely unknown in the West. The members of the Royal Society deemed it very worthy of investigation. Blagden was convinced that any discoveries connected to it would "prove likely quite new," as he wrote excitedly in September to Berthollet.[48] In July Sir Joseph Banks announced that the specimens of tabasheer were under chemical trial, and "it was much hoped that the results would be communicated to the society." Smithson—either because he volunteered and was accepted, or because he was hand-picked— was the one chosen to investigate the tabasheer. The selection was a telling marker of his excellent reputation already among the scientific elite at the Royal Society. His findings, "An Account of the Tabasheer," appeared a year later, his first publication in the Royal Society's prestigious journal, the *Philosophical Transactions*.

Smithson was, already by the age of twenty-five, developing the micro-chemistry experimental method by which he would be known all his life. Working in miniature required a high degree of technical dexterity, and the samples Smithson took from the parcels of tabasheer on which to conduct his experiments were minuscule; he admitted that "the largest of them did not exceed two or three-tenths of an inch cubic." On these tiny specimens Smithson executed hundreds of experiments to try to determine the physical properties of this unknown substance. He cut the pieces up and rubbed them together in the dark to see if they generated electric sparks, and he steeped them in mildly fermented red cabbage, a kind of primitive litmus paper, to test for pH. He subjected them to acids and alkalis and extremes of heat, repeating the experiments under a variety of conditions, using open and closed vessels, exposed to the light or hidden from it. His laboratory must have been sweltering, and filled with noxious fumes from hours of boiling the samples in "pure white marine acid" (hydrochloric acid) and "vitriolic acid" (sulfuric acid) or days of letting them stand open to the air in "spirit of wine" (alcohol). Many of the experiments lasted for weeks and some even for months.

Despite the tabasheer's vegetable origins, Smithson concluded that he had found a mineral substance in the bamboo. Tabasheer appeared to be "perfectly identical with common siliceous earth." The implications, though not part of his publication (Smithson as a true Enlightenment scientist, faithful only to that which could be observed and tested, declined to speculate extensively in print), were tremendously exciting to Smithson's peers. If the organic matter of the bamboo had created the mineral matter of the tabasheer, what might that mean for the origins of the earth? Chemistry looked to be the tool that could elucidate the link and unravel the mystery. The Royal Society, convinced that "farther Analysis of this singular substance may lead to a knowledge of the Composition of flint," was pleased to announce that Smithson had signaled "his intention of resuming the subject at some future period."[49]

Smithson's tabasheer paper was very well received, and his name was soon strongly identified with this publication all across Europe. Blagden promptly disseminated the results, reporting the discovery to Kirwan in Ireland and Berthollet in Paris. A notice appeared in the French *Journal de Physique* in December 1791, and in London the *Monthly Review* hailed Smithson's experiments as "very judiciously executed."[50] The work continued to be referenced in the years that followed. William Thomson promoted Smithson's tabasheer discoveries in his *Breve Notizia di un Viaggiatore* of 1795. Robert Jameson cited Smithson's work in a paper he delivered before the Royal Medical Society of Edinburgh in 1796. In 1803 the Genoa-based scientist William Batt was still hailing Smithson as "the chemical Mr. Macie (who analysed the Tabaschir)," and in 1805 likewise in his lectures on geology at the Royal Institution Humphry Davy referenced the tabasheer discoveries of "Mr. Macie."[51]

Smithson's paper also stood as evidence of the strong backing that he enjoyed among the most esteemed men of British science. During the course of his investigations, he had intrigued the Royal Society elite with his analysis of this strange concretion. Henry Cavendish had contributed to the work by conducting experiments on Smithson's behalf to determine tabasheer's specific gravity (its density). Smithson communicated with Joseph Black at exactly this time, and though the letter is lost it may well have concerned his work on tabasheer.[52] And at William Pitcairn's country place in Islington (the uncle of Smithson's Royal Society sponsor David Pitcairn), Sir Joseph Banks and other Royal Society luminaries traipsed with Smithson out to the glasshouses that ranged behind the house. They fanned out down the aisles, shaking and rustling the bamboo plants; Banks found one that rattled, a promising indication of the presence of tabasheer. They gathered around as Banks broke it open, Smithson reported, and were astonished to discover "not ordinary Tabasheer, but a solid pebble, about the size of half a pea . . . so hard as to cut glass!"[53]

In the course of just a few years Smithson had established himself as a chemist to watch. He had masterfully orchestrated his arrival in the world of scientific investigation in London. He was cultivating an extensive international network, offering himself up as a correspondent, eagerly taking on new research projects, and acting as a witness and assessor of public experiments. He had joined an elite group of men working in a field that was transforming life as they knew it.

The career of his close friend William Thomson, in contrast, the man who had helped him so much with his rapid advance, took a precipitous turn. In September 1790 Thomson hurriedly left Oxford under a cloud of scandal. Officials there wished to see him "most publically censured on a charge of suspicion" that he was guilty of "sodomy and other unnatural and detestable practices with a servant boy." The event in question had transpired some four years earlier, around the time of Smithson's last year at Oxford. No real details of the incident exist. Thomson confided to a friend that he was suffering "a most scandalous imputation from an Experiment performed on a man 4 years ago." He argued vainly that his activities had all been conducted in the name of science, but Oxford soon issued its ominous ruling: "et insuper eundem expellimus, bannimus et exterminamus."[54] Thomson was stripped of his studentship and his degrees, followed soon thereafter by the loss of his membership in the Royal Society and other societies. Since the time of Henry VIII sodomy was not only illegal in England, it was a crime punishable by death. The only safety lay in exile. Thomson fled from England, never to return. Smithson presumably helped his friend as best he could, perhaps sheltering him in London before he left England for the last time. After traveling the Continent, Thomson settled, appropriately enough, in Italy—a country long alluded to as "the Mother and Nurse of Sodomy," a place where "the Master is oftner intriguing with his Page than a fair Lady."[55] Smithson evidently promised Thomson he would see him in Italy before too long. He was headed to Europe soon himself, for some rest and recuperation, physically exhausted after the rigors of his chemical investigations.

Like all chemists of his age, Smithson used his own body extensively as an instrument for experimentation. When faced with an unidentified substance, an eighteenth-century chemist drew first from his own physical arsenal, relying upon tests of touch, smell, and taste. Perhaps the best-known body-altering experiments of the era were those that Thomas Beddoes and Humphry Davy conducted with nitrous oxide, or laughing gas, at their Pneumatic Institution in Bristol in the late 1790s. The St. Thomas' Hospital doctor George Fordyce, together with Joseph Banks, Charles Blagden, and others, conducted experiments in 1775 on human physiology in the face of extreme heat. Crammed into Fordyce's tiny experimental chamber, fully clothed, they measured how long they could expose themselves to temperatures of 150, and then 160 degrees. As the day wore on they stoked the cast-iron stove so hot that all but one of the primitive mercury thermometers eventually broke, their ivory cases buckling in the 200-degree-plus heat.[56] Smithson, when he began his experiments on tabasheer, employed all his senses to make a preliminary description of this foreign matter. He explained that it "could not be broken by pressure between the fingers; but by the teeth it was easily reduced to powder. On first chewing it felt gritty, but soon ground to impalpable particles. Applied to the tongue, it adhered to it by capillary attraction. It had a disagreeable taste, something like that of magnesia." Another of the parcels, when heated, "emitted a smell something like tobacco ashes, but not the kind of perfume discovered in that [specimen originating] from Hyderabad." Smithson's research throughout his life was littered with such observations. Analysis that depended on the senses—"No foetid animal smell was perceived during the combustion'[57]— provided essential clues for the identification of substances.

Such methods imposed a harsh price on the health of the practitioners. A quick survey of Smithson's friends provides ample evidence of the perilous demands of life in the laboratory. The French chemist Pierre-Louis Dulong lost an eye and two fingers in the discovery of "le chlorure d'azote" (the explosive nitrogen trichloride). Humphry Davy following up on Dulong's experiments triggered a similar explosion, sending a shard of glass slashing through his cornea; he was lucky not to have lost the eye completely. Likewise Joseph Louis Gay-Lussac was nearly blinded in his laboratory experimenting with caustic potash (potassium hydroxide), an accident which after a long period of suffering eventually caused his death. And the pharmacist-chemist Bertrand Pelletier was badly burned during his experiments with phosphorus after his clothes caught fire.[58] Smithson had a fairly delicate constitution to begin with, and it was not long before his chosen vocation began to take its toll.

It is likely that Smithson, as an inquisitive chemist, often self-medicated. For eighteenth-century scientists the body was another vessel to tinker with, a container of chemical events. Among the items in the Smithson Collection at the Smithsonian Archives is a "receipt book" filled with recipes for treatments such as Cox's Hive Syrup (which caused "Vomiting, Purging & Sweating'), Dr. Clarke's and Justice Bayley's Dinner Pills, an unguent for Hemorrhoids, and an Italian "Mistura per Gonorrhea."[59] Smithson's annotations in his cookbooks and his publication on "an improved method of making coffee" make clear that he commonly applied his laboratory talents in other arenas as well. He stayed abreast of all the latest medical ideas, becoming a fan, for example, of Brunonianism, the cultish theory of excitability that swept through Europe at the end of the eighteenth century. Brunonianism was the brainchild of Edinburgh medical man John Brown, who alleged that all diseases were due to an imbalance of nervous system energy and could be treated either by chemical stimulation or by depletion through purging or blood-letting. To one witty contemporary it was the idea that "human bodies are like lighted tapers in a constant state of Combustion," and he joked that "if this be true, Jesus how I pity the poor sweet Princess Royal! What a long time that large, fat, lubberly Husband of hers, the Duke of Wirtemberg, will take in consuming!"[60] Smithson, who probably tinkered at length with regulating his own system, unabashedly offered advice on medical issues to his friends. "I hope that you have found that I was right; that the formidable part of disorders, of which you complained when I waited on you last," he told Lady Holland, "was not quite as grave and real as you seemed then to apprehend, & that you have long since lost sight of all the black spots."[61]

By the autumn of 1791 Smithson was so ill that he had very nearly lost his hearing.[62] He could not face another winter like the two that had preceded it. In 1789, with the thermometer reading eleven below zero, the Thames had completely frozen. A frost fair had been erected on the ice beyond London Bridge, and newspapers

trumpeted tales of gaiety, but many lost their lives in the cold.[63] A
year later the river had flooded well beyond any previous known
heights. Solicitors had been ferried to their appointments at the law
courts in little boats atop the engorged river. Millenarians feared
that the apocalyptic weather patterns were retribution for the growing
political tumult. That winter had seen, Adam Walker told a friend,
"the most variable weather ever known in this variable Island:
Thunder Lightning, Rain, frost & wind, have taken place every 24
hours for the above time. . . . Much mischief has been done to the
land & sea, & great alarms still possess the People."[64]

Smithson settled on a sojourn to the Continent to heal himself.
The fresh air of the Mediterranean offered a time-honored cure for
bronchial infections and other ailments. As part of his recuperation,
he would probably have intended to devote a year or more to taking
in the pleasures and antiquities of Europe. Such a trip, a Grand
Tour, was a rite of passage for young English men of rank, an
essential component of their gentlemanly education. And for one
like Smithson so focused on his pretensions to the aristocracy, the
Grand Tour would have provided him an appropriately cultured
patina, as well as exposure to the best circles in Europe.

Smithson may well have planned to travel with his half-sister,
Philadelphia Percy, another of the duke's illegitimate offspring. She
was also ill, weak with consumption, and headed for the sunny south
of France "for the recovery of her health" in the fall of 1791. Perhaps
they set off together; it's not possible to know for certain. The
journey ended in tragedy, however, with her death en route to
Southampton to cross the Channel. She was buried at Westminster
Abbey at the end of November. Her casket was adorned with white
feathers and white silk, symbols of chastity and purity, and it was
laid to rest in a vault not far from that of her father, the Duke of
Northumberland. Smithson's other half-sister Dorothy, when she
died a few years later, while he was still abroad, was also buried at
Westminster Abbey.[65]

Smithson remained close to their unacknowledged mother,

Margaret Marriott, his entire life. At the time of her death in 1827, she entrusted Smithson with much of the childhood ephemera of these two girls, including their portraits, charging him in essence to be the guardian of their memory. And in her will Margaret Marriott carefully specified the details for her own funeral and burial. She wished her service to be celebrated exactly as those of Philadelphia and Dorothy had been performed, with the exception only that "Black feathers and Silk instead of White" be used. Most especially she desired to be interred in Westminster Abbey in the same vault with her "beloved" girls. The request would not be granted.[66]

Smithson, when he left finally for the Continent, enfeebled and unwell, probably also went with a heavy heart.

Six

Grand Tour, 1791–1797

I. Paris

I consider a nation with a king as a man who takes
a lion as a guard-dog—if he knocks out his teeth he
renders him useless, while if he leaves the lion his
teeth the lion eats him.

—Smithson to Davies Giddy, May 1792

S MITHSON RETURNED TO the narrow streets clustered
in the shadow of the Abbey of St. Germain, taking lodgings
at the Hôtel du Parc-Royal, just around the corner from
where he had stayed with Charles Greville three years earlier. The
weather was fresh and "exceedingly mild." The soft thin light of a
gentle winter invigorated him, and he soon changed his plans in
order to stay through to the spring. "I find myself better than in
London," Smithson told Greville, "and have entirely recovered my
hearing which I had nearly lost since several months."[1]

The setting was the same, but the Revolution had utterly
transformed everyday life. The Church, deemed to be in conflict
with the new ideals of a nation dedicated to liberty, was rapidly
being dismantled. New civic rituals replaced religious tradition.
Monastic vows were ended, and men of the cloth forced to swear
on the new constitution. Sainte Genevieve, the church of Paris'

patron saint, had been transformed into the Pantheon, a temple to
the martyrs of the Revolution and the civic heroes of the country;
thousands had crowded the streets when Voltaire's remains were
paraded up the cobbled hill in July 1791 to be interred there. "The
church is now here quite unacknowledged by the state," Smithson
wrote home, "and is indeed allowed to exist only till they have
leisure to give it the final death-stroke."[2]

A year after the Declaration of the Rights of Man and the abolition
of feudalism, the National Assembly in August 1790 had eliminated
the wearing of all decorations based on birth. The city that had long
been the center of a hierarchy visibly promulgated through fashion—
the lavish colors, the expensive lace, the latest cuts, the quality of
cloth and the amount of adornment—suddenly began to shun
distinction. Those in official positions donned tricolor sashes, a signal
attribute that was easily removable. The tricolor cockade, worn by
everyone in sympathy with the Revolution, quickly became popular
among the English visitors as well. "Mr. Davis, high sheriff for
Dorsetshire, left this town today," Smithson wrote to Davies Giddy,
who had recently been appointed high sheriff for Cornwall, "and
takes with him, it seems, a quantity of tricolor ribbon to deck his
men with the French national cockades, and I do not think this
example unworthy of imitation by those whose principles lead them
to consider with indifference and contempt the frowns of the court
party, to whom, doubtless, the mixture of red, white, and blue is
an object of horror."[3]

The nobility as a class was abolished, too. Titles, the word "de"
as part of one's name, liveries, and all armorial bearings were banned.
The Duc de Lauzan renounced all his privileges to become Citoyen-
Général Biron. The Duc d'Orléans rechristened himself Philippe
Egalité. Primogeniture was abolished. There was talk, too, of
abandoning the distinction between legitimacy and illegitimacy.
"Offspring of a sentimental union are sacred by nature," declared the
ex-monk Chabot in 1793. Cambacérès also saw the distinction "as
a vestige of ignorance and superstition."[4] These discussions had a

profound resonance for Smithson. Here finally he was witnessing the rebirth of a nation predicated on the idea that the circumstances of birth should not dictate one's path in life. "What kind of office," asked Tom Paine, "must that be in a government which requires for its execution neither experience nor ability, that may be abandoned to the desperate chance of birth, that may be filled by an idiot, a madman, a tyrant, with equal effect as by the good, the virtuous, and the wise?"[5] The King, who had humiliated himself with his attempted flight dressed as a valet in the summer of 1791, was in Smithson's eyes "a contemptible encumbrance." He hoped that "other nations at the time of their reforms" would also rid themselves of their monarchs.[6]

The National Assembly had finally succeeded in drafting a constitution in September 1791, and equality was now the theme of the future. Smithson had entered into a world where the crisis of identity that had gripped his childhood no longer ruled. He was filled with the language of enraptured republicans, the Dissenters who had joined the corresponding societies back in England and the radical Whig aristocratic followers of Charles James Fox, who had declared in the spring of 1791 that the French Revolution was "much the greatest event . . . that ever happened in the world."[7] The events in France "will compel great changes in every part of the globe," Smithson wrote to Greville back in London. James Watt, Jr., the son of the Lunar Society member and steam engine improver, who was also in Paris in 1792, likewise spoke of the import French actions had, "not merely for the liberty of their country, but for the defence of the liberties of mankind."[8]

James Watt, Jr., was traveling with Thomas Cooper, a member, like Smithson, of the Coffee House Philosophical Society. The two men presented a message to the people of France from the Constitutional Society of Manchester, one of many groups that had sprung up in England in support of the Revolution and principles of liberty; they expressed their desire to help build the foundations for "the Empire of Peace, and the happiness of Mankind." In April

1792 the two men were some of the stars of a triumphal parade in Paris, the largest civil ceremony the new regime had yet seen.[9] Their actions were widely publicized, and Edmund Burke condemned Watt and Cooper and other English Jacobins in Parliament. Fury at revolutionary sympathizers led to the passage of the Traitorous Correspondence Act of 1793, and trials for treason and sedition in London in 1794. Watt managed to return safely to work in England, but Cooper emigrated to the United States, as his mentor Joseph Priestley did soon thereafter. Decades later, from South Carolina, he would advise the U.S. Congress on the disposition of the Smithson bequest.[10]

Smithson, like these radicalized chemists and the Dissenting intellectuals who were their inspiration, wholeheartedly embraced the Revolution and its power to stand as a model for the rest of the world. Just as the radical Dissenting minister Richard Price had rejoiced "to see a diffusion of knowledge, which has undermined superstition and error . . . and nations panting for liberty," so Smithson did not see "what will conquer and restore to ignorance fifteen millions of people resolved upon success or death." A tolerant France, extending "its arm to the native of every latitude, to the sectories of every religion," would quickly outstrip all other countries in its progress. "Other nations can possibly maintain any competition with it," Smithson was convinced, "only by emulating and, if possible, exceeding it in its improvements."[11]

The abolition of inherited privilege, so exhilarating to Smithson and his fellow English Jacobins, struck fear in the hearts of many. Far off in Italy Vesuvius was enjoying a period of great activity, and the erupting volcano became a fitting metaphor for the events unfolding in Paris, regardless of how one perceived the Revolution. Smithson, thoroughly captivated, regretted missing Vesuvius, but he found consolation in the fact that:

I am here on the brink of the crater of a great volcano, from whence lavas are daily issuing, but whose effects are widely

different from those of the other that is laying waste one of
the finest countries in the world [and] is threatening with ruin
the noblest efforts of human art. While this on the contrary is
consolidating the throne of justice and reason, pours its
destruction only on erroneous or corrupt institutions,
overthrows not fine statues & amphitheatres, but monks and
convents.[12]

For the cautious American ambassador Gouverneur Morris, the
metaphorical eruption was distinctly more ominous. "We now stand
on a Volcano," he told Jefferson, "we feel it tremble and we hear
it roar but how and when and where it will burst and who may be
destroy'd by its Eruptions is beyond the Ken of mortal Foresight to
discover."[13]

The Revolution threw the scientific world of Paris, with its long-
standing, highly oiled system of patronage, into chaos. Little attention
could be devoted to research. The future of the royally funded Jardin
du Roi and Académie des Sciences seemed tenuous at best. In the
fall of 1790 the naturalists at the Jardin were permitted by the
Assembly to draw up a proposal for their own reform. They
envisioned a new Muséum d'Histoire Naturelle, a large multi-
disciplined research and teaching institute, a great foundation
dedicated to the increase and diffusion of knowledge, with salaried
professors and a collective approach to decision-making. But the
turbulent political situation prevented the proposal from even being
heard before 1793. Money allocated for the Jardin became scarce
and erratic, and Paris' once cohesive community of scientists grew
fractious and competitive. Balthazar-Georges Sage, for example, tried
to capture the mineral collections from the Jardin for his own purview
over at the Ecole des Mines. Throughout the first eight months of
1792, while Smithson was in Paris, the post of superintendent of
the Jardin remained vacant. Many scientists, driven by the same zeal
for the public good that had guided their scientific work, took to
the embryonic political system. The Marquis de Condorcet, the

permanent secretary of the Académie des Sciences, was only the most famous of these. The chemist Antoine Fourcroy and the naturalist the Comte de Lacépède were others. Berthollet removed himself to his place in the country outside Paris to work in tranquility, as he explained to a friend, but he found himself instead "continually distraught."[14]

The advance of the Revolution menaced every crown in Europe. They soon banded together to try to restore the French King to his throne, and Paris prepared both to defend itself and to export its message across the Continent. "Immense preparations are making for the war with the Princes," Smithson told Greville at the beginning of 1792. On April 20 that year France declared war on Francis II, King of Bohemia and Hungary and Holy Roman Emperor. By the summer the allied forces had invaded. They routed the French in the first battles, and Paris, threatened and exposed, descended into turmoil. As men went off to the front, the city fearfully turned on its own, looking to rid itself of any internal enemies, the better to fight the enemy advancing. It became increasingly difficult for those, like Smithson, who were identifiably gentlemen to stay in safety, regardless of their Jacobin leanings. The tricolor, long a popular token of revolutionary sympathy, became a compulsory part of one's costume; Arthur Young traveling in France pinned his on too carelessly and it blew off, subjecting him to the challenges and general hostility of a large crowd. A steady emptying of foreigners and French nobility from the city became by the summer a run. Smithson's Royal Society friends Charles Blagden and Smithson Tennant headed for Switzerland on August 9, 1792—unwittingly the day before the massacre at the Tuileries and the taking of the royal family.[15]

Smithson clearly left as well; Walter Johnson's 1844 article noted that Smithson's diaries chronicled various "tours on the continent, of which, one was made from Geneva to Italy, through the Tyrol, in 1792." But when finally did he decide that Paris was no longer such a good place to be? And what of his intention, as he had once told Greville, to visit "those provinces famous for their minerals" in the countryside of France, en route?[16]

The places that beckoned were probably the extinct volcanoes of the Auvergne, charted already by Smithson's friend the Abbé Soulavie in his multi-volume work. The basaltic formations of the Velay and the Vivarais, to the east of the Auvergne, which had been explored by the notorious Faujas de St. Fond, were surely high on Smithson's list as well. There was also the scientific court in Dijon, commanded by Guyton de Morveau, one of Lavoisier's collaborators and an intimate correspondent of Smithson's old mentor, Richard Kirwan.

Hoare's made three payments to the French banking house Perregaux & Co., on August 6, and again on September 4 and 11, repaying advances that had been made to Smithson. These indicate that Smithson was probably still in Paris into September, as the city descended into chaos. The streets resounded with the tolling of the tocsin; a steady drum beat called the men to arms, and alarm guns fired to warn of approaching threats. On August 10 the crowds stormed the Tuileries palace, slaughtering the Swiss Guards and taking the royal family hostage. The first days of September brought the massacres in the Paris prisons, where more than one thousand people, many of them clergymen, were brutally murdered. In the narrow streets by Smithson's hotel the mob surrounded carriages carrying twenty-three priests to the prison at St. Germain. They dragged the white-robed clerics out and slaughtered them, before the massacres moved inside to the prison. After peremptory trials by a "people's court," lasting each about a minute, hundreds of "conspirators and traitors" met their deaths by pike and saber. All night by the light of great bonfires in the courtyard, the bodies mounted. For five days and nights the same scene repeated itself throughout the city—at the convents of the Carmelites, La Force, La Salpetrière, and Bicêtre.[17] Smithson's friend the crystallographer Abbé Haüy, who like many clerics had been imprisoned after refusing to swear to the civil constitution, was saved only by the indefatigable petitioning of his student Geoffroy St. Hillaire. A few weeks later, on September 21, the monarchy was abolished. The following day was declared day one of Year I of the Republic. On September 24, Hoare's paid out £200 and change for Ransom & Co. notes, the eighteenth-century equivalent of traveler's checks. These notes were the means by which Smithson traveled when he was not in Paris or Rome—both cities that had a large English community and established bankers focused on that clientele. They would seem to indicate that he was by then on the move.

Records in Dijon, where Smithson might have stopped to see Guyton de Morveau and the Académie des Sciences there, yield nothing. No trace of Smithson's movements can be found in the archives for the Canton de Vaud or other Swiss repositories that contain passport control documentation. Throughout the summer of 1792 the lakeside towns of Geneva, Lausanne, and Evian continued to serve as a playground for England's wealthy, as they had for many summers prior. William Beckford was there with his four carriages, thirty horses, and a yacht on the lake. Georgiana, Duchess of Devonshire, too, was present, traveling in the area with her mother and her best friend Lady Bess Foster. Edward Gibbon, who had recently completed the final volume of his *The Decline and Fall of the Roman Empire*, lived nearby in a mansion with a vista over vineyards and the lake to the distant heights of the Savoy. He occasionally came to Georgiana's salons, where there was "much talk about chemistry & mineralogy." The duchess claimed that her "favourites of all favourites [wa]s mineralogy," and a series of scientists traipsed through her parlor to give lectures and demonstrations. Georgiana's exposure to science profoundly changed her, and she told a friend that "she now came to town with very different ideas from her former ones, to see the men of science and eminence."[18] (Not all fashionable women were so enamored; Lady Frances Ann Crewe, in Paris before the Revolution, was astounded at all the lectures on offer, and complained, "what, for God's Sake, have we poor women to do with Chimistry or Anatomy or rather what have we, or even the other Sex, to do with five or six sciences at once?

It is indeed very extraordinary to observe the Present Rage for both Frivolité and belle Esprit."[19])

Science was a pleasing distraction from the looming political turmoil. In the summer of 1792, as evidence piled up that the Revolution was taking a bloody, anarchic turn, and talk of Britain entering the war swirled through the salons, those enamored of chemistry were gripped by news of "animal electricity." The Italian scientist Luigi Galvani, observing a dissected frog that he had hung on an iron railing—by a pair of brass hooks attached to its spinal cord—twitch wildly, believed he had found proof of an electrical fluid coursing through the nerves of the frog. News of Galvani's experiment, the origin of the verb of galvanize, spread like wildfire, and countless demonstrators began replicating the experiments across Europe. Blagden in Switzerland went to witness "the experiments on nerves by Mr. Schmuck." Lady Webster (later Lady Holland) saw the phenomenon at an elegant dinner in Turin, where the host before the meal "sent for one of the Professors." Usually avidly interested in the latest scientific discoveries, she was appalled by "the cruel experiment upon a frog to prove animal electricity." Smithson must have been among those who witnessed a demonstration, and he probably set about replicating the experiments, as most of his scientific colleagues did, in order to investigate the phenomenon for himself. Blagden, for example, back in his rooms in Geneva, made his frog's legs jump, happily concluding in his diary, "Dr. Schmuck not a charlatan."[20]

A secret life force had been unveiled, and Smithson's community quickly began to examine the potential applications of such a discovery. Idealistic medical experimenters like Thomas Beddoes hoped to employ the power of animal electricity "so as to excite a new system of medicine."[21] And galvanism seemed to make real the possibility of reanimating a corpse, a notion that captivated the public imagination and ultimately inspired Mary Shelley to *Frankenstein* in 1817.

Galvani's theories were quickly challenged by Alessandro Volta, who developed the idea that the reaction originated not with a vital fluid in the nerves of the frog, but rather by the contact of certain dissimilar metals. A fierce controversy ensued, leading ultimately to Volta's invention in 1800 of the first electric battery (pairs of copper or silver and zinc or tin discs separated by pasteboard soaked in water). The battery, or voltaic pile, was found to readily decompose water; and Humphry Davy, in the first years of the new century, turned it into a powerful new experimental tool—successfully isolating a number of elements with the use of an electric current, by breaking down substances that had previously been considered already at their most elemental level. The battery became nothing less than a brand new lens on the nature of matter, a window to the world of the invisible. Davy told Coleridge that his discoveries "seem to lead to the door of the temple of the mysterious god of Life."[22]

But for Smithson, in the midst of traveling, the uneasy political situation probably continued to impinge on any opportunities for prolonged scientific research. Switzerland soon lost its sense of a safe haven. William Beckford, moving towards Italy in late 1792, reported that he was "obliged to cross over the lake in a violent hurry, for all Savoy is bedivelled [sic] and bejacobinized, and plundering,

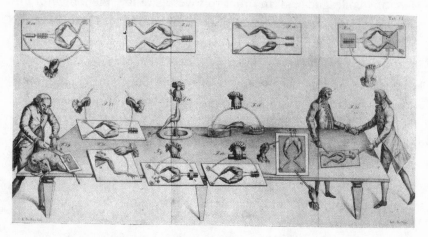

Luigi Galvani's experiments to showcase "animal electricity."

ravaging, etc., is going on swimmingly."[23] The Duchess of Devonshire's mother was likewise terrified during her travels. "Everything in these countries is in the greatest confusion," she wrote as she passed from Switzerland down into Italy. "The whole road and every Inn full of troops marching to the frontier."[24] By the autumn the only way to get to Italy was to pass through the Tyrol. Smithson did just that, as Walter Johnson's perusal of Smithson's diaries in 1844 showed.

Smithson's Tyrolean travel appears not to have been as fretful and hurried as most of his countrymen's journeys, however. He probably would have chosen this route even if the perils of wartime had not foisted it upon him, as the scientific communities in Paris and Geneva were abuzz over new discoveries in the southern Alps. Smithson's geologist friend Déodat de Dolomieu had recently determined that these towering white peaks of crystalline stone were not actually marble, as had long been assumed. Although the rock shared the same crystal structure as calcite, it did not react chemically the same way that marble (calcareous earth) should, suggesting that it was an entirely different substance. Dolomieu's findings had stunned Paris, because they called into question the French reliance on crystallography or crystal structure as the primary identification system for minerals. De Saussure's son boldly named this new substance "dolomite," and this region of the Alps became the Dolomites, in honor of Dolomieu's discovery.[25] Smithson passing through gathered as many good specimens as he could. Eager to impress all the learned men he was soon to meet, he planned to bestow these novelties, like precious jewels, on the collectors he encountered in his travels.[26]

II. Italy

Bello dev'essere l'acquisto fatto del diamante, ma
molto piu bello è quello dell'amicizia del Sre Macie,
che è il piu accurato di tutti i chimici che io
conosco—dunque coltivatelo, e specialmente per la
cristallografia. [Congratulations on getting the
diamond, but how much more exquisite is the
acquisition of Mr. Macie's friendship! He is the most
accurate chemist I know, so be sure to get to know
him, especially for crystallography.]

—William Thomson to Ottaviano Targioni-Tozzetti,
1793

Smithson's old Oxford friend William Thomson, who had hastily
fled England in the autumn of 1790, was now settled at Naples, in
the shadow of Vesuvius. Refashioning himself as Guglielmo
Thomson, he had successfully inserted himself into the fabric of the
community. The whiff of scandal had left him, and the Italians
lauded him as "già di Oxford"—once a lecturer at Oxford. He had
secured a position as physician extraordinary to the Pope, and he
was hailed as a celebrated doctor in one of the premiere destinations
for the recuperating English. No one questioned why he was there.
He was a scientist living at the foot of nature's original chemistry
set, positioned to be the first to comb through any finds from the
mountain, and he was already becoming renowned for his collection
of volcanic specimens.[27]

Thomson had been waiting for Smithson for nearly two years.
When Smithson left England in late 1791 he intended to travel
fairly swiftly through France down to Italy. Vesuvius, providing
frequent pyrotechnical displays, beckoned, and the gentle
Mediterranean air awaited him. Even when Smithson dallied in
Paris, finding the weather salubrious and the revolutionary spectacle

a cause worthy for delay, his plan remained to get to Naples by the winter of 1792–3. "It is my intention to spend next winter in Italy probably at Naples," Smithson wrote to Charles Greville on New Year's Day 1792, "and of course therefore a letter to your uncle will confer an obligation on me."[28] But, as so often happened on the Grand Tour, where itineraries were fluid and travel lasted years, plans did not unfold as expected. Smithson probably did not see Naples until the very end of 1793 or the beginning of 1794, if he got there at all.

It was July 1793 before Thomson finally received word of Smithson's whereabouts. The news was second hand, coming not from Smithson but rather from Ottaviano Targioni-Tozzetti, the professor of botany at the university in Florence—a letter that indicated Smithson had fallen in with the worthy *scienziati* in Florence, the men of the Accademia dei Georgofili. Thomson wrote back immediately to Targioni-Tozzetti, enclosing a letter to Smithson. He took another sheet to write to Giovanni Fabbroni, the number two in command at the museum and the most important member of Thomson's circle of colleagues in Florence. "Have you met Macie yet?" he inquired. "You must get to know him."[29]

While Thomson busied himself in Naples trying to orchestrate Smithson's reception in Florence, Smithson found himself already welcomed. Here in Tuscany the revolutionary tumult that had waylaid Parisian science had not yet infected the populace. Smithson discovered a thriving community of scientists, a place where he could focus with his colleagues wholly on his scientific work. The late Grand Duke of Tuscany, the philosopher-king Pietro Leopoldo, who had departed for Vienna in 1790 to assume the throne following the death of his brother the Holy Roman Emperor Joseph II, had been a great patron to science. The Imperial Museum of Physics and Natural History he had established in 1775 was already the most important scientific research center in the region and one of the largest museums in the world at the time. Located next to the Pitti Palace and the Boboli Gardens, it featured an astronomical observatory equipped with the finest English instruments. The museum also operated a large chemical laboratory, a library, a botanical garden, and an extensive and much-heralded wax model workshop. Several rooms at the museum were devoted to the display of these anatomical wax figure productions, which were as popular with tourists as they were with the medical students for whom they were created. In velvet-cushioned cases models like Madonnas from a Guido Reni painting-made-flesh reclined, their long hair cascading over shapely shoulders, their waxen stomachs split open, delicately exposing entrails for curious students. An entire room showcased pregnant torsos in various stages of giving birth, a graphic display that riveted Smithson's brother Henry Louis Dickenson when he passed through Italy.[30]

The Florentine circle of savants was as collegial as the coffeehouse community that Smithson had left behind in London. Smithson passed long hours in conversation with Ottaviano Targioni-Tozzetti, who shared Smithson's passion for mineralogy. He also breakfasted frequently with Giovanni Fabbroni, a classic Italian exemplar of the late Enlightenment man—a multi-lingual hub of information, pursuing knowledge in numerous branches of science, with correspondents in every major city. Fabbroni, when the museum was first being established in the late 1770s, had made a state-sponsored trip to survey the scientific communities in France and England, during which time he had become friends with Benjamin Franklin and Thomas Jefferson; Fabbroni's contemporary biographer even alleged that Jefferson had picked the name Monticello for his estate from a small village near Florence, in homage to Fabbroni.[31] Fabbroni had recently been one of those privileged to receive a copy of *Notes of Virginia*, Jefferson's pungent riposte to the Comte de Buffon's accusations of the degeneration of species in North America. In it Jefferson described the varied geography and climate of the United States, compared its flora and fauna with that of the Old World, and detailed the variety of native cultures and languages, the mysteries of geological formations, and the discovery of mammoth bones and teeth. The book laid out many of the issues that would dominate American science for the next several generations.[32]

The riches and the enormity of America were undoubtedly a topic of fascination in those salons Smithson frequented in Florence. The raw natural abundance of the land, which stood in such stark contrast to Europe, seemed a fitting metaphor for the fertile democratic experiment the United States was undertaking. Fabbroni had told Jefferson that he very much wanted to visit the "happy republic" of America.[33] Smithson's curiosity was evident in the marks he made in a two-volume guidebook to North America that he owned. He noted descriptions of "virgin copper . . . as pure as if it had passed through fire" from an island near Niagara; he commented on the architectural arrangements of slave plantations; and he even marked a logistical detail—as if he were making travel plans for himself—recommending the purchase of one's traveling equipage at Montreal if one intended to journey up the St. Lawrence. Smithson seems to have been particularly fascinated by stories of Native Americans, who were often viewed as America's own Rousseau-like primitives; he underscored the accounts of those men singled out by their desire for education and improvement, like the story of the six-foot-tall "Captain Thomas [Williams, or Te-ho-ra-gwa-ne-gen], a chief of the Cachenonaga nation [Caughnewaga in Quebec]," who spoke French and English and dressed like a white man, but who was not as respected as might have been a chief who had retained the habits of his nation. He also marked the story of the Mohawk war chief Joseph Brant, who had become close friends with Smithson's half-brother Lord Percy, with whom he had served in the British Army during the Revolutionary War.[34]

To the scientific men of Florence, their city was a near equivalent of America's "happy republic"—a prosperous, peaceful place where science could be successfully pursued. In Florence, furthermore, it was well funded. The Grand Duke, Fabbroni had told Jefferson, had been "the most humane prince in the universe" and Fabbroni had even named his son Pietro Leopoldo in gratitude.[35] Florence became something of an oasis for Smithson, too; he based himself here for much of the roughly three years he was in Italy, later finding, in addition to the thriving scientific community, an alluring group of liberty-loving English aristocrats.

In late 1793, though, after about six months in Florence, he set out towards Rome, on a roundabout itinerary in order to take in Livorno (or Leghorn, as the English called it), where he had heard there was a good mineral dealer. He was determined to continue his scientific tour, despite the rising political panic. The year had seen the guillotining of both the King and subsequently the Queen of France, and France's Revolution was rapidly turning into a world war; Britain had entered the fray in February, and Holland and Spain had followed soon thereafter.

In late 1793 Livorno, perched on the west coast of Italy, provided a clear vantage from which to survey the frightening progress of the war. The siege of the port town of Toulon, one of several cities in southern France staging counterrevolutionary uprisings throughout the summer, was preoccupying the British consul at Livorno, John Udny; England had gained control of the city in late August without firing a single shot, but was now on the verge of being forced to relinquish it (in a battle that proved one of the first triumphs for a young Corsican brigadier named Napoleon). In Florence Lord Hervey, the fanatically anti-French envoy-extraordinary to the Tuscan court, bullied the Grand Duke to renounce neutrality and eject the French minister and all "suspected Persons, Emissaries, Adherents or Partizans of the Regicide faction" in exchange for British protection of the Tuscan state.[36]

Smithson made no mention of the disturbances. He was interested more in Livorno's position near the mineralogical paradise of Elba. The spectacular specimens particular to the island of Elba represented an essential component of the cabinet Smithson was building of the crystallized produce of the earth. His trip to the Livornese lapidary was a wash, however; the man had nothing of worth. As Smithson explained to his friends in Florence, "I did not doubt that I should be able to furnish myself with specimens of all the bodies, of at least that part of Italy, which were interesting to me, but I found myself entirely disappointed in my expectations, for he had not any thing I wanted, or indeed any thing at all besides a few common shells."[37]

Smithson's disappointment in Livorno reinforced his sense that his best hope for building a comprehensive cabinet lay not in seeking out dealers but rather in working closely with his peers, those fellow savants who were also keeping cabinets. He asked his friends to hold onto any duplicates that they might have of his desiderata, and offered to reciprocate by filling the blanks in their collections of English productions. "It is only by exchange and mutual assistance," he believed, "that naturallists [sic] can possibly ever succeed in assembling together a collection of subjects of their study, which nature has made so numerous, and disseminated in such various and distant parts of the world."[38]

As he traveled along the edge of the Maremma towards Rome, on the main road south from Siena, Smithson passed through the Lagoni, a land of eerie and putrid vaporous hot springs much feared by the locals. He became friends with Paolo Mascagni, a Siena-based physician best known for his research into the lymphatic system, who was busily championing the Lagoni as an engine of economic advantage for the region. Mascagni had discovered a mineral there he called sassolino, which he determined to be boric acid in its solid state, a substance highly valued for use in manufacturing enamel, glass, pottery, and other wares.[39] The Lagoni were but one part of Smithson's scientific tour southwards. Fabbroni had plotted out the route for him, which was focused on "extinct volcanoes." It took him to the pyramid of Monte Amiata, terraced with vineyards; the medieval fortress town of Radicofani, perched high on a vertiginous pile of basalt; and the serene waters of Lake Bolsena, which, he told Fabbroni, "furnished me some bodies acceptable to my cabinet."[40]

In the last weeks of 1793 Smithson entered the gates of Rome, the omphalos of the English gentleman's Grand Tour. Piazzas, full of the music of conversation and splashing fountains, were crowded with outdoor cafés and people promenading. The English clustered around the Piazza di Spagna; the popular Café Anglais there, bedecked with murals by Piranesi, was a place where many collected their mail, their news, and their latest acquaintances. Artists congregated in this area as well, looking to capitalize on a captive clientele. The acclaimed painter of English aristocrats Pompeo Batoni was now dead, but others were taking his place. The sculptor Richard Westmacott was installed at the Palazzo Zuccari on the Strada Gregoriana, and the flirtatious painter Angelica Kauffmann was in residence at her studio near the top of the Spanish Steps; as a close friend of Smithson's cousin George Keate, Kauffmann might well have been someone for whom Smithson carried a letter of introduction. The Danish archeologist Georg Zoëga, engrossed in investigating the hieroglyphic inscriptions on Egyptian obelisks, was a good friend of William Thomson's and another whom Smithson would probably have sought out.[41]

Smithson, however, was not enthralled by Rome. Despite finding the city "so celebrated a Capital," he concluded it was "far removed from the mineral, the comm[er]cial and I had almost said, the scientific, world."[42] His friend Lord Wycombe, the son of Smithson's family friend Lord Lansdowne (as Lord Shelburne was now known), shared this disappointment. He too was in Italy at this time and wrote home: "Inhabiting Rome is like conversing with the dead, it exhibits a people as well as a city in ruins, it has no Society, no Spectacle; no commerce, no industry, and consequently no animation."[43]

These forward-looking Grand Tourists did not come to Italy simply to see the monuments of antiquity and to commune with the landscape that animated the classical texts that had been their school primers. The ruins did need to be examined, the paintings admired, and the churches visited; as Lord Wycombe went on to tell his father, "The objects of antiquity however, and those which the fine arts afford make ample amends to the stranger whose views do not extend to residence." But how could they leave behind all their ruminations on progress? How could they lay aside all the energies they were devoting to change and industrialization back home? They were living in times that seemed, finally, as brilliant as those of the ancients. Agricultural improvements, manufacturing inventions, medicinal advances, revolutions in living—all these things continued to possess men like Smithson. On their travels they cast an eye to see how these same challenges were being handled in other countries. They discussed them with each other at the *table d'hôte* in their *pensions* and with their newfound companions at the salons into which they were welcomed.

Even the few letters of Smithson's that survive are littered with such observations. He brought to Fabbroni's attention news of an exorbitant sale price for cattle in England, an apparent continuation of a discussion they had been having on the current state of agriculture. "You see what a footing agriculture is upon at present in England," Smithson concluded, "and you will not wonder that kings have farms, indeed at this rate, it will soon only be kings that will be able to have them."[44] In another letter he informed Fabbroni of "the new Telegraph," installed along the southern coast of England all the way to Land's End, with a signal system consisting of "balls, flags, and lanthorns [sic] by night."[45] Smithson's interest in this invention—yet another example of science in the service of society— was typical. Back in a Britain roiled by the French Revolution, however, reactionary factions viewed this development, along with many other technological advances, as the work of pro-French subversives. The caricaturist James Gillray depicted the opposition leader Charles James Fox as a gigantic, bulbous, hairy telegraph pole making signals in the dark. He stands as a beacon shining out across the black expanse of the Channel, a guiding light for the great wave of ships coming from France. With his other arm, a plank-like crossbar culminating in a finger-pointing hand, he directs the invading

Gillray's caricature of Charles James Fox, 1795.

force's attention to the dome of St. Paul's, the figurative heart of
the kingdom.

For Smithson Rome held one redeeming contemporary attraction.
The elderly, self-effacing Father Petrini at the Collegio Nazareno
provided a worthy scientific diversion in an otherwise
mineralogically vacant city. "I have derived here no small pleasure
and advantage from the acquaintance of Father Petrini, who is a
pleasing and informed man, and really possesses of a cabinet much
more extensive and complete than I should have expected," Smithson
wrote, thanking Fabbroni for the introduction. Gian-Vicenzo
Petrini's mineral collection, which he had started while teaching
philosophy and mathematics at the college, had become somewhat
famous; even the Emperor Joseph II had paid a visit, and he had
subsequently sent an outstanding collection of rare metallic rocks
from Hungary in thanks.[46] Georgiana, Duchess of Devonshire, and
many other fashionable English stopped in to meet Petrini while
in Rome; Lady Webster visited too, though she found Petrini

unutterably dull—"a more stupid personage I never knew in my life," she told Fabbroni.[47]

Smithson's visit was clearly the most exciting event of the year for Petrini. Smithson, in Petrini's eyes, was that rare landed gentleman, polished, humane and highly knowledgeable: "a *Cavaliere* in whom a vast and profound knowledge of chemistry, mineralogy, and physics is united in a character of sweetness, affability and grace." Petrini immediately wrote an ecstatic letter to Fabbroni, thanking him for the introduction to Smithson. "The obligations I owed you were already many and great," Petrini commenced. "But in presenting me with Mr. Macie they have grown almost to infinity."[48] In incantatory prose Petrini carried on writing about Smithson's visit to multiple correspondents; Smithson, in this world incumbent on giving and attending to favors, became a type of currency. Petrini even wrote to the Duchess of Devonshire, someone who had never heard of Smithson. His description of the young man was so incandescent that she felt compelled to ferret out some information about this Mr. Macie, and she turned to Sir Charles Blagden, secretary of the Royal Society, as her reliable source.

Blagden's response provides a fascinating window into how information was exchanged and relationships built in an era reliant on personal introductions. It is also a telling example of the curious fault line on which Smithson teetered, between the aristocracy and the world of science. Prickly old Blagden was hardly the advocate Smithson might have wished to be promoting his cause with the Duchess of Devonshire. Blagden had reason to be jealous of Smithson, a young man who had been steadily gaining a foothold with Blagden's patron Henry Cavendish. William Thomson "detested" Blagden, as he told Fabbroni,[49] and Smithson might well have shared some of this sentiment. Blagden was a character easily wounded; after some minor affront, for example, he insisted on corresponding with Sir Joseph Banks in a diffident third-person voice, despite Banks' repeated entreaties for him to desist. Blagden hadn't managed to make a good match, either. He never married, in fact, but unlike Smithson he suffered several public humiliations in his attempts to do so: he was rebuffed first by the widowed Madame Lavoisier and still later laughed out of town by the daughter of La Lavoisier's successful suitor, Count Rumford.[50]

And so, for Smithson, Blagden was able to muster only tempered praise. There was the reluctant acknowledgment that the young man was blindingly bright company. "The Mr. Macie of whom Father Petrini writes so favorably is indeed an excellent Chemist, with much information in many other parts of Science & great precision of ideas," he told the duchess. Blagden, however, was not willing to concur with Petrini's praise of Smithson's character, explaining that Petrini's description was "not exactly as I should have stated it." He refused to second Petrini's lyrical tribute, choosing instead to make some small put-down. He referred to Smithson in the past tense, and wrote that he had concluded his chemical career, before it had hardly begun:

Our friend Mr Cavendish liked him very much, & seemed to take great pleasure in his company. I was also frequently with him, and scarcely ever without acquiring some new ideas. He left England for his health, and, I was told, has, on the same account, entirely abandoned his chemical studies. The only thing of consequence that I know he has published is a paper in the Philosophical Transactions, giving the analysis of a remarkable concretion found not infrequently in the bamboo cane, & called in the Levant Tabasheer. This he discovered to be an almost pure siliceous earth, though generated in the middle of a vegetable; and further experiments showed him, that the substance of the bamboo itself contains some portion of the same earth; a fact which no doubt will be applied by those naturalists who conceive all the solid matter of our planet to be the produce of vegetables or animals, accumulated in a very long succession of ages.[51]

It is especially interesting to note that Blagden made no mention of Smithson's parentage. He had not been reluctant in the past to gossip about Smithson's supposed pedigree—back in 1784 he had reported to Sir Joseph Banks that Smithson "is said to be a natural son of the Duke of Northumberlands." The omission of Smithson's connection to the duke in this instance seems very deliberate. Blagden knew that such information would probably only raise Smithson in the duchess' estimation. It would have brought him into her circle in a way that Blagden could never have entered. In fact the duchess would probably have been more sympathetic to Smithson than Blagden could ever have imagined, as she had given birth to the child of her lover Charles Grey just the year before, in secret while on the Continent. The little girl had been taken away from her almost immediately, and she had been forbidden ever to acknowledge her connection to the child.[52]

It is important, too, not to overlook the speed of the gossip. Petrini, awed by the arrival of this young meteor, wrote immediately to the popular duchess. His letter traveled all the way from the frescoed vaults of the Collegio Nazareno in Rome to the shores of England, and from there into the countryside, to the pleasure town of Bath, where Georgiana and her family were taking the waters. She in turn, from her perch in the spa town, sent her query to Blagden. Her letter traveled out in the coach back to London, where it found the doctor in his rented lodgings near Hanover Square. Blagden, zealous to set the record straight, responded immediately. Hardly any time elapsed. The duchess was reading Blagden's letter, still in the first days of January. Smithson was whiling the time away in Rome, oblivious to the chatter. He had hardly even gotten around to thanking Fabbroni for the introduction to Petrini.[53]

Was there in the end a short visit in Naples? A month or six weeks, maybe? The archives yield nothing. The passports of foreign tourists are filed still in the cool courtyarded palazzo that houses the Archivio di Stato di Napoli, but there is a gap in the records for exactly the

critical years of 1790 to 1795.[54] Neither is there any evidence of
James Louis Macie in the trail of gossip amongst the traveling English.
Lady Palmerston was present, and Dr. William Drew, who was
falling for her. Bishop Winchester was there with his ailing wife
Lady North, and Count Rumford, too, himself on the verge of an
intrigue with Lady Palmerston. The English circle around Sir William
Hamilton swelled with visitors as the winter months approached.
"The Society here this Winter is very pleasing," Drew wrote to the
vivacious Lady Webster in Florence, trying to entice her down. "I
will not tell you who are, and who are not here; come & see."[55]
Even among the scientists there is no trace of Smithson. William
Thomson's letters to his Florentine friends in this period are curiously
silent. One expects the ringing of bells, great clarion trumpets of
publicity that the two old Oxford friends are reunited, that the
young Smithson who charmed everyone in the north has come now
to the sweet, indolent south and done the same.

At the same time, it seems impossible that someone so keen to
see Vesuvius would not have made his way just that much further
south than Rome. The mountain continued to signal that it might
bestow some theatrical fireworks on its eager audience. "Vesuvius
holds his breath as long as he can in tremulous expectation of you,"
another of Lady Webster's admirers coyly carried on to her, "but
an ardent sigh not unfrequently escapes from his lips & now &
then he utters a groan."[56] Smithson could have been sure of a red-
carpet welcome, as he was almost certainly equipped with a letter
of introduction to Hamilton, the central figure in British Naples,
from Hamilton's beloved nephew Greville.[57] Hamilton had wed
Emma, his living sculpture, just a few years earlier. Now she had
been brought to the Neapolitan court, befriended the Queen, and
was stopping the hearts of Goethe and all the lovers of virtù—
though perhaps not their wives, who were still unsure of her
respectability. She was Smithson's exact contemporary, and he
probably knew her well, having been exposed perhaps to much of
her rise and transformation after her arrival in Charles Greville's

London apartments from her life as an attending nymph in the quack doctor Graham's Temple of Hymen.[58]

The clearest sign of Smithson's presence in Naples can be found in his handwritten list of mineral specimens collected abroad. Smithson's "Catalogue of Some Minerals 1798" is littered with examples from the Neapolitan region. Many of these, along with those from Calabria and Sicily, were probably sent to Smithson by William Thomson. When Smithson returned to Florence in the spring of 1794, for example, he received a sample of a saline substance that had flowed out of a hole in the cone of Vesuvius, "with a request to ascertain its nature."[59] Nevertheless, it is quite likely that some of these specimens in his catalogue—"Phosphoric Marble, Vesuvius . . . . Group of Hornblend crystals [from] Naples . . . . Garnets from Naples for Exp[erimen]ts. . . . Porphyry lava cont[ainin]g iron crystals, Vesuvius"— do indicate a trip to Naples.[60] And there was so much to see beyond the mountain. Smithson's fellow scientific laborers were doing much to turn the region's resources to advantage; William Thomson's friend Scipione Breislak, who reconstructed the history of Vesuvius' evolution, was one such, guiding visitors around the alum works he operated at nearby Solfatara, a volcanic crater in the Phlegraean Fields (Campi Phlegraei). And the buried cities of Pompeii and Herculaneum, discovered only in the 1750s, offered up for scrutiny an ancient humanity caught in mid-breath. Tourists lunched on tables studded with the ring marks of round-bottomed cups from two thousand years earlier. In the museum at Portici, they gaped at the furniture and the trinkets and "some remains even of various kinds of victuals such as Eggs, Raisins, Bread, a Tart found in an Oven."[61] For Smithson the most indelible image of Pompeii seems to have been "the cast of a woman's breasts" captured in the hardened ashes, which he evoked decades later in one of the papers he wrote for the *Annals of Philosophy*.[62]

By the spring of 1794 Smithson had returned to Florence, where he apparently based himself for more than a year. He continued to socialize regularly with his scientific friends Fabbroni and Targioni-Tozzetti, availing himself of the museum's excellent chemical laboratory and extensive mineral cabinet. He also fell in with the fashionable Whig aristocrats who clustered around the English envoy to the Tuscan court. This was initially Lord Hervey, but after an outburst in which he called the Grand Duke a fool and a knave he was replaced by William Wyndham.[63] Most of this circle was younger even than Smithson, who, though still very youthful in appearance, was now nearly thirty. Although Florence's identity had long been stamped with homosexuality—even as early as the 1400s a German verb meaning to sodomize was "florenzen" and a sodomite a "florenzer"— the bed-swapping among the English resident in the republic in the 1790s was primarily heterosexual. Liaisons in this circle were complicated, ecstatic, and youthful, energized by the freedom these young men and women had discovered in travel and a life abroad.[64]

Many of them declared their love for Lady Webster, who sat at the heart of this set. She had arrived in Italy with the man she called "her tormentor," her depressive husband Sir Godfrey Webster, whom she had married when she was fifteen and he thirty-eight. Another of the figures Smithson came to know well was Mrs. Wyndham, the wife of the new envoy. She left her husband for Lord Wycombe, the first son of Lord Lansdowne—but he, as it turned out, was "not an enthusiastic admirer" of the state of marriage and eventually grew tired of the affair. It was Wycombe's cousin, best friend, and traveling companion, the gregarious twenty-year-old Henry Fox, the third Baron Holland and nephew of the legendary Whig leader Charles James Fox, who ultimately captured Lady Webster's heart. He had arrived in Italy fresh from an exotic tour around Spain, his complexion "partak[ing] of the *Moresco* hue." Lady Webster thought him "not in the least handsome," but she was soon won over, finding "his gaiety beyond anything I ever knew." It was not long before these two quietly began to court.[65]

It was a time of tremendous optimism and happiness for this set of friends, a time in which their own self-discovery coincided with a zeitgeist of hunger for knowledge and improvement. Lord Holland, like Smithson and most everyone in this set, was utterly in thrall to the French Revolution. Holland had been sent abroad to quiet the fires of his political enthusiasms, but the diplomat Earl Macartney, passing through Florence, reported that he was still "a little of a democrate." Lady Webster teasingly called Wyndham, who had spent time in Paris in 1791, "ce petit Jacobin." Lord Wycombe had recently returned from a great voyage around the United States and was full of stories. In 1791 he had met with George Washington and toured the site just chosen for the new capital, to be called after Washington, on the undulating marshy ground on the eastern branch of the Potomac, near the port towns of Georgetown and Alexandria. America was building an entirely new city, of immense classical grandeur, a bold manifestation of its unique experiment in democracy. "The plan exhibited [for the capital]," Wycombe told Lord Holland, "is on a most extensive scale. I know of no criterion of success except the price of lots [which were going for about one hundred pounds each, eight to an acre]." He likened the experience to "purchasing a ticket in the lottery" and confessed he "was not far from buying one, but happily escaped the scrape."[66]

The friendships Smithson forged in Florence continued much of his life. He carried on socializing with what became known as the Holland House circle back in London, though there is no evidence that he ever carried on amorously with any of them. Smithson's position in their world seems to have been primarily as a kind of scientific cicerone.[67] He was the one to whom they turned for news of the latest discoveries; he animated their understanding of new scientific principles, shared tales of travails from the laboratory, and helped organize their budding mineral collections. In a poem Lord Holland wrote in 1795 for Lady Webster's birthday, Holland ribbed her about her abundant passion for scientific knowledge, suggesting she would forsake her youth and beauty for a better understanding of the laws of nature: "In short for each enquiring wim / I'd sacrifice a sense or limb, / For beauty fades and youth decays, / But learning lasts me all my days!" The poem opened with Lady Webster calling upon the Muses, and upon her scientist companions, including Smithson:

Give me, indulgent Genius give
'Midst learned cabinets to live
'Midst curiosities, collections
Specimens Models, & dissections
With books of every tongue & land
All difficult to understand!
With instruments of various sorts
Telescopes, air pumps, tubes, retorts
With friends, fair wisdom to pursue,
Fontana, Macie, Blagden, Drew.
Give me in common sense defiance
Secure with Macie and his Science
On <u>floating bricks</u> superb to ride
O'er angry Oceans wandering tide . . .[68]

The poem, which carried on for many more lines, was only the
first in what became an annual tribute to Lord Holland's love for
Elizabeth Vassall, otherwise Lady Webster (and soon to become
Lady Holland). Every year on her birthday Lord Holland penned
another panegyric, even from Woburn Abbey when he was attending
the deathbed of his friend the Duke of Bedford and could not be
with his wife. Thirty-six years after this first tribute in Florence,
his celebration of Lady Holland's sixtieth birthday tenderly
concluded: "I loved you much at twenty four / I love you better
at threescore."[69]

The "floating bricks" that provided Smithson and Lady Webster
their seafaring carpet were yet another passing obsession of Smithson's
during his Italian sojourn, apparently gleaned from research
undertaken by Giovanni Fabbroni. Many of Smithson's
contemporaries attempted to divine the recipe for the cement the
Romans used in their construction, which was far superior in strength
to anything the eighteenth century had produced. Fabbroni in his
investigations of building materials had noted also that Pliny referred
to bricks made in Asia and Spain which floated on water. Thinking

that this invention might have useful contemporary applications, Fabbroni decided to try to reproduce them. Using Strabo as his guide—for he complained that no modern source provided him any useful guidance—he succeeded in finding the same chalky argillaceous earths—which had to have some plasticity and become hard under fire—that the ancients had employed, near Santa Fiore (Monte Amiata) in the Sienese countryside.

Fabbroni saw great potential for these bricks, especially in the construction of ships. His publication, read to the Accademia dei Georgofili in 1794, concluded by musing on the fate of the Spanish ships at the siege of Gibraltar a little over a decade earlier. All ten of these specially designed floating batteries had burned or exploded when subjected to the withering red-hot shot of the British, despite being fortified with six or seven feet of iron, cork, and rawhide; perhaps, Fabbroni suggested, floating bricks might have saved them.[70] Smithson, fascinated by the subject and eager to make himself useful, tried to aid Fabbroni in his experiments. "Mr. Macie passed this morning by the Public Cabinet, and also by via Cocomero [Fabbroni's house] without having the good fortune of finding Mr. Fabbroni," Smithson wrote (in French) to Fabbroni one evening. "Mr. Macie, when he was at Paris a year and a half ago or more, read in one of the English papers a notice on floating bricks, made in imitation of those of the ancients, but he has forgotten the details."[71] He clearly also shared his excitement over Fabbroni's research with his English *bon ton* companions.

Most of all, however, Smithson aspired to travel and live in the same aristocratic grandeur as these young English lords and ladies did. He had been schooled in similar circumstances and partook of their political and cultural outlooks. He would have claimed William Wyndham as a cousin, since Wyndham was part of the Seymour clan—Wyndham's brother George was Lord Egremont, heir to Petworth, the estate shaved off the Percy estates by the Proud Duke. And he shared the bond of illegitimacy with Wyndham's wife, who was the illegitimate daughter of Lord Baltimore. He was an Oxford

contemporary of Lord Wycombe, and their two families owned
neighboring estates in Wiltshire. Smithson, however, remained
something apart. Lady Webster thought he was a bit strange; "ha
una testa curiosa," she told Fabbroni—but Fabbroni, the scientist,
who saw things differently, said in reply that he found Smithson to
be a man of "rare merit," in whose company he would have happily
passed whole days had time permitted.[72]

While in Italy most of this group of English aristocrats
commissioned portraits from the French painter Louis Gauffier,
who had settled in Florence after the guillotining of Louis XVI.
He painted Lady Webster reclining in a chaise, her dog Pierrot
at her feet; Lord Holland in an elegantly turned chair, a bust of
his heroic uncle, Charles James Fox, beside him on the table.[73]
Smithson, too, might have commissioned a portrait of himself on
the Grand Tour. There is a Gauffier painting from Florence, dated
1796, whereabouts currently unknown, which shows an
unidentified young English gentleman who appears uncannily
similar to Smithson.[74] The young man has the same very long
nose, full lips, and distinctive brow. He also has the same wry,
languid gaze that Smithson had at five (if the Romney is counted
as a Smithson portrait) and at fifty (in the portrait made at Aix-
la-Chapelle in 1816).

The portrait, if it is Smithson, does not, as one might have
expected, give any indication of the abiding passions of Smithson's
life—chemistry and mineralogy. There are no scientific instruments,
no cabinets of crystals, no library of learned information in the
background. There is not even the slightest hint in the setting of
that pastime which probably occupied so much of his travel—the
exploration of an exposed cliff or cave or river bed that might have
yielded novel mineral specimens. Instead he presents himself as a
confident young Romantic, lace handkerchief in hand, his coat
nonchalantly abandoned atop a ruined column. The distinctive
skyline of Florence is visible in the distance, and his faithful dog
peers up at him devotedly. Smithson had been rapturously received

by the scientific community in Italy, and yet it seems that it was as a wealthy English gentleman on the Grand Tour that he wished to memorialize himself.

As if on cue, the volcano that was a metaphor for the era erupted in the most spectacular manner in June 1794. This explosion of Vesuvius was the biggest since the seventeenth century and one of the most massive ever in its history. Multiple torrents of lava coursed down the flank of the mountain, Sir William Hamilton reported to the Royal Society, uniting in a molten wave half a mile wide and some twelve to forty feet deep. The lava rushed towards the sea, swallowing vineyards and houses in its wake and finally engulfing much of the town of Torre del Greco as it slid into the bay.[75]

For William Thomson the event was exciting beyond imagining. At the very center of Torre del Greco, houses were buried up to their roofs, and only the church towers peeked out above the ruins. The town had become a mini-Pompeii for their own time, and he was poised to be its Pliny. Thomson clambered all over the ruins, scavenging the site with the idea of creating a cabinet of curiosities to illustrate the chemically transformative powers of the mountain. He found window glass that had folded in the heat and lost its transparence, becoming almost like porcelain of Réaumur. He collected iron window mullions that had mineralized and which under the microscope revealed nearly transparent rose-shaped crystals in vivid red and orange. In part of the church wall he discovered that ancient lava, used as a building material, had re-melted; once light and airy, it had become heavy and had sprouted crystal needles on its surface. Copper coins had been oxidized by the vapors of the lava, and he found specimens of the mineral olivine that had changed from green to red in the fiery heat. Thomson sent a complete set of his finds to his friends the Pictets in Geneva, who published his discoveries in their new journal, the Bibliothèque Britannique. He also sent Smithson a case of material. Among the treasures inside was a fragment of a bell from the church tower, encrusted in tiny brilliant crystals.[76]

On the day after the eruption of Vesuvius, many miles north of Naples a curious white cloud appeared around sunset, high in the sky over the little town of Lucignan d'Asso, in the Tuscan hills near Siena. Seven tremendous explosions, like the cannon fire of the gods, rocked the valley. The rumblings multiplied and a hailstorm of stones pelted the earth. Terrified peasants reported that they whizzed to the ground like rockets, some of them landing in water and emitting billows of smoke.

Word of this phenomenal event spread quickly through the network of scientific laborers and their patrons. Smithson immediately rode over the Chianti hills to Siena to see the fruits of the spectacle for himself, according to a published account of the Siena fall. Massimiliano Ricca's book on the Siena meteor shower reads in parts like a fairytale, in the way it evokes Smithson's arrival, underscoring at the same time how heralded Smithson was among his scientific contemporaries in Italy: "There was in this year also traveling in Tuscany the illustrious Chemist, J. L. Macie, today J. Smithson, whom I personally introduced to Father Soldani." Father Ambrogio Soldani, a Sienese naturalist best known for his studies of fossils from Tuscany's ancient seas, had quickly become the central figure collecting and studying the strange black stones. Ricca related that Smithson studied the specimens that had been brought together and penned a description of his findings "to his friend Mr. Cavendish" back in London, to spread the word of this extraordinary happening— a letter of which, of course, no trace remains.[77]

Everyone puzzled over where the pebbles had come from. The extravagant Earl of Bristol, Lord Hervey's father, was another who promptly arrived in Siena to view the stones. Bristol had long been passionate about geology; he had even singed his foot on a trip up Vesuvius in the 1770s. Like many, he was already convinced that the rocks that fell from the sky had actually been catapulted up the length of Italy from the Vesuvian eruption. William Thomson, who could hardly tear himself away from his study of the effects the lava had wrought on the ruined city of Torre del Greco, soon ventured up to Siena as well. He wrote back to his Neapolitan friend Scipione Breislak that he remained unconvinced that the stones could have come from Vesuvius. He believed instead that they must have been thrown from some extinct Tuscan volcano, which had inexplicably reawakened from centuries of slumber. He fingered Santa Fiore (Monte Amiata) or the heights of Radicofani as possibilities. Further study revealed, however, that neither place boasted any opening in the earth that might have emitted such stones. Thomson then worked up an idea that many found preposterous—that the stones had come from space, emitted from a volcano on the face of the moon.

Difficult as it was for some to accept that the stones' origin was extraterrestrial, the idea nonetheless began to gain currency. Soldani in his *Sopra una pioggetta di sassi*, which was dedicated to the Earl of Bristol, put forth the idea that the stones had condensed from the atmosphere. The Abbot Domenico Tata's *Memoria sulla pioggia di pietre*, which included Thomson's analysis of the stones, agreed that the stones had come from the sky; and Thomson himself suggested that the substance of the stones be called soldanite, in honor of Soldani's tireless researches.

Smithson was as confused as the rest by the mysterious stones. He clearly took seriously his friend William Thomson's hypothesis, even if much of polite society still found the suggestion laughable. Back in London in 1797 the subject of the Siena fall came up at a dinner party. "Macie is my delight," Dr. William Drew recounted afterwards. "His Brain, like my own, is fruitful in Whimsies, and then he is of such easy faith! I gigled [sic] inwardly at his credulity about the Sienna Pebbles . . . the dear Pebbles—how innocently he fell into my hypothesis that they were projected from the Moon."[78]

The Siena fall was the first meteorite shower to be observed by such a large number of people that its authenticity could not be challenged. Smithson, though not an eyewitness, was there from the very beginning. Despite never publishing on the subject, he seems to have followed developments very closely. Over the course of his lifetime Smithson enjoyed friendships with many who played a prominent role in the foundation of what became known as the science of meteoritics. It was William Thomson who actually first identified the Widmanstätten pattern, the signature internal crystalline pattern visible in meteorite metal. Another of his acquaintances, Edward C. Howard, published a ground-breaking chemical analysis of samples from numerous different suspected falls in the Royal Society's *Philosophical Transactions* of 1802. And Smithson's European friends Jean-Baptiste Biot and Martin Klaproth were others who published important contributions on meteoritics.

Smithson's collection as it came to the United States in the 1830s contained "a valuable suite of meteoric stones, which appear to be specimens of most of the meteorites which have fallen in Europe during several centuries."[79] In the years after the Siena shower an astonishing number of other notable falls were witnessed: the stone which fell like a "Phaeton from heaven" at World Cottage, Yorkshire, of 1795; one at Evora, Portugal, in 1796; the spectacular Benares, India, fireball of 1798; the shower of some three thousand stones at L'Aigle in Normandy in 1803. The French scientist Fleuriau de Bellevue gave Smithson a personally inscribed copy of his pamphlet on the 1819 meteor fall at Jonzac. Through his wide network it would not have been difficult for Smithson to obtain specimens from these falls and from earlier meteorite falls as well. As the acceptance of meteorites became widespread, scientists scoured historical treatises to identify possible falls from earlier centuries. Samples from many of these soon made their way into the hands of scientists and collectors. Charles Greville's collection contained a specimen, once part of the Viennese mineralogist Ignaz von Born's cabinet, from a stone said to have fallen in 1754 near Tabor, Bohemia. The British Museum had among its meteorites an example from the mythic Mesón de Fierro stone in Argentina, first reported by European travelers in 1576. From Peter Simon Pallas, a professor at St. Petersburg, Smithson had obtained some mineral specimens; he may well have also acquired a sample of the famous Pallas Iron from Siberia, which William Thomson analyzed.[80] Perhaps Smithson's cabinet even included an

example of the then oldest known meteor, the thunder stone of
Ensisheim, which for three hundred years had sat in a local church—
before it was briefly appropriated during the Revolution for display
at a new National Museum at Colmar—near an inscription that
proclaimed the year of its arrival, 1492. Today the Ensisheim meteorite
is the only known example from a pre-eighteenth-century European
fall. Had Smithson's collection survived the Smithsonian fire of 1865,
his suite of meteorites from "several centuries"—with its handwritten
catalogue notes indicating each stone's provenance—would surely
have proved of immense value.[81]

Both Lady Webster and Lord Holland on separate occasions in 1794
and 1795 went south to consult with William Thomson regarding
their health. Smithson continued to travel in Italy through late 1794
and 1795 (and probably even into 1796)—he was in Venice briefly
in July 1794[82]—but he did not return to Rome or Naples. Petrini
in his letters to Fabbroni and others in Florence endlessly sent his
compliments to the "noble," the "worthy," the "splendid" Mr.
Macie. At the end of March 1795, though, he confessed to Fabbroni
that neither he nor Thomson had heard from Smithson since
Smithson had been in Rome more than a year earlier.[83]

Smithson was a notoriously irregular correspondent. Thomson,
frantic to discover back in 1793 when he might finally see his friend
after he had learned that Smithson had arrived in Italy, got no answer
to his frequent pleas for information. "Since it always takes a century
to hear from Mr. Macie," he beseeched Ottaviano Targioni-Tozzetti,
"won't you please tell me where he is headed, Rome or elsewhere."
When, weeks later, he had still received no response, he chastised
Targioni-Tozzetti in a letter full of playful profanity: "You still haven't
told me . . . when is Macie leaving Florence and where is he headed?
Many are the positive qualities of this gentleman [Smithson], but I
wouldn't like to see you copying his *trascuratezza* on this stupid
affair! *Razza di cose! Buona crusca!*"[84] It's difficult to understand
Smithson's insensitivity to these friends. Perhaps he felt some need

to keep Thomson, who could well have been in love with him, at arm's length. But with the mild, self-effacing Petrini, Smithson's silence seems particularly strange or cruel.

At some point, perhaps in the summer of 1795, Smithson set out to pass some time in the Alps. Intending to return "to spend the winter at Milan," Smithson left a large box of books in the care of the Auberge Royale in that town. He wasn't ready to leave Italy just yet. "But," as he wrote to an Italian friend nearly a decade later, "the French deranged all my plans, and I have not heard a word of my case of books since."[85] There were still plenty of English in Milan through the winter of 1795–6; Smithson, however, seems to have grown into a very cautious traveler. France's bedraggled Army of Italy lurked in the foothills of the Ligurian Alps. In March 1796 they gained a galvanizing young commander named Napoleon and proceeded in a matter of days to capture the kingdom of Piedmont. Infused with money, supplies, and confidence, Napoleon's troops pressed on to victory at Lodi and the occupation of Milan. Leery of the political situation, Smithson had already headed up towards Germany.

III. Germany

Germany? But where is it? I don't know how to find
such a country?

– Goethe and Schiller, 1797

It was not easy to travel in the Germany that Smithson visited in the mid-1790s. One's passport and papers had to be in good order. Border crossings were frequent, since the territory, ruled by the Holy Roman Empire, was divided into some three hundred principalities. Travel was slow and difficult. Rivers were only partly navigable; sandy roads turned to mud with the rain, creating great ruts that engulfed carriage wheels. A trip from Frankfurt to Berlin took nine days. Even the modest distance from Berlin to Potsdam was made by a coach only once a day and lasted six hours. Walking was hardly better, as notorious thieves and gangs roamed the byways and highways.[86]

Smithson did not develop any great love for the region. He told Lady Webster, when he finally returned to England in 1797, that while in the German states "among twenty-six million people he found only one with common sense, that one being an unknown chemist."[87] Smithson's perceptions reflected popular prejudices amongst the classically minded English, who on the whole disdained both the country and its inhabitants; they found that the happy intersection of court life and cultural discourse common in England and France did not really exist in most of the German states. The chemist Richard Chenevix told Sir Joseph Banks, "I define a German thus—German is the passage from man to brute. Man is capable of manual and intellectual operations: Brutes incapable for the most part of either. Germans capable of the former, incapable of the latter."[88] A new book reviewed in the September 1797 issue of the *Monthly Review*, a magazine Smithson regularly read, stated that Germany was "an immense country, composed of a little magnificence and a wide extent of misery; a country where you travel a hundred miles without finding a town in which a person of any taste or spirit could bear to reside, or a single villa like those which so much abound in England."[89]

Despite the desolation that the English perceived, the country was highly literate; it boasted some thirty universities compared with England's two.[90] And as Romanticism took hold of the English imagination, the long-standing dismissal of German culture began to yield; poetic pilgrims like Coleridge sought out the wild and lonely Harz mountains, its mossy slopes carpeted with pines and haunted with witches and spirits. Smithson toured these mountains, too, but his exploration was, unsurprisingly, more grounded in his study of the country's centuries-old mining traditions (some "slag from off the copper works, Hartz" became specimen No. 1401 in his collection).[91]

This region boasted some of the earliest mining academies in the

Members of the Society of the Dilettanti, with Sir Joseph Banks at far right, clinking glasses with Charles Greville, who looks back at him; Lord Carmarthen sits in the right foreground, showing off a gem.

world, and in the mining regions of the Harz, the Erzgebirge, and Slovakia, chemical instruction—as related to metallurgy and minerals at least—had been a fixture since the second quarter of the eighteenth century. Many of the members of this burgeoning German chemical community had ties to England and to Smithson's old mentor Richard Kirwan in particular, and Smithson presumably carried letters of introduction to many of them. Intent on building his mineral collections, Smithson was also keen to inform himself on the state of scientific instruction and learning in Europe.[92]

Upon leaving Italy, Smithson might well have first headed east, perhaps to the mining academy of Schemnitz (today in the Slovak Republic). His itinerary is not known.[93] His mineral collection included specimens from "Chemnitz in Hungary" and a "small group of native gold in 24-sided crystals from Vöröspatak in Transilvania" (Verespatak or Roşia Montană, in Romania, one of the most famous gold crystal localities in the world). It also featured "White Calamine" from Bleiburg and Hüttenberg in Carinthia (a mining area in southern Austria), specimens that became central to one of Smithson's most significant investigations: his identification of hydrozincite and the mineral that was later named smithsonite in his honor.[94]

One of Smithson's principal stops was in Dresden, hailed as Florence on the Elbe for its elegant and picturesque architecture. The city was the capital of Saxony, seat of the electors, and home to one of the oldest and richest mineral collections in the world. Smithson had an excellent entrée to Dr. Karl Heinrich Titius, the curator of the royal mineral cabinet. He arrived in Dresden armed with a commission from Lady Webster for a set of wooden crystal models. These large-scale blocks were used to demonstrate the principles of crystallography and were popular as erudite displays in European salons.[95]

Dresden boasted a large community of English, whose activities were often coordinated by Hugh Elliot, the British envoy to the Saxon court. Smithson lodged at the Hôtel de Pologne, one of the most fashionable hotels in the city, where Mozart and also Sir William and Emma Hamilton had stayed a few years earlier. Among the

English present was Lord Carmarthen (Francis Godolphin Osborne, fifth Duke of Leeds), the former foreign secretary. Carmarthen was part of the Wiltshire elite that Smithson claimed; his aunt the Duchess of Newcastle had lived in a house at Queen Square near to Elizabeth Macie in the 1760s, and both families employed Elborough Woodcock as their solicitor.[96] Carmarthen was also a member of the Society of the Dilettanti, and thus a friend of Smithson's friends Charles Greville and Sir Joseph Banks.

Here in Saxony, then, a good way to be remembered to Sir Joseph Banks presented itself. As Smithson was not especially knowledgeable about botany, and Sir Joseph Banks not that interested in mineralogy, Smithson had not felt able to curry favor with the president of the Royal Society as much as he might have liked during his travels. But he had noticed an unusually vivid blue flower en route into town, and Carmarthen obligingly agreed to carry a small packet back to England. So Smithson collected a few specimens for Banks' herbarium and sent them along with a letter:

I hope my total ignorance of botany will plead my excuse for troubling you with them & that you will see in the action only the evident desire to be of use to you, and wh[ich] of it has not more shown itself during my travels has been occasioned by the fear of being more troublesome than useful from the extreme wealth of your collection and my entire unacquaintance with the subject. I have met during my journeys with a good many new substances which had escaped the notice of mineralogists, but will not fatigue you at present with any account of them as it is not I know, the part of natural history to which you are partial. If I can be of any sort of use to you in this country I beg of you to command me and to believe me to be

Dear Sir

yr most obdt servt

James L. Macie[97]

While in Saxony, Smithson also toured Freiberg, the home of the first mining academy in Europe. He presumably met Abraham Werner, director of the academy and renowned as the founder of the Neptunist theory of the earth. Smithson obtained a number of specimens, including a "Feldspat crystal not mackled" and "Five crystals of sulphate of lime" from Johann Friedrich Wilhelm Toussaint von Charpentier, director of the mines at Freiberg. In nearby Meissen, home of the famous porcelain factory, he collected a suite of pitchstones (the dark, glassy, igneous rocks called pechstein in German) and sent them off to his friends back in Florence.[98] And at Berlin, the seat of the Prussian Academy of Sciences, Smithson became good friends with one of the most respected analytical chemists in Europe, Martin Klaproth. Klaproth, who by the late 1790s had already discovered uranium and zirconium, gave Smithson some "crystallized antimony" for his cabinet. Berlin, presumably on account of Klaproth, became a place Smithson returned to a number of times in his life, when because of the wars he found himself passing entire years in the German states.[99]

Smithson was forced, because of the war with France, to travel home via the turbulent North Sea, a much longer and more unpleasant crossing than that of the Channel, especially in early March. Many English travelers were not above trying to find a way through enemy France, so preferable was it to the lengthy passage and sickeningly rough waters of the North Sea. Smithson's friend Sir Lionel Copley was one of many who found himself stuck in Switzerland unsure of how to get home. According to Lord Wycombe, who wrote a droll account of his encounter with Copley to his father Lord Lansdowne, Copley learned that a fellow Englishman had applied to the French government "for a passport to go home through France, alledging [sic] his wife's ill health as a reason. The passport was given. My friend Sir Lionel a newly elected Member of Parliament without a wife thought this scheme convenient; he has accordingly written to Paris and is waiting for an answer."[100]

Smithson, not so crafty, found himself thoroughly miserable on the interminable, storm-tossed crossing. It was a trip so devastating that, when faced with making it again six years later, he would instead wait four years on the Continent, endlessly postponing the journey in the hopes of a development in the war that might afford him an alternative route, a decision that in the end nearly cost him his life.[101] If Smithson ever contemplated a visit to America, this North Sea voyage probably confirmed that as an impossibility. James Smithson and sea travel did not mix.

SEVEN

London: Citizen of the World, 1797–1803

Of Mr Macie I still expect much. How can a person of his ardour ever be idle?

– Richard Kirwan to Sir Joseph Banks, a few weeks after Smithson's return from the Continent, April 1797

"OUR FRIEND THE philosopher Macie is here, come from Germany," Lady Webster wrote to Giovanni Fabbroni in March 1797.[1] Smithson, ravaged by the rough sea crossing, had stopped to rest en route back to London with his Grand Tour friends from Florence, Lord Holland and Lady Webster. The trial Lord Webster had brought against his wife for her scandalous adultery with Holland had recently concluded, clearing the way for her future as Lady Holland; the marriage took place in July. Smithson's presence must have stirred memories of their courtship—heady, happy days spent in the city of the Medici, times that now in the face of interminable war seemed distant and blissfully untroubled.[2]

England in the spring of 1797 was in a state of crisis. Everyone was terrified of an invasion. The French were on the doorstep, their troops massing across the Channel. Only a few months earlier they had nearly succeeded in landing in Ireland, where they had hoped to convince a restive populace to turn with them against England. There had been a run on the Bank of England in late February, and, as fears grew for England's finances, the Bank suspended specie payments for the first time in its history. The unprecedented stoppage, followed by the introduction of an emergency paper currency, seemed to augur the crumbling of the country. The King on his way to open the Parliament the previous season had been greeted with hisses and hoots instead of huzzas, an immense mob crying out, "Peace! Peace! Give us bread! No Pitt! No Famine! No War!"[3] There were food riots and demonstrations, and protests against new registration laws for the military. The Royal Navy, the mightiest aspect of England's defense, mutinied at Spithead and at the Nore in the Channel in April and May, further shattering the country's sense of security and prestige. Everyone seemed exhausted with the war. Lord Holland, who had been so passionate an admirer of the French, wrote: "I know not which way to direct my wishes for both sides seem equally dead to all feelings of humanity & all sense of their real interests and welfare, which can never be found in bloodshed massacre devastation & misery."[4] Smithson caught up on the state of affairs in England while staying with his friends, in conversations that evidently included advice on the most reliable financial investments at the moment. Not even back in London yet, he sent directions to his bankers to purchase £1,000 worth of the Bank of England's 5 percent annuities.[5]

Smithson returned to his mother's house on Upper Charlotte Street, off Fitzroy Square, where he seems to have based himself for about a year and a half before setting up his own residence. As word of his return spread, there were probably many reunions with family and friends, and letters of congratulations and welcome arriving by post. Smithson's Cornish friend John Hawkins, upon his return from the Continent in 1798, received at least twenty-four such letters, which are still carefully bundled together in the Hawkins Papers at the Cornwall Record Office. Randle Wilbraham, one of those who sent Hawkins congratulations, was another young man who had himself only recently returned from a similar tour, where he had obviously imbibed all the new thoughts stirring the Continent; his hair, he warned his mother before he arrived home, was now stunningly free of powder and at Naples he had cut it short "à la Brutus."[6] Reading these letters, glowing with friendship and adventure, provokes yet another pang-filled reverie for the losses in the Smithsonian fire of 1865. Who was waiting at home for Smithson, and how had the Continent transformed him?

One of the first people Smithson apparently contacted was his old mentor Richard Kirwan up in Dublin—since Kirwan immediately wrote to Sir Joseph Banks, full of enthusiasm for Smithson's "ardour" and prospects.[7] Kirwan had grown increasingly eccentric in his old age. He spent his time now bundled in front of his fire, his hat on regardless of the company, surrounded by Irish mastiffs and a pet eagle. Although the letter from Smithson is lost, it was probably filled with breathless tales of collecting escapades, new specimens discovered, great personages met, and alliances kindled.

Smithson's Grand Tour from a scientific point of view had been a tremendous success. At his mother's house, he organized the great hoards of material that he had collected on his travels, writing up a "Catalogue of Some Fossils from Journey Abroad." (In Smithson's lifetime, the word "fossil," from the Latin *fossus*, meaning "dug up," encompassed everything from under ground—minerals, fossils, bones, and more.) There were specimens of Carrara marble containing pyrites, iron crystals from Stromboli, and colored iron crystals in quartz from Altenberg ("neat bit," Smithson wrote in the margin); there were crystals of mica from Rome, yellow porphyry from Freiberg, and a "bottle of the residuum of the water from Dresden." He had Siberian topaz, tourmaline from the Harz mountains, and a crystal of carbonate of lime given to him by the pharmacist Bertrand Pelletier in Paris ("bad," Smithson commented). Most importantly, Smithson had also amassed an enormous network of colleagues with whom he could now make exchanges of duplicates and rarities.

Peter Christian Abildgaard, a Danish mineralogist whom Smithson had met in Venice, sent a case full of mysterious unidentified stones; Smithson added "unknown green grains from Ahrendal [Arendal in Norway]" and "black, plated, unknown matter from Ahrendal" to his collection. William Thomson, too, from Italy sent a box of treasures for Smithson to examine—including "vitriolated tartar, probably with copper, spewed out liquid f[ro]m a small aperture in the cone of Vesuvius" and "a bit of Egypt[ia]n brick, evidently made with straw, why?"—via a mutual friend named Dr. Robertson.[8] Now that Smithson was home he could pick up his correspondence once more. "The times have passed, my dear Sir, when I had the good fortune to enjoy your company and talk with you about chemistry and mineralogy," he wrote—in French—to Ottaviano Targioni-Tozzetti in Florence. "Now our conversations can only take place over the lengthy route of letters!"[9]

One of the first people he probably saw upon his return was Margaret Marriott, his father's old lover. She was now grieving the loss of both her daughters, his half-sisters. Dorothy had died in 1794, three years after her sister Philadelphia, having endured, as one newspaper solemnly opined, "the slowly consuming ravages of that most painful of all poisons grief—with almost unexampled resignation."[10] In the newspaper accounts Smithson would have seen that Dorothy and Philadelphia were openly referred to as children of the Duke of Northumberland, as both girls' obituaries named them as half-sisters to the current Duke of Northumberland and the Earl of Beverley. They had those things that Smithson most craved: support from their father, who had financed their education in Paris; the carrying of the family name; and public acknowledgment of their relation to the duke, at least insofar as being afforded the opportunity to be buried practically at his side in Westminster Abbey.

Smithson seems to have grown exceedingly close to Margaret Marriott, whom he called "a most particular and intimate friend of mine."[11] While this language was not uncommon in the eighteenth century and does not necessarily connote a physical relationship,

Smithson did give Margaret Marriott two portraits of himself, both "painted in Oil Colours one very large and one smaller."[12] She is the only person so far identified to have been singled out in such a way. A portrait, a miniature especially, was an intimate memento, to keep one's beloved close during times of separation. As Prince Lee Boo gleefully replied, when Smithson's cousin George Keate asked whether he understood the purpose of a portrait, pointing first to Keate and then to the painting of him: "Lee Boo understand well—that Misser Keate die,—this Misser Keate live!"[13]

Margaret Marriott and the Percy girls, probably more than anyone, understood Smithson's anguish over his father. Even as the sisters had enjoyed many advantages that Smithson had not, they had not been accepted into the ducal household; Mrs. Marriott had attempted, following the duke's death, to have the girls raised by the duke's second son Lord Beverley and his wife, but Lady Beverley had apparently refused.[14] Dorothy Percy in her last days worked out a way to express the acute sympathy she felt for Smithson. Two weeks before her death, she added a codicil to her will. In it she left "unto my half brother James Macie Esquire natural son to his late Grace Duke of Northumberland the sum of three thousand pounds."[15] The money was not to come to Smithson until after the death of Mrs. Marriott, an event which occurred only in 1827. The heft of these words in Dorothy's will, though, was much greater even than the monetary gift. Dorothy's bequest, her legacy to Smithson—the act of a devoted friend, a sister in spirit—was the act of naming. It represented, finally, a public acknowledgment of Smithson's paternity. There in writing, in an official document, was notice of his birth.

Dorothy's death was probably a strong reminder to Smithson of his disenfranchisement, and the corresponding need he felt to be recognized as a man of quality, a wealthy noble-born gentleman. Most young gentlemen returned from the Grand Tour to settle on to their estates. Smithson had no such realm. His mother had sold Great Durnford Manor in 1791, the estate that had been in the Hungerford family since the fifteenth century. She still retained the

Macie property of Weston House in the countryside near Bath, and she was expending astronomical sums bringing it into the latest fashion, but it was not destined to be his. She may also have been renting Elm Grove near Mortlake, a bucolic Thames-side community of villas and pleasure grounds where Smithson passed some time this first summer.[16]

Smithson had yet to establish his own domain, but he was a gentleman returned from the Grand Tour, and he intended now to live in a manner reflecting that status, despite the continuing suffering of the country at war. In early 1799 he found a house to rent on Clarges Street off Piccadilly and began to decorate lavishly. Payments flowed out of Hoare's to the cabinet makers Gillow & Co., to Thomas and Richard Chippendale, to the wallpaper manufacturers Jeffrey & Co., and to one of London's leading glass suppliers, John Blades. At a house sale run by the auctioneer Christie's he laid out £70 for a large collection of items, including a mahogany card table, three separate fireplace sets—each with fender, irons, and hearth rug—and a pantheon stove. He prepared for entertaining on a large scale with the acquisition of eighteen oval blue and white china dishes and a vast set of decanters and wine and water glasses. He also took home a handsome "three-foot achromatic telescope by Watkins, on a pillar and claw," as well as quite the most expensive item in the sale, "a magnificent Vauxhall plate of glass," nearly six feet high and four feet wide, cased in an "elegant carved and gilt frame."[17] Eager to stock his library shelves, Smithson roamed the booksellers of London, including the French émigré De Boffe's shop in Soho. Among his purchases was Mercier's *Mon bonnet de nuit*, or "night cap" thoughts, the two-volume pocket-sized French edition published in London in 1798. This luminous meditation on quotidian life in Paris—a kaleidoscopic parade of images: bolts of silk in shop windows, snatches of conversation from the theatre boxes, and the songs of oyster sellers in the market—provided wistful Francophiles something to luxuriate in while they were still prevented from crossing the Channel.

Smithson immersed himself in the company of the Whig aristocrats he had met on the Grand Tour. "Would you have the kindness to re-tell me the shop where your dinner services were made," he asked Lady Holland, "and if you would grant me the loan of one of them, to guard against the little mistakes to which the petulant genius of English workmen expose them, of taking black for white, blunt for sharp-pointed, &c &c &c it would still add to the favor. You know that by your own calculation you will save me two years of the time required for my getting settled in my house." When he returned the items a few weeks later, he thanked her profusely before joking, in regard to the tripling of wheat prices and the bread riots around the country: "I believe that I should have done more wisely not to [have] bespoken any, as knives, plates, and every other article, in any way, connected with eating, must be very soon, in this country, most perfect inutilities."[18]

At Lord and Lady Holland's rambling Jacobean mansion on the outskirts of town, he found a happy simulacrum of his European existence. Their unorthodox courtship and subsequent marriage had stunned London society, and her divorce trial had only compounded the scandal of the liaison. Shunned by many of the court regulars, she and Holland proceeded to set up an alternative court at Holland House, which soon became one of the most important centers of opposition politics and culture in the country. It was the closest thing London had to a European salon—and it was one, like those of Madame de Staël or Madame Récamier, run by an alluring, opinionated woman. At its famous dinner parties the table was crammed with visitors, scientists mingling with poets and politicians. As Holland recalled years later, "geology, chemistry and electricity were the fashionable topics of conversation."[19] Lady Holland imperiously presided over all; "Make room," she called down to a guest on one occasion, who replied, "It certainly must be made, for it does not exist."[20]

One of the many acquaintances Smithson met at Holland House was the wealthy American William Loughton Smith, a congressman from South Carolina who was on his way to a posting as American minister to Portugal. Smithson turned to Smith for help when Mrs. Marriott ran into trouble with "a very considerable" property in South Carolina that she had inherited from her uncle. Margaret Marriott had been born Margaret Goodwin on the island of St. Helena, near Beaufort, South Carolina.[21] "A rascally executor," as Smithson explained to Lord Holland, was preventing her from obtaining the property. Smith's brother, Joseph Allen Smith, one of America's first art collectors and philanthropists and a key member of South Carolina's merchant and planter elite, had been "mentioned to her [Mrs. Marriott] by many people as the person in the world most able, and best qualified, to render her service, both from his station and the excellence of his moral character." Smithson was convinced that "if our Mr. Smith [William], his brother, would prevail upon him to undertake the affair they say that the recovery of the property is indubitable."[22]

Unfortunately, no details regarding this particular American connection have yet been found in the archives of either England or the United States. For someone like Smithson, though, trafficking in the Establishment culture of England and Europe in the late eighteenth century, America was not a remote and foreign land. Many of Smithson's friends and associates had traveled there, whether to fight—as his half-brother Lord Percy, now the second Duke of Northumberland, had—or to explore, as had Count Paolo Andreani or Lord Wycombe or Sir Charles Blagden or any number of Smithson's acquaintances. Others of his acquaintances drew much of their fortune from property there, as Margaret Marriott probably did; Lady Holland, for example, was the granddaughter of an American loyalist who had left her a life interest in a vast estate in Maine on the Kennebec River.[23] And there were lots of Americans abroad. American diplomats formed part of the circles in which Smithson moved; and on the Continent wealthy, sophisticated Americans like the Smith brothers were frequently to be met on the Grand Tour.

Smithson had come of age during the extraordinary decade that witnessed the surrender of the British at Yorktown, the formal recognition of an independent United States, and the unprecedented creation of a constitution based on self-government. He had learned of these epochal events and discussed them—in the politicized circle of chemistry devotees at Oxford, amidst the congenial philosophers of Edinburgh, and in the radical coffeehouse culture of London— in communities of men who were profoundly sympathetic to the democratic ideals of this new nation.

Smithson and his fellow philosophers, the men of the English Enlightenment, were focused on constructing a public sphere, a community that fostered scientific advancement and the happiness of mankind. They understood that liberty was essential to the success of their pursuits. When Joseph Priestley fled to the United States in 1794 seeking protection from the persecution that trailed him in England, the radical United Irishmen published a public letter of sympathy and support; "But be cheerful, dear Sir, you are going to a happier world, the world of Washington and Franklin," they assured him. "The attention of a whole scientific people [here] is bent to multiplying the means and instruments of destruction . . . but you are going to a country where science is turned to better use."[24]

Smithson's Enlightenment aspirations had had in his lifetime their most perfect realization to date in the United States. The architects of the American republic, statesmen like Franklin and Jefferson, were many of them scientists and leaders of scientific societies; the election of 1800, which pitted Jefferson against Adams, was also the contest of the president of the American Philosophical Society against the president of the American Academy of Arts and Sciences. America's leaders regularly praised the pursuit of science, highlighting the role that democratic forms of government could play in the fostering of progress. Jefferson argued that liberty was "the great parent of *science* and of virtue; and that a nation will be great in both, always in proportion as it is free."[25] And George Washington, in his final address as president, exhorted: "Promote, as an object of primary importance, institutions for the general diffusion of knowledge. In proportion as the structure of a government gives force to public opinion, it is essential that public opinion should be enlightened."[26]

In April 1799 Sir Joseph Banks invited "Louis Macie" to become a proprietor of just such a new establishment, the Royal Institution. The brainchild of the American-born inventor and soldier of fortune Count Rumford, the Royal Institution was to be devoted to "the applications of Science to the common Purposes of Life."[27] It was a dramatically new kind of forum for the spread of knowledge, both in its scientific focus and in its intended audience. It was to be dedicated to applied science, to the discoveries that materially improved the human condition—research into the properties of heat and fuel, and the processes of tanning, bleaching, and dyeing—work that Rumford had long championed. By providing laboratory facilities, it would offer the country's first institutionally backed place of research. And with the creation of a lecture hall, teaching became possible. This utilitarian approach, so markedly different from the gentleman-scholar-oriented program of the Royal Society, which lacked both laboratory and lecture hall, was coupled with a brand new target audience: the working man. The Royal Institution in its earliest iteration was an idealistic effort to bring science to the masses. The higher echelons of society were to be entertained with lectures illustrating the beneficial applications of new discoveries to daily life, while artisans, bricklayers, and other tradesmen—"whose deficiency in knowledge proves one of the greatest drawbacks to the progress of art"—were to be served by a school for mechanics.[28]

Smithson was one of about one hundred original subscribers or "Proprietors" solicited within the first two months to provide financial backing; by the end of the first year this number had grown to two hundred and eighty. These men were for the most part not scientists at all, but rather aristocrats and wealthy gentry; at fifty guineas a subscription, only the rich could afford to be listed supporters of the new endeavor. Smithson, hungry for recognition of his gentlemanly status, seems to have been content to become a patron. He found himself in the company of some of the most prominent philanthropists in England: the Earl of Winchilsea, who took an active role as the first president of the Managers, the men picked by the Proprietors actually to run the business of the Institution; the entrepreneurial aristocrat the Duke of Bridgewater, who spearheaded the canal mania that swept the country in the late eighteenth century, and was invited to be president of the Royal Institution but declined; and Thomas Bernard, the treasurer of the Foundling Hospital, who served as the first secretary of the Royal Institution. Many of the backers, Bernard especially, had been involved in the creation of the Society for the Bettering of the Condition of the Poor and had also been active on the Board of Agriculture. They were for the most part improving landowners— enlightened aristocrats riding the latest developments in science to better their agricultural yields and more effectively exploit the natural resources of their properties.

Chemistry was promptly established as a central preoccupation of the new institution. Humphry Davy, twenty-two years old and fresh from his experiments with nitrous oxide (laughing gas) at Thomas Beddoes' Pneumatic Institution in Bristol, was hired in the first years of operation as a lecturer. Davy was a brilliant, dynamic speaker, taking his audiences on an exalted tour of the civilizing forces of chemistry. His lectures were filled with references to poetry, metaphysics, and ancient history, and were punctuated by spectacular demonstrations. Electricity could be summoned, for example, with loud explosions and brilliant colored lights, to burn out the letters S-C-I-E-N-C-E on a luminous sheet of gold leaf. Davy's lectures soon became an essential part of fashionable entertainment in the capital, and on evenings when Davy was speaking Albemarle Street became so clogged with carriages rushing well-dressed ladies and gentlemen to the proceedings that it was made into London's first one-way street.[29]

Smithson's initial involvement in the Royal Institution signaled his ever-increasing involvement as a gentleman patron and his ascent to roles of leadership in London's scientific community. Over at the Royal Society he was elected to the governing council for the first time at the anniversary meeting of 1800.[30] Among those with whom he was to serve were his friends John Hawkins and Charles Greville, as well as Greville's uncle Sir William Hamilton, who was then, together with Emma and Lord Nelson, enjoying a hero's welcome back in London, his posting at Naples finally at an end. Just as Smithson seemed ready to take a more commanding position in the scientific world, however, he dropped out of sight. He failed to attend a single meeting of the Royal Society council following his swearing in in January 1801.

The start of the new century was an absolutely calamitous period for Smithson, a time filled with the deaths of many in his closest circle, including his mother. His cousin George Keate had died shortly after Smithson's return from the Continent in 1797. Now Keate's wife Jane-Catharine passed away, forcing the sale of all Keate's extraordinary collections. The sale of the books alone lasted for three days, the coins for two, and the lots that comprised the rest of the museum, when finally sold more than a year later, filled an astonishing eleven days. Smithson, as he witnessed this spectacle, might have wondered about Keate's legacy—and whether it could have been handled in a different manner. Might Keate's name have been better remembered if he had specified in his will that the museum be kept intact? Certainly, this was something on the minds of others. "It is to be lamented," declared *The Times*, "that the valuable and choice Museum of the late George Keate, Author of the Pelew Islands, which will begin selling at King's in Covent-Garden, on Monday next, was not disposed of altogether, for although it will enrich the cabinets of the first Collectors in Europe, it certainly ought to have become a national purchase."[31]

Smithson's old guardian Joseph Gape, the family solicitor who had sponsored his naturalization and who might well have been the nearest that Smithson had to a father figure during his early childhood, also passed away around the turn of the century. So too did the solicitor Albany Wallis, who took to the grave much of the staggering and mysterious £8,000 that Smithson had loaned him a few years earlier; his death provoked Smithson into filing a lawsuit against Wallis' heir for the recovery of the money, the only time—in contrast to his extraordinarily litigious mother—that Smithson ever went to court.[32] Most traumatic of all was the death of his mother.

To her last days, Smithson's mother had remained the widow Elizabeth Macie. And yet, at the end, she did not come to rest next to her first husband in the Macie ancestral grounds at Weston, near Bath. Neither did she elect to be interred amongst the Hungerfords at Bremhill in Wiltshire, where her brother lay. In 1803 her sister Henrietta Maria would be buried in Salisbury Cathedral, surrounded by those medieval Hungerfords who had once brought fame to the family. Elizabeth Macie instead came to lie in Brighton, a louche watering hole popularized by the King's wayward son (later George IV) on the south coast of England. She had evidently developed some roots there, as she chose to be buried at St. Nicholas' and requested that the parish officers distribute twenty guineas worth of bread to the poor on the day of her burial. Why she settled in Brighton, and who or what kept her there, is a mystery.[33]

Smithson immediately threw himself into sorting out the morass of her affairs. Among his many responsibilities was the vacating of the premises at Weston, according to the terms of John Macie's will. There were problems as well at Great Durnford, the Hungerford property Mrs. Macie had sold in 1791. Smithson had a testy exchange over water rights with the new owner, Lord Malmesbury. He extended the offer that his mother had made, "to take back the Estate, and restore to you the price of it." Failing that, Smithson told Malmesbury, they would have to settle the matter in court, though he concluded, "To me, as to you, my Lord, the object is null—the money in dispute is nothing—the amount of it, and more, will be wasted in the struggle." Smithson felt insulted by Malmesbury's accusations, and he believed the honor of his late mother was drawn into question, too, by the dispute. Malmesbury's proposed solution, simply to split the monies in question, Smithson sarcastically called "an ingenious device by which wrong becomes inevitable." He exhorted Malmesbury to come to an amicable agreement. "From the imperfections intrinsically interwoven in human nature, there are no transactions between men in which there are not some flaws on which rigid precision may not fix. But Nature has infused candor in the human heart, my Lord, for the purpose of supplying the defects which she had left in the human head, and checking the jars which, else, would endlessly have perturbed society."[34]

But first of all he tended promptly to the resolution of his public identity. Immediately following his mother's burial he instituted efforts to change his name from Macie to Smithson. No longer was there to be any secrecy surrounding his paternal lineage. He appealed to the Crown for a formal change of name, which was ultimately accepted in February 1801 and printed in the *London Gazette*. The first place the change was registered was in his banking records at Hoare's, in June 1800—about a month after his mother's burial.[35] Clearly, it was a move he had been contemplating for some time.

There are few examples of how his friends reacted to the name change. The bald striving for acknowledgment that lay behind the decision seems to have been evident to most—and was even on occasion a source of amusement or ridicule. The catty Sir Charles Blagden, seeing Smithson in Paris in 1814, well over a decade after the name change, wrote in his diary: "Teased to B[ertholle]t that he [Smithson] was the same man as Macie."[36]

Despite the fact that Smithson was not socializing much during these days, one person he did see with regularity was his cousin Georgiana Henderson, the only child of his cousin George Keate. On the last day of the auction of Keate's immense museum collections, Smithson went to dinner at Georgiana's town house on Devonshire Street, near Portland Place. He played with her children and supped with her husband, the collector and amateur artist John

Henderson. At half past eight Henderson and Smithson climbed the stairs to take tea with Georgiana in her room. For the rest of the evening the three of them, just as they had three nights earlier, pored endlessly over the Hungerford family papers. Smithson, Georgiana reported in her diary, "did not go away till Twelve o'clock."[37]

These two cousins, now orphaned adults, shared a deep bond. Both lived unacknowledged, deprived of any public claim to their family. George Keate had mysteriously and vitriolically turned against his daughter at the time of her marriage, despite having been supportive of John Henderson for several years prior. Keate cut Georgiana out of her inheritance and shunned any of his friends who carried on their friendship with his daughter. Georgiana's invitation to her father to bestow a name upon her firstborn child, who arrived at the end of that first year of her marriage, was met with silence. She lived now, like Smithson, in a state of dispossession.[38] As Smithson battled with Lord Malmesbury over Great Durnford Manor and Georgiana watched her father's collections go under the gavel, Smithson and Georgiana wrote letters and saw each other constantly. In the lamplight of Georgiana's study they consoled themselves with the litany of their family history, tracing its ancestry, reviewing its deeds and titles. Both believed in the chimera of its potency.

Following his mother's death, Smithson focused ever more intently on his wealth and how best to put it to use. In July he sold £13,350 of the 5 percents and reinvested the enormous sum—£5,350 of which may have been his mother's shares—in exchequer bills. He had long been a shrewd investor in relatively safe, blue-chip Bank of England investments—the 5 percents, the 3 percents, India bonds and others—but he now also turned his attention to bankrolling technological innovations that promised a better economic future for England. Many of the projects Smithson might have been involved in will probably remain unknown, as it is possible they were funded from other caches of money or paid out to intermediaries.[39] His bank accounts seem far from presenting a complete picture of his finances.

First, and most successful, among these investments was the Grand Junction Canal. Designed to provide a direct waterway for industrial goods from Birmingham to London, the Grand Junction was part of the canal mania that had swept the country in the preceding decades. Originally, the contribution of Londoners to this growth was minor. The Grand Junction Canal was unusual in that it sought its investors in London, and Smithson when he joined found himself in the company of some of the richest and most prominent men of England. Its chairman was the well-connected banker William Praed, and the Duke of Grafton, the Earl of Clarendon, the Earl of Essex, and the Earl Spencer were all on the board. The financial troubles of 1797–8 complicated the completion of the canal and caused construction estimates to spiral well beyond their original projections. Simultaneously, however, the threat of invasion and the urgent need to move troops and stores securely around the country underscored the strategic importance of the canal project. In 1801 the Grand Junction Canal finally opened onto the Paddington Basin, and a few years later the Blisworth Tunnel, the last part of the route, was completed.[40] It immediately showed a return, and Smithson continued to receive dividends from it all his life. He was even carrying with him at the time of his death in Genoa a large packet of papers concerning the canal company.[41]

Smithson's enthusiasm for industrial progress seems to have stayed close to home, focused primarily on the London area and on projects aimed at improving transport and communication. The efficient movement of people and goods was essential to bringing about a modern and materially successful society. Smithson invested in the New Croydon Canal, though it did not in the end yield much in the way of dividends. And he joined a number of local industrialists to serve as a financial backer to one of the Croydon Canal's biggest competitors, the Surrey Iron Railway, which carried goods from the Thames at Wandsworth south through Colliers Wood to Croydon. Canal companies often owned the tramways or other byways that linked various canals and endpoints; the Surrey Iron Railway, however, established by an Act of Parliament in 1801, was the first railway independent of a canal.[42] Smithson also backed the construction of an abortive tunnel under the Thames. The sprawl of London made the need for a better method of traffic between the two banks an absolute imperative—but bridges, which impeded the passage of large ships, were considered less than ideal solutions. The impresario-engineer who proposed the tunnel emphasized its usefulness in moving troops, and Parliament passed the Act to make the tunnel in 1799. Smithson bought up several hundred pounds' worth of shares to fund the project—but it never actually came to fruition (Brunel's tunnel, the one that was finally built, did not start construction until 1825).[43] All of these investments reflected Smithson's enduring belief in the social benefits of scientific progress. They also evince a strong interest in promoting the economic strength of his homeland, England.

Despite the emotional drain of these first years of the new century, Smithson continued his scientific work. Mention in his catalogue, in 1799, of some new examples of what Smithson suspected to be fluorspar, from Matlock in Derbyshire, suggests that perhaps he made a mineralogical tour or two around England in the years following his return from the Continent, in pursuit of representative specimens for his cabinet.[44] Of the laboratory experiments he was conducting during this period, he brought one to the level of presentation, a paper that turned out to be the most significant of his career. With some calamines he had purchased from a dealer in Germany, he began a series of experiments that led to the paper he presented to the Royal Society at the start of the new season in November 1802. This work, the first official public outing of his new name Smithson, eventually led, appropriately enough, to the naming of the mineral smithsonite.[45]

When Smithson began his investigations of calamine, there were many confusing accounts of it circulating among mineralogists.

Miners and artisan metalworkers had long known that some calamine produced zinc that was useful in the making of brass, while other specimens—which appeared identical—produced only slag. Although the eighteenth century had seen the development of zinc smelting techniques, it remained economically viable to mine calamine. There was a decided value to finding a reliable means of distinguishing between these different kinds of calamine. Smithson collected numerous samples for his study. He had specimens from the Mendip hills in Somersetshire, from Derbyshire, from Regbania in Hungary, and from "Bleyberg in Carinthia [Bleiberg, Austria]." His analyses revealed that what was called "calamine" was not in fact a single substance but multiple distinct minerals—zinc carbonate (that which became smithsonite); zinc silicate (now hemimorphite), which was also called electric calamine on account of its pyroelectric qualities, the ends of the crystals becoming electrically charged when heated; and that which was eventually named hydrozincite.

Smithson's calamine paper exuded a confidence that had not been in evidence in his tabasheer paper of a decade earlier. The species had already been studied by two of the most prominent mineralogists of the eighteenth century—the Swede Torbern Bergman, champion of chemical analysis in mineralogy, and the French founder of crystallography René-Just Haüy. Smithson, at the opening of his paper, unabashedly announced that his experiments had shown "how wide from the truth have been the opinions adopted concerning them [these ores of zinc]." Haüy had not even been convinced that zinc silicate existed, but in light of Smithson's work he quickly revised his position.

In addition to putting forward these new identifications, Smithson also ventured some theoretical speculations based on his findings. He had observed the constituents of calamine to be combining in regular proportions. He cautiously suggested that the application of mathematical calculations to check laboratory results might "introduce a degree of rigorous accuracy and certainty into chemistry, of which this science was thought to be ever incapable." He probed further, stating, "A certain knowledge of the exact proportions of the constituent principles of bodies, may likewise open to our view harmonious analogies between the constitutions of related objects, general laws, &c., which at present totally escape us."[46] In the coming years Smithson argued more forcefully for the "importance of a knowledge of the true quantity in which matters combine."[47] John Dalton soon thereafter formulated his atomic theory, explaining how the weights of an element's atoms combined in fixed ratios, coining the laws of definite proportions and of multiple proportions. Smithson, on account of these musings, which he mentioned in other papers as well, was credited in the first decades of the nineteenth century as one of those instigators who had been crucial to discovering an underlying chemical theory.[48]

At the end of 1801 Smithson stood atop the cliffs of Dover, staring across to France. Gone were the crowds that had massed there a few months earlier seeking the pyrotechnics of a confrontation between their own sails and those that menaced from across the Channel. Alone on the windswept chalky bluffs, Smithson drolly painted the scene for Lady Holland back in London. "Vapid flags of truce tamely" waved from every direction, and there were a few "old and crazy edifices, shaken in the passed storm, tottering on their foundations and forewarning of the approaching moment of their fall." He lamented his inability "to enrich my letter with interesting details of the destruction of fleets and the conflagration of cities, but helas, before I came hither exhaustion had already forced a pause in the noble scene, and satiety has since quenched, for a time, the thirst of human blood."[49]

During the war the Continent lay off bounds for wealthy Grand Tourists, and the *bon ton* had to content themselves instead with holidays at the English coastal resorts. Smithson's cousin Georgiana Henderson typically spent several months over the late autumn and winter at Dover and the Isle of Wight in the years leading up to the Peace of Amiens. His mother likewise had passed her last seasons in Brighton. Smithson over the winter of 1801–2 spent more than three months in the Dover area. He probably dabbled in the pleasures of society there, partaking of gambling and dinners and dances. He also explored the windswept countryside, ranging from Kent into Sussex, with hammer and chisel in hand and a collecting sack over his shoulder, looking for specimens. Mindful of currying favor with well-placed friends, he sent off "a small box, containing some of the productions of this neighbourhood" to Lady Holland. "All the specimens are <u>perfectly fresh</u>," he told her, "having been dug out from the strata where they were formed. It being proper that they should travel a grave and philosophical pall, they will not pay their respects to you for some days."[50]

A few weeks of observing life on the coast instilled Smithson with tremendous optimism. He abandoned the wry and cynical tone with which he'd described the scene at Dover in his letter to Lady Holland. The elation of peace after such wrenching bloodshed and upheaval, like the release of a long pent-up breath, had infused him with hope for the future. Writing now to her husband, he sounded both amazed and joyful. "Only the being contemporary to the wonderful event, and an eyewitness to the truth of it," Smithson told Lord Holland, "could render credible the change which, in the space of a few short years, has taken place, thro'out all Europe, in the minds of men." Smithson felt the surge of communal sympathy and acceptance that follows the survival of a harrowing ordeal. People from warring nations now suddenly conceived of themselves as part of one universal society. Smithson could hardly believe the transformation:

> Indeed I scarcely meet with an individual who is not in fact become a citizen of the world, who does not already consider the Globe as his country; and express a determination to take up his residence in that part of it where he can live most secure, most free, most happy, whatever may be the meridian in which this may be.

His letter to Holland was steeped in the language of Enlightenment, equating freedom of movement with liberty and light, and the privations of war and oppression with darkness and ignorance. Smithson told his friend that when peace finally arrived the opening of the ports would be "like the destruction of a dike—like the bursting of a mine—the people will issue as a huge wave; will rush out as by explosion from this damp dungeon, the dark den of want and melancholy—the lurid cell of maniac puritanism."[51]

The declaration of amnesties on October 1, signaling the coming peace, enabled countless émigrés and royalists hiding in England to return to their homeland. And even before the official Peace of Amiens was signed in March 1802, the stream of curious English across the Channel turned to a flood. The French likewise made their way to England. "The number of French people daily landing here is quite astonishing. 20, 30, 50 come over in a vessel I am told," Smithson informed Holland. "The two countries seem going completely to exchange their inhabitants." Many of the French visitors were hailed as celebrities. Madame Récamier was mobbed in Kensington Gardens, and the French aeronaut A. J. Garnerin, the first ever to parachute out of a balloon, was received with wild applause when he arrived with his wife to make some theatrical ascents. Smithson no doubt wished to be among those rushing off to France, but 1802 passed in its entirety, and several months of 1803 as well, before he finally crossed the Channel.

He was probably waiting for his brother, Henry Louis Dickenson, to return. The two of them had not seen each other in more than ten years, and now, with their mother dead, they had only each other. Dickenson, the second son, had not gone on to university. After flirting briefly with an apprenticeship at the family solicitors, he had bought a commission in the Army. His subsequent, not especially illustrious career had taken him to Holland, Cape Town, and India.

Now on leave, he drew out his trip home, taking nearly six months to travel from the Red Sea back to London. It was a journey

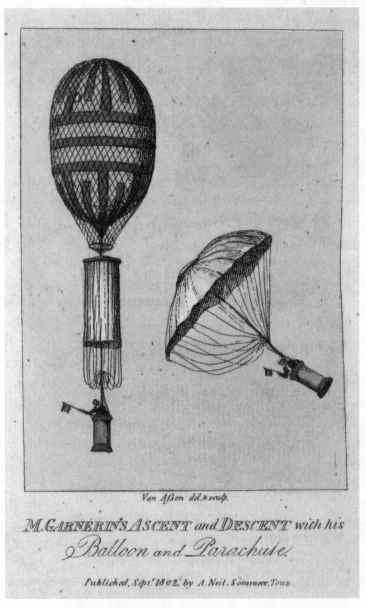

Van Afsen dd.& sculp.

M. GARNERIN'S ASCENT and DESCENT with his
Balloon and Parachute.

Published, Sept. 1802, by A. Neil, Somners.Town.

The frontispiece from one of Smithson's books, showing Garnerin's
balloon launch and his parachute jump.

filled with sightseeing, Dickenson's own version of the Grand Tour. In Egypt he picked up a little figure of Isis to bring back to his brother Smithson, who later analyzed the pigments that had been used to color it. The view from the top of the pyramids marked, he said, "the first time in my life that my imagination had fallen short of the reality." After crossing from Alexandria to Malta, he carried on to Naples, saw Pompeii and Herculaneum and climbed Vesuvius. In Rome he was presented to the Pope, whom he found "totally deficient in dignity." Traversing the Alps at Mont Cenis, he delighted to see ice again for the first time in so many years. At the end of November 1802 he arrived in Paris and stayed a month, visiting "everything worthy of curiosity." When he finally reached London, Smithson, who had inherited almost everything from his mother, including money in trust for his younger brother, quickly began to pick up Dickenson's bills. Their overlap, however, was brief. Although they had much to catch up on, Smithson was eager to taste the delights of Paris for himself. He probably intended to be gone only a few months at most.[52]

In late February 1803 Smithson made the requisite trips to get his passport documents—first to Lord Hawkesbury at Whitehall and then to the French ambassador. He was ready finally to leave for the Continent by the end of the month. Once again, however, a death in the family intervened. On March 10 his aunt Henrietta Maria Keate Walker Hungerford, the last of the "heiresses of Studley," as she and Smithson's mother had called themselves, died at her house near Cavendish Square after a long illness. The burial did not take place until the end of the month. It was held at Salisbury Cathedral, where the Hungerford family had long ago dominated in medieval splendor. There amongst her ancestors, adjacent to the seventeenth-century brass plates commemorating Sir Giles Hungerford and his wife Dame Margarite, and near the worn and displaced fifteenth-century stone tombs of Walter Lord Hungerford and Catherine his first wife, Henrietta Maria Hungerford found her resting place. She was the last of the Hungerfords to be buried at Salisbury.

The Hungerford chapel at Salisbury before its demolition, 1788.

More than a decade earlier, Horace Walpole had decried the loss of the Hungerford chapel at Salisbury Cathedral. This exquisite, traceried temple to the family name had been destroyed during the renovations of the cathedral in the late 1780s. "I shall heartily lament with you, Sir, the demolition of those beautiful chapels at Salisbury," Walpole wrote to the antiquarian Richard Gough. "It is an old complaint with me, Sir, that when families are extinct, chapters take the freedom of removing ancient monuments, and even of selling over again the site of such tombs. A scandalous, nay, dishonest, abuse, and very unbecoming clergymen!"[53] The Hungerford family, in most eyes, was already extinct by the close of the eighteenth century. Smithson was not to be counted as an inheritor of the Hungerford line. And when Sir Richard Colt Hoare penned his history of the Hungerfords in 1822, he neglected even to mention

Smithson's mother, listing her siblings Lumley and Henrietta Maria as the only Keate descendants of their branch, ironically ensuring Smithson's further obliteration. Smithson was not, of course, to be found in the lists of the offspring of the Duke of Northumberland either. On the pages of history being recorded around him, James Smithson did not see himself inscribed.

In late April 1803 Smithson finally set sail for the Continent, his servant and baggage in tow.[54]

EIGHT

The Hurricane of War, 1803–1807

I left England on a trip to Paris, was overtaken by
the hurricane of war, and cast away onto this
desolate country.

—James Smithson in Germany to Lord Holland,
November 1805

BY THE TIME Smithson crossed the Channel in April 1803
England had been consumed for over a year by all things
French. As soon as peace was proclaimed, fashionable society
had raced over to see the changes that "twelve years of virtually
uninterrupted cataclysm"—as Henry Yorke described it in his *Letters
from France*—had wrought on the aristocracy's favorite country. They
were astonished at the latest fashions: tailcoats, wide lapels, and tight
cravats for the men, and for the ladies diaphanous high-waisted
Grecian gowns that left little to the imagination. They marveled at
the new Musée Napoléonienne at the Louvre, bursting with
antiquities and masterpieces plundered from Italy. Above all they
went to see the man himself, Napoleon. Once a month he held
receptions at the Tuileries palace, and on Sundays throngs of carriages
crowded the road en route to Josephine's entertainments at
Malmaison. Those not so fortunate as to gain an audience still had

plenty of opportunity to see Napoleon, as Smithson's brother had, at one of his frequent reviews of the troops.[1]

Much of the country had been ravaged by a decade of revolution. Monasteries and churches lay in crumbled ruins, tombs and religious monuments mutilated and sacked. The roads were miserable, save that from Calais to Paris—which Napoleon had shrewdly overhauled for Cornwallis' arrival to the treaty negotiations at Amiens. But Paris itself glittered. The English discovered in the capital a flourishing neoclassical wonderland. Old buildings had been recast as new, with names redolent of optimism and celebration: the Palais Royal—the center of English pleasure-seeking—found fresh life as the Tribunat, and the old Café de la Rotonde in the leafy garden courtyard was rechristened the Pavilion of Peace. The site of the gruesome guillotine had been renamed the Place de la Concorde. Eager to put memories of the Terror behind them, the populace and their English visitors reveled in luxury. Bonaparte's installation of himself as Life Consul inaugurated a new type of court existence, fully as ravishing and opulent as that of the *ancien régime*. Life in Paris was dedicated once more to frivolity. Theatres were packed to the rafters, and the political cafés—where speeches had once stirred fiery pledges of sacrifice, and pamphlets had raised men's thoughts to revolution— lay empty and forgotten.

Smithson hardly had time to savor the changes, however. Already when he set sail in April 1803 tensions between the two countries were running high. The peace was a fragile, poorly brokered one, and in the eyes of England the price was steep. After nine years of war and many victories at sea, England had handed back virtually everything to France. All it retained was Spanish Trinidad and Dutch Ceylon—though Smithson was delighted at news of the latter, which meant he might be able to procure some of the reddish crystals (corundum) the Dutch used "as a substitute for emery" found in profusion on the island.[2] The English eyed with suspicion the French factories that continued to churn out munitions and the shipyards filled with the clamor of workers. Napoleon still had troops stationed in the Netherlands, and he continued aggressively to expand France's borders into Italy and Switzerland, annexing Elba and Piedmont. Reports from India and the Levant hinted at intrigues there as well. Through the sale of the territory of Louisiana to the Americans (the Louisiana Purchase) he brought $15 million into his coffers and simultaneously eliminated the threat of the United States having cause to join England against him. England in consequence reneged on their promise to relinquish Malta, in order to retain some advantageous position against any possible attack Napoleon might launch against Egypt or India. Less than a month after Smithson arrived in France the truce between England and France finally ruptured. "I was so unfortunate as to get into France just at the time that it became necessary to leave it," he wrote to a friend in Italy, "and indeed was out of it only two days before the English were so traitorously arrested."[3]

Within days of Britain's declaration of war on May 18, 1803, Napoleon retaliated by announcing the unprecedented arrest of all English males between the ages of eighteen and sixty in France. Napoleon's order contravened every tradition of conduct between nations at the time; it was a gross violation of international faith and goodwill, and it set the stage for the modern state of total war. In the eighteenth-century conception of warfare, only crowns were at war and only crowns' armed and paid forces were fighting. Gentlemen like Smithson had always been able to travel above the fray. With Napoleon's edict, people like Smithson for the first time became an inseparable part of war.[4]

The net thrown captured hundreds of English indiscriminately, shopkeepers together with peers. Lord Elgin en route back from his post at Constantinople—without the Parthenon marbles, which were traveling separately by sea—was arrested, despite brandishing his passports and pleading diplomatic cover. Lord Yarmouth, the future founder of the Wallace Collection, in Paris picture-hunting with his wife, children, and eight servants, likewise found himself shipped off to Verdun—without his wife, who was left in the hands of the Governor of Paris, General Junot, and promptly became the general's mistress. Doctors and clergymen, historically exempt from capture even if they were accompanying the military, were also rounded up. Most were taken to walled fortress towns which, on account of Napoleon's extensive land grabs, now lay well within France's new borders. Verdun soon became the most famous depot, a reputation gained not for any cruel punishments meted out there but because of the lavish lifestyles the detainees managed to lead. The English continued their gambling, horse races, and parties; Yarmouth kept on collecting paintings, with help of a Parisian dealer. By the end of 1803 Napoleon had decreed that all gentleman prisoners should be sent to Verdun. Throughout the wars the town always had an especially high concentration of English wealth. English shopkeepers, arrested alongside their traditional clientele, set up their stands, transforming the walled city into a mini-Bath or Tunbridge Wells. Many of those arrested spent years immured there, some until peace was declared in 1814.

Smithson was one of the few lucky ones. He left France shortly before the declaration of war, setting out for the Low Countries. Soon thereafter he removed himself to a further safety in Germany, "in what I swear to you seemed at the time an excess of precaution," he told one friend.[5] In those weeks before the recommencement of hostilities, everyone believed the English would be given ample warning for departure. *Argus*, one of the English language papers in Paris, assured its readers it was safe to remain in France, even after the departure of Lord Whitworth from the embassy; France after all, they argued, was no longer ruled by a Robespierre.[6] But Smithson, like Bertie Greatheed, clearly heard "the buzz of war."[7] Time soon showed, in fact, that his zealous self-preservation was not an overreaction.

Smithson was a voracious tourist, and from the marks he made in his guidebook it seems he did pause for some sightseeing as he moved swiftly over the Rhine. The tradition of observation begun when he was still in his teens he retained all his life. He filled dozens of little pocket diaries. But these all vanished in the Smithsonian fire, and the stories they contained have been lost forever—tales perhaps from the first days of balloon flight, of the streets of Paris during the Revolution, of Vesuvius erupting or meteors "from the moon"; accounts of laboratory accidents, sudden discoveries, or even Smithson's reflections on fame, his family, and the future. His collection of books is all that remains, and from the myriad faint pencil markings in his guidebooks have to be gleaned a shadowy sense of the mind of the traveler.[8]

Smithson's marginalia reflect his Enlightenment obsessions with utility, improvement, and novelty. Outside the towns he tracked the natural resources that fueled men's fortunes—like the marble quarries of Nancy and the iron mines of Dinant—and he looked for specimens that might augment his own growing collection. He made notes on the windmills surrounding Lille, busily churning out colza oil, and the well-known pin factory at Venloo. Often it was the use of local clays or stones that gave each region its distinctive architectural flavor, and Smithson was quick to identify monuments that had been built in a particular vernacular style or tradition. He traced every town's source of water: the lavish fountains at Dieppe that gushed night and day, drawing water from a league away through subterranean aqueducts; the cisterns at nearly every house in Calais, where there were no fountains; and how at Bruges, which had no fountains either, the city was threaded with canals whose waters raced onward towards the sea. Ever on the lookout for ways to improve his health, he took care to note those mineral waters that were especially prized.

Historical events, both recent and long past, also drew his attention. At Cologne he inspected the swords that the villagers used to battle Charles of Burgundy in 1474; at Mayence he noted with interest the special currency that had been coined during the 1793 revolutionary siege against the Austrians. He took in art, admiring the high-style artifice of Rubens' *The Descent from the Cross* in Antwerp Cathedral and the fantastical Château de Retz built by the ducs of

Valois. And he sampled the gastronomic delights of each locale: the wild chicory root that was drunk instead of coffee around Liège, the duck pâté of Amiens and the white-raspberry jam of Metz. He savored the excellent haricots of Soissons, the little cakes of Nanterre, and the wine from the town of Worms so delicious it was nicknamed "the milk of our Lady."

Smithson seems finally to have been attracted by anything unusual. A distinctive ivory Christ on the cross in the Eglise des Capucins at Brussels was depicted in death with shocking realism, his mouth gaping open instead of the more customary and decorous closed position; this drew from Smithson a long dash in the margin. In the crypt of the Cordeliers at Brive, Smithson was fascinated to learn that the bodies exhumed from the tombs were discovered intact, the earth in which they lay having desiccated them without destroying them. He was equally titillated at the possibility that one of the cadavers was "la belle Paule," the famous teenage beauty from Renaissance Toulouse, so exquisitely formed that parliament had decreed she must show herself to the public at least once a week in a place that would permit the multitudes to gaze upon her.

Most of all Smithson desired information, and when his sources disappointed him he did not hesitate to unleash a disparaging critique. "No Proof," and "Nonsense," he scribbled next to the description of the astronomical clock in the cathedral at Strasbourg, which the author explained no longer worked because there were no longer men smart enough to fix it. The clock had long been considered one of the most sophisticated mechanical creations in existence; philosophers like Locke had famously employed it as a symbol of the Newtonian universe in action, with God as clockmaker and master of the intricate inner workings, and humans capable only of admiring the rotating calendars, the allegorical paintings, and the mechanical rooster which sprang to life at the ringing of the hours. Smithson, of course, had devoted his life to discovering the secrets of matter itself, in company with many brilliant colleagues; it is not surprising, he found the guidebook's statements preposterous.[9]

Amidst his touring—his taking in of pictures, sculpture, and architecture, and the natural marvels of mineral deposits, sources of springs, or particularly interesting crops—Smithson continued to muse on the notion of philanthropy. In his guidebook he was drawn to the story of the foundation of the Hospital of St. Mathias, in the ancient Roman town of Trèves, the last principal town before entering the Low Countries (now Trier in Germany).[10] Two centuries earlier a *marmiton*, or kitchen boy, had served the monks of the Abbey of St. Mathias. He left the abbey and attached himself to a nobleman, or *seigneur*, who eventually left the scullion all his worldly goods. The *marmiton* then returned to the abbey to establish a foundation for the poor, the Hospital of St. Mathias. In highlighting the story Smithson underscored the word "seigneur"—lord, or gentleman. It was a word he frequently used to describe himself, signing his letters "James Smithson, Seigneur Anglais." At Trèves Smithson seemed more interested in the role the nobleman played in the establishment of the foundation than that of the lowly kitchen boy. At the time of the guidebook's publication in 1802, more than two-thirds of the city's inhabitants were dependent upon the generosity of the convents. Here was an excellent example of a *seigneur*, like himself, whose money—enjoyed during a lifetime—had later transformed a community.

Fresh from London where he had been immersed in the foundation of the Royal Institution, Smithson was probably filled with ideas for instruments to improve society. It is conceivable he was thinking already of a forum for his own riches. He was nearing forty, unmarried and without an heir, and through his investments he was amassing a tidy fortune. Smithson's community—his family, in a sense— were his fellow savants, the people who, like him, considered themselves citizens of the globe. They believed, as Smithson wrote, that "It is in knowledge that man has found his greatness and his happiness."[11] They perceived themselves to be the future leaders of the world, a meritorious elite, engaged in a constant, ongoing dialogue on the advancement of society—wrestling with schemes for the amelioration of the poor, the diffusion of educational opportunity, the abolition of the slave trade, the improvement of agriculture, and the increase of patronage for scientific research.

By late 1803 Smithson was in Kassel, the capital of lower Hesse, a land of thickly forested hills and fertile valleys rolling golden in wheat at harvest time. Kassel, straddling the River Fulda, was a royal city, born out of a prince's Enlightenment aspirations. The houses of the new town, neat and classical, were all of stone. Wide, clean *allées* radiated out in all directions, lined with pollarded trees and illuminated by a thousand street lights. Nearby were the fashionable pleasure grounds of Wilhelmshöhe, the Versailles-like summer palace of the electors, high on a hill overlooking the city, where Smithson searched for specimens while strolling among the gothic ruins and Italian follies.

Kassel was a place friendly to the English, an area historically loyal to the Hanoverians. Much of the electorate's wealth had come from George III's hiring of Hessian mercenaries to execute his battles, especially in the American colonies. It was also a city extremely well suited to a mineralogist and collector, harboring a number of scientifically minded residents, multiple private mineral collections, an observatory, and the colossal Museum Fridericianum. One probable friend of Smithson's in Kassel was his fellow Royal Society member, the Irish chemist and mineralogist Richard Chenevix. Another Smithson friend here might have been Johann Gottlieb Groschke, the translator of Martin Klaproth's works and a member long before, with Smithson, of the Society for Promoting Natural History.[12]

Smithson seems to have based himself in Kassel throughout much of 1804. He already wished to be back in England, but the simplest way home, across the Channel, remained off-limits: "A feeble constitution makes it preferable for me to wait in Germany rather than expose myself to the rude and disagreeable passage home via the North Sea, a route I was once forced to undertake."[13] Napoleon's advances, furthermore, meant that no end to Smithson's wait lay in sight. A few months before, on December 2, 1804, in an extraordinary ceremony at Notre-Dame that borrowed elements from Charlemagne's coronation, Napoleon, wearing royal red robes and ermine, had crowned himself Emperor with a laurel wreath of gold. For Wordsworth, who like Smithson had ardently embraced the Revolution in its first years, this act was the final blow, "the dog returning to his vomit."[14] Smithson, too, had come to believe that the

> French republic sprouted up much too quickly, and on too recent ruins to be of any duration. A plant of so rapid a groth [sic] could have but very little root. It could be but a mushroom which would not survive the gloomy day w[hic]h produced it . . . The amiable part of the French character, the desire, nay the ambition, to please, is unfortunately a good resulting from an innate propensity to dependance [sic] and was it not so, french impetus is too great not to pass thro' liberty to anarchy, and recoil back from anarchy to despotism.[15]

His aspirations for the Revolution's transformation of society had faded, but Smithson, happily, was cynical enough not to miss an opportunity to profit from his perceptions of the French character. Before he had left for Europe he had wagered a friendly bet with Lord Holland over whether monarchy would return to France. With Napoleon's coronation he saw that his little one-guinea gamble was going to bring him one hundred in return, and he promptly wrote off to Lord Holland in Spain to collect on it.[16]

He continued to fill his notebooks with observations on the topography, the stratigraphy of the rockbeds, the types of industries, architecture and more. He explored Hanau and Frankfurt, the basalt quarries in Stenheim and the spa town of Wilhelmsbade, studying the volcanic evidence of the region's terrain. "Green clay found by self near Frankfort," he scribbled. "I found it adhering to/coating one side of/a mass of lava lately extracted from the earth. It had probably formed in a fissure of the lava stratum."[17]

In the spring of 1805 he headed south towards the Alps, hoping perhaps to distance himself from the convulsions of the war. At some point en route, however, a packet of papers he was supposed to receive was lost or misdirected. The loss agitated him greatly. It was important enough that Smithson began to retrace his steps, losing a week or more of travel time. And then, on a bridge over the Rhine between Strasbourg and the fortress town of Kehl, Smithson was spotted by an undercover French policeman on the lookout for runaway English *détenus*, disgraced émigrés, or potential foreign agents.[18] Smithson—a lone traveler who showed a confident familiarity with his surroundings—had the potential to be any of the three. The policeman, named Mengaud, began to trail Smithson, initiating a wild-goose chase all through the region, a two-man odyssey of furtive layovers in hotels, casinos, and bars at all hours of the day and night. The encounter proved a serious drama for Smithson, but it was nothing compared to the ordeal that awaited him, when in 1807 he decided finally to attempt the North Sea passage home to England.

Mengaud's avid scrutiny of Smithson affords us an amazing first-hand description of him at age forty. Smithson, in the eyes of a stranger, appeared fairly well built, around five foot eight inches in height, with brown hair and eyebrows, and distinctive little sideburns.[19] He was without doubt a man of fashion. He wore blue trousers and a round hat, and Mengaud was especially interested to note that his grey redingote (a double-breasted outercoat or riding coat) was American in style.

But he seemed a chameleon-like figure, able to slip amongst different national identities, befriending many and assuming their poses. At one point Mengaud "shivered with horror" to discover Smithson chatting with an émigré in the doorway of the "Auberge du Soleil d'Or" in Strasbourg; at another he saw him masterfully carrying on in German; and at yet another point he watched Smithson at a communal table in a hotel successfully pass as an émigré himself. But Mengaud heard an accent, and at night in the casino he watched

Smithson reading only the English newspapers. Over dinner at the *table d'hôte*, as the assembled raucously recapped the news of the taking of Jamaica, Smithson, Mengaud smugly told his superiors, "took the side of the English too passionately not to be one himself." He decided finally that Smithson had "all the turnings of an Englishman."[20]

Convinced his target was a spy, Mengaud slipped into Smithson's empty hotel room one night, rifled through his belongings and pocketed the passport he found nestled in the linens. The passport, which sits today in Smithson's police report in the Archives Nationales in Paris, was a single piece of paper covered with scrawled signatures, dates, and various seals. As Mengaud perused it, his suspicions grew. The passport had clearly been deliberately falsified. It appeared to have been authorized by the French ambassador in London on February 22, 1804, and by the Grand Judge in Paris on April 22, 1805. But there was no longer a French ambassador in England in 1804, and the man who signed as the Grand Judge was not the head of the police service in 1805. Both dates had actually been 1803, and Smithson or an accomplice had tampered with the passport, changing the years. Mengaud began to envisage an elaborate storyline for this Englishman who went by the name of Smithson—a story featuring a portmanteau of secret papers collected in France and ferried across the Rhine in a small boat at some unpopulated spot, and coded handshakes and messages passed between Smithson and the postilion of an empty carriage—with whom Mengaud had twice spotted Smithson talking. Mengaud filed a full report of his surveillance of Smithson, including his fantastical theories, and sent it off with the passport to the highest ranking person he could think of: the mercurial Talleyrand, Minister of Foreign Affairs.

Talleyrand turned over Mengaud's reports to the head of police in the region, giving him full power to investigate the "comings and goings" of this Mr. Smithson. Consequently, Smithson must at some point have been dragged in for questioning. His distress over a lost packet of letters, coupled with Mengaud's overactive imagination, had alarmed an entire region. The letters were most likely of a personal or financial nature, though they might possibly have contained scientific notations and observations. Count Rumford, who had a trunk of papers containing "the result of whole years of intense study and of innumerable experiments" stolen outside St. Paul's as he was re-entering London after a stint on the Continent, wrote to Lady Palmerston: "I feel myself poor for the first time in my life . . . It does not appear to me to be possible for anything to ever make me smile again, or to remove the sad gloom which overspreads the whole universe."[21] Smithson's lost material was important enough to him that he was willing to lose a week or more doubling back on his route to Switzerland. Mengaud's misinterpretation of this potential loss is predictable, since he was not of this distinct species of man, the savant. His reaction was akin to the incomprehension that greeted Smithson when he landed in Oban with the treasures that he had found on Staffa, which the innkeeper viewed as only "rocks and dirt."

Smithson, later, when he really was suffering as a prisoner of war, lamented most the potential loss of his research and work. Facing his own mortality, he worried above all for the two papers he had not yet finished, "as I should be sorry that they were all lost by my death after all the pains & time they have cost me."[22] Smithson believed that labor for the increase and diffusion of knowledge constituted man's highest calling. Its endangerment was the source of some of his deepest despair. For a non-scientist like Mengaud, on the other hand, there could only be one explanation for such concern over some lost papers: the man with the little brown sideburns, who spoke excellent German and had the airs of an émigré, was probably in reality an Englishman, and an English spy at that.

In the end the letters were never recovered, and no evidence of espionage was found. Smithson was released. His police shadow Mengaud revealed himself to be a bumbling, hapless investigator. He executed his sneaking maneuvers so leadenly that eventually the Strasbourg police hauled *him* in and demanded an explanation of his activities in the area. Smithson, too, had quickly realized he was being followed, and in Strasbourg, when Mengaud was eavesdropping through the window of the hotel bar, Smithson had given him a cheery wave. When it was all finally over, Smithson congratulated himself on having survived unscathed an encounter with the dreaded French government. The episode became primarily a farcical anecdote. "You have not an idea perhaps what a terrific object is an *agent d'Angleterre*, whose presence in a country draws down upon it the destructive wrath of the almighty one," Smithson told Lord Holland. "In a trip I took last summer to Switzerland, taken for such, I moved like a comet spreading dismay, and foreboding, it was thought, as I appeared the fall of governments and of states."[23]

Smithson ultimately carried on to the snow-covered summits of Switzerland unmolested, trying to maintain the belief that he could continue as the Grand Tourist he once had been. Through Basel, Neuchâtel, and Zurich he focused once more on augmenting his mineral cabinet. But even in Switzerland he did not find things much easier. "In Switzerland," he wrote home, "an english face had the effect of that of Medusa, and froze the blood of all who beheld it."[24]

In late July he was at Karlsruhe. The muddled Mengaud thought he had heard Smithson say he was headed ultimately for Vienna. If Smithson did intend to carry on from Switzerland to Vienna, that plan was thwarted, once again, by the depredations of the French. Napoleon, on the coast menacing England during the summer of 1805, abruptly abandoned his plans for invasion. Recasting his forces as La Grande Armée, he turned them south and sent them 200,000 strong across the Rhine in late September. On course to converge at the Danube, masses of troops marched swiftly all through the area in which Smithson was traveling, filling the roads with their rumbling caissons and seizing what food and supplies they could from the terrified locals. Napoleon had cannily predicted the Allied governments' next offensive, and the campaign he devised was unprecedented in its scale. In a rapid and stealthy attack he surrounded the Austrian General Mack at Ulm, forcing his surrender. The occupation of Vienna soon followed, as well as a series of brilliant maneuvers that culminated in the demolition of the third coalition at Austerlitz on December 2, 1805, the very anniversary of Napoleon's coronation.

Smithson was safely back in Kassel by November 1805. He remained convinced, as he told Lord Holland, that he would soon be coming home.[25] It was a hope he had cherished already for two years. He was weary of the war and eager to be in contact with friends. "Mankind has been in a state of agony from one pole to the other surely full long enough," he declared. But as long as the only route home was the dreaded North Sea passage, Smithson was willing to sit and wait. He simply was not physically strong enough to face the journey. He never wanted to repeat "the wild and endlessly-circuitous road of Embden; equally terrible in the part which is land and the part which is sea."[26] With this route, as one passenger explained, a "most fortunate passage of forty-eight hours fine weather and no hard gales" qualified as quick and uneventful; but even that often meant being "most terribly sick for the first nine or ten hours."[27] The seasickness occasioned by the rough waters seemed nearly insurmountable to the acutely sensitive Smithson, and there remained the threat of capture by the privateers skulking in the waters around England.

As the war ravaged Europe, fewer and fewer options remained to Smithson, and there was correspondingly an increasing dearth of communication. Smithson was isolated both from friends and family back in London and from the community of scientists that formed his family in Europe. The English newspapers he read in the inns and casinos where he passed his time gave him notice of those friends whose rank was such that they were objects of general attention. In this way probably he learned of the death of Lord Lansdowne and the ascension of his friend Wycombe to his father's title. But as far as personal letters went, Smithson, like most, was far less fortunate. Fanny Burney, alone in France with her French husband, lived in such a news blackout that she didn't even learn of the English victory at Trafalgar until 1812, seven years after the event.[28] When Smithson had no word from Lord Holland, he assumed that "my letters or yours, partaking in the spirit of the times, have deviated from their right road or been intercepted." He diligently wrote twice more over the next six months, near copies of the information contained in the first. Back in London Sir Lionel Copley likewise heard nothing from "Mr. Macie Smithson" on the Continent; the Royal Institution nevertheless generously permitted Copley to renew the lecture ticket Smithson had loaned him.[29] Several letters Smithson had written to William Thomson went unanswered, and he no longer even knew whether his other Italian friends were still alive. "The troubled state of Europe for so many years," he lamented, "has prevented my keeping up that correspondence with my mineralogical friends in Italy, which I should have wished."[30]

The upheaval his friends were experiencing in Italy was more even than Smithson could have imagined. The French had invaded Rome in 1798 and had, according to one disillusioned English painter, carted off everything but the Sistine Chapel.[31] The elderly Father Petrini had undergone a complete conversion to the republican cause, and his passionate embrace of Jacobinism had cost him not only his position at the Collegio Nazareno but also his entire association with the Church. Once defrocked, he slunk quietly off to Lucca, the site of his childhood. His mineral collection had perforce been left behind, and Petrini lamented its future. "Hadrian's Museum at Tivoli lasted forty years after the emperor's death," he told Fabbroni; "the collection at Nazareno won't survive forty days after mine."[32] In Siena in the spring of 1799 the French had installed the physician Paolo Mascagni in a position of authority, set forth as an example of Napoleon's prizing of science and scientists. The appointment, however, was short-lived. In late June a violent counterrevolutionary brigade from Arezzo invaded the city. The marauding Aretini turned their attention first to the Jewish ghetto, but they soon focused on the Jacobins and members of the new French administration. The hatchet-wielding mob found Mascagni at his home, which was sacked as they carried him off. At the Piazza del Campo, where the murdered Jews were being burned in a sacrificial pyre on the site of the French tree of Liberty, Mascagni narrowly escaped being caught in the hysteria. He was locked instead in a stifling, filthy prison, where he remained for months.[33] For William Thomson the arrival of the French in Naples had been likewise catastrophic, though he at least had been able to continue with his scientific work. He had hurriedly debarked with the entire English circle around Sir William Hamilton to Sicily. Secure in the shadow of Etna, and for a while enjoying the company of England's savior Nelson—then in thrall to Hamilton's wife Emma—he had carried on augmenting his volcanic collections.[34]

In this time, as Smithson called it, "of unexampled calamity," Kassel remained something of a refuge. A tiny coterie of English society was still putting on masquerades and concerts, centered mostly on the house of Mrs. Heathcote, mother of Ralph Heathcote, the young secretary to Brook Taylor, Britain's Minister Plenipotentiary to the Landgrave of Hesse-Kassel.[35] The city was also an island of quiet that allowed Smithson to carry on with his experimental work. In March 1806 he wrote to Sir Joseph Banks to announce a discovery: "a new, and perhaps it may be thought an interesting, species to the ores of lead. I have found *minium* native in the earth." Minium, or "red lead," was a lead oxide highly sought after for use as a pigment in paints, dyes, and glazes. It had been manufactured since at least Roman times, as its occurrence in nature was extremely rare. Smithson, while perusing the offerings at a dealer, thought he spied something that looked like this "factitious" or manufactured minium. It was "vivid red with a cast of yellow," in a "pulverulent state," and attached to a specimen of zinc carbonate—the very mineral Smithson had identified in 1802, later named smithsonite.[36]

Excited at his find, Smithson subjected his little specimen to a thorough battery of tests to confirm its identity. He took a few grains, placed them on a hollowed-out charcoal block and submitted them to the blowpipe, chronicling the transformations under the blowpipe's varied flames. The sample melted, contracting into a small roiling ball as the oxygen escaped, leaving only lead. "On the charcoal," Smithson confirmed, "it reduces to lead." He then approached the sample with chemical reagents, mixing up some aqua regia, in an effort to offer his readers further proof that the metal he had uncovered was lead and not one of the noble metals, such as gold or silver or platinum.

Smithson's publication provides another example of his masterful use of the blowpipe, but it also offers a window into his inventive experimental approach. With a very limited sample—Smithson apologized at the start for not being able to conduct as many experiments as he would have liked—he was able to plan a careful sequence of tests to confirm what had probably been a strong hunch from the moment he spied this curious scarlet matter on the specimen from the lead mines of Breylau in Westphalia at the dealer's shop.

Smithson was still in Kassel in the late summer of 1806, although he curiously made a point of informing one friend that he was "not resident there." It may have been that he was simply on the verge of departure. At the end of July 1806, having seen yet another summer come and go, he told his friends that he planned to travel soon to the spa town of Pyrmont. His health problems must have been acting up, and he probably intended to follow a course of the waters there.[37]

Napoleon, however, was determined to make the German states virtual colonies of France, and Smithson was inadvertently headed directly into the heart of the conflict. It would be more than three years before he finally reached the shores of England. With the dissolution of the Holy Roman Empire in the summer of 1806, and the abdication of Emperor Francis II, Napoleon reorganized sixteen of the German states into the Confederation of the Rhine. William IX, whose father had been the son-in-law of George II, owed too much to England to allow Hesse-Kassel to follow suit. Like Prussia it remained neutral. Central and northern Germany enjoyed what Goethe called "a doubtful safety."

On October 1, 1806, Frederick William III of Prussia reluctantly declared war on France in response to their violation of the Treaty of Schönbrunn. The war, once declared, was short-lived; in one spectacular week Napoleon defeated Prussia, whose army had not so long ago, under Frederick the Great, been the most famed in Europe. The crushing battles at Jena and Auerstädt laid an enormous swathe of land under French control. Virtually all the coast of Germany along the North Sea and the Baltic, including the stronghold of English trade on the Continent, Hamburg, fell to the French. Napoleon arrived in Berlin for a triumphal procession under the Brandenburg Gate and down the Unter den Linden on October 27, 1806. A month later he announced the Continental Blockade, preventing any vessel originating in Great Britain or her colonies to enter a port of the Empire. His decree signaled a blistering escalation of tactics. France was ready to deal the crippling blow to England, and it seemed she had land and power enough to enforce it.

The defeats in Prussia left Hesse badly exposed. The Hessian court rapidly demobilized their troops and tried to obscure the fact that they had been quietly supporting Austria and Prussia, going so far as to post signs along the roads proclaiming "Electorat de Hesse: Pays Neutre."[38] Failing to gain a late admission to the Confederation of the Rhine, they sought to interest Napoleon in whatever they could offer him. As Smithson had joked with Holland:

It is reported that a large body of French troops are coming here avowedly to eat, having like locusts devoured every thing in Hesse Darmstadt. A person is hastened to Paris to remercier, in the french sense of it, his Imp. Majesty for his partiality to this country. It is hoped that he has been furnished by the Elector with a sufficiency of weighty arguments to have effect, for the people here have at present scarcely enough to eat for themselves.[39]

Vivant Denon in Kassel examining pictures to take back to Paris for the Musée Napoléonienne (the Louvre), 1807.

By the beginning of November 1806 the French had taken Kassel. Prince Wilhelm fled up into the Schleswig-Holstein peninsula, to his brother's castle at Gottorf. His abandoned citizens watched as a French general installed himself in the palace. In January 1807 Dominique-Vivant Denon, the acclaimed head of the Musée Napoléonienne and one of the savants who'd accompanied Napoleon to Egypt, arrived in Kassel to survey the pictures. Fresh from his plunder of the royal collections at Potsdam and Berlin, where he had also stripped the Brandenburg Gate of its golden quadriga, he found an unexpected world of riches in Kassel. Over the course of nearly a month a delighted Denon selected his spoils from the picture gallery and the Fridericianum and shipped the material off to Paris.[40]

Where Smithson spent the winter of 1806–7 is a mystery. Only one clue sheds any light: a pamphlet in his collection on the November sack of Lübeck.[41] It recounts the final chapter in the humiliating destruction of Prussia, the story of how Blücher, unable to cross the Elbe and driven back by the French, took refuge in the free Hanseatic city of Lübeck, only to see the town invaded and pillaged. Was Smithson there? Why did he own this particular pamphlet? And why, if he had already made his way up into Schleswig-Holstein, did he not decide finally to brave the North Sea and attempt the journey home?

NINE

Vibrating between Existence and the Tomb, 1807–1810

I have been above a year, since the middle of August last year, always in hot water, & without one single moment of real peace & quiet. So much worry is more than my constitution in its present enfeebled state will be able to endure much longer. When I came here my wish, in conformity to the orders of my physicians, was to have gone to Aix la Chapelle, & the south of France in Winter, but I have totally lost all inclination to stay among the French. My wishes are now to return to England; or at the least to get set at liberty & be the master of my own person and motions.

—James Smithson to Sir Joseph Banks, September 1808

I N THE SUMMER of 1807 Smithson reluctantly turned, finally, to the North Sea passage. He had already delayed his journey several years in order to avoid the stomach-churning violence of that itinerary, which had proven such an unpleasant experience in 1797. He had lingered too long, though, and the wait would nearly cost him his life. Most of continental Europe was now under

French control. In July 1807 Napoleon had met Tsar Alexander on a raft in the middle of the Niemen River to sign the Treaty of Tilsit, in which all of Prussia's territories west of the Elbe were yielded up, cementing Napoleon's dominion of northern Europe. The route Smithson had taken home in 1797 was no longer even an option for him. Napoleon's Continental Blockade prevented any English ships from docking in ports like Hamburg, and England in turn had instituted its own counter-blockade, ruthlessly patrolling the mouth of the Elbe. All trade and travel had been shunted north into the Schleswig-Holstein peninsula, territory controlled at that time by neutral Denmark. It was there that Smithson headed.

Smithson's destination was the medieval walled village of Tönning, perched at the mouth of the Eider five miles from the open sea on the western coast of the Schleswig-Holstein peninsula, which at that moment was functioning as the unlikely epicenter of commerce for northern Europe. While Hamburg and other bustling trading metropolises shuddered to a painful halt with the war, the quiet fishing village of Tönning found itself instead in the midst of the most extraordinary boom time it ever experienced, before or since.

The harbor at Tönning, 1805.

Over the course of nearly five years between 1803 and 1807, Tönning enjoyed a fleeting golden age, when it essentially assumed the work of the massive commercial port of Hamburg. A stately new customs house was built, and wooden shacks on stilts sprang up at the exit of the harbor, bringing all the debauchery of a large port—five dance halls alone—to the village. Between March and early summer of 1807, nearly three hundred ships left Tönning's harbor for England. Americans too were actively using the route, and in August, around the time Smithson arrived there, some twenty American ships were at anchor in the port.[1] The passage was safe and flourishing. No wonder then, that Smithson, despite his reluctance to be buffeted about the North Sea, eventually turned to this route as the way home.

But as Smithson made his way up through the marshy fenlands of Danish Schleswig-Holstein in the long, still days of early August, a menacing flotilla of English ships of the line simultaneously sped across the North Sea towards an unsuspecting Denmark. England, operating on intelligence that Napoleon intended to coerce neutral Denmark into joining the French, had decided to strike preemptively— a second chapter, of sorts, to the Battle of Copenhagen Nelson had fought in 1801. Fearful that France would gain an insurmountable advantage with the control of Denmark's large navy, England began to mass troops in the area immediately following the signing of the Treaty of Tilsit. In the first days of August, George III's fleet— twelve ships of the line and numerous other smaller vessels—arrived in the sound by Elsinore.

On August 8 the British envoy Francis James Jackson met the Danish foreign minister to unveil England's ultimatum. The English tried to argue that they had been left no other course of action. Their demands, they explained, were simple: if Denmark would permit England to carry away the Danish fleet, England promised to take good care of it until the cessation of hostilities, at which time it would be promptly returned—"with all its Equipments, in as good State as it is received."[2] Denmark, a neutral sovereign state, unsurprisingly found the request outrageous. Denouncing the unparalleled arrogance and perfidy of the English, the Danish minister repaired to Copenhagen to prepare for battle. Overtures were made immediately to Paris, and on August 13 the Danish King issued a proclamation, alerting his countrymen that hostilities were imminent. Within a few days Denmark ordered its men to take arms. The English diplomacy had gone so abysmally wrong and relations had deteriorated so rapidly that Charles Fenwick, a Foreign Office attaché in Elsinore, abandoned his post for the safety of Helsinborg in Sweden.

Thirty thousand English troops landed on the mainland and began to close in on Copenhagen. Denmark reacted swiftly, issuing another proclamation on August 17, ordering the sequestration of all British property. Simultaneously, throughout the region, regardless of circumstance, the English were arrested. There was, shockingly, no warning given, no order to leave the territory. Smithson, newly arrived in Tönning, found himself seized along with dozens of others. He was thrown into a barren warehouse on the edge of town that was pressed into service as a makeshift prison.[3]

Smithson had long believed himself a victim of "the hurricane of war," tossed aggrieved onto an unwelcoming Germany back in the first days of his tour through France. But despite having been accused of being a spy in 1805, he hardly seems to have traveled with much urgency or fear. During the summer of 1807, en route to Tönning, he apparently stopped in Kiel for some time, where he found a congenial philosophical community and the facilities to conduct some chemical experiments. With his arrest in Tönning, however, must have come the realization that he had in fact been traveling these last few years as if becalmed in the eye of the storm. This desolate village in the fenlands of Schleswig-Holstein—"whose climate," Smithson railed, "is highly prejudicial to all foreigners whatsoever"—was the blinding maelstrom on the other side.[4]

On September 1, 1807, the commanders of the British sea and land forces wrote to the governor of Copenhagen offering one last opportunity to surrender the capital, to avoid "the further Effusion of Blood." The indignant city replied: "If you are cruel enough to endeavour to destroy a City that has not given any the least Cause to such a Treatment at your Hands, it must submit to its Fate; but Honour and Duty bid us reject a Proposal unbecoming an independent Power; and we are resolved to repel every Attack, and defend to the utmost the City and our good Cause, for which we are ready to lay down our Lives."[5]

A day later England began the bombardment. It lasted three days and nights and wrought devastation on Copenhagen. Two thousand were killed, and much of the city—including the cathedral and the university area—was lost to fire. Desperate to stem the civilian casualties, Copenhagen yielded up its ships. The English took control of all those that were serviceable, burned the ones in process of being built, and confiscated stores worth some two million pounds. On September 7, Jackson wrote back to his superiors in Whitehall that the capitulation of Copenhagen was complete. Papers had been signed and he was now headed home. He told the Foreign Office that he would take a boat from Tönning back to England. When Jackson tried to land at Tönning, however, his flag of truce unfurled and waving high, he was rebuffed. The English assault on Copenhagen had hardened the spirits of the Danes, and no one was permitted to come ashore.[6]

As it turned out, the capitulation in Copenhagen had been signed in ignorance of the Danish King's declaration of war. The Danes were bitterly defiant of the English presence and the enforced ceasefire mandated by the September 7 document. Even George III had questions about the morality of England's actions in Denmark. Throughout September and October Denmark seethed, and English travelers such as Smithson, caught by chance in the middle, received the very worst of this pent-up fury.

In early October the English imposed a blockade on the Eider as well, and all neutral traffic ceased. In Tönning the whaling ships bound for Greenland that had clustered at the mouth of the harbor disappeared, as did the men crowding the docks loading up provisions in barges headed for the new Schleswig-Holstein canal. Smithson and the rest of the town fell into utter isolation. Tönning's brief moment exultantly shouldering the weight of a continent's trade vanished as rapidly as it had arrived. By the end of the month an angry Denmark joined the side of the French with the signing of the Treaty of Fontainebleau, and a few days later England officially declared war on Denmark.

Throughout Denmark all the English had been swept up in the net. The arrests were violent and chaotic, and as Smithson reported, "the vigorous manner in which the English were treated . . . occasioned the death of several."[7] A mild-mannered English teacher who had been resident in Hamburg without incident throughout the French occupation was seized in neighboring Danish-controlled Altona, where he had gone to teach lessons; his arrest occasioned an impassioned twelve-page letter from a concerned Hamburg citizen. In Tönning itself, Smithson's fellow prisoners included the Englishman George Harward, a former Consul General to the Austrian Netherlands who had been unable to resist imprisonment despite broadcasting his Foreign Office connections, and an American sea captain named Reuben Smith. Harward spent fully two years as a prisoner in Denmark before finally being given permission to return to England.[8] Reuben Smith probably fared better, having the power of an indignant U.S. consul in Hamburg on his side.[9]

Letter upon letter wended its way to Danish authorities, each calling for mercy and justice. Prisoners clutched at any connection, no matter how meager, to gain a chance at freedom. The clerk to the Scottish consul to Denmark, swept up while returning from a trip to Norway, sent a plaintive message to Count Weddel Jarlsberg. "If Your Excellency recollects," the clerk beseeched him, "I am the same person who had the Honour to wait on You, when Your Excellency was in Edinburgh, to inform You about the Ship Your Excellency was to Embark in at Grangemouth."[10] Some went so far as to decry their own "vile" governments. One Englishman ingeniously offered as a condition for release to "exert every means of returning in one month afterwards to Norway unless my beloved sovereign will consent to the immediate release, as exchange for me, of one hundred of your Majesty's subjects now detained in Great Britain."[11] Another begged only, on behalf of her husband and children, to be permitted "the consolation of being Prisoners in the same House." She pleaded for compassion "for a poor family who never knew what it was to be in want of the necessaries of Life till very very lately."[12]

James Smithson was no different. His letters likewise would have appealed to a sense of honor and decency, to the old code of warfare. He was the son of a peer and a brother to a current duke. He had a fortune and a family through his maternal line that was of equally important and ancient lineage. He was, in short, an English gentleman. These distinctions had once counted for something; he believed he should have been considered above reproach. "Since equallity [sic] is abolished in France I should have expected to have met with something more regard here than I have done," he wrote indignantly, "owing to the situation I hold in life from the rank of my mother & my father."[13] He was, furthermore, desperately sick. The chaos of the arrest brought on once more his bronchial afflictions, and Smithson began frequently spitting up blood. Darkness arrived earlier each day. Rain lashed at the warehouse prison, and the wind whistled across the flat, marshy lands, bringing a damp chill to the air. Deprived of fresh air and exercise, the prisoners languished in this limbo, easy prey to the twin demons of depression and illness. Smithson knew he needed to find a way out of Tönning. "My life depended on my immediately quitting the Danish territory," he later said.

He had a doctor draw up a report documenting his poor health, which he included with his petition for freedom. Smithson asked for permission to travel to Kassel, where he still had contacts who could help him. From there, he apparently wished to go on to Paris, perhaps in the hopes of gaining safe passage to England.[14] This idea

Gillray's caricature of "An Experimental Lecture on the Powers of Air" at the Royal Institution, with Humphry Davy behind the table holding the bellows and Count Rumford standing off to the right.

The fire of 1865 at the Smithsonian, in a photograph taken and retouched by Alexander Gardner.

James Smithson, around age fifty, in a portrait painted
at Aix-la-Chapelle by Henri Johns, 1816.

was only one of several he entertained, however; he also contemplated retiring for a while to the baths at Aix-la-Chapelle (Aachen) and then eventually passing to the south of France for the winter, places where he hoped to recover his strength after the punishing dampness of Denmark.[15] But the bleak and frigid winter months advanced, and he heard nothing about his case. Desperate for help, Smithson sought some consolation in the arena that had brought him the most happiness in his life: the pursuit of knowledge.

"You will readily believe that under such circumstances I have not been able to do much for Science," he wrote to Sir Joseph Banks. "However," he hastened to add, "I wrote a paper at Tonningen a little before being taken ill, which I have promised, in a letter to M. Greville, to send him the moment I can hunt for it. I have several others in some forwardness, I have also collected a considerable mass of detached notes & observations, & I have a certain number of new substances. I have besides with me many of the papers of two more considerable works on which I have been long engaged. I wish much to get to England to arrange & finish them, as I should be sorry that they were all lost by my death after all the pains & time they have cost me." In a letter focused on securing his own release, Smithson went to great lengths to show how he continued to dedicate himself to useful research, even in the most challenging and inhospitable environment. He did not want to be forgotten by the world of science.

Unless this Tönning paper he promised to Greville is one that was lost and never published, it can probably be identified as Smithson's "On the Composition of the Compound Sulphuret from Huel Boys, and an Account of its Crystals," which was read to the Royal Society in London on December 24, 1807, and published shortly thereafter in the *Philosophical Transactions* of 1808. It was based on research he had conducted in Kiel en route to Tönning, a continuation of an analysis of the compound sulphuret of lead, antimony, and copper that had been put forward in the *Philosophical Transactions* of 1804 by his colleague Charles Hatchett. Smithson's next paper was not published until 1811 and was clearly based on work done in London. Smithson was apparently so distraught when he wrote to Banks that he forgot that he had already mailed this paper.[16]

Finally, in early spring 1808, Smithson's luck turned with the acquaintance of John Thornton, a well-connected English merchant operating in Hamburg. Thornton offered to help Smithson, and "powerfully desired to do so"; he submitted an appeal on Smithson's behalf to the French in Hamburg. But because Smithson was still under the control of the Danes there was little that could be done until he secured his own traveling papers.[17]

The promise of a plan in Hamburg seems to have effected his release. Smithson gained papers to travel and made his way towards Hamburg, clutching a letter of invitation from the French minister to the city, the venal Louis Antoine Fauvelet de Bourrienne. He was probably the "Herr von der Smissen" who checked into the Paetzhold guesthouse in Kiel on May 8, 1808.[18] During Smithson's stay in Kiel in the summer of 1807 he had probably become friends with the Danish physician Joachim Dietrich Brandis, then professor of medicine at Kiel and later physician to the royal court in Copenhagen. Brandis was in all likelihood one of those doctors Smithson referred to so proprietorially in his letter to Sir Joseph Banks—where he casually boasted, "My breast being thought in the greatest danger, my physicians were all of opinion that my life depended on my immediately quitting the Danish territory . . ." Brandis was an authority on dangerous illnesses, and he seems to have developed a special regard for his know-ledgeable English patient. In the midst of chaotic and desperate wartime, the two of them found solace in each other's conversation. Brandis left Smithson with a particularly treasured token of his esteem—a bust carved by Denmark's greatest living sculptor, Bertel Thorvaldsen, then the toast of artistic circles in Rome. It remained with Smithson all his life.[19]

Weakened and sick, Smithson finally limped into Hamburg at

the end of June 1808, anticipating only a brief stay to sort out his papers. Hamburg, overrun with French soldiers, was by then a city on its knees. It had been greatly affected by the blockade of the Elbe, and its coal, which traditionally came to the city from England, was in low supply and very hard to come by. Prices had skyrocketed; Edward Thornton, Britain's minister at Hamburg, had been constrained to maintain a tiny establishment, not even allowing himself an equipage.[20] Even before the crisis, Hamburg had not impressed some; Linnaeus, for one, had referred to the city as an open sewer. One Englishman believed it needed large impressive buildings; to describe the city to his mother, he compared it to London: "If London had not Westminster and Southwark, no docks, and only one-eighth part of its shipping, if the town were also sunk below the surface of the earth, Hamburg would be like it. In other words, London was like Hamburg three or four centuries ago."[21]

Smithson promptly presented himself in person to Bourrienne, a former schoolmate of Napoleon's and a man notoriously amenable to bribery. He assured Smithson that he "might stay in the town in perfect safety and quiet." Smithson, however, on his very way back from meeting the minister, was promptly arrested. Locked in a room with two boisterous guards, he soon relapsed into the worst of his illness, repeatedly coughing up blood. The guards stayed on through day and night, week after week, behaving "in a very riotous manner," according to Smithson, who grew weaker and more disturbed by the day. From the confines of his crowded, unpleasant room he watched July turn into August, bringing with it the ominous first anniversary of his status as a prisoner. Irrepressible embitterment clouded his thoughts. He had placed all his faith in John Thornton— a man "much employed by Government & whom I thought that I could trust"—and he had been abandoned. "I am really here in a most untoward situation," he complained to Sir Joseph Banks, "in fact an utter stranger to every body, deserted by those on whom I had depended, not perhaps to say worse, & vibrating between existence & the tomb."

Thornton's supposed betrayal played into all of Smithson's historic anxieties—his feelings of abandonment and his belief that he was entitled to special treatment but often denied it. One senses that behind the little phrase "not perhaps to say worse" lies all the venom and despair that Thornton's disappearance unwittingly unleashed in Smithson. Smithson could not have known, however, that Thornton had in April 1808 found himself, like Smithson, in hot water. Napoleon, placing the Hanseatic cities under his special protection, had specifically ordered the dissolution of the banking house Thornton & Power. The French secret police were convinced that the company, with branches in Paris, St. Petersburg, Constantinople, and Spain, was a cover for the English government, disbursing money to foment dissent and fund émigrés, spies, and recruiters. They speculated, too, that Thornton was illegitimate, from a disreputable branch of the family that had furnished Edward Thornton, England's minister to Hamburg. In Hamburg the police readily relieved John Thornton and his partners of any special privileges and immunities they had previously enjoyed. Thornton was denied access to his country house and found himself the object of particularly zealous scrutiny by the local authorities, who were eager to carry out Napoleon's wishes. In order to regain his country house, Thornton was ordered to renounce all relations with England. Smithson was an inevitable casualty.[22]

While Smithson was trapped in Hamburg, the English lurked in the waters to the north, just beyond the horizon. The coast was extensive and porous, and Napoleon, despite his conquest of northern Europe, was stretched thin, having opened up another front in the Spanish peninsula. As contraband slipped through the blockade, so too did information. English agents quietly stirred ideas of insurrection. The red-cliffed island of Heligoland, not far off the coast from Tönning, became their command center. Small boats launched frequently for the mainland, bringing papers, pamphlets, and other supplies to shopkeepers and agents throughout the north of Germany. News of Spain, news of Napoleon losing his footing infiltrated the

towns; insubordination mounted, and desertions increased. The
French in the summer of 1808 grew skittish and uneasy. Bourrienne
in Hamburg, alarmed at the insolence of two soldiers who refused
to salute their officers, ordered all who were denounced to him to
be executed.[23] Prisoners were a burden, especially English gentlemen
prisoners. Some years earlier, in December 1803, Napoleon had
decreed that all well-born *détenus* should be concentrated at the depot
of Verdun. Smithson's handlers undoubtedly felt Verdun was the
sensible place for Smithson, too. The guards continually harassed
their frail, scholarly charge with the threat of an enforced march.
Smithson, "vibrating between existence and the tomb," believed that
being dragged off to Verdun meant certain death.

Into the breach stepped another English merchant and banker,
Richard Parish. Parish's family was, like Thornton's, actively
working the trade routes around Europe. They had even begun
to focus on developing business in the United States, which Parish's
brother David was convinced was "the only country where a
person could look forward to enjoy for half a century at least, a
state of tranquility and security."[24] Richard Parish, as Smithson
told it, "hearing of my situation was indignant at it, & answering
in his person & property for my not quitting the territory of
Hamburg got the guard removed." Smithson thus found himself
"again at liberty to take a walk & a little air when my strength &
state of health will allow of my doing so, but I still remain in the
very disagreeable situation of a prisoner."[25]

Now able to move about some, and bolstered by the goodwill
and energies of Richard Parish, Smithson made strides to help
himself. Soon, in London under the sign of the Golden Bottle on
Fleet Street, "postage of a packet to Heligoland" began to be
charged to Smithson's accounts at Hoare's.[26] His bankers finally
knew his whereabouts; they funneled correspondence to him, paid
his bills. They stood ready to aid his efforts to get released. Smithson,
apologizing for his pathetic state—"I am so weak & my head is
so confused"—penned a long letter in September 1808 to Sir

Joseph Banks. He hoped that Sir Joseph would put in a good word with the Prince de Ponte Corvo, the head of the French military command in the region, as he remained "always in apprehension of their dragging me off to France." It was, however, only one element of his efforts to gain his own freedom. He did not expect, as he confided to Banks, "that it [a letter from Banks] would be sufficient for my entire release."

Smithson underestimated the strength of the international scientific community. For nigh on a decade now Banks had been laboring to keep channels of communication open between French and English men of science. Single-handedly, he had tirelessly dedicated himself to securing the safety of Royal Society members all over Europe and aiding in the release of French savants imprisoned in England. By the time Smithson wrote, Banks' efforts had gained him the unshakeable admiration of the French scientific community. He had managed to secure release of the vast natural history collections amassed by the botanist La Billardière, which had been impounded by the British after La Billardière was detained in Java with all his scientific colleagues. He had also worked every imaginable channel to free the highly regarded French geologist Déodat de Dolomieu, whose imprisonment at Taranto on his way back to France in 1799 following Napoleon's expedition to Egypt had caused a "sensation . . . in the Literary world" of London.[27] In 1801, when France's National Institute (the reconstituted Académie des Sciences) elected their new foreign associates, Sir Joseph Banks was the first to be chosen.

Smithson and his scientific colleagues had long decried the difficulties that the war had placed on their communications. When Lavoisier had been guillotined on May 8, 1794, his fellow scientist Joseph Louis de Lagrange had famously mourned, "It took them only an instant to cut off that head but it is unlikely that a hundred years will suffice to reproduce a similar one."[28] Although it was Lavoisier's work as one of the loathed tax collectors, or *fermiers généraux*, that had been predominantly responsible for his sentence, his correspondence with numerous members of the Royal Society had played no small part in his condemnation "for conspiracy with the enemies of France against the people."[29]

Despite the dangers, scientists around the world embraced their foreign correspondence with increasing urgency amidst the complications and senselessness of war. They railed against the strictures placed on their work and reaffirmed their devotion to a higher calling—the increase of knowledge and the advancement of society as a whole. "The Sciences are never at war," the English physician Edward Jenner wrote to the French Institut around 1803. "Peace must always preside in those bosoms whose object is the augmentation of human happiness." And Faujas de St. Fond, when in 1797 he finally published his account of the trip to Staffa he had taken with Smithson back in 1784, added a little postscript. Discussing the atmosphere of cordiality at the Royal Society, he noted: "The sciences, like the muses, should be sisters, and ought to know no distinction of country or of government."[30]

James Smithson ardently espoused this fraternity of science. While in Kassel in 1806 he had eagerly advanced some research for the prominent French zoologist Georges Cuvier. The work gave Smithson a chance to affirm his commitment to scientific cooperation despite the fact that their countries were at war with one another. "It seems to me, Sir," he wrote to Cuvier, "that the man of genius who through his important discoveries extends the realm of the human spirit is entitled to something more than a simple and sterile admiration. . . . The work of savants being for all nations, they themselves should be considered citizens of the world."[31] This creed, which had already sustained Smithson many years, soon took on ever more talismanic power. For it was the universal brotherhood of science in the end that finally secured Smithson his freedom.

Having received Smithson's letter, Sir Joseph Banks wrote off to the astronomer Jean-Baptiste Delambre, secretary of the French Institut, to plead "the case of James Smithson Esqr. a gentleman of property and of letters &c. and Fellow of the R. S. [Royal Society] of the class of those who labor effectively for the promotion of science." Only a few months earlier the men had been in communication regarding the plight of the French scientists François Arago and Jean-Baptiste Biot, captured in Spain while on their expedition to measure the meridian.[32] Banks lamented the restrictions that the English government had recently placed on his ability to help foreign savants. "I cannot however resist cherishing the pleasing hope," he concluded, "that my friend [Smithson] will in some way or other find an amelioration of his destinies through the intercession of those who as friends of science must also be friends to him." Banks' letter was read out to the Institut in March 1809. The following month Delambre relayed Banks' "pressing letter in behalf of his friend, reminding us of the various reasons why M. Smithson is entitled to the esteem of savants," to the minister of war. The plea of clemency for this Hamburg prisoner slowly traversed its way through the halls of government. On June 19, 1809, at the Institut meeting, Delambre was pleased to read into the record the response from the minister of war. Napoleon had formally approved Smithson's release.[33]

Smithson was once more the master of his own person—and he seems to have audaciously tested the fullness of that liberty. Remarkably, after all that he had been through, Smithson does not appear to have taken the first boat home for England. According to Walter Johnson's review of Smithson's journals (before their destruction in the Smithsonian fire), Smithson traveled between Berlin and Hamburg in 1809. Apparently, rather than scurry home to the safety of England once he'd secured permission to travel, Smithson took one last journey on the Continent, to the city of his old friend Martin Klaproth.

Why would he possibly have undertaken any travel that might have further endangered him? Prior to his arrest he apparently toured fearlessly around much of France at a time when virtually all Englishmen were locked up in depots like Verdun. With his aristocratic bearing and his excellent French, Smithson easily passed for an émigré, as the police officer Mengaud who trailed him in 1805 attested. And he had tampered with his passport, changing the issue dates to times well after the outbreak of the war, which probably gave him a feeling of invincibility. Perhaps he felt that he traveled with the status of one protected, an Englishman who had been singled out for special treatment by the French, honored with permission to pass through enemy lands—as Humphry Davy would be with his assistant Michael Faraday in 1813, or as the American diplomat Ninian Pinkney did in 1807–8. Smithson owned the book Pinkney later penned of his tour through France "by a route never performed, made with permission of the French Government," and he may even have come across Pinkney in his travels; he littered the margins of the book with pointed and vitriolic criticisms that seem motivated by real personal dislike.[34] Smithson had even been stopped by the French police and released. But all that travel had taken place before the shocking arrests in Tönning. Why Smithson, after having learned the terrible consequences of truly being caught up in the hurricane of war, would have taken any additional risks by traveling to Berlin remains a mystery. But it seems also to be a pretty telling measure of his self-assurance, determination, and bravado.

He traveled to Berlin at a pivotal moment in that city's cultural and intellectual history, and the events that occurred during this time may well have contributed in some way to Smithson's future dreams of a Smithsonian Institution. Berlin's French occupying forces had vacated the capital at the beginning of 1809. But the timid King Frederick William and his court were still sheepishly ruling from the relative security of Königsberg and continued to do so until the end of the year.[35] Inside the parlors of the city's many intellectuals, however, the air bristled with new prospects, the stirrings of Romanticism and the birth of German nationalism. Classical Berlin was a melting pot of widely varying cultures and influences. Jewish women ran some of the most learned and prominent salons in the city; the philosophers Schleiermacher, Fichte, Schelling, and Hegel were challenging the limits of Enlightenment, laying the groundwork of their idealist philosophy; reformers were setting down the tenets of the Prussian civil code; and Schinkel and other architects were designing a modern city that drew obvious parallels with classical Greece.[36] Much of the talk in this so-called Athens on the Spree was of the plan for a new university. Wilhelm von Humboldt, brother of the explorer Alexander, had recently returned from Rome to take up an appointment as head of Prussia's educational system. The German states had long been strong in learned endeavors. Humboldt's ambitious plan, however, was unlike any other. It became profoundly influential, serving as the very model of the ideal university for much of the nineteenth century, all over Europe and the United States.[37]

Humboldt's radical idea was to gather together all the learned societies and institutions of the capital under one umbrella. The new university at Berlin was to form part of an organic whole that would include the academy of sciences, the academy of arts, the observatory, the botanical garden, and the state's collections of art and of natural history. Research, for the first time, was to be included as part of the essential work of a university. Humboldt's university would be, in essence, a single, enormous foundation dedicated to the increase and diffusion of knowledge.

In the process, Humboldt envisioned that this revolutionary educational institution, this *Lehranstalt*, would restore Prussia's wounded pride. Officials planned to revitalize the state and counter the dominance of Napoleon's empire by cultivating German intellectual creativity. Humboldt hoped it would "exert a significant influence on all Germany."[38] Once given the go-ahead, Humboldt immediately began selecting the faculty for this new enterprise. He was determined to secure the cream of each profession; he wanted his choices to show that the university would be the finest ever seen. Smithson's friend Martin Klaproth was offered a prominent role. Klaproth became the head of chemistry, a position he held until his death in 1819. Lectures had already begun by the summer of 1810, as the university took firm root. Here in Berlin Smithson had first-hand exposure to the creation of a brilliant new institutional endeavor, one intended to advance knowledge and at the same time lift the spirit and life of a country.

It is unclear when exactly Smithson made it back to England. News of Napoleon's approval of Smithson's release was read into the record at the Institut in Paris in June 1809, so it is likely that sometime in the months thereafter he was given permission to travel. Assuming he then made his improbable trip to Berlin, it may well have been close to the end of 1809 before he returned to London. By what route he returned is unknown; there are few indications of Smithson's movements in these years. His bank records remain practically the only source of information regarding his activities during this time.

In September 1809 Hoare's Bank made the first payment out to Henri Honoré Sailly, a servant to whom Smithson remained connected for the rest of his life, one he remembered in his will. After the demeaning treatment Smithson endured in Hamburg he told Sir Joseph Banks that he had "totally lost all inclination to stay among the French." And yet at some point during this time Smithson took on Sailly for the intimate role of manservant or *valet de chambre*. Perhaps Smithson brought this Frenchman back with him to London as a kind of trophy. The eccentric household at Holland House boasted a number of continental servants, and William Beckford kept as one of his favored inner circle a malodorous dwarf from the Savoy named Pierre de Grailly. Henri Honoré Sailly could have been Smithson's own exotic appendage, evidence of his triumphant survival at the hands of the enemy—an acquisition to be prized perhaps much as black servants were a generation earlier; Smithson's half-brother Lord Percy, later the second Duke of Northumberland, had brought back the former slave Bill Richmond from Revolutionary America, who went on to a career as the famous pugilist, "the Black Terror."[39]

On November 30, 1809, at the Royal Society's annual anniversary meeting, Smithson was elected to the governing council. This vote was a reassuring affirmation of his colleagues' regard for him and evidence of his respected place amongst the contributing members of the society; it was probably also hearty congratulations for having survived such a long period of suffering. But Smithson was not sworn in to his place of honor with the other newly elected members in the meetings that followed the election. His own induction to the council did not take place until June 1810. He missed every single monthly meeting of the governing body for the first half of the year.

There remains no proof then that he was back in the public eye, heralded and among company. It is possible that Smithson's election to the council followed on the news that he had been released as a prisoner and was on his way home, and perhaps the fact that he was not sworn in immediately should be taken as an indication that he had not yet arrived in London. Or, more likely, he could have returned and been sequestered at home, in feeble health. Beginning in the late autumn of 1809 there are small indications of his presence in London, mostly showing that he was deeply engrossed in his laboratory work. On New Year's Day 1810 Hoare's ledgers recorded a payment to Allen & Co., which was probably the establishment of the Quaker chemist William Allen at Plough Court, a place at the heart of supplying London's burgeoning industrial community and active in a number of chemistry and mineralogy philosophical societies.[40] In February 1810 Smithson conducted some experiments on the "Fossile wood" he had picked up at Meissner. "I could not saw it. The saw was however not a good one" was his first observation; "A bit put into the flame of a candle burned with a large vivid flame & fell to a white ash. It had an odd smell" was his second.[41]

The first real indication of Smithson's re-entry into London society is the payment, on April 21, 1810, into his account of £100 by Lord Holland. The baron, who had become an important MP and opposition leader, finally ponied up the £100 he owed Smithson on their one-guinea wager over whether a king would once more sit upon the throne in France. Napoleon, having crowned himself emperor, could no longer be seen as quite the revolutionary hero that Lady Holland would have liked to have painted him. One wager still remained outstanding between them—the question of whether the Bourbons would sit once more upon the throne. Smithson had bet yes, and he surely intended to wait and see if he would collect.

On June 22, 1810, less than a week before his swearing in at the Royal Society council meeting, Smithson paid out twenty-one pounds from his Hoare's bank account to the Royal Society, in trust for the family of the late George Gilpin.[42] It was not an extravagant sum of money, but to a family which had recently lost its principal means of support it was enough to live on for several months. Gilpin's widow, the society had discovered, had been left "wholly unprovided for." She had two sons, only one of whom was employed, and five daughters. The Royal Society came together to raise support for the family.[43]

George Gilpin had been the clerk of the Royal Society for twenty-five years, and before that had served as an assistant to Neville Maskelyne at the Royal Observatory. It was Gilpin who had conducted the trials of Cavendish's experiments that Smithson had been invited to witness back in late 1787. Gilpin was never made a Fellow, though he did contribute two papers to the society deemed worthy of publication in the *Philosophical Transactions*. Gilpin had simply, quietly, for a quarter of a century, administered the business of the society. He wrote and transcribed correspondence, carried out the dogsbody work of many large-scale experiments, and calmly took care of the details when Sir Joseph Banks was out at his rural retreat of Revesby Abbey. All ran so smoothly that he faded into the background. In the end George Gilpin was so unremarkable that the Royal Society today has no biographical information on him whatsoever.[44]

With this gesture, the compassionate act of a man who had just been through his own grueling ordeal—and who no doubt felt deep gratitude to the Royal Society's president for his efforts in securing his freedom—it is safe to assume that James Smithson, Esquire, was back in the thick of things in London.

London: A New Race of Chemists, 1810–1814

"The ancient teachers of this science," said he, "promised impossibilities, and performed nothing. The modern masters promise very little; they know that metals cannot be transmuted, and that the elixir of life is a chimera. But these philosophers, whose hands seem only made to dabble in dirt, and their eyes to pore over the microscope or crucible, have indeed performed miracles. They penetrate into the recesses of nature, and show how she works in her hiding places. They ascend into the heavens: they have discovered how the blood circulates, and the nature of the air we breathe. They have acquired new and almost unlimited powers; they can command the thunders of heaven, mimic the earthquake, and even mock the invisible world with its own shadows."

—Mary Shelley, *Frankenstein* (1818)

F ROM HIS NEW rented apartments on St. James's Place, fast by the gambling dens and smoking rooms of the gentlemen's clubs of Brooks's, White's, and Boodle's, Smithson returned to the rhythms of his London life.[1] He was soon reunited with his brother Henry Louis Dickenson, and he discovered that during his long incarceration abroad he had become an uncle. Dickenson had sold his commission and retired from military life; on his last tour in India his common-law wife Mary Ann had given birth in Pondicherry to a son. The child was fair-haired and blue-eyed, with the tell-tale broad, high expanse of forehead and long, aquiline nose both his father and uncle shared. He had been christened Henry James Dickenson—the middle name a tribute, in all likelihood, to his talented, charismatic uncle James Smithson.[2]

Everywhere Smithson turned there were indications of his warm welcome back into the inner circle of high science in London. He went as Humphry Davy's guest to the Royal Society Club dinner.[3] He was elected to the Royal Society Council, a post to which he was returned the following year; he was also elected to the new Committee of Chemistry, Geology and Mineralogy at the Royal Institution, an appointment that was renewed virtually every year until the disbandment of the Committee. And his library began to fill once more with the latest scientific publications of his friends, many cordially inscribed from the authors.[4]

In print, too, Smithson received some notice from his peers. Tilloch's *Philosophical Magazine* referred to him as "this ingenious mineralogist," and a new book included him as one of the "new race of chemists' keeping Britain at the forefront of science. Smithson still believed that the work of science transcended national interests, and that scientists should be considered "citizens of the world" and benefactors of mankind. But as the war with France trundled on towards the tenth anniversary of the resumption of hostilities, this viewpoint was one increasingly in the minority. Discussion of scientific accomplishment took on a nationalistic tinge, and Smithson became one more drafted into the fray. Thomas Thomson's history of the Royal Society, published in 1812, explained how the victory of the French chemists over the doctrine of phlogiston "drove all the British chemists out of the field." It described the creation of a new nomenclature and a new theoretical system for chemistry as a humiliating setback in the history of British science and ingenuity. "By degrees, however," Thomson continued, "a new race of chemists arose . . . [T]he reverence, almost approaching to absurdity, which was paid to the French School, wore off, and the natural genius and invention of British philosophers began to appear." Thomson singled out about ten men from the Royal Society, all alive and active, whose work had "restored Great Britain to the first rank among the improvers of chemistry." Smithson was among them.[5]

Chemistry enjoyed a privileged position now, credited with a primary role in the advent of modern living. And the chemist himself had become a figure of admiration and allure, a transformation due in large part to Humphry Davy. In the years of Smithson's absence, Davy had become the most famous and celebrated chemist in England. Since his 1801 arrival in the capital as a young man of twenty-three, dreaming of "greatness and utility," Davy had risen to the heights of cosmopolitan society. His lectures at the Royal Institution were a magnet for the fashionable. Thomas Carlyle teasingly suggested that Davy had transformed the Royal Institution into "a kind of sublime Mechanics' Institute for the upper classes."[6] They "come in their carriages for their weekly luncheon of philosophy," one observer commented wryly, "just with the same intention, & with as much advantage, as they go in the evening, to hear Madame A. or Signora B. squall at the opera." Women were a large part of this constituency, and a slew of new books aimed at this audience, such as Jane Marcet's hugely popular *Conversations on Chemistry*, underscored the acceptability of such study. Davy praised women's interest, proclaiming that the study of science "refined and exalted" the imagination. Everyone could benefit from an understanding of nature's secrets.[7]

Davy's lectures ushered in a sense of wonder and awe for the quest for knowledge. "The philosopher who has made a discovery in natural science, or the author of a work of genius in art or in literature, is a benefactor," he explained, "not only to the present generation, but likewise to future ages." He cast himself, and by extension his fellow chemists, as a channeler of nature's powers, submitting to dangers and toiling endlessly in his effort to comprehend the processes of life. The scientist, he said, was a "mariner voyaging for discovery," out on the gusting ocean, and the new facts and truths he was accumulating were like the green branches that were "the omens of the land." Davy invited his audiences to marvel both at the extraordinary progress that had been made to date, but also at that which was to come. He blazed a heroic path for the scientist in society creating the romantic identity of genius that has stayed with us ever since.[8]

Smithson would have seen that the Royal Institution, with Davy as impresario, boosting the profile of people like himself who had dedicated themselves to chemistry, was now established on a firm footing. In 1810 Parliament had passed an Act establishing a single class of membership for the institution, abolishing the Proprietors, the landowning elites who had frequently bailed out the institution in moments of financial hardship. It had become a publicly owned entity dedicated to the improvement and prosperity of the nation as a whole. Davy, explaining the changes, announced that the Proprietors were "giving up their private interests for the purpose of founding what may be called a National Establishment." He told the country, "Our doors are open to all who wish to profit by knowledge."[9]

Under Davy's dynamic public leadership, the Royal Institution probably appeared to Smithson as a powerful vehicle for the promotion of science in society. The reactionary 1790s had severely compromised the movement for Enlightenment science, and many of its strongest proponents—like Joseph Priestley, or Smithson's old Pembroke associate Thomas Beddoes—had been tarred by their enthusiasms for revolution and change. Davy himself had struggled to shake off his reputation as one of those anarchic experimenters from his early successes exploring the hallucinatory effects of nitrous oxide at Beddoes' Pneumatic Institution in Bristol. But now the Royal Institution under Davy generated tremendous energy, bringing a much greater audience than before for science.[10]

Organizations modeled on the Royal Institution began to spring up across the British Isles. In Ireland the Cork Institution for the Application of Science to the Common Purposes of Life was founded by a follower of Joseph Priestley. Cornwall, Liverpool, and Manchester all gained their own versions of a Royal Institution— the Royal Institution of Cornwall, the Liverpool Royal Institution, and the Royal Manchester Institution.[11] Closer to home the London Institution for the Advancement of Literature and the Diffusion of Useful Knowledge was founded in 1805, and the Surrey Institution, dedicated to promoting scientific and literary knowledge, followed a few years later.

Smithson's naming of the Smithsonian Institution suggests that the model might have been rooted in the establishments that proliferated in these years.[12] They catered to large popular audiences, offering well-stocked libraries and dozens of lecture courses. Although lectures covered a wide range of topics—in the Surrey Institution's domed "Rotunda," for example, Samuel Taylor Coleridge talked of belles-lettres and Shakespeare, and William Hazlitt covered the English poets—they focused especially on the natural sciences.[13] These institutions provided at the same time sophisticated facilities for a corps of professional scientific researchers. In the basement of the Royal Institution, the members of the Committee of Chemistry, Geology and Mineralogy—a group which included Smithson— gathered regularly to witness Davy's work.[14] Although Smithson did not specify in his will the functions of a Smithsonian beyond "the increase and diffusion of knowledge among men," his life in London was immersed in a world where forums for the cultivation of science were flourishing—providing places both for cutting-edge investigations and for enthusiastic, growing audiences for science.

Upon his return, Smithson seems to have flung himself into the business of catching up—renewing his correspondence, updating the catalogue of his cabinet, and reading the latest literature. The scientific advances that had been made while he had been away on the Continent were dramatic. John Dalton had unveiled his atomic theory, the idea that the atoms of each element had a unique "atomic weight" and that they formed compounds by combining in small, regular numbers. His theory introduced the first mathematical theoretical underpinnings for chemistry, and Thomas Thomson promptly hailed it as "the greatest step which chemistry has yet made as a science."[15]

But perhaps the most exciting development during Smithson's absence was Davy's command of the voltaic battery. Control of this animating force had given him powers previously unimaginable. Substances that were thought elemental a few years earlier he was now able to identify as compounds—and then proceed to break them down into their constituent parts. Myriad new elements were discovered in these early years of the century. His first successes came in 1807 with the isolation of potassium and sodium. These soft metals generated dramatic reactions; when Davy threw the particles of potassium into water, they "skimmed about excitedly with a hissing sound, and soon burned with a lovely lavender light." Davy's brother described him "delirious with joy," dancing around the room, when he realized the significance of his finds.[16] He had harnessed a new tool for chemistry and cut a path forward for his fellow scientists. Priestley saw it as the way "the glory of the great Sir Isaac Newton . . . [could] be eclipsed."[17] And in France the chemist Louis Jacques Thenard when he heard of it also took to running around the room, shouting, "How beautiful! I would give my right arm to have made this discovery!"[18] In the years that followed Davy announced the discovery of calcium, magnesium, strontium, barium, and other elements. Though the periodic table would not be established properly until the 1860s, many of the pieces came together now in these first decades of the new century.

These developments led many to believe that the science was already undergoing another rebirth, just a decade or so after Lavoisier's groundbreaking discoveries.[19] New publications appeared, such as Nicholson's *Journal of Natural Philosophy*, wholly dedicated to scientific matters. New instruments were invented, new technologies mastered, and entirely new fields of study introduced. Geology, which had not even been mentioned in the 1797 *Encyclopedia Britannica*, had become its own discipline; it was given a long write-up in the next edition, in 1810. Humphry Davy delivered a highly successful series of geology lectures at the Royal Institution, exclaiming that one day the field would have its own Newton. In 1807 the Geological Society of London had been founded, one of a number of specialist societies that cropped up in the early years of the nineteenth century, but the first one to have its own journal and the first really to challenge the hegemony of the Royal Society.[20]

Smithson published three papers during these years in London, 1810 to 1814. They stand now as practically the only remaining clues to his activities and thoughts at this stage in his life. They show a man avidly reconnecting with the state of scientific knowledge. But they also reflect the interests of a man in poor health, and one who had been separated for a long time from his collections, his community, and the trajectory of his own life. His health had probably deteriorated greatly while abroad, and he appears to have kept pretty close to home. The trials of his years as a prisoner seem to have left their mark.

All three papers focused on specimens that Smithson had analyzed or collected years earlier, in his teens and twenties. "An analysis of zeolite," published in the *Philosophical Transactions* in early 1811, gave him an opportunity to recall his very first triumph, the trip to Staffa so many years earlier, at a time when that island had only just come under the scrutiny of naturalists. His analysis of ulmin and his account of a "saline substance" from Vesuvius were both based on specimens that his old friend William Thomson had sent him years earlier. The ulmin, a black gum-like substance, had been sent him "adhering to the bark from Palermo in Sicily by Dr Thomson with the following label 'Saline gum from an old elm tree under my window. Palermo June 1800.'" There would be no more packets from Dr. Thomson, however; he had died in Palermo in 1806, aged only forty-six.[21]

The papers were highly analytical works, spurred by research that others had done, which Smithson felt the need to question or to better. The zeolite paper, which was notable also for coining the term "silicates," originated with a sample the French crystallographer René-Just Haüy had sent—an indication, too, that Haüy and Smithson had managed to renew their correspondence, despite the war. The work on ulmin began soon after Smithson read an account of the substance in Thomas Thomson's new *System of Chemistry*, which described it as possessing "qualities totally peculiar and extraordinary." His friend the Berlin chemist Martin Klaproth, whose sample had also come from William Thomson, had been the first to analyze and name it; Smithson's investigations might well have been motivated by a robust sense of competition, to see if his results differed from Klaproth's. And in his third paper, the analysis of a "saline substance" from Vesuvius called vitriolated tartar [potassium sulfate], Smithson discovered "no less than nine distinct species of matters, and a more rigorous investigation, than I was willing to bestow on it, would probably add to their number."[22]

The papers, with their many references to recent journal articles, reflect Smithson's keen desire to remain current on the latest developments, and to continue to contribute to the scientific community. But in many places that we might have expected to find him active in London, there is no trace of him. He never joined the Geological Society, despite being friends with a number of prominent members and clearly keeping up with their publications.[23] The Geological Society had its roots in the mineralogical chemistry community; many of its members had been active in the Askesian Society and the Mineralogical Society, groups that Smithson, had he been in London, probably would have taken part in. Something seems to have been pulling Smithson away, detaching him from the social fabric of this community.

There are no letters from these years revealing any of the issues that might have been preoccupying him, but there are small indications of problems. After he returned to London, Smithson severed his long-standing ties with his bankers Hoare's, opening up a new account with Drummonds. Hoare's had been his bankers since his university days, and they had also served his mother and her extended family, as well as the Duke of Northumberland in his last decades. They had presumably been involved, too, in the efforts to secure Smithson's release from prison. Perhaps Smithson had become disgruntled with their performance during that time. The reason for the rupture will remain a mystery, but it must have been something quite significant.[24]

He no longer took many guests to the Royal Society. He occasionally brought his brother or his cousin Georgiana Keate Henderson's husband, and a few times he invited an as yet unidentified "Mr. Cox."[25] He sponsored no new members. Few foreign scientists were paying visits to the capital, on account of the war. The celebrated Swedish chemist Jöns Jakob Berzelius, though, was one who came to town in 1812; he was a frequent guest of Smithson's friends Humphry Davy, Smithson Tennant, and Alexander Marcet, but Smithson does not appear to have met him during this visit. Smithson no longer appeared in the Dinner Book lists at Holland House, nor did he form a part of the King of Hearts—the informal conversation club of which Lord Holland and Smithson Tennant were members, along with a number of other men Smithson knew. And Smithson was most especially absent from the valuation of his close friend Charles Greville's mineral collection—a collection to which Smithson had contributed and knew intimately.[26]

Greville had died in May 1809, while Smithson was still away, and for a year his villa at Paddington Green had been shuttered and closed, its furniture, pictures, books, and wine all inventoried. For a week in the spring of 1810 a group of eminent scientists entered the gloomy, abandoned house at the direction of the House of Commons to assess Greville's extensive mineral collection. Most of the men appointed—Charles Hatchett, Esq., the chair of the group; the Comte de Bournon, the French émigré mineralogist Greville had supported during the Revolution; Richard Chenevix; Humphry Davy; Robert Ferguson; William Hyde Wollaston; and Dr. Babbington—were acquaintances of Smithson. And Smithson was soon serving with a number of them on the Royal Institution's new Chemistry, Mineralogy and Geology Committee, which was chaired by Davy. This group, admittedly, could have been formed while Smithson was still away on the Continent. Its evaluation was carried out after he had returned, though, and Smithson was notably missing from this clique.

The assessment of Greville's mineral cabinet was very much of the Establishment and for the nation. As Greville's brother Robert said, Greville had been keen to see the collection go to the British Museum, and thus be "secured, to the advantage of the British Nation, & perpetuating the Memory of the Person, by whom this Collection had been so industriously, & scientifically made [emphasis Robert Greville's]." The committee stated in their report that the collection, numbering some twenty thousand specimens, scientifically arranged, had been "selected with very great Judgement, both as to their utility & beauty." In the end, the men concluded, "they considered the Entire Collection to be equal in most & in many part superior to any other similar Collection which any of these Gentlemen have had opportunity for viewing in this & other Countries." They valued it at more than £13,000. Parliament promptly allocated the money, and Greville's minerals were purchased for the benefit of the nation.[27] The British Museum, long disparaged for its inadequate mineral cabinet, finally owned a collection worthy of the country.

Greville's cabinet consisted of many large, spectacular specimens, eminently suited to a national collection. Smithson might well have believed his own collection was of great importance, too, for different reasons, geared as it was for scientific research rather than show. He had annotated his finds, attaching little pieces of paper to each specimen, and he had also prepared a written catalogue, where each specimen was numbered and described. As a book he owned on building a useful mineral collection explained, "All specimens must be numbered and strictly described in a register. Every mineral collection without such a register is like a body without a soul."[28]

What did Smithson imagine was the future of such a collection as he was building? Was he thinking about the disposition of his own life's work, imagining what place might best benefit from his labors?

Although there is little beyond his published laboratory work that remains from these years, it is evident that Smithson was still expanding his circle of scientific acquaintances and reaching out to cultivate the next generation of scientists, an activity he pursued later in Paris with tremendous energy. He met the young Irish geologist William Fitton, who had come to London in 1809 to study medicine.[29] And he became friends with Sir Alexander Johnston, a neighbor in St. James's who had recently returned from a stint abroad as the Chief Justice of Ceylon, and had a number of interesting mineral specimens for Smithson's cabinet.[30] Smithson also spent time with Edward Howard, younger brother of the Duke of Norfolk and author of a landmark paper on the chemical analysis of meteorites. Howard was best friends with the chemists Wollaston and Smithson Tennant, men Smithson was presumably seeing regularly in London.[31]

Smithson, like Tennant and Wollaston, was still pursuing micro-chemistry. He still believed that his work was leading him towards a serious contribution, something of real potential. And he felt that his way of working, on "a very diminished scale of experiment," was "highly to the advantage" of chemistry and mineralogy.[32] There were some, however, who couldn't see the point of such work; Coleridge dismissed it as "empirical compilation," and wondered how his scientific friends could imagine that the solution to nature's secrets would be found by accumulating "a cumulus, a Rubbish Hill, of Descriptions of the appearances which this bit of mineral and that, and of another only to the ten thousandth presents or may be by fire, & chemical tests—be made to assume." Coleridge sought instead a unity of science and the spiritual. His was a philosophical hunger that could perhaps have been sated more readily by the spectacle of Davy's colossal battery at the Royal Institution, which Davy was using to explore a new theory of the affinity of matter.

Davy's work also lay at the heart of the rivalry with the French. Davy with his battery, Thenard and Gay-Lussac with theirs on the other coast, were, it was said, like Wellington and Napoleon, generals squaring off. After the French had awarded Davy their highest honor for his electrical discoveries, Napoleon had underwritten the cost of the French one to compete. No such governmental support was forthcoming in Britain, and so Davy raised money amongst his genteel audiences, telling them that the voltaic battery was "an alarm-bell to experimenters in every part of Europe."[33]

Gentlemen scientists—men with wealth at their command—began to work on obtaining their own batteries. J. G. Children, for example, built one for his well-equipped laboratory in Tunbridge Wells, a place where Davy came occasionally to work. The Quaker chemists at Plough Court set one up as well. But the Royal Institution's battery was to be larger than all of these, capable of experiments beyond those that had previously been conceived. Smithson, with his wealth, certainly could have been one of the gentlemen patrons like Children underwriting the latest technology. He continued to work instead in an older tradition, grounded in the Enlightenment ideal of science as a civic enterprise, with simple equipment accessible to all.

But Davy's ability to attract support for large-scale electro-chemical work marked the crumbling of the old Enlightenment way of science. There were, finally, limitations on the contributions that an individual with small, typically portable, instruments could make. In the promise of Davy's battery was foretold the end of an era, and the beginning of modern, institutionalized, large-scale laboratory-based science.

ELEVEN

Paris: Private Vices, Publick Benefits, 1814–1825

Some years since in Paris I made the acquaintance of a distinguished foreigner, of great wealth, but in wretched health, whose life, save a few hours given to repose, was regularly divided between the most interesting scientific researches and gambling. It was a source of great regret to me that this learned experimentalist should devote the half of so valuable a life to a course so little in harmony with an intellect whose wonderful powers called forth the admiration of the world around him.

—François Arago, speaking of Smithson, 1836[1]

A T THE END of March 1814 the allies marched into Paris. News of Napoleon's subsequent abdication soon reached London, and three euphoric nights of illuminations followed. At Carlton House, home of the Prince Regent, sparkling lights looped around the columns in front and along the roof and cornice lines. Drunken shouts of joy and hoarse huzzas joined the ruckus of drums, trumpets, bells, and pistol shots to fill the skies above Pall Mall. Days later a frail Louis XVIII, who had been waiting out the war in Buckinghamshire, arrived in the metropolis, the first King of France to enter the city in some four hundred years. Tens of thousands, many wearing the Bourbon white cockade and a sprig of laurel, thronged the roads as far as a mile outside London to catch a glimpse of him. They perched in trees, lined walls and roofs, and crowded every window along the procession route.[2]

Smithson, in a manner that cannot have endeared him to his old friend, promptly called in the bet he had wagered with Lord Holland over a decade earlier: one guinea on one hundred that the Bourbons would be restored to the throne. Before the peace was even officially signed on May 30, Smithson had pocketed his winnings and was back in Paris.[3] Once more he formed part of an enormous wave of English tourists eager to soak up French culture. "Where are the French?" one traveler wrote home to his wife. "Nowhere. All is English; English carriages fill the streets, no other genteel equipages are to be seen. At the playboxes all are English. At the hotels, restaurateurs—in short, everywhere—John Bull stalks incorporate."[4]

Smithson was undoubtedly swept up in the social gaiety, attending salons and parties, touring the Louvre with all its looted works of art, and gambling in the city's glittering gaming houses. The streets overflowed with the glint of swords and the colors of all the Allied armies. High-ranking officials and nobility from all across Europe had arrived for the festivities marking the restoration of the monarchy. That winter, it was said, there were more balls than had ever before been held. The world was waking as if from a dream, *Galignani's Messenger*, an English paper in Paris proclaimed; France had "hurled from his throne the tyrant, who, vampyre-like drained her of her best blood . . . and the native princes of the French nation are recalled to the throne of their ancestors." The stage to which they returned had changed dramatically. Paris was littered with marble monuments to Napoleon's aspirations for an imperial capital— triumphal arches, new bridges over the Seine, the arcaded rue de

Rivoli, and classical temples such as the one for the Bourse. The new regime immediately set to dislodging the symbols of its predecessor. The statue of Napoleon atop the Colonne de la Grande Armée was toppled; the golden quadriga stolen from Venice pulled down from the Arc du Carrousel; the "N"'s on the buildings, marks of Napoleon's dynastic aspirations, lifted off; and in the carpets and tapestries of the palaces the bees and eagles—his emblems—were embroidered over with the royalist fleur-de-lys.[5]

Smithson probably watched this activity with wry amusement, having predicted as much, a full decade earlier:

> To reinstate former institutions is the mode by which nations
> endevour [sic] to return to former times, to recall former
> happiness, and avert those further evils with w[hic]h innovation
> is still pregnant. Such was the conduct of the English in the
> time of Cromwell, such will be that of the French in the time
> of Buonaparte. The Bourbons will reascend the throne of
> France, amidst the acclamations, the sincere and harty [sic]
> acclamations of the whole nation.[6]

Smithson's reconnection with Paris was not exactly like that enjoyed by most other English visitors. His reacquaintance with the city was above all a reunion with the community of scientists from whom he had been separated by the wars. While the majority simply marveled at the splendor of the gas lamps that illuminated the Passage des Panoramas in 1816, for example, the first gas lighting of a public place in Paris, Smithson was interested in the mechanics of the system and was a friend of the Englishman who had arranged it.[7] Paris lay at the center of scientific discourse, and every significant figure passed through the city at some point. Smithson's circle in Paris was large, and it included many of the most important people. Some of them, like Berthollet, Haüy, and Cuvier, he had known already twenty years or more.

Chemistry in Paris was flourishing, and the scientific community enjoyed a thriving day-to-day existence. "I am living entirely among 'soda' and 'potash'—between [Louis Jacques] Thenard and [Joseph Louis] Gay-Lussac," wrote the German explorer Alexander von Humboldt after settling in Paris in 1808. "'Ammonia,' M. Berthollet, comes to see us occasionally; and then we all think ourselves to be hydrogenated."[8] Jöns Jakob Berzelius exclaimed upon his arrival to the city in 1818, "The amount of work in chemistry that is done in Paris is completely incredible. I believe that there are here more than 100 laboratories devoted to research."[9] The center of much of the activity was the Société d'Arcueil, which had been set up by Berthollet and the physicist Simon Laplace at their neighboring villas in the countryside outside Paris in the first years of the century. Berthollet and Laplace provided critical laboratory space, a place to share ideas and "cook muck" together, as Berzelius described it. The Société d'Arcueil provided France its first opportunity for something like a shared research program to arise. They founded their own journal and vetted each other's papers, which were then often delivered at the weekly Monday seances in town at the Institut. The members of the society were mostly brilliant young "polytecniciens," men who had trained at the Ecole Polytechnique and would go on to play a tremendous role in French science throughout the first half of the nineteenth century. Smithson, perhaps through introductions forged in the pastoral Arcueil, became friends with many in this next generation—the physicist and chemist Joseph Louis Gay-Lussac, the astronomer François Arago, the mathematician Jean-Baptiste Biot, and the chemist Pierre-Louis Dulong in particular.[10]

At least one account of Smithson's presence at a gathering of the Société d'Arcueil exists, a visit in the autumn of 1814, recorded by Sir Charles Blagden, who was then staying with Berthollet. Smithson arrived in Arcueil accompanied by the sloppy, genial Smithson Tennant, who was in France on a brief tour, having just completed teaching his first course of mineralogy at Cambridge (Tennant's idea of packing for a trip was to dump the contents of his dresser drawers into his tablecloth).[11] Many of the society's regulars were in attendance, including Laplace, Gay-Lussac, Arago, Dulong, and Humboldt, who was in the midst of preparing the account of his epic journey to South America for publication.[12]

Although Blagden did not describe the specific conversation of that evening, beyond mentioning how much Humboldt "talked away as usual," his diary is filled with the ideas that were percolating at the time—topics that likely reflected the conversation in the circles in which Smithson moved. Blagden was immersed in the recently published folio volumes of Napoleon's 1798 expedition to Egypt, in which Berthollet had played such a leading role; the archeological discoveries documented in these volumes fueled the Egyptomania that dominated the decorative arts and architecture of the early nineteenth century. Entering Berthollet's study was in fact like taking a fantasy trip to Egypt. The walls were painted with scenes of the ruins at Thebes and Dendera, and the furniture was all Egyptian in style, including a desk specially built for the folios in the shape of a temple.[13] Another topic of fascination was the Hottentot Venus, who was then being displayed at the Jardin des Plantes; the discussion of her physiognomy, though, because it was held in mixed company, was all "kept within the bounds of decency."[14] There was talk, too, of Britain's torching of the U.S. capital city of Washington, which was being trumpeted as a great vindication and triumph in the English papers; the men of science, in contrast, frowned upon it. "Told of capture of Washington by English, blowing up the Capitol, & proceeding to Baltimore," Blagden recorded. "We all agreed that Baltimore [was] a proper subject of attack [because of its port] but better have left Washington alone: it w[oul]d rather incite the people against us."[15]

The idyll of these days of scientific camaraderie was shattered a few months later, when Smithson Tennant, en route back to England in February, was thrown from his horse near Boulogne. He died almost immediately. His loss must have been especially devastating for Smithson, who had passed so much time with Tennant in those last months of his life. In Paris they had worked together; the purpose of Smithson's 1819 publication "On Native Hydrous Aluminate of Lead, or Plumb Gomme" was to assert Tennant's posthumous priority over the analysis in the face of a publication by Berzelius.[16] And they had played together, both being lifelong bachelors with a love of gambling. They spent one of Tennant's last nights gambling in Paris, in fact, and the news that Tennant had beaten Smithson—to the tune of £100—had quickly made the rounds among their friends. Blagden, still with Berthollet out at Arcueil, was disgusted; he wrote in his diary, "Tennant & Smithson at gaming house: former won latter lost. . . . Told B[ertholle]t what I had heard of Tennant, added that I knew him to be a man of property but could answer for no one who went to a gaming house."[17]

Immediately following the "catastrophe" of Tennant's death, as one of Smithson's friends described it, "came that of the resurrection of Bonaparte, the tiger who broke his chains to come torment mankind."[18] The news of Napoleon's escape from Elba struck terror in the hearts of the royalist bourgeoisie and frightened many in the scientific community as well. Berthollet especially felt himself to be in grave danger. He owed his phenomenal wealth to Napoleon's patronage, the fruit of a relationship built in Egypt. In publishing the first memoirs of the Société d'Arcueil he had virtually dedicated the work of the group to Napoleon. At the time of the allies' entry into Paris in 1814, however, Berthollet as a member of the Senate had been forced to sign a document deposing the Emperor. Napoleon, reflecting on these events towards the end of his life, in the purgatory of exile on St. Helena, "was often heard to exclaim— 'What Berthollet! . . . on whom I thought I could rely with such confidence!'"[19]

Napoleon's landing in France, on March 1, 1815, and his uncontested march up to Paris, which he entered triumphant twenty days later, sent the English racing for home. The road to Calais became "one immense length of cavalcade." Every horse, donkey, and mule was pressed into service; there was "not a horse to be had" in Paris, Lady Dalrymple Hamilton wrote in her diary.[20] It would have been natural for Smithson to have returned to England at this time, as a frightened Blagden and hundreds of others did. Everyone was haunted by images of a repeat of the random imprisonment of all English citizens, the march to Verdun that had followed the renewal of hostilities in 1803. Smithson was elected once more in June 1815 to the Royal Institution's Committee of Chemistry, Geology and Mineralogy, which suggests that he might have been in London at this time.[21] His bank ledgers at Drummonds, however, do not yield any indication of his living locally. They are filled only with charges for letters of credit. The biggest outlays in the months prior to Napoleon's resurgence are to the French banker and bon vivant, Jacques Récamier, husband of the glamorous hostess, Madame Récamier—which raises the interesting possibility that Smithson enjoyed the company of one of the most celebrated salons of Paris.[22]

The defeat of Napoleon at Waterloo on June 18, 1815, marked the end of the Hundred Days and diminished once and forever Napoleon's hold on the imagination of Europe. The fallen emperor returned to Paris, where he attempted to arrange passage to the United States. Such a sanctuary was not to be, however, and at length he gave himself up to the British Navy. For Smithson, who saw the imprint of his ancestry writ in the world around him, it must have seemed inevitable that the ship that carried Napoleon off to his permanent jail on the remote island of St. Helena was called the *Northumberland*.

Whether Smithson returned to London during the Hundred Days or not, he soon settled himself completely in Paris, where he remained virtually until the end of his life. There were probably many reasons why Smithson chose France as his permanent home. It was much easier on this side of the Channel to live lavishly on less money. Paris and Boulogne were in fact havens for English gentlemen like Smithson's friend George Mills, who were having difficulty affording their lifestyles in England. Mills, who called on Smithson in Paris, was so profligate he was even accused of having become a Member of Parliament solely in order to avoid going to jail (MPs were not subject to imprisonment for debt).[23] Sir Charles Blagden, too, chose to settle mostly in Paris, for much the same reason. One English friend wrote to him: "You judge most wisely in my opinion to prefer being where you are [Paris], & if you invest 7 or £8000 in French securities you may there enjoy the income of it & find that quite enough for a Philosopher. . . . were I younger & in better health I would not have a shilling in this country nor stay in it a fortnight. The best plan would be to have one's property in America which seems very flourishing, & to live, not there, but in almost any part of Europe except England . . ."[24]

And Smithson, always the outsider, probably took easily to the role of foreigner. Davies Gilbert (né Giddy), seeing him late in life, after years on the Continent, observed that Smithson had "manners and habits more foreign than English."[25] What family he had left was also here, as his brother Henry Louis Dickenson had chosen to settle in Paris, with Mary Ann and their child, Smithson's nephew, eventually ending up in a place near the site of the old Temple on rue Charlot.[26]

But, above all, Paris was a place where the stigma of illegitimacy did not loom over Smithson. Here he was simply an alluring figure, "a distinguished foreigner, of great wealth," as his friend Arago recalled. Styling himself a "Seigneur Anglais," he lived with more than one servant, moving often from one large furnished apartment to the next, much as he had in London in years past.[27] And immediately upon his arrival in freshly monarchical Paris, he added an aristocratic "de" to his name, becoming "Monsieur de Smithson."[28]

This pompous inflation of his name, and with it the ironic transformation into patrician elegance of a name that in England telegraphed illegitimacy, belies the fact that Paris completely freed him of the gnawing knowledge that he was not heir to anything. The emotional needs that haunted Smithson in England appear to have plagued him still in France. In the books he bought during these years he invariably, poignantly, marked the margins whenever the Northumberlands were mentioned. He lined the passages of Louis

Dutens' book that mentioned the extravagance of his father's expenditures, and in a guidebook description of Waterloo—"the spot on which the battle was lost, and won, that has given peace to the world"—Smithson noted the hotel the Duke of Wellington had used as his headquarters; it was from here, the text explained, that the great general had "sent his important despatches to England by Major Percy [Smithson's half-brother]."[29]

Smithson commissioned at least two portraits of himself at this time, motivated perhaps by feelings of mortality. In 1816, while on a trip to Aix-la-Chapelle, he had himself painted by the miniaturist Henri Johns. This half-length portrait, in which he gazes penetratingly at the viewer, may well be one that he gave to Margaret Marriott, the mother of his half-sisters Dorothy and Philadelphia Percy.[30] A year later he commissioned Pierre Joseph Tiolier, who had just retired as Engraver General of France, to make a bust medallion. It shows him in profile, and on the reverse he attached a little tag which read, "My likeness."[31]

By the time Smithson left for France he had apparently decided on the Royal Society as the future repository for much of his fortune. He intended his money to be devoted to "the publication of scientific memoirs and researches." As scientific research was not yet the object of extensive philanthropy, Smithson was probably confident that posterity would laud his generosity and good sense. His name would be repeated through the ages, embossed perhaps on the front of publications, gratefully acknowledged at the presentation of new work. He would be linked to exciting future discoveries, his name identified forever with the support of science and the quest for knowledge. The Royal Society, as the oldest and most reputable establishment in England dedicated to fostering the promotion of science, and one that had early recognized Smithson's talents, was a natural beneficiary of his largesse.

Smithson's relationship with the Royal Society, however, seems to have come to an abrupt and stormy end. The dispute apparently occurred, according to the physicist Sir Charles Wheatstone, in the late 1810s when Smithson "became offended with the [Royal Society] Council for having stricken out some sentences from a communication which he presented."[32] The famed Swiss naturalist Louis Agassiz's telling of this conflict—the only other account of the incident—differed slightly. He said that "Smithson had already made his will and left his fortune to the Royal Society of London, when certain scientific papers were offered to that body for publication. They were refused; upon which he changed his will and made his bequest to the United States."[33] The details of the controversy are lost to posterity, unfortunately, as no trace of the episode remains in the Royal Society archives. The Smithsonian learned of the story first through Wheatstone, around 1870; Agassiz's reminiscences were published much later, in *Science* in 1919. If Wheatstone's reflections are the more accurate, then the conflict might well have erupted over Smithson's last publication with the Royal Society, "A Few Facts relative to the Colouring Matters of Some Vegetables," which was published in 1817.

"A Few Facts" is a minor paper indeed to have elicited such a calamitous rupture, and Smithson essentially admitted as much. In the opening paragraph he explained that he was presenting the work not because he had conducted new research or because he was interested in investigating the topic further; on the contrary, he said, "I have now no idea of pursuing the subject." He made the contribution because he wanted to be useful. He thought that some of the observations he had recorded were worth distributing for the use of others: "In destroying lately the memorandums of the experiments which had been made, a few scattered facts were met with which seemed deserving of being preserved." The paper described Smithson's investigations into the natural coloring of a variety of organic matter, including red cabbage, mulberries, and violets, many of which acted as indicators for pH levels. "Is the colouring matter of turnsol a compound, analogous to ulmin, of a vegetable principle and potash? Its low combustibility gives some sanction to this idea," Smithson asked, in an observation typical of the paper. Perhaps some "few scattered facts" like these were censored by the Royal Society Council prior to publication, causing Smithson to take offense.

There are other indications, even from the scant archival material that remains from these late years, of how acutely sensitive Smithson was to the handling of his message and reputation. He was often driven by a desire for retribution, a patterning impressed upon him perhaps by his mother's besieged perspective on the world; "the man who feels," he had written years earlier, "does not sit down easy under the sense of being wronged and nor my family, or myself, have been inured by habit to the sensation." When he had first arrived in Paris, the *Journal de Physique* had just published a French edition of his paper on ulmin. Smithson was unhappy with the translation, however—enough so that he acted as his own translator for the French edition of his zeolite paper, which followed in August. He submitted a lengthy list of the errata he had found in the ulmin piece, which was published in a subsequent issue. But he quickly found fault with that, too. In his own personal copy of the printed corrections, Smithson scribbled further revisions to the published list of errata—amendments, of course, that no one would ever have seen.[34] The effort is typical of the intensity Smithson brought to his experimental practice, the constant checking and testing of his work. But it seems also an indicator of how very easily slighted he was, and his defensiveness appears only to have grown stronger as he aged. "There may be persons who, measuring the importance of the subject by the magnitude of the objects, will cast a supercilious look on this discussion," he stated testily towards the end of one of his publications; "but the particle and the planet are subject to the same laws; and what is learned upon one will be known of the other."[35]

Whatever the details of the conflict with the Royal Society, the break appears to have had a galvanizing effect on Smithson. The Royal Society's publication organ, the *Philosophical Transactions*, had served as Smithson's primary publishing venue for all his life. Now he looked elsewhere for an outlet. And while he had typically published a paper in the *Philosophical Transactions* every few years, after this slight Smithson began publishing with a vengeance. These years in Paris, which lasted now practically until the end of his life, were a fury of productivity, despite his declining health. Seventeen of his twenty-seven known published papers were written in this time, a period of only six years. In 1819, his analysis of a native sulphuret of lead and antimony, for example, was followed three days later by his paper, "On native hydrous aluminate of lead, or plomb gomme." Likewise, "On the Detection of very Minute Quantities of Arsenic and Mercury," and "Some improvements of lamps," both debuted in August 1822. The following year, 1823, saw six of Smithson's papers reach publication—from "A means of discrimination between the sulphates of barium and strontium" to "An improved method of making coffee."

And though he wrote them in Paris, he continued to focus on English journals as the organ for his writing, as if driven by a desire to prove his worthiness, to show his English colleagues that they had misjudged and undervalued him. When in 1823 he identified chloride of potassium, "a new species in mineralogy," in the veins of "a red ferruginous mass . . . which was said to have been thrown out of Vesuvius during a late eruption," he decided to donate the type specimen to the British Museum. In 1823 he was still thinking of the British Museum as the repository he wished to augment, the place of record for his finds and discoveries.[36]

In these last years, however, Smithson's health caused him endless trouble, and it was primarily gambling that eased his physical sufferings. Smithson had a liking for "Rouge et Noir," and needed "the excitement of the game."[37] Risk had probably been an important part of chemistry's allure for him, the exhilaration of discovery in the laboratory heightened by the danger of explosion, the thrill of specimen-hunting in the field by the perils of an unknown cave or crumbling cliff-face. Now in his old age, Smithson seems to have found that rush primarily in gambling; it was, he said, the one thing that kept his mind off his feeble state. But by the 1820s Smithson's gambling was spiraling out of control. "I keep such very late hours," he wrote to Berzelius, apologizing for not having seen his friend in such a long time, "& generally rise so late that I have indeed no day left."[38] His friend Arago despaired to see so talented a mind wasted. He watched as Smithson, whose wins and losses frequently canceled each other out, began to believe that he could beat the bank "largely through a run of luck." Arago decided to stage a kind of intervention. To Arago, the "analytical formulas of probabilities offer[ed] a radical means, the only one perhaps of dissipating this illusion." And so he proposed to Smithson "to determine in advance, in my study, the amount, not merely of the loss of a day, nor that of a week, but of each quarter. The calculation was found so regularly to agree with the corresponding diminution of the bank-notes in [Smithson's] pocketbook that a doubt could no longer be entertained."[39] Chastened by this presentation of scientifically gained evidence, Smithson curtailed his gambling. He could not, as he confessed to Arago, give up the game of chance completely—it was too effective a palliative—but he could set limits on how much of his fortune he was going to commit to the green-baize tables.

The social nature of scientific interaction in Paris, as evidenced by Arago's playful intercession, also seems to have bolstered Smithson in his last years, when he was frequently debilitated by his illnesses. In the winter months he kept a small portable bed made up in the room he occupied during the day.[40] Colleagues dropped by for breakfast, and he invited them, too, to join him "for a very plain dinner." Some came seeking encouragement from Smithson; "I work incessantly trying to verify my first observations," the young chemist Antoine-César Becquerel explained in a note he left at Smithson's door. Others left seeds of inspiration. "M. Ampère, a few days ago, accidentally in conversation, mentioned a fact to me which much excited my attention," Smithson related in the introduction to his paper "On Some Capillary Metallic Tin."[41]

And still others, like the Danish chemist Hans Christian Oersted, came to observe Smithson's laboratory work. Oersted was in Paris for several months in the winter of 1823, where he was received as a celebrity, having a few years earlier discovered electromagnetism; his research had sparked a flurry of investigations into electrodynamics, inquiries that led ultimately to the technologies behind the radio, the generator, and much else. "Among my new acquaintances is the English Chemist Smithson," he wrote home to his wife. "Recently, I spent 3 hours with him in order to understand his method of experimenting with very small amounts. The tools he uses cost hardly a Daler [two Danish crowns]. Some of them are so small that children would regard them as toys, but he uses them with the greatest skill. He often yields the constituents of amounts so small you can scarcely believe, amounts that often do not weigh $\frac{1}{10}$ gram."[42] Smithson took tremendous pleasure in "the great beauty of deriving knowledge from so diminutive a source." Already by 1819 he boasted that his experiments were being carried out on "particles little more than visible."[43]

In Paris, as Oersted discovered, the scientific community passed their days in scientific conversation and their evenings at parties. Most houses had an evening of the week when they regularly entertained; Georges Cuvier held enormous Saturday Receptions, filled with ministers, scientists, and men of letters, and Lavoisier's widow hosted concerts every fortnight, as well as salons twice a week; Smithson seems to have often hosted gatherings on Wednesdays.[44] "Once you are introduced into a home," Oersted explained to his wife, "you can therefore without notice go there such an evening without grievances. You leave again when you want to without ceremony. You may stay for $\frac{1}{4}$ of an hour or two to three hours, as you like. You may therefore easily, if you want to, visit several parties in one evening."[45]

Smithson's home was open to a liberal mix of scientists, philanthropists, reformers, radicals, and eccentrics, based on the calling cards and clipped signatures in the Smithsonian archives and on the inscribed books in his library. The philanthropist Comte Charles-Philibert de Lasteyrie du Saillant was apparently a regular.

He had opened the first lithography workshop in France, where the illustrations for many natural history books by Cuvier and others were printed, and he was also a founder or director of the Philanthropic Society, the Society for the Encouragement of National Industry, and the Society for Elementary Education.[46] The elderly Jens Wolff, who had served in London as Danish consul, gave Smithson a copy of his book *Runakefli le Runic Rim-stock*, an investigation of the mythological figures depicted on ancient Northern wooden calendar staves. And the Italian political intriguer and firebrand César Airoldi, who had been forced into exile after the Neapolitan Revolution of 1820–21, was another who called on Smithson. He had been a dedicated mineral collector in Sicily in the late 1790s, but he was now immersed in politics, and his efforts to raise money for the cause back home made him the subject of frequent surveillance by the French police.[47]

Perhaps the most curious figure known to have been in Smithson's orbit was the young Pierre Henri Joseph Baume, born in Marseilles, the son of a wigmaker freemason who had abandoned his family. Baume was excitable, naive, and somewhat paranoid, but he managed to ingratiate himself into many elite positions—from tour guide for the English explorer John Guillemard (Davies Gilbert's brother-in-law) to secretary to the cosmopolitan Count Castelcicala of the court of the Kingdom of the Two Sicilies. Baume made himself wealthy in the meanwhile, trafficking in state secrets and acting as a debt collector for the Prince Regent. In Paris he found work through a friend whose job was making certificates of loan for the Spanish court. How Baume and Smithson came to know one another is a mystery, but they seem to have met by 1822; it is very likely that Baume was behind Smithson's purchase in 1822 of Spanish stock.[48]

Awed by Smithson, Baume soon became something of a disciple. Throughout his life he called himself by a slew of false names, "Bold Honesty," "Mr. Browne," "F. Mason," "John Blunt," and many more. One of these names was F. Steward—the F standing for Faithful, reflecting Baume's self-image as a trusty companion. The initials

F. S., however, also stood for yet another of his aliases: Frank
Smithson. Late in life Baume came to believe that he was Smithson's
illegitimate son. Years after Smithson died, he convinced himself
that Smithson had fathered him "through some American
connection."[49]

Baume's diary offers a revealing window into Smithson's life, both
for the actual information he delivers and for the perspective from
which he imparted it. Most of the people known to be colleagues
or associates of Smithson in Paris were famous, at least in their day;
it was their signatures and calling cards that were kept by the next
generation as mementoes, as indications of proximity to greatness.
Their notes in the Smithsonian archives constitute the major part
of what remains as evidence for the texture of Smithson's Parisian
existence; it is inevitable that any portrait of that time based on
them will emerge as skewed. But Baume, who believed Smithson
to be one of the greats, was simply a curious, slightly sycophantic
hanger-on, and a wonderfully oddball one at that. His naivete and
enthusiasms—his diary is punctuated with hundreds of exclamation
marks—put Smithson's views in heightened relief.

On one afternoon Baume found Smithson enjoying the early
eighteenth-century philosopher and satirist Bernard de Mandeville's
The Fable of the Bees, or Private Vices, Publick Benefits. Eager to follow
suit, Baume picked it up, as well, but was horrified at Smithson's
embrace of the theory "that *virtue* can lead to Decadence in an
Empire; and that *Vice* can lead to the greatest Prosperity." Mandeville
argued that altruism tended to stifle ingenuity and advancement, and
that it was vice—greed, envy, and man's hunger for luxury—that
stimulated invention and progress. Mandeville's philosophy
foreshadowed the Utilitarianism or "greatest happiness principle"
fostered by Jeremy Bentham and John Stuart Mill in the 1820s.
Baume, who lived a life of avowed deprivation as part of his effort
to benefit others, was one of many who found Mandeville's views
an affront to morality and religion.[50]

On another visit to Smithson's apartments, Baume recounted that

"Smithson showed me a little phial full of Viper's Venom which a scholar had sent him from America which he had collected by making them bite on a piece of glass, onto which they threw their Poison; but in spite of all Smithson's efforts by repeated experiments, he had never been able to reproduce this toxic material!"

Baume's report is riveting first of all for the news that Smithson did after all have at least one contact in the United States. It is possible that this correspondent was Dr. John Edwards Holbrook, a professor at the Medical College of South Carolina and a leading nineteenth-century herpetologist. Holbrook as a young man had come to know a number of prominent European naturalists while at the Jardin des Plantes in Paris in the early 1820s.[51] Whoever the mysterious snake-venom correspondent was, Smithson had American colleagues and was engaged with the work being done to examine and catalogue the natural riches of the New World.

But Baume's diary record is interesting as well for a glimpse of the research Smithson was conducting that was never published. Some two hundred manuscripts came to the United States in the 1830s, only to be lost a few decades later in the Smithsonian fire. Many of the discoveries of Smithson's generation brought accolades by chance or luck; frequently, a colleague had come close to the same conclusion and would have found it shortly, or had already discovered it and neglected to publish. What avenues had Smithson begun to explore, what new directions were contained in his papers? His attempted analysis of snake venom was, and still is, an incredibly ambitious experiment. His research may also have formed part of a larger inquiry into poisons generally. He had recently published a paper on the detection of "very minute quantities of arsenic and mercury," which had proved of great interest to the medical community and was referenced in the Spanish chemist Matthieu Joseph Bonaventure Orfila's landmark tome, *Traité de Toxicologie*, the work that launched the science of toxicology.[52]

From his published work alone it is clear that Smithson's interests and his inquiries ranged over very wide spectra in these last years.

In one paper he shared his invention of a small wax lamp, which he found useful when traveling, made in a china cup with a single cotton thread as a wick; in another he divulged the improvements he had made in the economical preparation of coffee and tea. He was an early examiner of the properties of some compounds of the volatile, mysterious fluorine, an element that was not properly isolated until the 1880s, and he also attempted to discern the crystallography of ice. And taking a fragment of the tomb of King Psammis, which he acquired from a man who had accompanied the famed circus strongman Giovanni Belzoni to Egypt, Smithson investigated the composition of the paint colors used by the ancient Egyptians.[53]

His last major paper was a refutation of the theories linking the universal deluge and geological history, a subject gripping the scientific community in England. In 1818 the King had endowed a chair of geology at Oxford, and William Buckland, acceding to the position, had delivered a lecture to the university the following year entitled *Vindiciae Geologicae; or the Connexion of Geology with Religion Explained*. It was not a lecture that Smithson would have listened to with much patience. Buckland was an adherent of catastrophism, a variant of diluvialism that sought to reconcile the biblical story of creation with the growing scientific evidence that showed the earth to be much older than a few thousand years. The deluge, in this argument, became only the most recent in a series of cataclysmic events that had destroyed the earth, and its varied plant and animal life, many times over.[54]

The discovery in 1821 of the Kirkdale Cave in Yorkshire, filled with fossil bones, gave Buckland an opportunity to test his theory. He concluded that the cave was the lair of hyenas that had lived in pre-diluvian times, and their bones had been covered in mud deposited by the Flood. In his flamboyant lecture style he painted a richly detailed portrait of prehistoric Yorkshire from his forensic examinations. "The hyaenas, gentlemen, preferred the flesh of elephants, rhinoceros, deer, cows, horses, &c.," he told the members of the Geological Society at one dinner, "but sometimes unable to procure these & half

*William Buckland entering Kirkdale Cave, a caricature
by fellow geologist William Conybeare.*

starved they used to come out of the narrow entrance of their cave
in the evening down to the water's edge of a lake wh.[ich] *must* once
have been there, & so helped themselves to some of the innumerable
water-rats in which the lake abounded . . ."[55] The resulting book,
*Reliquiae Diluvianae, or Observations on the Organic Remains attesting
the Action of a Universal Deluge,* published in 1823, became a best-
seller, and the Royal Society awarded him the Copley Medal for
discovering firm evidence for the Flood.

Granville Penn was another who took a turn at interpreting the
finds of the cave. Penn was a biblical literalist, for whom there had
only ever been two catastrophic events in the earth's history, the
Creation and the Deluge. He believed that the bones in the cave were
those of tropical animals swept across the globe and deposited there
by the Flood. As the waters drained away, clusters of animals had sunk
into the calcareous mud, which had eventually dried and become

the Kirkdale limestone, but not before the putrefying bodies had emitted tremendous amounts of gas, pushing the limestone paste outwards to form the Kirkdale Cave.[56]

Smithson weighed in decisively with a lengthy analysis of the subject, despite—as he informed the journal—not having actually seen much of Buckland's or Penn's writings. It was nevertheless better to speak out, he felt, "than to risk by silence letting a question settle to rest, while any unsupported assumptions are involved in it." He did not bother to make any great distinctions between the two men's ideas, but simply laid out an elaborate case against the entire idea of the universal deluge. And he enjoyed himself immensely while doing it. He refused to mention the Bible by name, referring to it only as "a book held by a large portion of mankind to have been written from divine inspiration." He then proceeded to query the logic of the reasoning behind the Deluge. If the Flood had left a bed of calcareous mud on England and Germany, he posited, then it must have done so all over the earth. How was it that the settlers at Botany Bay had found no limestone and had been forced to collect shells on the beach in order to make the lime that they so desperately needed to build shelters? And how had Noah and the animals reached dry land again, if all the earth was a thick layer of mire? Did they not sink in the muck? Where had the herbivorous animals found plants to eat? "What a time must have elapsed," Smithson concluded in mock distress, "before Noah could cultivate the vine!"[57]

He helpfully tried to come up with a plausible geological explanation for Granville Penn's theory. All the world's volcanoes, if they had not been extinguished in the Deluge, he suggested, must have poured carbonic acid into the ocean in order to bring about conditions to allow for the solidification of the rock in so short a time; but then, he surmised with a sigh, "it is also utterly impossible to believe that the beings in the ark, already not a little inconvenienced for respiration, could withstand the suffocating effluvium."

On a more serious note, there were two points especially that

Smithson knew made his case incontrovertible. One was the "total absence in the fossil world of all human remains, of every vestige of man himself and of his arts." All the millions of men who roamed the earth before the Flood should have been found along with these bones. Evidence of their work and manufactures should have turned up as well; "embalmed within the substance of the diluvian mud, entire cities, with their monuments . . . would remain. Every limestone quarry should daily present us with some of these most precious of all antiquities, before which those of Italy and Egypt would shrink to nothing." Smithson's second point was that the fossil animals that had been found were clearly not those that existed at the time of the Deluge, as "the multifarious wonders of the ark had for sole object their preservation." If the animals that live today were the ones shepherded onto the ark, he argued, then examples of them too should be found in the earth.

In "Some Observations on Mr. Penn's Theory Concerning the Formation of the Kirkdale Cave," all Smithson's musings over the question of extinction, the march of time, and man's place in the universe came to the fore—controversies that only intensified in the decades following Smithson's death. The paper was the longest he ever published, and unusual in that it was primarily a refutation of someone else's theory. His comments were nevertheless rooted in a lifetime of restless exploration and information gathering, and they reflected his disdain for the superstitions of religious authority. He buttressed his argument with references to experiments he had conducted over thirty years and to the specific geological character of places all over the world—including the Alps, the Andes, Pompeii, Carlsbad, and the Calabrian shores of Italy. Many of these places Smithson had visited personally, such as the "Stunsfield slate" region near Oxford or the sea at Dumbarton. Others he had studied vicariously, often through the crystals that had entered his cabinet via friends and correspondents, and through the travel accounts he had read.

Smithson was fascinated with the existence of ancient civilizations and intimations of pre-history. "More than commonly incurious must he be," Smithson wrote, "who would not find delight in stemming the stream of ages, returning to times long past, and beholding the then existing state of things and of men."[58] His generation had been the first to extend the age of the earth beyond its biblical conception. He had been only nineteen when he had met James Hutton in Scotland and traveled through the imagination over great expanses of geological time. Here in Paris Georges Cuvier, another catastrophist, had found in the stone quarries of Montmartre, excavated for Napoleon's massive building program, the flora and fauna of multiple lost worlds. From the bones he collected, Cuvier had reconstructed the skeletal forms of strange and exotic beasts that had once walked the earth, turning the globe that had popularly nurtured an Edenic fore-story into an alien place of wild and woolly monsters. The work elevated him as a giant in the public's eyes—though his ever-expanding girth also contributed to his nickname "the Mammoth." Balzac called him nothing less than the "greatest poet of our century" for having "rebuilt cities by means of teeth, peopled anew a thousand forests with all the wonders of zoology thanks to a few chips of coal and rediscovered races of giants in a mammoth's foot."[59]

Smithson had an agile mind, and he had spent a lifetime making observations and weighing evidence. He had repeatedly been confronted with rapidly changing realities and huge shifts in scientific understanding, such that he had little trouble envisioning change occurring over periods of millennia, rather than just centuries. In a letter to Lord Holland, written from the Continent during the Napoleonic Wars and musing on the fate of France, he entwined geological time and the development of society:

The disposition of a nation alters as slowly as the climate of their country, and probably with it. . . . When the Romans expelled their kings, it was a fierce banditti, grown numerous which rose against its captain, & continued their predatory excursions under several leaders. When the Romans submitted

to their Emperors, not only civilization and the afflux of
strangers had insensibly produced a new people, but nature
herself had worked towards the change. The volcanic
mountains round Rome had probably smouldered down, their
forests, their snows, their glaciers, had probably disappeared,
the Tiber had ceased to freeze, and the present climate of
Rome had succeeded to that of the Alps.[60]

Smithson's Kirkdale paper was above all a cogent and passionate
defense of a life dedicated to knowledge. This was, ultimately, his
reason for speaking up, and in it he made his most powerful
articulation of the Enlightenment ethos that had guided his life. "It
is in his knowledge that man has found his greatness and his happiness,
the high superiority which he holds over the other animals who
inhabit the earth with him," he argued. "No ignorance is probably
without loss to him, no error without evil . . ."

But the brilliant discoveries of Smithson's generation had altered
the way that man inhabited the world in more ways than one.
Peering out into the sublime vastness of the solar system, imagining
a tumble through the abyss of geological time, Smithson and his
contemporaries could not help but think, too, of how infinitesimal
the moment of their own existence now appeared. To the
Romantic soul, how futile seemed the span of an individual life.
"We wonder, crushed as we are under so many worlds in ruin,"
Balzac mused, "what can our glories avail, our hatreds and our
loves, and if it is worth living at all if we are to become, for
future generations, an imperceptible speck in the past."[61] Against
this smallness, Smithson and his friends dreamed of posterity. They
hungered for fame and for utility, and they hoped for a lasting
monument.

Within the year he headed to London to write his will. He had
been back to London at least once before, in 1820, to probate the
will of his brother, who had died aged forty-nine—after a particularly
brutal winter in Paris, the first time the Seine had frozen in nearly

forty years.[62] They had buried him at the new cemetery of Père Lachaise, on the eastern outskirts of Paris, one of the only places available for Protestant burials in France. Dickenson had entrusted his estate to Smithson, rather than his partner Mary Ann, the mother of his son; and he had left instructions for Smithson to provide for Henry James, who was then a teenager in school, "in such manner as shall appear best to my Brother."[63] This Smithson had evidently done, and more as well; sometime between 1822 and 1825 Henry James Dickenson had at Smithson's request changed his name to Henry James Hungerford.[64] The name change probably reflected Smithson's decision to leave his fortune to his nephew and to that young man's future heirs. It is logical to assume that this much of the thinking behind his bequest, at least, Smithson discussed with his nephew. In the spring of 1825 he headed back to London to prepare his papers.

TWELVE

London: The Will, 1825–1829

I James Smithson Son to Hugh first Duke of
Northumberland, & Elizabeth, heiress of the
Hungerfords of Studley & niece to Charles the
proud Duke of Somerset, now residing in Bentinck
Street Cavendish Square, do this twenty third day of
October one thousand eight hundred & twenty six,
make this my last will & testament . . . .

—James Smithson, October 1826

W HEN SMITHSON CROSSED the Channel in the
spring of 1825, sailing towards the white cliffs of Dover,
it must have seemed as if he were headed in the wrong
direction. Fashionable society was teeming over to France, on their
way to the biggest social event of the year: the coronation of King
Charles X, held at Reims Cathedral on May 29, 1825. The roads
from Paris were clogged with carriages, and every lodging in the
region around Reims was let, sometimes at prices well over the cost
of the entire house. Tens of thousands not privileged enough to be
inside for the ceremony pressed into the square before the cathedral,
as the King, in ermine robes and laden with jewels, made his way
down the nave. When it was over the artillery thundered from the

ramparts and all the bells in town set to swinging, the last element
of a monumental piece of theatre designed to reaffirm the glory of
the Bourbon monarchy.

Smithson steered clear of this spectacle, and it cannot have been
lost on him that the person England sent as ambassador-extraordinary
was none other than the Duke of Northumberland, now the third
duke, the son of Smithson's half-brother Hugh Percy. The
Northumberlands had arrived in Paris months before the ceremony,
and were ubiquitous in society, even calling on Georges Cuvier to
see the collections at the Jardin des Plantes.[1] The duke famously bore
the whole cost of the mission, and his performance in France was so
voluptuous that a young poet at the outset of his career named Victor
Hugo dubbed him the "Arabian Nights ambassador." The night of
the actual coronation the duke hosted a ball, "a magnificent, fairy-
like spectacle," in which every lady found a diamond in her bouquet.
Upon his return to England the Crown rewarded the duke for his
"exceptional magnificence" with a diamond-hilted sword.[2]

Smithson had once sworn, "My name will live on in the memory
of men when the titles of the Northumberlands and Percys are
extinct or forgotten." There had been a time in his youth when
excitable earls had stood on tables in Revolutionary Paris and
renounced their titles and all hereditary privileges; there had been
a time, he had believed, when it seemed likely that the system as
it had long existed would cease to support itself and a new egalitarian
society with reason as its queen would triumph. He had now lived
to see three Dukes of Northumberland parading their magnificence
across the stage of society. With every passing year it became ever
clearer that—despite the progress of science—the Northumberlands,
each more ostentatious than the last, were thriving.

Smithson, in contrast, had not yet succeeded in bringing eternal
fame to his name. He had known many of the scientific greats of
his era, the "Men," as he called them, "to whom it is given to make
alone the progress of a century."[3] But he was not apparently destined
to enter that league himself. A lifetime dedicated to augmenting the

store of natural knowledge had resulted in no ground-breaking discoveries. And now he was back in London, a city where it was much harder to ignore the family story that so preoccupied him. Hungerford Market, on the site of his maternal family's ancestral palace, sat cheek by jowl with Northumberland House at the head of the Strand, around the location of Charing Cross station today. On a stroll to see the latest prints in the glass-fronted shops of the Strand, Smithson would have passed in quick succession the Northumberland Coffeehouse and the Hungerford Coffeehouse, an inevitable reminder of his rich illicit parentage.

Soon after his arrival in London he was welcomed back to the Royal Society Club, attending the dinner as the guest of his friend Sir George Staunton—who had recently hosted Smithson's raffish Paris associate Pierre Henri Joseph Baume for almost two months at his "bachelor's villa" in the country.[4] He toured the city's latest attractions, taking in the popular show at the Egyptian Hall on the wonders of Ancient and Modern Mexico, which included a panorama of Mexico City and a live Mexican Indian living in a hut. And he perused the specimens of native filigree silver from Saxony and the "rarissime" crystallized serpentine from Pennsylvania in the auction of minerals held at Mr. Thomas' great room on King Street.[5] But Smithson's journey back to London in 1825—around the time of his sixtieth birthday—seems to have been one primarily dedicated to putting his house in order. This was to be, as he most likely knew, his last trip to England; it was a time to organize his possessions and write his will. He may well have been the Mr. Smithson who sold some paintings in the fall of 1825 at Edward Foster's auction house on Greek Street.[6] Over at Drummonds bank he tended to his finances, selling a series of Exchequer bills totaling more than £7,000 and reinvesting the money in Bank of England stock.[7]

Even while going through his possessions Smithson found material that he deemed worthy of publication. One was an old letter from Joseph Black, dated 1790, which he published with commentary as

VIEW of the EXHIBITION of ANCIENT and MODERN MEXICO.

The exhibit of Ancient and Modern Mexico, from a pamphlet in Smithson's library. The Mexican Indian is seen talking to a visitor in the foreground.

"A letter from Dr. Black describing a very sensible balance," in the *Annals of Philosophy* in the spring of 1825. The article afforded Smithson the opportunity to publicize the cordial relationship he had enjoyed with the late and much revered chemist of the Scottish Enlightenment. It also gave him the chance to promote a tool he had long found useful in the manipulation of very small samples— an instrument emblematic of the micro-chemistry experimental method that stood at the heart of his reputation both at home and abroad. He praised the balance as "a very valuable addition to the blowpipe apparatus, as it enables the determination of quantities in the experiments with that instrument, which was an unhoped-for accession to its powers."

He was probably pleased to see the article republished within the year in Thomas Gill's monthly magazine, the *Technical Repository*. Smithson's 1823 paper, "Method of fixing particles on the sappare," had also been reprinted by this periodical, which was geared towards transmitting useful information to working men and entrepreneurs, people who could apply new knowledge to their practices. It was hoped that the diffusion of such information might in turn engender new discoveries; in the mind of utilitarians like Smithson, the diffusion of knowledge was another way of spurring the increase of knowledge. One did not need to have specialized equipment, or specialized knowledge, in order to contribute materially to the store of natural knowledge. The reprinting of these two papers in the *Technical Repository* would have satisfied Smithson in another way as well; the publications enabled Smithson to pass on information about a body of working methods that had served him well for decades, techniques that were rapidly becoming obsolete in the face of the latest advances in chemistry.

The other paper Smithson published in London, entitled "A Method of Fixing Crayon Colors," was an account of his clever transformation of a pastel portrait in order to preserve it while traveling. Smithson informed the editor that he wished "to transport a crayon portrait to a distance for the sake of the likeness, but without the frame and glass, which were bulky and heavy." He consulted various authorities but was dissatisfied with all their proposed solutions on how best to fix the colors. He settled finally on a solution of his own making: the shellacking of the portrait with "a drying oil diluted with spirit of turpentine." He proceeded cautiously, coating first the back and waiting a few days for it to dry before applying the mixture to the front. And then, he informed the journal with delight, "my crayon drawing became an oil painting."[8]

This kind of work sat at the heart of Smithson's interests, his faith in the amelioration of the human condition through the spread of knowledge. For him no object was unworthy of study; he had analyzed his lead pencil, the Napoleon coin in his pocket, and the indelible green stain left by crushing a gnat on paper. No discovery was too minor to be shared. Some small observation could prove the missing ingredient, the unresolved question, in some other scientist's labors. "When the sole view is to further a pursuit of whose importance to mankind a conviction exists," he argued, "all that can do so should be imparted, however small may appear the merit which attaches it." He chastised his fellow scientists for not publicizing the improvements they had developed in their apparatus and their working methods. Finding a better way of doing something translated into a saving of time, money, and resources. And it benefited not only other scientific laborers like himself; it had ramifications for society as a whole. "In all cases means of economy tend to augment and diffuse comforts and happiness," Smithson emphasized. "They bring within the reach of the many what wasteful proceedings confine to the few."[9]

Smithson would have found on his return to London in the mid-1820s a group of reformers alight with such thinking. The London Chemical Society's radical journal *The Chemist*, which praised Smithson's work a few times during its short one-year existence, condemned the elitism of high science in the capital—especially as embodied in the dandified president of the Royal Society, Sir Humphry Davy. While the scientific establishment shunned the working classes, George Birkbeck, the head of the London Chemical Society, determined to bring education to the masses. Drawing on his experiences lecturing at the Andersonian Institution in Glasgow, where he had developed classes for working men after "observing the intelligent curiosity of the 'unwashed artificers,'" he launched the London Mechanics' Institution. It offered evening classes in chemistry, mathematics, and electricity; the program was phenomenally successful. By 1826 every large town in England and many small ones had mechanics' institutes.[10]

The Society for the Diffusion of Useful Knowledge was also founded at this time, the brainchild of Birkbeck's friend and fellow Scot, the Whig reformer Henry Brougham. It had similar goals, seeing science—chemistry, in particular—as an essential subject in the dissemination of knowledge in society. "The pleasures of Science go hand in hand with the solid benefits derived from it," Brougham argued, and "they tend, unlike other gratifications, not only to make our lives more agreeable, but better; and that a rational being is bound by every motive of interest and of duty, to direct his mind towards pursuits which are found to be the sure path of virtue as well as of happiness."[11]

The year 1825, when Smithson returned to London, also marked the beginning of what came to be called University College, London. Like the Scottish universities—and in distinct contrast to Oxford and Cambridge—the university in London was open to all regardless of religious beliefs. It signaled the first break in the tradition of elite channels, it stressed the widening of possibilities for all, and science featured prominently in the studies offered. The university quickly gained support from Brougham and other leading utilitarians; pamphlets circulated promoting the scheme, and a joint-stock company was founded to manage the funds raised.[12]

It is likely that Smithson was aware of many or most of these developments. He was an avid consumer of news, and these institutions addressed matters that had long been at the heart of his interests. But Smithson was not solicited, as he had been at the founding of the Royal Institution, to be a patron of any of these new ventures—despite the fact that many who served as shareholders of the new university in London were or had been prominent leaders at the Royal Institution, and some, like the radical politician Henry Warburton, were good friends.[13] If by chance Smithson was feeling unappreciated or overlooked by the London community of philanthropic reformers, perhaps he learned of a new quarter where his work was being well received and eagerly consumed. In 1825 the *American Journal of Arts & Sciences*, the leading scientific journal in the United States, which was otherwise known as "Silliman's Journal" after its founder Benjamin Silliman, reprinted Smithson's "Method of fixing particles on the sappare"—which was retitled simply "Blowpipe Experiments." And in May 1826 the *Franklin Journal and American Mechanics' Magazine*, based in Philadelphia, reprinted Smithson's article on transforming the pastel portrait into an oil painting.

The United States over the preceding decades had slowly been developing its own native culture of science. Scientific societies, like the relatively long-standing American Philosophical Society in Philadelphia and the American Academy of Arts and Sciences in

Boston, had been joined by a growing number of specialist departments at universities, as well as new scientific journals and literature. America was still dependent on Europe in many ways, and it had nothing like the traditions of patronage and institutional support that Europe enjoyed. Its audience was smaller, too, as many fewer men had the leisure to devote themselves to the pursuit of science.[14] But President John Quincy Adams had urged his countrymen to "return light for light," to cultivate knowledge and send it back in the direction of Europe. Adams had advocated the establishment of national institutions for the promotion of science: an astronomical observatory, a national university, and an exploring expedition.[15]

Even if Smithson was unaware of the reprinting of his papers in American journals, he had probably long had his eye fixed on the United States. Europe, by the 1820s, viewed America as the future. It was a country that seemed admirably unburdened by many of the troubles that plagued the Old World. "Our countrymen do not believe that America is more advanced in knowledge and refinement than Europe," the *Edinburgh Magazine* explained to its readers, "but they know that, with slight divergencies, both hemispheres are in this respect nearly abreast of each other. And they know that, both being yet far from the goal, their generous transatlantic rivals start unencumbered by many old prejudices and social trammels which we cannot here escape from."[16]

These opinions on the unencumbered status of people in the New World, now reaching general circulation, were ones that Smithson, who had spent a lifetime brooding over the disenfranchisement caused by the circumstances of his birth, had likely mulled over for a very long while. He probably watched with interest, and perhaps even pleasure, as the elite of London engaged in debates about England's decline. Prince Meckler-Muskau, touring England in 1826–8, concluded that the country had outlived her "highest greatness, and is already declining." And Charles Babbage, inventor of the difference engine, the forerunner of modern computers, published his controversial *Reflections on the Decline of*

Science in England in 1830, attacking the leadership and dilettantism of the Royal Society.[17]

And in the late summer of 1826, as Smithson turned his attention to the writing of his will, America was very much in the news. July 4 marked the fiftieth anniversary of the Declaration of Independence, and the United States had planned extensive festivities for the jubilee anniversary. Around the country men hailed the genius of America, celebrating its traditions of self-government—while in the same breath often condemning the corrupt and aged institutions of Europe. In the days that followed July 4, however, the celebrations took on a completely new and even more exalted cast, when the news spread that both Thomas Jefferson and John Adams, two of the last founding fathers, had passed away on that milestone day. President John Quincy Adams first learned of Jefferson's death on July 6. "A strange and very striking coincidence," he wrote in his diary. It was only three days later, as he headed north to be with his ailing father, that he learned belatedly of his father's death and comprehended truly the magnitude of the event. "In this most singular coincidence," President Adams proclaimed, "the finger of Providence is plainly visible!"[18]

Ten days before he died, Jefferson penned one last paean to the idea of America. "The general spread of the light of science has already laid open to every view the palpable truth," he declared, "that the mass of mankind has not been born with saddles on their backs, nor a favored few, booted and spurred, ready to ride them legitimately by the grace of God."[19] America's democratic experiment had already inspired several generations of utopian visionaries. Coleridge's Pantisocracy, his unrealized communitarian living experiment on the banks of the Susquehanna River in Pennsylvania, was one of a number of such schemes birthed during the turbulent 1790s. Now, in 1826, a voyaging band of scientists and educators, in a boat named *The Philanthropist*, were making their way down the Ohio River to their experimental settlement at New Harmony, Indiana. The "Boatload of Knowledge," as it came to be known, was the visionary idea of Robert Owen, the reformer who had revolutionized working conditions at the New Lanark mills in Scotland. His Utopia was to be a place where the pursuit of knowledge, fostered by progressive educational theories, could thrive, in America's "new fertile soil, new for material and mental growth."

It is not known whether Smithson knew of the plans for New Harmony. Accounts of life on the settlement had already reached Europe by the fall of 1826, as Goethe, for one, was talking of it. William Maclure, a Scottish geologist turned American citizen who was one of the leaders of the New Harmony community, had been a friend of the late William Thomson and perhaps knew others in Smithson's circle. Smithson's protégé Baume might have been another conduit of news; he was awestruck by Owen and developing a close relationship with him (Owen, in fact, would later christen the illegitimate son Baume fathered in an incestuous relationship with his sister). The New Harmony project was one, presumably, that Smithson would have admired. It embodied the belief that scientific knowledge could enlarge and empower the human mind; and it evinced, too, the faith that reformers placed in the United States, "the cradle," as Owen called it, "of the future liberty of the human race."[20]

Smithson's will as he finally penned it is unique in the annals of testaments. Many of his contemporaries, the men of the English Enlightenment who had, like him, dedicated themselves to advancing the frontiers of knowledge, were also approaching the end of their lives in the 1820s. A number of them had become very wealthy over the course of the years, as during their lifetimes science had started to become a career in which one could make one's fortune. In their wills, some of them made gestures of support for science, but none of them suggested a Smithsonian-like instrument for their wealth that would dramatically impact the direction of science or society.

Humphry Davy, whose scientific genius netted him a knighthood and an heiress, believed there was no better use for a man's wealth than the promotion of science. As the abstemious William Hyde

Wollaston, who had made a fortune in processing platinum, lay dying, Davy told his wife, "So will W. die! with perhaps two or three hundred thousand; yet these men might have applied money to the noblest purposes."[21] Wollaston did leave £1,000 to the Geological Society and £2,000 to the Royal Society. At the Royal Society the dividends from this sum were to be used to promote experimental research. Although this bequest represented a small percentage of Wollaston's total wealth, the Donation Fund, as it was called, nevertheless formed the first money that the Royal Society received enabling it to patronize scientific research in any systematic way.[22]

But Davy hardly made much of a donation to science himself when it came to the end. He wrote his will in 1827, at a time he was "feeling more than common symptoms of mortality." He died two years later, on the Continent, where he had penned the romantic discourse *Consolations in Travel, or the Last Days of a Philosopher.* His fortune at his death totaled close to £30,000. Most of it he left to his wife and sole executor, Lady Davy. To his brother he entrusted some plate he had been awarded, with instructions that if it was not used by the family it be melted down or sold and the proceeds go to the Royal Society to found an annual medal for the most useful discovery in chemistry in Europe or America.[23]

Smithson's old mentor Henry Cavendish, acknowledged as one of the wealthiest men of science in England, left an estate worth close to £1,000,000 in 1810; Smithson's estate, in contrast, totaled a little over £100,000. Most of Cavendish's wealth reverted to his family. Little was left to science; his old assistant Sir Charles Blagden declared that he was not a "person who gave the £40,000 [annual income] to hospitals." Cavendish left Blagden £15,000, but Blagden was virtually the only scientist so honored.[24]

Count Rumford, who birthed the Royal Institution, was perhaps one figure who might have served as something of a role model for Smithson. He spent much of his life involved in philanthropic activities—most with the added goal of enhancing his own reputation. In addition to improving enterprises such as the workhouse in

Munich and the Royal Institution in London, Rumford had endowed scientific prizes in his own name at the Royal Society and the American Academy of Arts and Sciences, making it quite clear at the outset that he hoped very much to be awarded the first medals. America, the place of his birth, featured prominently in his final bequests. Upon his death in 1814 he left all his books and military designs to the United States government for the use of any military academy they might found. Like Wollaston and Davy, he left a sum to promote scientific research; Rumford's gift was to Harvard College, an annuity of $1,000, to endow a Rumford professorship dedicated to "the utility of the physical and mathematical sciences for the improvement of the useful arts, and for the extension of the industry, prosperity, happiness and well-being of Society."[25]

Smithson's last testament did not in the end resemble any of these men's. It was a highly irregular document, its language strikingly informal and inexact. Solicitors were paid handsomely for drafting legal documents precisely to avoid the vague descriptors that cluttered Smithson's text. Defining one's mother as "Elizabeth, heiress of the Hungerfords of Studley, & niece to Charles the proud Duke of Somerset," with no last name, address, or other identifying details, invited challenges and problems in probate. This is not to say that eighteenth-century gentlemen did not write quirky wills; the opening clause of the antiquarian Francis Douce's will read: "I give to Sir Anthony Carlisle £200., requesting him either to sever my head, or extract the heart from my body, so as to prevent any possibility of the return of vitality."[26] But in light of the size of the estate and Smithson's unusual intentions for it, it is remarkable, not to say almost unprecedented, that he did not consult with a professional in the drafting of his will.[27]

Smithson left all of his property in trust to his bankers, Messrs. Drummonds, instructing them to put it under the management of the Court of Chancery. He remembered first of all his servants John Fitall and Henri Honoré Sailly, leaving Fitall a £100 annuity and permitting Sailly to keep the outstanding bills and bonds signed by

Smithson's nephew
Henry James Hungerford.

Smithson for five years at an interest of 5 percent. He then specified that "To Henry James Hungerford, my Nephew, heretofore called Henry James Dickinson [sic], son to my later brother, Lieutenant-Colonel Henry Louis Dickinson [sic], now residing with Mr. Auboin [sic], at Bourg la Reine, near Paris, I give and bequeath for his life the whole of the income arising from my property of every nature & kind whatever . . ." He empowered his nephew to make a jointure should he marry, ensuring that any wife might also be provided for. The whole of his property "of every kind absolutely & forever" was to go to any children that Hungerford might have. Smithson was careful to note—in language that was exceedingly rare—that these included children legitimate or illegitimate; Smithson's father's will had, by contrast, reflected the traditional manner of citing children, repeatedly stating "lawfully begotten being always preferred."[28]

Only then, after he had laid all of these instructions out, did he write, "In the case of the death of my said Nephew without leaving a child or children, or the death of the child or children he may have had under the age of twenty-one years or intestate, I then bequeath the whole of my property, subject to the Annuity of One hundred pounds to John Fitall, & for the security & payment of which I mean Stock to remain in this Country, to the United States of America, to found at Washington, under the name of the Smithsonian Institution, an Establishment for the increase & diffusion of knowledge among men." There was no further elaboration. He did not set out any program of operations or suggest how the management of such an establishment might be organized. And he made no special dispensation for any particular possessions, like his mineral cabinet or library or scientific apparatus, items that might have immediately benefited a research institution or university.

There seems little question that Smithson wrote the will on his own. He had to hand a little guide called *Plain Advice to the Public, to Facilitate the Making of Their Own Wills*, which had just been published in August 1826. The book's intended audience was "the man of middling possessions," not the gentleman of fortune like Smithson. The proprietor of "large and extensive possessions," the author explained, could "well afford to pay for the assistance of a legal adviser." For various, evidently painful reasons, however, Smithson did not have great swathes of family real estate to devise nor complicated entails to draft. His holdings were mostly in the form of bank stock, and the number of people to whom he wished to bequeath his fortune was, by this stage in his life, few. He could dispose of his fortune in a relatively simple manner.[29]

Smithson was probably attracted to the author of the pamphlet's stated desire "to infuse into his work as much as possible of that valuable ingredient—*practical utility*." He evidently followed the booklet closely in many of its recommendations. Included in the back of this little how-to book were a number of "fictitious wills" to be used as models, the mention of which Smithson noted clearly with a dash in the margin. He heeded all the suggestions regarding how best to remember faithful servants, including the language "free of legacy duty" in Joseph Fitall's annuity and indicating that it was to be payable quarterly, with the first payment to come three months after Smithson's death.

But there were, obviously, other ways in which Smithson departed dramatically from the advice imparted by the booklet. In writing a will that spoke to his deepest needs, he seems ultimately to have followed no guide but himself. He signaled what was most important to him in the very first sentence: his ancestry. For Smithson, the opening lines, presenting his inflated portrait of his parentage, were about as significant as the ones that decreed the possible future Smithsonian. They were his final opportunity to set the record straight, to broadcast his lineage and assert his claim to his father. The guide that Smithson consulted recommended commencing with "a formal introduction," one that identified the author through his domicile—street, city, and county, and in the case of someone like a merchant marine, his occupation. There was no direction to list one's parents, especially not in such vague and grandiose terms.

Likewise, the idea for a Smithsonian Institution was not one that could be found in any book. In the matter of charitable giving, the guide suggested "a bequest to a public charity," recommending in one example a gift of £100 to benefit the poor of the parish of Islington and in another £100 "to the president, treasurer, and governor of Christ's Hospital, London, for the use and benefit of said institution." The author of *Plain Advice to the Public*, of course, even in his wildest, most imaginative suggestions, never came close to proposing that the beneficiary be all of mankind, in the form of a bequest to the government of a distant land.

Having written his will and tidied up his affairs, Smithson went back to Paris. He may have returned as early as November or December 1826, as his friend John Guillemard recalled last seeing him in Paris in that year.[30] In early June 1827 he was reunited with his eccentric protégé Pierre Henri Joseph Baume, who had just completed a long religious pilgrimage and was living in a monastery in Paris, his hair all grown out and people mistaking him "for a Moor," to his great distress. "Smithson very long conversation," Baume reported in his diary. Several times more that month the two of them met to talk, and in early July Baume set off on a trip to London via Brussels, a commission from Smithson in hand. The details of this commission remain unknown. Baume at this point in his life was fascinated by Robert Owen and programs for universal education; he harbored dreams of perfecting agriculture, and he was also entertaining ideas of setting up a society called "the Friends of Truth," whose members should be well versed in medicine. In 1821, dismissed from the court of Naples, he had taken a tour of "public institutions." It is possible that this trip to Belgium included a fact-finding mission on matters of educational or scientific institutions for Smithson; but it is equally possible, of course, that this commission was simply a request for books or Belgian lace. Whether Smithson discussed his bequest with any of his friends is not known; Baume never made any mention of it in his diaries.[31]

Smithson was still in Paris in the summer of 1828. On July 8, 1828, he loaned the exorbitant sum of 20,000 francs—quite enough for a gentleman to live on for an entire year—to his former servant, Henri Honoré Sailly, who was then running the Hungerford Hotel on the rue Caumartin.[32] At some point thereafter, he packed up his things and headed south to the Mediterranean, accompanied by his servant Herman Fropwell. He traveled across the Continent in grand style, in his own private carriage, carrying himself, as ever, as the English aristocrat. Smithson brought many things with him on this journey—books, papers, his telescope, a large collection of silver, two gold snuff boxes, many fine pieces of gold and diamond jewelry, and "two paste board boxes containing medals coins stones &c." For his toilette he had assembled forty-four pocket handkerchiefs, nineteen cravats, seven waistcoats, thirteen pairs of stockings, two pair of underwear, three nightcaps, and more. He was not, however, carrying all of his belongings; the artworks he still owned, much of his library, probably much of his mineral collection, his scientific instruments, his gun, and his extensive china service he seems to have left behind in London or Paris—either in storage, or perhaps in the care of his nephew and sister-in-law.[33]

Presumably Smithson hoped to recuperate for a season or more along the coast somewhere. He settled for a while in Genoa, a sprawling amphitheatre of a town perched high on the hills, with broad vistas out to the sea. If he was beyond the point of taking long walks into the countryside, the city's views remained a salve to the spirit. Mary Shelley was another visitor who took in "the theatre of Nature from my windows," during the melancholy months following her husband's drowning off Livorno in 1822.[34]

Genoa, while not a spot traditionally sought after by those with pulmonary complaints, did offer plenty of comfort to the wealthy tourist, especially one scientifically minded, and it was a place to which Smithson had long been attracted.[35] The city boasted an excellent museum of natural history, a large mineral collection, and a botanical garden; and at the university the first chemistry professorship had been held by the English physician William Batt, a man Smithson had known back in his Grand Tour days.[36]

It was in Genoa, at the end of June, that Smithson passed his final hours. Death was the ultimate experiment for the men of the Enlightenment, the final opportunity to observe and record, to try to collect useful information. Smithson's friend Wollaston, who had died the year before of a brain tumor, spent his last day trying to communicate his state of alertness—"endeavouring," it seemed to one friend, "to convert his death into a grand philosophical experiment, to give data for determining the influence of the body on the mind, and to try whether it was possible for the latter to remain until the very last."[37] Likewise, when Amédée Berthollet, the son of Smithson's good friend, committed suicide in 1810, he did it in a manner that his bereft father must have reluctantly admired; he stuffed all the cracks and crevices of the room, set a watch upon the table, lit a charcoal brazier, and proceeded to catalogue the effects of carbon monoxide poisoning, until his writing descended into illegible scribbles and finally trailed off altogether.[38]

How did Smithson die? And what of, in the end? There is no record—only the knowledge that the English vice consul, summoned probably by Smithson's servant, hurried to the house that same day, June 27, 1829. He came with a Mr. Gibbs, an English agent resident in Genoa who had served as Smithson's banker. Together the two men made arrangements for a funeral. The vice consul inventoried all Smithson's possessions, making special note of his "Geneva gold watch," which Fropwell the servant had taken into his custody "and for which the said Herman is to account for." The vice consul then "put the papers and the most valuable objects in boxes and a trunk on which he placed the Consular Seals, except for the underwear and clothes of the deceased. A part of these would have to be washed. He had, however, left these under the care of a servant of the deceased, a person to be fully trusted; and wrote to the relatives of the deceased in order to have their instructions." Going through the belongings the men had found a receipt of the will, which Smithson had carried with him.[39]

At the annual anniversary meeting of the Royal Society that year, held on November 30, 1829, Davies Gilbert, Smithson's old friend from Pembroke, sat in the chair as president. "In no previous interval of twelve months," he declared, "has the society collectively, or have its individual members, experienced losses so severe." The Royal Society had lost from its ranks William Hyde Wollaston, Thomas Young, and most especially Sir Humphry Davy, all three of whom represented Britain as Foreign Associates of the Institut in Paris. Gilbert took some time to recall the particular contributions that each had made to science before going on to list the further deaths the society had suffered: Dr. Edward Ash, Lord Buchan (David Steuart Erskine), Lord Oriel (John Foster), and, finally, James Smithson. Smithson, Gilbert reminisced, "was distinguished by the intimate friendship of Mr. Cavendish, and rivalled our most expert chemists in elegant analyses."[40]

Smithson died far from London, out of sight of this scientific community, and public notice of his death was slow in coming. Davies Gilbert at the Royal Society had probably learned of the loss of his friend only shortly before that anniversary meeting at the end of November, following the probate of Smithson's will. *The Times* observed it a week or so later, printing the will in its entirety and finally bringing word of Smithson's extraordinary contingency bequest to light. The *Gentleman's Magazine* commemorated him in a few paragraphs in early 1830, mistakenly reporting the death as having taken place in October 1829, "In the South of France." Its obituary opened by quoting from the will Smithson's ostentatious description of his own family heritage: "Son to Hugh first Duke of Northumberland, & Elizabeth, heiress of the Hungerfords of Studley & niece to Charles the proud Duke of Somerset." The editors immediately disparaged Smithson's ancestral claims, stating that "in the account of the family in Sir R. C. Hoare's *Hungerfordiana*, we find no Elizabeth, nor the name of Macie, which was that which Mr. Smithson originally bore."[41]

From scientific quarters there were few observations of Smithson's passing. There was no *éloge* at the Institut, that true marker of statesmanship in international science, though Smithson's friend Georges Cuvier sat in the chair. It was in fact only at the Royal Society's anniversary meeting in November 1830, a year and a half after Smithson's death, that the president Davies Gilbert communicated a more complete recognition of his college friend. Gilbert's tribute consisted primarily of "the trifling but characteristic" recollection of Smithson's delight over his analysis of a lady's tear— a story, Gilbert told the assembled, that Smithson relished to tell. "Smithson, once observing a tear gliding down a lady's cheek, endeavoured to catch it on a crystal—one half of the drop escaped; he preserved the other, however, submitted it to the re-agents, and detected what was then called microcosmic salt, with muriate of soda, and other saline substances, held in solution."[42]

The recollection is a charming one, conjuring up from an earlier century the picture of a festive salon where elegantly dressed ladies together with gentlemen in starched stocks and silk coats peruse fine

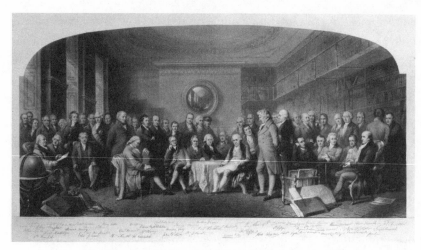

"Distinguished Men of Science Living in 1807-08,"
featuring Cavendish, Davy, Herschel, Dalton, and many others
(including Joseph Bramah, inventor of the unpickable lock, at far right, pictured
facing backwards because there was no known portrait of him). When this image
was created in the 1860s, Smithson, it seems, had already been forgotten.

faceted gems and competitively vaunt their Romantic affectations. There in the middle is Smithson, leaping forward theatrically with an outstretched crystal to catch the tear as it rolls down a powdered cheek, to take this little symbol of sensibility and submit it to Science. Smithson's clever party favor, the scientist in service to society— gay, *bon ton* society this time—belongs to another era. Even that which Smithson analyzed was known then, as Gilbert reminded his listeners, by another name. Time has moved on, science moved forward, and the bit players standing at the margins have begun to recede. Although they commanded the respect and admiration of their colleagues in their day, history has no room for them. Smithson stands for many of them.

THIRTEEN

America:
The Finger of Providence

A stranger to this country, knowing it only by its
history, bearing in his person the blood of the Percys
and the Seymours, brother to a nobleman of the
highest rank in British heraldry, who fought against
the revolution of our independence at Bunker's Hill—
that he should be the man to found, at the city of
Washington for the United States of America, an
establishment for the increase and diffusion of
knowledge among men, is an event in which I see the
finger of Providence, compassing great results by
incomprehensible means. May the Congress of the
Union be deeply impressed with the solemn duties
devolving upon them by this trust, and carry it into
effect in the fulness of its spirit, and to the increase
and diffusion of knowledge among men!

—John Quincy Adams, *Memoirs*, January 10, 1836

H ENRY JAMES HUNGERFORD was in Paris when he
learned of Smithson's death, and he wasted no time getting
his traveling papers in order. By July 6, 1829, he and his
servant were headed to Genoa. A month later they were at Calais, on
their way to London so that Hungerford could begin the process of
sorting through his uncle's affairs and gaining access to his inheritance.[1]

Smithson's nephew was just reaching his majority in 1829. Free from Monsieur Aubouin's boarding school in the leafy environs of Paris, where he had been sent for cultivation, the world expanded around him. The suit for his inheritance was successfully concluded by 1831, netting him some £4,000 of annual income—he was entitled only to the interest off Smithson's estate, as the principal was destined for his as yet unborn heirs. He gave a generous annuity to his mother, who now had two small children by her second husband, Théodore de la Batut, and he apparently set immediately to spending the rest of it. He took a suite at the Hôtel Britannique, rue Louis le Grand, in a fashionable quarter of Paris convenient to the city's numerous theatres. He also changed his name, brazenly abandoning the Hungerford name that his benefactor uncle had requested he adopt. He took instead the lyrical name of his stepfather, de la Batut; and then, even more ostentatiously, he began calling himself a baron, despite not having any claim to the title. In this way, as Baron Henry de la Batut, the illegitimate Henry James Dickenson made his entrance in towns throughout Europe. It was, in a sense, fitting; he had affected only a more grandiose version of his uncle's own pretensions as Monsieur de Smithson, Seigneur Anglais.[2]

The nephew was like his uncle in another way as well. He was plagued with poor health, and he traveled to Italy, just, it seems, as Smithson had, with only a servant as company, in search of curative air. He left Paris in June 1834, headed for Marseilles, intending to travel on to Naples. He does not seem to have ever arrived there. In late May 1835 he presented himself to the English consul at Livorno and installed himself in a hotel overlooking the Arno in Pisa. A few days later, the high-flying, self-styled Baron de la Batut, aged twenty-six or twenty-seven, unmarried and without children, was dead. It had been only six years since Smithson's death. There was not even money enough left in his account to pay his debtors or his funeral expenses.[3]

The death of this obscure young man set in motion an

extraordinary sequence of events, which led ultimately to the birth of the Smithsonian Institution. In London a group of solicitors appeared on the doorstep of the American chargé d'affaires, bearing with them the startling news that an Englishman named James Smithson had left a "very considerable" estate to the United States of America, "to found at Washington, under the name of the Smithsonian Institution, an establishment for the increase and diffusion of knowledge among men."[4] This information, when delivered to Washington, elicited mostly bewilderment. President Andrew Jackson was not even sure that he possessed the authority to accept such a bequest. No one had ever left this kind of gift to the United States government before. Especially puzzling was the news that the donor had no connection to the country or any ostensible reason for such largesse. There was simply no precedent for such a sweeping gesture. After some deliberation, Jackson turned the matter over to Congress, leaving it up to them to decide whether or not Smithson's donation could be received.[5]

Smithson's mandate was entirely contained in one brief, single-sentence directive. The location and name of the proposed foundation were clear. Its purpose was much less apparent. What exactly *was* an establishment for the increase and diffusion of knowledge? Was it a national university? A library? A laboratory? A museum? These questions would later preoccupy Congress for nearly a decade.

More immediately, however, people questioned the motivation behind such unprecedented philanthropy. Few could believe that the bequest was really an act of enlightened generosity. The whole story exuded an air of megalomania. A man had given a huge gift to a country he had never even seen, all—it appeared—in order to have his name on a building in the nation's capital. The chargé d'affaires in London suggested, privately, in his report on the matter, that there was some question as to whether "the Testator labored under some degree of mental aberration at the time it [the will] was made."[6]

John Quincy Adams, now serving as a congressman after having been president, thought he understood better than anyone the aspirations behind James Smithson's gift. A near exact contemporary of Smithson, Adams had been raised in the courts of Europe, enjoying a cosmopolitan, well-traveled childhood with his diplomat-president father; he nursed a keen interest in scientific research, and he believed that the government could be a force for improvement and scientific advance. As president he had campaigned in his very first address to Congress for the establishment of a national university, the sponsorship of scientific expeditions, and the creation of an astronomical observatory—this last a cause he renewed when presented with the opportunity of the Smithson bequest. He was appointed chairman of the congressional committee convened to consider the bequest, and he argued eloquently for its acceptance. For Adams, Smithson's bequest "signalized the spirit of the age," and he hoped that Congress might show its appreciation of Smithson's "comprehensive beneficence" by unanimously approving a bill to accept the bequest.[7]

The promise, however, of a national institution to be located in the capital posed a significant threat to those in the South who championed the issue of states' rights. In the Senate the news of this eccentric legacy ran headlong into the brewing storm of a north–south divide. Both senators from South Carolina vehemently opposed accepting the Smithson bequest. John C. Calhoun railed that it was "beneath the dignity of the United States to receive presents of this kind from anyone." William Preston believed that Congress should not "pander to the paltry vanity of an individual," and the city should not be used "as a fulcrum to raise foreigners to immortality." Otherwise, he ranted, "every Whippersnapper vagabond that had been traducing our country might think proper to have his name distinguished in the same way."[8] Ultimately, at the beginning of July 1836, Congress agreed to condone the appointment of an agent to go to England to secure the money. Beyond that nothing was assured.

Immediately, the appeal of a prominent sinecure, representing the government abroad, lured prospective suitors to the door of the

White House. "It would be gratifying to my pride and conducive to my political fortunes here," gushed one hopeful, "to receive some appointment from the President as he is going out of office. I know of none that I would accept but the agency under the Resolution of the Senate in relation to the Smithson bequest. I should like that appointment, because it would introduce me to the men of business, and give me as much of an official character as I could wish, without chaining me down to a particular spot. The salary is nothing—my own fortune is ample . . ."[9] Wealth was, in fact, an important criterion for the job. The agent would have to be circumspect, a gifted diplomat, skilled in legal matters, and rich. To ensure that he would not abscond with the Smithson monies, he would have to post a bond of half a million dollars.[10] Jackson's choice, in the end, was excellent.

Richard Rush was a lawyer, a seasoned diplomat, and the son of the noted Philadelphia physician Benjamin Rush, one of the signatories of the Declaration of Independence. He had extensive contacts in London, where he had lived for nearly eight years as the United States' ambassador to the Court of St. James's.[11] It took Rush little more than a few weeks to put his affairs in order and raise the money for the bond. He sailed in early August to Liverpool, arriving in London in the first days of September 1836.

Rush quickly learned the particulars of the case from the solicitors—and the problems that faced him. Smithson had indicated, in quite an unusual clause in his will, that the money was to be left to legitimate or illegitimate children, and it would take some doing to prove that there was no secret love child somewhere. Discreet inquiries would have to be made in Italy, France, and England, without drawing attention to the vast sum involved—which Rush was sure would invite fraudulent claimants.

There was also the matter of the nephew's mother, Madame de la Batut, who was pressing for her share of the money. Rush quickly dismissed such talk, but it was not at all clear that she did not have a right to at least some compensation. A portion of Smithson's

"A Chancery Suit!" A caricature from 1828 highlighting the endless delays in Chancery; the plaintiff goes from dandy to pauper, while the solicitor does the opposite.

fortune had come from his brother, and Dickenson in his will, when leaving his estate to Smithson in trust for his son, had wished for her to enjoy half the income during her lifetime. Smithson had in fact, following the death of his brother, made payments to his brother's widow from time to time, and the nephew had continued the tradition.[12]

And lastly, there was the question of whether or not Smithson's servant, John Fitall—the only other person with a claim to the money, as he had been left an annuity in the will—was still alive. This last point, at least, would not be difficult to figure out.

Rush hoped that the case could be concluded without it having to appear before the infamous Court of Chancery. In the mid-1830s the court was some eight hundred cases in arrears, a backlog that had already reached legendary proportions. "A suit in this Court is become proverbial for something interminable," one visitor to London observed.[13] Charles Dickens immortalized the process in *Bleak House*, set in a lurid and murky 1830s London. Tom Jarndyce, one of the players in the epic suit Jarndyce v. Jarndyce, who eventually kills himself in a coffeehouse on Chancery Lane, likens the experience to a slow, drawn-out torture. "It's being ground to bits in a slow mill," he says; "it's being roasted at a slow fire; it's being stung to death by single bees; it's being drowned by drops; it's going mad by grains."[14]

Rush was understandably daunted by the prospect of the Smithson bequest being smothered by red tape, a term in fact inspired by the red ribbons wrapped around the voluminous case records at Chancery. Unfortunately, the lawyers, when Rush was finally able to sit down with them, promptly ruled out the possibility of avoiding the labyrinthine court system. True to Rush's fears, the fabled delays set in. It was February 1, 1837, five months after Rush's arrival in England, before the first hearing on the case was held.

During what he called "the first interval in my little Smithsonian steps," while he waited for the opening hearing, Rush filled his time with weekend parties at the great country houses and sightseeing in

London.[15] These intervening months, however, were hardly free of trouble for the Smithson case. The President of the United States v. Drummonds & Co., the executors of Smithson's will, represented the first instance of the U.S. ever launching a suit in a court of law in England. In January 1837, as the case drew towards the first hearing, the Attorney General for His Majesty—who had been made a party to the case—moved to have the bequest declared void and the Smithson money passed to the Crown. "A complication of illegitimacy" had arisen, Rush reported back to the State Department. Keen to keep the Smithson money from leaving the country, the Crown argued for the will to be set aside on the grounds that Smithson's provision for any illegitimate children of his nephew to inherit under his will was invalid. And on the grounds of the ancient doctrine of escheats, which governed estates left ownerless or in limbo, the Crown stated that Smithson's estate should pass to it in the absence of a valid will. Although this line of argument was quickly dropped, the circumstances of Smithson's birth, amazingly, haunted his estate even beyond the grave.[16]

The de la Batut family proved another serious challenge for Rush. Madame de la Batut's husband came to London to press the family's "moral claim" to some portion of the estate. Since the Smithson bequest was intended to promote knowledge, he argued, his children should be entitled to an allowance for their education. Rush grew increasingly exasperated with the demands of the family, telling the U.S. government later that "To no one can I give the remotest encouragement . . . and least of all to one so unreasonable, so exacting, and apparently so bent upon thwarting the rights of the U.S. as Monsieur la Batut."[17]

The de la Batut family was, however, in many ways the only source who could supply the information critical to bringing the case to a quick close: proof that Smithson's nephew had died without heirs. Congress had allocated $10,000 for the total costs of securing the Smithson bequest, and Rush found the money slipping away at an alarming rate. "It seems that something is to be paid for every step taken," he lamented, "every line written, and almost every word spoken by counsel, senior and junior, solicitors, clerks, and everybody connected with the courts, and officers attached to them, under the extremely complicated and artificial judiciary systems that exist here."[18] In an effort to hasten the proceedings, he soon concluded that it was best to compromise in regard to the family and allow their claim to go forward.

Rush's decisions were on the whole outstanding—and in the sea of unending, generation-breaking lawsuits that was Chancery, the Smithson case sailed sturdily through in less than two years. "I assure you it was considered a thing next to impossible that you should succeed," one of Rush's English friends finally told him, once it was all over.[19] In May 1838, the court awarded the bequest to the United States. They also determined that Mary Ann de la Batut was entitled to an annuity—her portion of the interest due her during her lifetime, as per Dickenson's will. She was granted a payment of £150 a year, backdated to September 1834—the time when Smithson's nephew dropped off making regular payments to his mother. A sum of £5,015 was left in stock in England to generate income enough to cover this annual payment.[20]

Rush decided to bring the money, which was mostly in the form of annuities (the equivalent of government bonds), back to the United States as gold coin. It totaled a little over £105,000. Using the common retail price index, which measures purchasing power, this would be the equivalent of a little under £7,000,000 today; using other indicators, however, such as one reflecting the per capita share in the GDP, it could be valued at as much as £97,000,000. Over the course of the next few weeks, with the help of the savvy U.S. consul, he carefully monitored the markets in England, looking for the most opportune time to cash in Smithson's holdings. The country was in a dizzied state of excitement over Queen Victoria's coronation, and Rush worried that if the young Queen took sick, "only think how the stocks would come down." The sheer volume of trading that Rush was contemplating held its own dangers; he was warned that unloading all the bank stock at once might well depress the market. He decided to sell off Smithson's holdings in several smaller pieces. Rush in the end was triumphant at his successful playing of the market, telling the U.S. government that what he had brought in for the 3 percent consols was, he believed, the highest price that had been seen in nearly eight years.[21]

Finally, at the end of July 1838, he prepared to set sail. Smithson's belongings had been stored in a warehouse in London, and Rush had the boxes opened to make a fresh inventory of the contents. Packed haphazardly years earlier, they were already suffering the effects of mold and dirt. It quickly became clear that a number of things from the original inventory were now missing, including Smithson's gun, an assortment of china, a pair of glass candlesticks, a "Derby spar vase" (made of the dark violet fluor-spar, or "Blue John," found near Castleton), and two small oval portraits—probably those of the two Percy girls, Smithson's half-sisters Dorothy and Philadelphia, willed to him by Margaret Marriott.[22] These objects, the solicitors concluded, had most likely been taken by the nephew and were now gone. The Americans carefully repacked the trunks and secured them with the consular seal, and Smithson's possessions joined the 104,960 gold sovereign coins that comprised the Smithson bequest—packed in leather bags, and sealed in eleven boxes—on the transport ship that was to carry Rush home. In the first days of September 1838, after a turbulent, month-long crossing filled with "squalls, gales, and headwinds," the aptly named *Mediator* sailed into view of the friendly, steeple-topped harbor of New York. More than two years had passed since Rush had set out to claim the Smithson bequest.

Anxious to complete his mission to the utmost, Rush personally escorted the gold coins to the U.S. Mint in Philadelphia. There the sovereigns were recoined into American currency, Queen Victoria's profile replaced by an American eagle. The conversion yielded $508,318.46—a sum that represented about $\frac{1}{66}$th of the entire federal budget for 1838.[23] The successful prosecutor of the Smithson suit then returned to his lawyerly life in Philadelphia and his comfortable family idyll, Sydenham, in the countryside outside town. His battles on behalf of the Smithson bequest, however, were, as it turned out, not yet over.

Even before the deposit of the Smithson fund to the U.S. Treasury, Congress had begun contemplating the proposed Smithsonian Institution. Most members were in agreement on the benefits that such a foundation might bring to the country, but there was still widespread confusion over what was to be the principal purpose of the new institution. The Secretary of State appealed to men of science across the country for their ideas, eliciting a proposal for an agricultural school that could serve as a "nursery of scientific agriculturists for the whole Union," another for a university to teach "Latin, Greek, Hebrew and the Oriental languages," and one for an institute for research in the physical sciences, among other suggestions.[24]

Rush weighed in with an idea for a wide-ranging cultural institution that included a natural history collection, a collection of antiquities, and "courses of lectures which should be free to a certain number of young men from each State."[25] Thomas Cooper, a chemist and mineralogist who had recently retired as president of South Carolina College (today the University of South Carolina), wrote that he objected to any plan to teach "belles-lettres and philosophical literature, as calculated only to make men pleasant talkers." Cooper had long ago been a member, like Smithson, in the Coffee House Philosophical Society, though he never claimed to have known Smithson. Like Smithson, too, he believed in the power of science to advance society, and he argued that a university devoted to practical science—promoting research that would "multiply the comforts of existence to the great mass of mankind"—was the best use of the fund.[26] Cooper's views were popular in the Senate, but in the House, John Quincy Adams, the most ardent champion of the bequest, made a case for an astronomical observatory—that project for which he had so passionately advocated during his presidency.[27]

The House and Senate established a joint committee to discuss the Smithsonian. These two bodies had such divergent aspirations for the trust, however, that the committee was soon dissolved. A few members in the Senate, in fact, continued to question the constitutionality of accepting Smithson's money at all. John C. Calhoun remained virulently opposed to the idea of Congress establishing a national institution in the District of Columbia. "We must look carefully at the extent of our own power," he warned. "This Government is a trust, established by the States, with a specific capacity, education not included, and all the powers which are not granted are expressly reserved to the States. . . . [W]hat are we to do with the money? There is no difficulty in that; it must be returned to the heirs."[28]

Outside of Congress, the Smithson bequest tapped into an ongoing discussion about America's status in the international scientific community. The United States lacked a public face like the new British Association for the Advancement of Science, an umbrella organization that could spur professional development and promote public interest in science. And the state of scientific knowledge generally was considered poor. "Our newspapers are filled with the puffs of quackery," decried one of America's most important scientists—Joseph Henry, the man who later became the first head of the Smithsonian—"and every man who can burn phosphorus in oxygen and exhibit a few experiments to a class of Young Ladies is called a man of science."[29] Clearly, the Smithsonian, if it could be established with an effective program, had the potential to make a significant contribution to American life.

In 1840 the National Institution (later Institute) for the Promotion of Science was founded in Washington, in large part with an eye towards becoming the logical repository of the Smithson monies.[30] The brainchild of South Carolinian Joel Poinsett, a former secretary of war and the man for whom the poinsettia plant is named, the National Institute put forth an ambitious agenda—one that was ultimately unsuccessful but did have a considerable impact on the formation of the Smithsonian. The National Institute planned to establish a national museum of natural history, ideally to showcase the collections amassed by the U.S. Exploring Expedition, which Poinsett had helped to organize. They also proposed an observatory, botanical and zoological gardens, and "apparatus for illustrating every branch of Physical Science." They did gain control of the government collections from the Exploring Expedition, displaying them at the Patent Office—over the disgruntled objections of the Commissioner of Patents. They also managed to secure Smithson's possessions, which were transferred from Philadelphia.[31] But despite all these maneuvers, Poinsett and his faction were unable to unite their fortunes to the Smithson bequest. Lacking funds and strong congressional support, accused of operating out of "self-aggrandizement" rather than for "the promotion of science," the National Institute after a rapid ascent failed to gain momentum.[32] It faltered along, having been granted a twenty-year charter at its inception, ironically watching the Smithsonian, when it was finally founded, embrace nearly everything to which it had aspired.

As the years passed, and resolution after resolution was tabled without any successful legislation, Adams privately fretted in his diary that the money might be "squandered upon cormorants or wasted in electioneering bribery." The only successful action that had been taken regarding the bequest was driven by just such special interests. The money after its deposit in the Treasury had been invested in the state bonds of Arkansas, Michigan, and Illinois. Within a few years the states had defaulted on their payments, and the Smithson fund seemed in danger of being lost. On top of everything, the Smithson money now had to be rescued from what Adams called "the fangs of the State of Arkansas."[33]

Ten years after Congress had first green-lighted the United States' acceptance of the Smithson bequest, there finally began to be some movement on a bill for a Smithsonian. Many had stepped forward to champion their own pet projects, and proposals for botanical gardens, cabinets of natural history, and educational foundations had all been mooted, but none had succeeded in becoming law. In late

1844 Senator Benjamin Tappan of Ohio proposed a bill for an institution combining a natural history museum, mineralogical cabinet, lecture hall, chemical laboratory, and a ten-acre agricultural station. Rufus Choate of Massachusetts led a contingent who believed a "grand and noble public library . . . durable as liberty, durable as the Union," was the best use of the fund, and he succeeded in having a library provision added to Tappan's bill. On January 21, 1845, with the Senate's ratification, it became the first Smithsonian bill to pass either branch of Congress.[34]

Brought to the House for approval, the bill foundered for a year before Robert Dale Owen, the son of the utopian New Harmony, Indiana, founder Robert Owen (friend to Smithson's eccentric protégé Baume), was able to get his own substitute bill considered. Owen took out the provision for a library, disdaining the idea of trying to compete with Europe. "Shall we grudge to Europe her antiquarian lore, her cumbrous folios, her illuminated manuscripts, the chaff of learned dullness that cumbers her old library shelves?" he asked. He championed instead a teacher training college, an opportunity to spread knowledge across the nation through the improvement of the common school system.[35] His plan, which also encompassed a natural history collection, an experimental garden, and a laboratory, gained a large measure of support, but John Quincy Adams railed fervidly against the idea of a common school as contrary to Smithson's wishes. At the last moment William J. Hough, a first-term congressman from New York, proposed a substitute bill that omitted the educational component; the backers of the library, meanwhile, managed to slip in an amendment increasing the appropriation for a national library. Finally, a Smithsonian bill had been drawn up that met with the satisfaction of a majority of members—though not without "almost a death struggle," according to Owen's father.[36] On April 30, 1846, the House sent word to the Senate that they had passed a bill enacting the Smithsonian.

The Senate promptly established a commission to assess the bill and add their own amendments. As they lingered in their debates, letters poured in urging Congress to act. In Albany, New York, a convention of county superintendents "could not suppress their deep mortification and painful regret" that the United States had not yet carried out any plans for such a "noble and exalted" gift as Smithson's.[37] But it was not until August 10, 1846, the very last day of the session, that the Smithsonian bill was finally brought up for review. "The day," wrote Adams in his diary, "like all the last days of a Session of Congress was a Chaos of confusion." At noon the final meeting of the session would adjourn, regardless of the work in progress. As the trains idled at the station, waiting to take members away from the swelter of Washington and home to their districts, the question was asked: "Shall this bill pass?" Thirteen said nay, but twenty-six senators replied yea. It was done.[38]

The Smithsonian, miraculously, had been legislated into existence. Twenty years after Smithson wrote his will, the unique secondary clause he had included had been brought to life. It had very nearly not happened. At dozens of points the story of the Smithsonian could have taken a markedly different turn. Smithson's nephew Henry James Hungerford, the primary beneficiary of Smithson's will, might have married and had children, relegating the bequest to an amusing family anecdote about quirky old Uncle James. The United States Congress could have refused the gift outright in 1835, rendering it a casualty of the nascent states' rights battle that eventually gave birth to the Civil War. Richard Rush could have failed in his suit at Chancery, or brought home a pittance of the original sum, had the case dragged on for years as most at that time did. The *Mediator*, which carried Rush home to America, could have sunk with its gold coin cargo in any one of the terrible storms it encountered crossing the Atlantic. And of course, without the vigilance of John Quincy Adams and others, Congress' eight years of debates on the nature of a Smithsonian Institution might well have ended in stalemate or oblivion. Time and again Smithson's gift foundered or fell by the wayside, only to be resurrected.

The fights over the purpose of the Smithsonian, unsurprisingly perhaps, hardly ended with the passage of the act enabling the institution. The legislation was a classic example of the art of congressional compromise. It was bursting with programmatic directives; squabbles over the allocation of resources were inevitable. The 6 percent annual interest that comprised the budget amounted to about $30,000—a pretty modest amount to fund a natural history museum, library, gallery of art, and a chemical laboratory, not to mention salaries, publications, and lectures. Compared with other private endowments in the United States, the Smithson fund was an impressively large sum of money, exceeded only slightly by that of Harvard University. Smithson's gift, furthermore, as the donation of a single individual, existed in a league of its own; Harvard's endowment had already been accumulating two hundred years by the mid-nineteenth century. But compared with the resources of the federal government—the Smithsonian's annual budget was one-quarter that of the government's Coast Survey, as an example—the Smithson bequest was relatively insignificant. It was hardly enough money to undertake properly all the myriad activities specified in the legislation, much less construct a large, ornate building on top of it all.[39]

In December 1846 the newly appointed regents of the Smithsonian— a governing board that included the Vice President, the Chief Justice, the Mayor of Washington, three senators and three congressmen, two members of the National Institute, and a handful of private citizens—picked Joseph Henry to be the first secretary of the Smithsonian. A much sought-after professor at the College of New Jersey (Princeton), Henry was the most prominent experimental physicist in the United States. He was also an extremely pragmatic and hard-nosed leader. He saw quite clearly the challenges and risks that such a liberal mandate posed to the future effectiveness of any Smithsonian Institution. He also saw the potential the Smithson gift held to transform American science. Drawing up a careful program of organization, he offered his interpretation of how best to carry out James Smithson's mandate. Henry believed that the Smithsonian could play a vital role in America by funding basic original scientific research and disseminating it through publication. "The increase of knowledge," he explained, "is much more difficult and in reference to the bearing of this institution on the character of our country and the welfare of mankind much more important than the diffusion of knowledge. There are at this time thousands of institutions actively engaged in the diffusion of knowledge in our country, but not a single one which gives direct support to its increase."[40] He advocated economy in the creation of a building and argued that the permanent staff supported by the bequest should be kept small. Stern and high-minded, Henry came to see himself as the only one who could properly carry out Smithson's wishes. He dedicated himself to the future of science in America, passing up other lucrative offers to do it—thinking perhaps, like Smithson, of posterity.[41]

The regents, however, who included Richard Rush and Congressman Robert Dale Owen, were keen to uphold the broad mandate of the legislation. In the first decade of the institution Henry battled with the building committee, who were intent on creating an architectural showpiece for the nation; he fought the librarian, who angled to position the Smithsonian as the platform for a national library; and he derided the placement of a lecture hall in the Smithsonian building for similar reasons, believing it was "a perversion of the trust," because the hall could reach only a local audience and not all of mankind as Smithson intended.[42]

The biggest conflict of all was over the museum. Henry struggled to keep the Smithson fund independent of the government, even as the Smithsonian was drawn ever more deeply into the role of custodian of federal collections. The Smithsonian's founding coincided with the birth of Manifest Destiny, the belief that God had blessed America with abundant land to spread the experiment in democracy. Government expeditions fanned across the continent, sending back trunkloads of specimens to Washington; the

Smithsonian's new building emerged as an ideal public exposition space, and it was one not yet filled. It was only a matter of time before it would be claimed as an essential repository for a national museum.

In 1858 Henry agreed to the transfer of the government scientific collections from the Patent Office, in exchange for financial support of his meteorological program—a decision that would have an extraordinary impact on the future direction of the Smithsonian. For the first time, Henry negotiated a large appropriation from Congress to underwrite the upkeep of the museum. Federal support was something he had long opposed, for fear of congressional interference in matters of scientific research. He remained determined to maintain the Smithsonian's independence, and he worked hard to keep the museum under a separate administrative umbrella. The overwhelming amount of work involved in maintaining the collections, however, soon dominated the activities of the institution, and the multi-faceted Smithsonian evolved primarily into a museum, the role for which it is known today. This trajectory was halted only briefly, with the fire of 1865.[43]

The fire of 1865, for all that Henry personally lost with the destruction of his papers and correspondence, gave him another opportunity to reshape the agenda of the Smithsonian; and he took full advantage of it. In an effort to concentrate the institution's resources once more on scientific research, he sent the library up to the Library of Congress, the herbarium to the Department of Agriculture, and the art to the new Corcoran Gallery. He made no request to have the lecture hall rebuilt, and he had the building properly fireproofed. Henry's agenda lasted until his death in 1878; his successor, Spencer Baird, who had been in charge of the museum under Henry, made the museum the centerpiece of the institution.

Joseph Henry also used his position as an expert scientist and leader of the Smithsonian to advocate for federal support for the sciences outside of the institution; while he labored to protect the Smithson fund, he encouraged the government to underwrite expeditions and inventions and original research. He was instrumental in the founding of the American Association for the Advancement of Science and eventually served as its president, and he did likewise with the National Academy of Sciences.

In Henry's efforts to develop a profile for American science, Smithson's money, poignantly, did for the United States what Smithson had attempted to do for himself all his life: bring legitimacy. It did more as well. In Henry's able hands, it became a powerful example of what private funding could accomplish for scientific research in the United States. A great surge of philanthropy supporting scientific research and education followed on Smithson's gift. Observatories, universities, libraries, museums, and other learned institutions were erected by generous patrons seeking to spread scientific enlightenment among the people. John Lowell bequeathed to Boston the Lowell Institute, with an endowment of $250,000 to bring distinguished lecturers to the city. The eccentric James Lick, looking for a way to memorialize himself, entertained visions of a pyramid larger than the Great Pyramid at Giza to be built in his name in downtown San Francisco before being convinced in the 1870s to endow the Lick Observatory in the Diablo Range, east of San Jose, California, which became the first permanent mountaintop observatory in the world. George Peabody set up the Peabody Institutes and the Peabody Education Fund, bringing a richer cultural life to Baltimore and other cities; and Peter Cooper established the Cooper Union in New York City, with the very Royal Institution–like mission of advancing science and art in their application to daily life.[44] Levi Woodbury, Treasury Secretary under President Jackson and later Supreme Court justice, invoked Smithson's name as he urged his fellow Americans to develop the country. "Every act well done," he said, "may become the parent of a numerous progeny, by attracting imitation, through the esteem and admiration of all who witness it." A gesture as modest as planting a single tree mattered; that person still, Woodbury argued, "to a certain extent, becomes a public benefactor." One person, he suggested, might create a hospital for the destitute, or "another, like Smithson, create a fund for the noble end of diffusing knowledge among mankind."[45] Smithson's gift took on a new life in America, and so too did Smithson. The benefactor became a model for future philanthropists.

Even before the fire of 1865, however, the context that gave rise to the ideals behind Smithson's bequest—the ferment of knowledge that comprised what is often now called the English Enlightenment—had virtually vanished. Smithson's belief in scientific exchange and opportunity had been forged in the coffeehouse societies of Revolutionary Europe; his models were likely bodies like the Royal Institution, dedicated places of research that sought also to make scientific education accessible to all. The Smithsonian as it emerged in the 1840s and 1850s took shape as a product of Victorian America. Its organization and interests reflected the needs and goals of a different culture and a very different scientific climate. In this transplanted environment, the Smithsonian's founder became simply a name, his motivations a mystery.

In 1861, the Smithsonian learned of the death of Madame de la Batut, the mother of Smithson's nephew, in France. They also discovered that the money left in England to generate her income had appreciated greatly in the intervening years. The £5,015 lodged twenty-three years earlier in England realized $54,165.38 for the institution.[46]

The passing of Madame de la Batut was not the last that the Smithsonian heard of this curious tangent from the Smithson story, however. Throughout the late nineteenth century her children clamored for recompense, in letters that decried the defrauding of their mother—and, by extension, themselves. "Great nations honor themselves by their gratitude to their benefactors," Emma Kerby de la Batut wrote, "and on this score the United States owe us a reparation."[47]

The first aggrieved letter from this next generation arrived at the institution in the mid-1870s. In it Georges Henri de la Batut stated that he had sent a letter a few years earlier but had heard no reply, and he wondered if the Smithsonian had thought it was a hoax. "No, Sir," he announced, "I am the half brother of Henry James Hungerford and it is from some rubbish left by him that I find myself the possessor of this portrait [of James Smithson]. I have thought that it would be much better in the care of the Institution than in the hands of a disinherited person and I have decided to send it to you." Along with this miniature de la Batut also eventually sent a copy of Smithson's will written in his hand, a portrait of Henry Louis Dickenson, and one of the nephew. For the Smithsonian, which had lost nearly everything connected to Smithson in the fire of 1865, the news of these objects was extremely welcome. They promptly dispatched an agent to pay a visit to the de la Batuts in Brittany.

The Smithsonian representative found only two people in the little town who spoke any English, a Navy lieutenant in charge of the Morbihan River oyster beds and an English jeweler married to a Frenchwoman. A wary Georges de la Batut, a local justice of the peace, received the men. Then in his early forties, about five feet eleven inches, with brown hair and blue-grey eyes, de la Batut had a "heavy English figure, and in features [was] not unlike the Prince of Wales." He was suspicious of his visitors, and the Smithsonian official soon determined that the family was deeply embittered at the loss of the Smithson fortune. They still believed that they were entitled to some money from the estate.[48]

De la Batut nevertheless, as he had promised, went and "hunt[ed] through his mother's effects and his own papers" for memorabilia related to Smithson and his brother Dickenson. He mailed the Smithsonian a number of treasures—those items already mentioned, along with some scraps of letters indicating Smithson's social circles in Paris, an engraved portrait of the Duke of Northumberland, the passport papers of the nephew, the diary of Smithson's brother. A few months later, though, he was writing again to the Smithsonian. He complained that he had not been thanked, and he was genuinely irked to learn that the lieutenant in the village who had served as translator had been sent a set of books and engravings from the Smithsonian. The Smithsonian promptly mailed off a barrage of gifts to France—including twenty-five volumes of Smithsonian publications, eleven volumes of the Pacific Railroad Survey, ten volumes of the Geological Survey of the Western Territories, four volumes of the Fisheries Commission, a mineral map of New South Wales, three dozen stereoscopic views of national parks in the United States, and a photographic portrait of Joseph Henry. The damage, however, had already been done. De la Batut's next letter closed with this ominous warning: "When the Institution thinks of disinterring the remains of Smithson let it remember that I will be in the way. If he has given away his fortune, his remains still belong to his family."[49]

Decades later, these words came back to haunt the Smithsonian. In the first years of the new century, the Smithsonian learned that the city of Genoa was planning to move the bodies interred in the cemetery where James Smithson was buried. The city was steadily reclaiming the cypress-covered heights of San Benigno, quarrying the great chalk cliffs overlooking the harbor—"slowly but surely eating its way towards us from the sea," in the words of one member of the cemetery committee. While most of the Smithsonian regents greeted this news with indifference, content to let Smithson's resting place remain in Italy, one member of the board saw in the dilemma a momentous opportunity.[50] For Alexander Graham Bell, the famous inventor of the telephone, James Smithson was somebody worth remembering. In Bell's eyes Smithson's legacy had profoundly altered the direction and development of an entire country. His gift had marshaled the energies of the young government of the United States and provided a focal point for the collective organization of scientific research. It had provided an organ for the dissemination of knowledge and a repository for the immense and irreplaceable national collections of natural history specimens. Smithson's faith in the American government as the instrument to implement his bequest elicited Bell's deepest respect and gratitude.

Bell identified strongly with Smithson's philanthropy. Despite the fact that he was only fifty-six, Bell was in appearance already the avuncular white-bearded man of legend. His invention of the telephone, when he was still in his twenties, had transformed society and the way that man contemplated communication; the liberal patent that had been granted such a fundamental discovery had ensured him an ample fortune. Bell had since devoted much of his wealth to fostering scientific research in America. He had established the Volta Laboratory Association in Washington to support research on deafness. He had underwritten the magazine *Science*, headed the National Geographic Society, and had actively supported the manned flight or "aerodrome" experiments of the man now heading the Smithsonian, Samuel Pierpont Langley. The Smithsonian's founder, in Bell's opinion, deserved a proper measure of homage. James Smithson's remains should be brought to America, he said, and "interred with due honors in the grounds of the Institution which he founded."[51] Bell's proposal, however, found no support. He felt so strongly about the matter that when he saw the rest of the board uninterested in taking action, he even offered to pay the expenses of relocating Smithson's remains out of his own pocket. But the regents remained unconvinced, and time was running short. At the end of November 1903, the Smithsonian was informed that Genoa had expropriated the cemetery land. Their intentions regarding the disposition of Smithson's remains had to be communicated to Italy before the first of the year.

It was Bell's dynamic son-in-law, who became the first full-time editor of the *National Geographic*, Gilbert Grosvenor, who turned the tide. Grosvenor published a lengthy editorial in the *New York Herald*, entitled "Should Smithson's Bones be Brought to America?," in which he put the case to the nation. "James Smithson, the founder of the Smithsonian Institution, is about to be turned out of his grave, in Genoa, Italy, to make room for a quarry," he announced. "We should place him where he may rest in peace—not for another seventy-five or one hundred years, but for as long as the great nation lives for which he showed such complete confidence and respect." The piece was reprinted across the country, from the *Virginian-Pilot* in Norfolk to the *Salt Lake Tribune* in Utah, and America responded. Soon enough, an about-face amongst the regents had Bell and his wife on a steamer to Europe.[52]

The Bells arrived in Genoa on a dark and dreary Christmas Day. Bell had caught a cold on the train from Paris, which was "aggravated by a chilly ride on Christmas Day without wraps." Confined to his hotel, he doodled in his notebooks, musing about the lime-dissolving liquid in which a hen lays an egg and its potential as a rheumatism remedy, while his wife explored the steep cobbled streets of the city.[53] From his room Bell tried to coordinate plans for the removal of Smithson's remains. There were permissions to secure, health officers to contact, and shipping arrangements to make. But beyond these bureaucratic stumbling blocks there lay an even more formidable obstacle. An employee of the city had excitedly produced a paper some twenty-five years old, in which a man in France ostentatiously stated his claim over the bones of James Smithson. The bureaucrat had been able to recall the exact location of the letter in his files because, he said, in all his years of work he had never seen anything like it. The Smithsonian, it appeared, was not going to be able simply to cart Smithson away.[54]

Back at Bell's hotel, the U.S. consul fretted nervously about the state of affairs. He was aghast that the legal claim to the site was not absolutely free and clear. It was only after lengthy consultation with the mayor of Genoa and the British consul that the exhumation was arranged, but Bell still decided to take only the remains. He left behind the monument—which was decisively carved with the inscription "This monument is erected, and the ground on which it stands purchased in perpetuity, by Henry Hungerford, esq., the deceased's nephew." The Smithsonian subsequently retrieved the sarcophagus later in 1904.[55]

William Henry Bishop, the American consul at Genoa,
photographed holding up Smithson's skull by Mrs. Bell, 1903.

High on the heights of San Benigno, in the midst of a snowstorm
made that much more intolerable by the cold whip of the wind,
the exhumation proceeded. Snow collected on hat brims and the
collars of woolen coats as the men peered into the chasm of the
tomb. Mrs. Bell toiled in the background taking photographs.
Smithson's skeleton, once exposed, lay coated in a fine layer of red
dust, the remains of the thin wooden coffin in which he had been
buried. "The effect recalled to me, on a large scale," the U.S. consul
said later, "that of a desiccated leaf." He held up Smithson's skull
in contemplation for Mrs. Bell's camera. Together they created a
series a pictures they impishly called the "Alas, poor Yorick" set.[56]

For the next few nights, guarded by the gardener, Smithson's
remains, now sealed in a strong zinc coffin, rested in the cemetery's
mortuary chapel, a little Doric temple surrounded by cypress trees.
Bell, from his hotel, worried about what lay ahead. "It is to be
hoped," he confided to his diary, "that these few bones—almost all
that really remains of what was once the wealthy gentleman and
scientific student—will escape the fate that has befallen all his other

possessions which have preceded him to America!"[57] On the morning
of January 2, 1904, they held a brief ceremony at the chapel; the
coffin was draped with an American flag, Mrs. Bell placed a wreath
of leaves from the gravesite, and the others contributed flowers.
Smithson's remains were then transferred to the steamer *Princess Irene*
in the harbor below.

Bell's son-in-law had not been idle while Bell had been in Italy.
Gilbert Grosvenor had gone over the heads of the Smithsonian
regents and gained the backing of President Theodore Roosevelt
for an elaborate reception. Smithson's arrival in Washington was
marked in grand style. The president ordered the Navy to send a
boat to escort the *Princess Irene* into harbor, and Grosvenor arranged
for a troop of U.S. Cavalry to accompany the casket from the Navy
Yard to the Smithsonian. On the morning of January 24, 1904, as
the Marine band played "Nearer My God to Thee," Smithson's
coffin, draped in the American and British flags, was winched over
the side of the ship to begin the stately trip to the Smithsonian.
Men on the sidewalks doffed their hats as the solemn cortege passed
down Pennsylvania Avenue; the mounted soldiers were followed
by the carriages carrying the dignitaries in their best dark suits and
silk top hats, and by the large-wheeled caisson with the flag-draped
coffin. They drew up to the porte-cochere of the old red sandstone
Smithsonian building, and Smithson was carried upstairs and placed
in state in the regents' room—the very room where long ago his
personal effects had been displayed.[58]

Soon after the arrival of Smithson's remains, the Smithsonian
solicited designs for a memorial to the institution's founder. They
called on prominent artists and architects around the country,
including Augustus St. Gaudens; Gutzon Borglum, the sculptor who
went on to create Mount Rushmore; and Henry Bacon, later the
architect of the Lincoln Memorial. Washington in these years lay
in the grips of the City Beautiful movement, its landscape undergoing
a transformation from a clutter of Victorian red brick into a city of
magnificent axial vistas and gleaming marble monuments. The

Henry Bacon's design for a mausoleum for Smithson, 1904.

proposals for Smithson's tomb, following these general artistic trends, were a parade of images of neoclassical splendor. One presented a bust of Smithson on a pedestal under a classical pergola. Another resembled the Mausoleum of Halicarnassus, one of the seven wonders of the ancient world. Borglum proposed a monumental "heroic" statue of Smithson, sitting like Rodin's *The Thinker*, contemplating a mineral specimen in his hand.[59]

Had the money been appropriated, and one of these designs built, Smithson's monument on the Mall might today have rivaled the Lincoln Memorial in size. In the end, bowing to financial constraints, the Smithsonian opted to dedicate a room at the entrance to the Castle as a crypt for Smithson's remains. The original marble sarcophagus, when it arrived finally from Genoa, was reunited with Smithson's coffin and installed in the room. It is still today Smithson's Crypt. For one brief glimmer of a moment, however, at the opening of the twentieth century—with a state reception at the shores of the nation's capital and the drafting of a mausoleum on the Mall by several of America's leading architects—James Smithson was elevated to the status of an American founding father.

1832

We hope that the name "smithsonite" will not meet
with any opposition as it recalls the name of a
scientist to whom we owe several important
accomplishments in a time when the science of
chemistry had made but few advances.

—François Beudant, *Traité Elémentaire de
Minéralogie,* 1832

IN 1832, THREE years after Smithson's death, the French
mineralogist François Beudant coined the name "smithsonite"
to describe the calamine that Smithson had identified as zinc
carbonate. The attribution was published in the second edition of
Beudant's multi-volume *Traité Elémentaire de Minéralogie.* This work,
the labor of a lifetime of cataloging and describing, joined a long
procession of such encyclopedias, reference works that sought to
place the productions of the earth in a systematically ordered
framework. Smithson's age had seen the birth of mineralogy as a
science, a massive flowering of system-building after centuries of
silence. Mineralogical classification had changed little since the
Renaissance before the burst of activity that began in the mid-
eighteenth century. The advances made in Smithson's lifetime, in
many fields, but in chemistry and mineralogy especially, marked the
beginning of what is generally recognized as the modern

quantification of science. And Smithson's labors throughout his life fell in the midst of these developments.

But Beudant addressed the memory of Smithson as if he had flourished a generation earlier, and not as if he were someone who had been dead only three years and actively publishing in the 1820s. Already in 1832 Smithson formed a part of a group rapidly receding into history, whose work and advances were quickly becoming obsolete. No longer could an amateur or self-taught man make a sizeable contribution to the world's store of knowledge. The year itself, stamped by the passage of the Great Reform Act in Parliament, has come to symbolize the sweeping away of old systems, and the obliteration of antiquated, corrupt modes of operation. As in government, the Church, and the world of education, science, too, underwent tremendous change and reform. Around this time William Whewell is credited with coining the term "scientist" to replace that archaic moniker "natural philosopher." And in 1832 the British Association for the Advancement of Science was enjoying the anniversary of its first year of existence. Established to give a common platform for the rapidly proliferating branches of scientific inquiry, it represented the beginning of a professional identity for the scientific community.[1]

When he allied Smithson's name with this alluring and useful mineral, Beudant could justifiably have believed that he was providing the best and greatest memorial the world would ever have of one James Smithson. In his lifetime Smithson had published no great scientific tome, no account of his travels or his associations with famous people, no philosophical tract elucidating his beliefs or aspirations. His meticulous, minutely scaled analyses, while eliciting the praise and admiration of his contemporaries, resulted in no clever invention to change the way science was conducted. The limitations of the era—the lack of precise measurements, the difficulties in calculating temperature or time or weight—were all soon overcome in subsequent generations. Smithson's earnest and well-intentioned publications on how to build a balance or enhance the workings of a blowpipe hold appeal today mostly for their quaintness and for the evocation of the exigencies of laboratory work two hundred years ago. For all Smithson's desire to ensure his name should outlive that of the Percys and the Northumberlands, it was in fact François Beudant who first committed the name of Smithson to the pages of history.

It was only the death of Smithson's nephew Henry James Dickenson a few years later in 1835, in a hotel on the banks of the Arno at Pisa, that set the Smithson bequest in motion. If this young man had not passed away at such an early age, if he had instead gone on to have children, the name of smithsonite would stand today as the only notice of James Smithson's life and work. It was this single death that brought Smithson's name to the shores of the New World and out of obscurity.

In 1832 Smithson's twenty-four-year-old nephew was roaming the Continent with all the world in front of him, buoyed by a bank account swollen by his uncle's largesse. He felt no compunction to expand the store of the world's knowledge, that lofty aim of his uncle's; it seems he was a disciple more of that other part of his uncle's character, the witty and dissipated casino haunter, the gambler, the coxcomb. Hungerford may also have been something of an amateur artist; he left behind several sketchbooks.[2] His debt to his uncle and benefactor he had paid with the commissioning of an elaborate neoclassical monument in the English Protestant Cemetery at Genoa, on which he had ordered the inscriptions:

Sacred to the Memory of James Smithson, Esq.[re] Fellow of the Royal Society London, who died at Genoa the 26. June 1829. aged 75 years.[3]

This monument is erected, and the ground on which it stands purchased in perpetuity, by Henry Hungerford, esq., the deceased's nephew, in token of gratitude to a generous benefactor and as a tribute to departed worth.

Smithson's tomb in Genoa.

More than half a century later, the astrophysicist and head of the Smithsonian Samuel Pierpont Langley, standing in front of that marble sarcophagus on the cypress-topped cliffs of San Benigno, would be shocked to find no mention of the Smithsonian in the dedication. How could the founder of such an important American institution lie so utterly neglected and unacknowledged?[4]

In 1832, however, when the nephew was still alive and the sarcophagus newly erected, Smithson's "establishment for the increase and diffusion of knowledge among men" survived merely in the realm of dreams. It was a sentence in a will buried in the offices of a dead man's solicitors, or a paper filed at Chancery Court during the proceedings to entail the nephew. Fleetingly perhaps, when the will was published in *The Times* six months after Smithson's death, the idea might have circulated as a curiosity in the salons of fashionable London. How extraordinary, they might have said—as we still do today—how bizarre, to leave your fortune to a country you had never seen. The potential windfall for the burgeoning United States of America piqued the curiosity of a sharp-eyed editor in New York, who published a notice of Smithson's will in his *New-York American* in January 1830.[5] But three years later the chatter had, if it ever existed, without question disappeared. Consigned to history, the Smithson bequest existed only as a curious artifact of one man's fantastical imagination.

Yet it was also a brilliant example of the collective will of the "citizens of the world," a remarkable extension of the ideals embraced by one who came of age in the exploding culture of knowledge and revolution in the late eighteenth century. Smithson's bequest exemplified the faith that he and his circle shared in science as a vehicle for progress and enlightenment—and the place that America occupied in their imagination. The future they imagined was one in which talent and industry would be rewarded above all else, where the increase and diffusion of knowledge would bring society to a state of happiness and prosperity.

Smithson seems never to have abandoned those beliefs. In his last papers he argued still that "no researches can be undertaken without producing some facts, leading to some consequences," and he extolled the virtues of spreading "comforts and happiness" to the widest possible community. In the scathing marginalia he added sometime in the late 1810s or 1820s to Col. Pinkney's *Travels through the South of France*, Smithson wrote, "noble things!" next to a description of "ancient chateaux," and a sarcastic "Oh! No!" next to Pinkney's lament that many of the ancient châteaux "were indeed in ruin from the effects of the Revolution."[6]

But Smithson had been powerfully imprinted by his mother's

world, a society that took for granted a belief in the nobility of blood. His embrace of democracy seems to have been at least partly grounded in what for him was the retribution of equality, in an awareness of how it might have rewritten the story of his life. For all his scientific promise, for all the acclaim he garnered from such a young age, he never stopped hungering for the validation of his family history. Even in his last years he was still writing letters to the solicitors of his cousins trying to establish claims. He styled himself as "Monsieur de Smithson," and he made a series of efforts to ensure the Hungerford name was carried on into the future, funding the establishment of the Hungerford Hotel in Paris and making his nephew and heir change his name from Dickenson to Hungerford.

He seems to have straddled these two worlds, never able fully to inhabit either. In the world of science he was defined in part by his fortune, and he constantly took himself out of circulation, through travel and gambling and his quest for the aristocratic sheen he felt was his birthright. These ellipses of engagement were compounded by times that he was removed from the scientific arena against his will, caught up in the geo-political maelstrom of his war-torn era. Unlike so many of his Oxford scientific peers, he did not explore the roles opening up to his generation, the possibilities for teaching, for founding manufactories or charitable institutions, for becoming scientific leaders in diverse ways. These friends, for the most part, unlike Smithson, seem to have been less preoccupied with questions of their status in society; many of them did not have extensive personal incomes like Smithson's. Perhaps, had he not so desperately needed to fill a void, to find the respect and credibility that he felt came for him in the guise of *seigneur* first of all, he might have lived a less restless life. Perhaps he might have chanced on a scientific discovery that could have made his name.

Smithson grappled all his life with the extraordinary facts of his own life story. He had enjoyed a *jeunesse dorée*, a youth that coincided with Europe's own time, as Wordsworth said, "at the top of golden hours." And yet he was a man haunted by the specter of what could have been, had just a few things been different, or one thing changed. "It is the character of human nature, even when no extraordinary motives to it have occurred," Smithson once told a friend, "to cherish the past above the present, both because youth is in the past, & because fr.m something unaccountable in man what is irretrievably lost is ever most valued."[7] He wrote this when he was only forty years old. He was looking back already, even before the disappointments and setbacks that marred his later years: the brutal incarceration during the wars, the break with Hoare's, his long-time bankers, the even more profound rupture with the Royal Society. Of course, the most significant and irretrievable loss Smithson suffered occurred before he ever clutched it in his hands. Acknowledgment from his father, an identity of legitimacy, and a secure and admired position in society were all taken from him before he had even arrived.

For a story lined with sadness and unfulfillment, the ending is purely American. It is a very sweet twist of fate that Smithson's last grasp for posterity—the leaving of his fortune to the government of the United States in a secondary clause of his will—gave birth to a legacy greater than he could have ever imagined. The bequest has made him the founder of one of the world's great museums, a place that serves as curator of America's dreams and memory, a much beloved "nation's attic." Smithson's gift in the end was a spark from the last embers of the English Enlightenment, one that managed— against unimaginable odds—to land across an ocean in the dry brushfield of a nation hungry for identity, prestige, and progress.

SMITHSON'S FAMILY TREE

*"The best blood of England runs through my veins.
On my father's side, I am a Northumberland,
on my mother's I am related to kings . . ."*

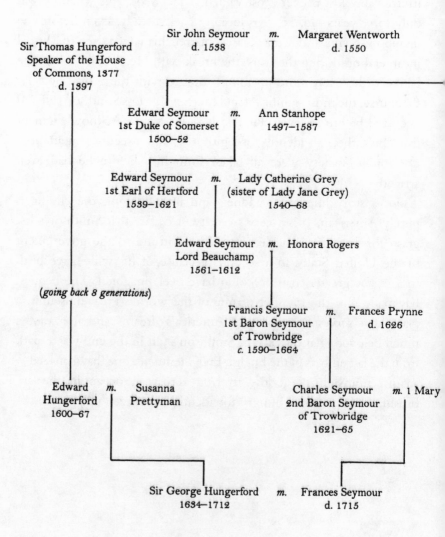

Sir John Seymour
d. 1538

m.

Margaret Wentworth
d. 1550

Sir Thomas Hungerford
Speaker of the House
of Commons, 1377
d. 1397

Edward Seymour
1st Duke of Somerset
1500–52

m.

Ann Stanhope
1497–1587

Edward Seymour
1st Earl of Hertford
1539–1621

m.

Lady Catherine Grey
(sister of Lady Jane Grey)
1540–68

Edward Seymour
Lord Beauchamp
1561–1612

m.

Honora Rogers

(going back 8 generations)

Francis Seymour
1st Baron Seymour
of Trowbridge
c. 1590–1664

m.

Frances Prynne
d. 1626

Edward
Hungerford
1600–67

m.

Susanna
Prettyman

Charles Seymour
2nd Baron Seymour
of Trowbridge
1621–65

m. 1 Mary

Sir George Hungerford
1634–1712

m.

Frances Seymour
d. 1715

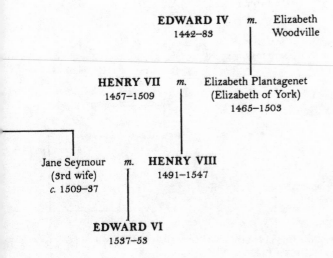

EDWARD IV *m.* Elizabeth
1442–83 Woodville

HENRY VII *m.* Elizabeth Plantagenet
1457–1509 (Elizabeth of York)
1465–1503

Jane Seymour *m.* **HENRY VIII**
(3rd wife) 1491–1547
c. 1509–37

EDWARD VI
1537–53

m. 2 Elizabeth Bennett
daughter of 1st Earl
of Arlington

Charles Seymour *m.* Elizabeth Percy
6th Duke of Somerset 1677–1722
"The Proud Duke"
1662–1748

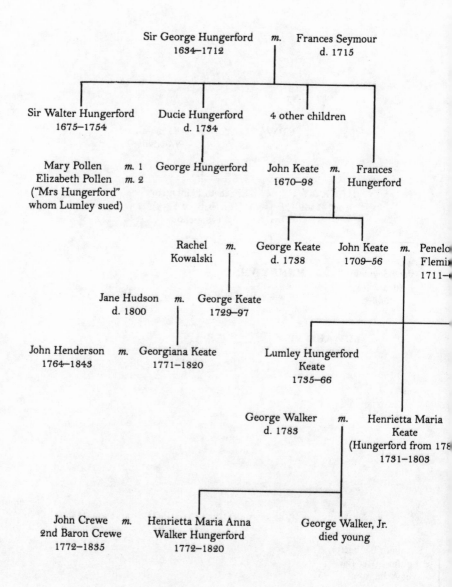

Sir George Hungerford   m.   Frances Seymour
1634–1712   d. 1715

Sir Walter Hungerford   Ducie Hungerford   4 other children
1675–1754   d. 1734

Mary Pollen   m. 1   George Hungerford   John Keate   m.   Frances
Elizabeth Pollen   m. 2   1670–98   Hungerford
("Mrs Hungerford"
whom Lumley sued)

Rachel   m.   George Keate   John Keate   m.   Penelo
Kowalski   d. 1738   1709–56   Flemi
1711–

Jane Hudson   m.   George Keate
d. 1800   1729–97

John Henderson   m.   Georgiana Keate   Lumley Hungerford
1764–1843   1771–1820   Keate
1735–66

George Walker   m.   Henrietta Maria
d. 1783   Keate
(Hungerford from 178
1731–1803

John Crewe   m.   Henrietta Maria Anna   George Walker, Jr.
2nd Baron Crewe   Walker Hungerford   died young
1772–1835   1772–1820

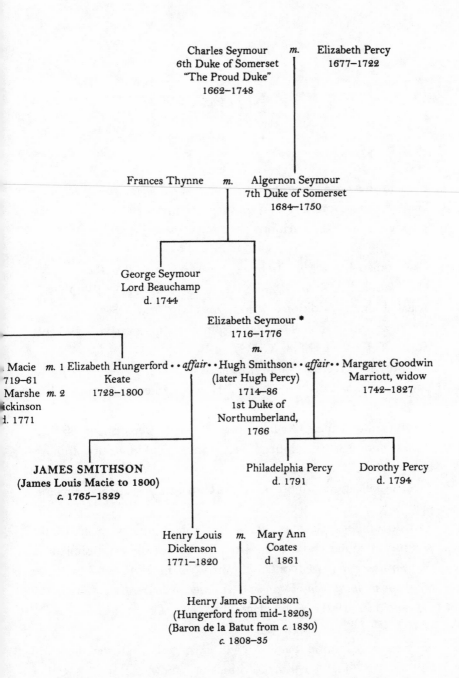

Charles Seymour   *m.*   Elizabeth Percy
6th Duke of Somerset   1677–1722
"The Proud Duke"
1662–1748

Frances Thynne   *m.*   Algernon Seymour
7th Duke of Somerset
1684–1750

George Seymour
Lord Beauchamp
d. 1744

Elizabeth Seymour *
1716–1776
m.

Macie   *m.* 1 Elizabeth Hungerford · · *affair* · · Hugh Smithson · · *affair* · · Margaret Goodwin
719–61   Keate   (later Hugh Percy)   Marriott, widow
Marshe *m.* 2   1728–1800   1714–86   1742–1827
ickinson   1st Duke of
d. 1771   Northumberland,
                   1766

JAMES SMITHSON   Philadelphia Percy   Dorothy Percy
(James Louis Macie to 1800)   d. 1791   d. 1794
c. 1765–1829

Henry Louis   *m.*   Mary Ann
Dickenson   Coates
1771–1820   d. 1861

Henry James Dickenson
(Hungerford from mid-1820s)
(Baron de la Batut from *c.* 1830)
c. 1808–35

* NB   Hugh Smithson's legitimate children by Elizabeth Seymour were:
      Hugh Percy, later 2nd Duke of Northumberland, 1742–1817
      Algernon Percy, later 1st Earl of Beverley, 1750–1830

Notes

Citations here are given in full at the first mention in each chapter. Translations of foreign language texts are my own unless otherwise specified. Some abbreviations used throughout are:

Smithsonian Institution Archives, Record Unit (SIA, RU)
The National Archives, Public Record Office (TNA: PRO)
British Library, Additional Manuscripts (BL Add MS)
American Philosophical Society, Fabbroni Papers (APS B F113)
Cornwall Record Office (CRO)
Edinburgh University Library, Manuscripts Collection (EUL)
Dawson Turner Collection, Natural History Museum, London (DTC)

Rush Family Papers, Manuscripts Division, Department of Rare Books and Special Collections, Princeton University Library. Published with permission of the Department of Rare Books and Special Collections. Abbreviated as Rush Family Papers, Princeton.

The documents related to Richard Rush's term as agent for the Smithson bequest and the legislative history of the establishment of the Smithsonian are contained in William J. Rhees, ed., *The Smithsonian Institution: Documents Relative to its History, 1835–1899* (Washington, 1901). Abbreviated as Rhees, *Documents*.

Smithson's scientific papers have been collected together and published as "The Scientific Writings of James Smithson," together with William J. Rhees' 1880 biography "James Smithson and His Bequest," and Walter R. Johnson's 1844 "Memoir on the Scientific

Character and Researches of James Smithson," in *Smithsonian Miscellaneous Collections* 21 (Washington, 1881). I have referred below to the individual publications by journal title and year, without reference to this volume.

Smithson's book collection is housed in the Joseph F. Cullman 3rd Library of National History, Special Collections Department, Smithsonian Institution Libraries. Abbreviated as Smithson Library, SIL.

Another resource are the volumes produced by the Joseph Henry Papers editorial project, especially: Volume 6, *The Princeton Years: January 1844–December 1846* (Washington, 1992); Volume 7, *The Smithsonian Years: January 1847–December 1849* (Washington, 1996); Volume 8, *The Smithsonian Years: January 1850–December 1853* (Washington, 1998), and Volume 9, *The Smithsonian Years: January 1854–December 1857* (Science History Publications/USA, 2002). Abbreviated as *The Papers of Joseph Henry*.

Prologue 1865

1 *Evening Star*, January 23, 1865, p. 1.

2 *Smithsonian Annual Report of 1854*, p. 9.

3 Marcus Benjamin, "Meteorology," in G. Brown Goode, ed., *The Smithsonian Institution, 1846–1896: the history of its first half century* (Washington, 1897), pp. 659–61.

4 Cynthia R. Field, Richard E. Stamm, and Heather P. Ewing, *The Castle: An Illustrated History of the Smithsonian Building* (Smithsonian Institution Press, 1993), p. 77. In 1858 Joseph Henry wrote, "it is hoped that Congress will in due time purchase the portraits belonging to Mr. Stanley, which will become more and more valuable in the progress of the gradual extinction of the race of which they are such faithful representations." *Smithsonian Annual Report of 1858*, p. 42. See also Michael Kraus, "America and the Utopian Ideal in the Eighteenth Century," *Mississippi Valley Historical Review*, vol. 22, no. 4 (March 1936), p. 490, fn. 12.

5 The account of the fire is taken from three sources: *Report of the Special Committee of the Board of Regents of the Smithsonian Institution relative to the fire* (February 1865), Senate Rep. Com. No. 129, 38th Congress, 2nd Session; newspaper accounts of January 24 and 25, 1865, in the *Daily National Intelligencer* and the *Evening Star*; and the diary of Mary Henry, SIA, RU 7001, Box 51.

6 Mary Henry diary, entry for January 26, 1865.

7 Mary Henry diary, entry for January 25, 1865.

8 Testimonials of the fire, January 1865; SIA, RU 7081, Box 14.

9 There remains some confusion as to what exactly survived from the regents' room in the south tower. The report investigating the fire states vaguely that among the losses is "a part of the contents of the regents' room, including the personal effects of Smithson, with the exception of his portrait and library." Smithson's library and portrait survived because they were kept in the west wing of the building (which was unharmed in the fire), where the institution's library was housed. Some scraps of Smithson's mineralogical notes were salvaged, which John McD. Irby in 1878 compiled and bound with transcriptions in a red leather book now kept in the Smithsonian Archives; SIA, RU 7000, Box 2. And one other piece of Smithson ephemera survived the fire, though no mention is made of it in the 1865 report: a painting of a landscape by Nicolæs Berchem. Henry arranged for Smithson's books to be displayed to the public in the library in 1858; it is likely that at this time he also moved the portrait of Smithson as a student, the Nicolæs Berchem landscape, and the scraps of mineralogical notes—all those things of Smithson's that survived the fire—down for display in the west wing as well. Henry Desk Diary, March 4, 1858; SIA, RU 7001.

10 This phrase was first published before the Smithsonian fire, in the *U.S. Magazine*, vol. IV, no. 1 (January 1857). "He [James Smithson] declared, in writing, that though the best blood of England flowed in his veins, this availed him not, for his name would live in the memory of men when the titles of Northumberlands and Percies were extinct or forgotten." It is probable that Rhees or someone else who perused the diaries for some elaboration of Smithson's intentions for a Smithsonian Institution landed on this sentiment as the closest expression of a motivation. Having paraphrased it using the third person for the 1857 article, Rhees seems after the fire to have taken this phrase and transformed it into a direct quote.

11 William St. Clair, *The Reading Nation in the Romantic Period* (Cambridge, 2004); personal communication with the author, March 2006.

12 Walter R. Johnson, "A Memoir on the Scientific Character and Researches of James Smithson, Esq., F.R.S." (Philadelphia, 1844).

13 Spencer Baird, prefatory advertisement to William J. Rhees, "James Smithson and His Bequest" (Washington, 1880).

14 James M. Goode, "Exhumation and Reinterment of the Remains of James Smithson," memorandum for the record, October 5, 1973; SIA, Smithson reference file.

15 John Sherwood, "Smithson Skeleton Unearthed," *Washington Star-News*, October 5, 1973; J. Lawrence Angel, "The Skeleton of James Smithson (1765–1829)," October 15, 1973; SIA, Smithson reference file. I'm very grateful to Dr. David Hunt for spending time discussing this report with me. The graphologist JoNeal Scully has suggested that the deformation of the right metacarpal may have been the result of a thyroid irregularity; personal communication with the author, June 2005.

16 Richard Kirwan to Sir Joseph Banks, April 9, 1797; DTC, vol. 10, ff. 119–121. Many thanks to Neil Chambers and the Joseph Banks Archive Project for their assistance. Dr. William Drew to Lady Webster, n.d. [June to July 5, 1797], BL Add MSS 51814, ff. 37–38.

17 See Macie v. Hungerford, 1766; TNA: PRO C 12/1019/4. Macie v. Blaake, 1767; PRO C 12/1250/27. Macie v. Dickinson, 1770; PRO C 12/1028/19 and C 12/56/39. Macie v. Cowdrey, 1771–2; C 12/1038/11. Macie v. Cocks, 1772–3; C 12/1035/12. Macie v. Walker, 1782–4; PRO C 12/1261/38. Leir v. Macie, 1773; PRO C12/1626/19. Macie v. Baldwin, 1792; PRO C 12/471/70. Leir v. Macie, 1796; PRO C 12/2181/16. Rhees, "James Smithson and His Bequest," p. 1.

18 Smithson, "A Chemical Analysis of Some Calamines," *Philosophical Transactions of the Royal Society* (1802).

19 William Drew to Lady Holland, October 27, 1798; BL Add MS 51814, ff. 62–63.

1. Descended from Kings

1 Elizabeth Macie died in Brighton on May 22, 1800. A death notice was published in *The Sussex Weekly Advertiser* or *Lewes Journal*, Monday June 2, 1800, vol. 52, no. 2805. I am grateful to Hugh Torrens for sharing this find with me. Her burial is recorded in the burial register of St. Nicholas', Brighton [ref. PAR 255/1/1/7]. Her bank records are at Hoare's, London. In her will she bequeathed Smithson "all the Manors Messuages Lands Tenements and Hereditaments both Household Copyhold Customary and Leasehold and also all my ready money Securities for money money in the public funds and all my Goods Chattels Personal Estate whatsoever and wheresoever . . ."; TNA: PRO, PROB 11/1343. The multiple lawsuits Elizabeth Macie filed and those lodged against her are at TNA: PRO; in the 1790s, she was suing the celebrated Bath architect Thomas Baldwin, who had renovated her house in Weston, near Bath, for money he owed her (TNA: PRO C 12/471/70), and she was being sued by the Leirs, the cousins of her first husband who were due to inherit Weston after her death, who accused her of squandering the estate (TNA: PRO C 12/2181/16). The record of the 1791 sale of Great Durnford is located in the Hampshire Record Office (Hants RO), 7M54/20.

2 Smithson to Lady Holland, May 1, n.y. [1801]. BL Add MS 51846, ff. 104–5.

3 The name change was noted on June 18, 1800; Hoare's Bank Archives, vol. 68 (1800–1801), ff. 67–68. W.P.W. Phillimore and E. A. Fry, *An Index to Changes of Name under authority of Act of Parliament or Royal Licence 1760–1901* (London, 1905), p. 296. It was also announced in the *London Gazette*, February 16, 1801, p. 202.

4 The description of Smithson's appearance is based on a painting by Louis Gauffier, *Portrait of a Young Gentleman in Florence*, 1796 (whereabouts unknown), that might possibly be of Smithson. The wax seal is on one of his letters to Fabbroni in Florence, located in the SIA, RU 7000, Box 1; I am grateful to my friend Massimo Pelligrini for his research into the iconography of the seal, which appears to be based on the sculpture of Eros and Psyche in the Capitoline Museum in Rome; personal communication with the author, September 2001.

5 Smithson, beginning sometime in early 1799, nearly two years after his return from the Continent, took lodgings at No. 19 Clarges Street, a house he maintained until he left for France in 1803; *Boyle's Court Guide*, 1799–1803. I do not know for certain that he established a library and laboratory at this address, but it seems likely; Sir Charles Blagden reported in 1790, soon after Smithson moved into new quarters on Orchard Street, that Smithson was busy "setting up his library and laboratory." Blagden to Richard Kirwan, March 20, 1790; Royal Society (RS) Archives, Blagden Papers 7.322. In May 1797 Smithson paid out £70 to Christie and Co.; he was probably the "Mr. M" who bought a large number of items at a Christie's house sale at that time; see May 1, 1797, sale in Christie's Archives.

6 Elizabeth Macie to John Harris, Lord Malmesbury, September 3, 1777; Hants RO, 9M73/160.

7 Smithson to Lord Malmesbury, February 28, 1802; Hants RO, 9M73/G2215.

8 Smithson to Sir Joseph Banks, September 18, 1808; Sutro Library, California. Published in A. Grove Day, "James Smithson in Durance," *The Pacific Historical Review* 12, no. 4 (1943), pp. 391–4.

9 Horace Walpole to Horace Mann, May 7, 1775; *Correspondence of Horace Walpole* 24 (1967), p. 99; quoted in H. S. Torrens, "Smithson, James (1764–1829)," *Oxford Dictionary of National Biography* (Oxford, 2004).

10 Phillimore and Fry, *An Index to Changes of Name*, p. 296.

11 Davies Giddy diary, June 11, 1789 (note added to this day's entry, written c. 1826); DG 14, CRO; reprinted in the Smithsonian's *Annual Report of 1884*, p. 4.

12 Smithson knew his family tree well enough to refer to his fellow chemist Smithson Tennant as a "distant relative." The relationship between the two was so obscure it eluded any explanation; and it was only in the 1970s, after Tennant's biographer devoted much of his retirement to the problem, that it was determined the two were related not on the Smithson side, as one might suspect, but instead on the Hungerford side of the tree (and it was necessary to go all the way back to the 1660s to find the connection). A. E. Wales, biography of Smithson Tennant, unpublished. I have not been privileged to see the manuscript, but Wales' son, Dr. John Wales, generously shared the genealogical chart and other Smithson-related materials with me.

13 My assumption that they were a London-based family comes from three sources: a title deed listing "John Keate of the City of Westminster, Esq.," December 1, 1746; Z1/47/1, Devon Record Office; and the fact that at the time of his Oxford matriculation Lumley Keate hailed from the parish of St. Margaret's, Westminster, as did Elizabeth Keate at the time of her marriage in St. Paul's Cathedral in 1750. J. Foster, *Alumni Oxonienses* (Oxford, 1888), p. 780; J. W. Clay, *Register of St. Paul's Cathedral* (Harleian Society, 1899), p. 163.

14 Anne Pollen, *John Hungerford Pollen, 1820–1902* (London, 1912), p. 3. Thanks to Louis Jebb for this reference.

15 A. G. Stewart, *The bounds of sodomy: textual relations in early modern England*, unpublished Ph.D. (Queen Mary and Westfield College, 1993), pp. 196–8.

16 Rev. Richard Warner, *Excursions from Bath* (Bath, 1801), pp. 25–35.

17 Lumley is referred to as "Hungerford Keate" in a letter from Lord Northumberland to George Grenville, March 17, 1765; BL Add MS 57824, f. 115. Henrietta Maria Keate changed her name from Walker to Hungerford on March 17, 1789; Phillimore and Fry, *An Index to Changes of Name*, p. 169. That Smithson requested his nephew change his name is noted in John Guillemard to Richard Rush, July 4, 1837; Rush Family Papers, Princeton.

18 The Proud Duke was the third husband of the famous child heiress Elizabeth Percy, who as the only surviving offspring of Josceline Percy, the eleventh and last Earl of Northumberland, brought with her to the marriage all the titles and estates of the House of Percy.

19 Northumberland's intimacy with the head of the new government, the Earl of Bute, George III's former tutor, was cemented by the marriage of Northumberland's eldest son to one of Bute's daughters in 1764—a disastrous liaison as it turned out, concluded by scandalous divorce proceedings, but a formidable alliance at the time. Gerald Brenan, *A History of the House of Percy* (London, 1902), vol. 2, p. 446.

20 Lady Northumberland compiled a list of "persons from whom being descended I ought to have Prints." Alnwick Castle MSS, D20/242.

21 Henrietta Maria Walker to Earl of Shelburne, June 14, 1782; BL Bowood Papers, B50, ff. 7–12.

22 Henrietta Maria Walker to Earl of Shelburne, June 14, 1782. For Lumley Keate's perquisite see Northumberland to G. Grenville, May 10, 1763, Morgan Library [Aut. Misc. England], and March 17, 1765, BL Add MS 57824, f. 115.

23 John Macie died at their Queen Square house "after a tedious Illness," in 1761, aged forty-two. "Universally beloved while living, lamented when dead," he was buried, like all his family, at the church in Weston. *Bath Journal*, March 30, 1761, p. 4, col. 3; *Bath Chronicle*, April 2, p. 4, col. 4; April 9, p. 4, col. 4. Elizabeth's description of the worth of the Macie estates is in TNA: PRO C 12/1028/19.

24 Louis Dutens, *Mémoires d'un voyageur qui se repose* (London, 1807), vol. 3, p. 108; Smithson Library, SIL. Roy Porter gives comparative earnings, showing that the agricultural laborers on Elizabeth Macie's properties, for example, might not earn £800 in a lifetime; Porter, *English Society in the Eighteenth Century* (London, 1982), pp. 63–4.

25 In 1764 Horace Walpole told a friend, "I have been this evening to Sion, which is becoming another Mount Palatine. [The architect Robert] Adam has displayed great taste, and the Earl matches it with magnificence." Horace Walpole to the Earl of Hertford, August 27, 1764; Peter Cunningham, ed., *The Letters of Horace Walpole* (London, 1891), vol. 4, pp. 265–6. For a discussion of the work done at all three residences, see Eileen Harris, *The Genius of Robert Adam* (London and New Haven 2002), pp. 64–103.

26 Walpole to George Montagu, June 8, 1762; Mrs. Paget Toynbee, ed., *The Letters of Horace Walpole* (Oxford, 1904), vol. 5, p. 211.

27 Photographs of Weston House taken prior to its 1970 demolition are at the National Monuments Record, BB74/5778–95. See also Joan Hargood-Ash, *Looking Back at Weston* (1964); John Collinson, *The History and Antiquities of the County of Somerset* (Bath, 1791), vol. 1, pp. xxxix, 156–66. The mention of the laundresses is in Pierce Egan, *Walks Through Bath* (Bath, 1819), p. 186. The Jane Austen letter is quoted in Constance Hill, *Jane Austen: Her Homes and Her Friends* (John Lane Bodley Head, 1901), p. 126.

28 R. E. Peach, *Historic Houses in Bath and their associations* (London, 1883), p. 60. Bath Record Office, SRO D/P/Wal. SW 4/1/1.

29 Alfred Barbeau, *Life & Letters at Bath in the XVIIIth Century* (London, 1904), pp. 53–62.

30 *Bath: A Glance at its Public Worship, Style of Dress, Cotillons, Masquerades, &c. &c.* (Bath, 1814), p. 6.

31 Diaries of the Duchess of Northumberland, July 29, 1760 and February 6, 1763; Alnwick Castle MSS. There are also many entries concerning her anonymous lovers "500" and "9" throughout 1763–65, which were all edited out of the published edition of her diaries.

32 The mention of the declaration of love is quoted in James Grieg, *The Diaries of a Duchess: Extracts from the Diaries of the First Duchess of Northumberland (1716–1776)* (New York, 1927), p. 58. The maxims are from the Duchess' original manuscript diaries.

33 Diaries of the Duchess of Northumberland, November 17 and December 19, 1761; the movements of the duke are charted from his correspondence. Alnwick Castle MSS.

34 Will of John Macie, July 16, 1761; TNA: PRO PROB 11/867. Judith Schneid Lewis, *In the Family Way: Childbearing in the British Aristocracy, 1760–1860* (Rutgers University Press, 1986), p. 39.

35 There is a microfilm at the Archives de Paris of those records reconstructed in the late nineteenth century from other sources; it contains no record of Smithson. It would in any case have included Smithson only if his mother had chosen to have him baptized a Catholic; Protestants were not permitted official records of birth, death, or marriage in Paris at this time, and had to worship in private. The naturalization petition expressly states that Smithson was raised in the Protestant faith, despite being born in Paris. There has been some speculation that Smithson might have been born at the Abbaye de Penthemont, one of the most aristocratic convents in Paris and highly fashionable with the English (the grizzled and worldly Abbesse, Madame de Béthisy de Mézières, had an English mother and grandparents who had held positions in the household of James II). The Duke of Northumberland paid for his illegitimate daughters, Smithson's half-sisters Philadelphia and Dorothy Percy, to be educated there. Thomas Jefferson was another who placed his daughters there, during his stint in the city in the late 1780s; he was quick to explain to relatives back home that the convent had "as many protestants as Catholics, and not a word is spoken to them on the subject of religion." Jefferson to Mary Jefferson Bolling, July 23, 1787. Quoted in William Howard Adams, *The Paris Years of Thomas Jefferson* (New Haven and London, 1997), p. 221. See also François Rousseau, "Histoire de l'Abbaye de Pentemont, depuis sa translation à Paris jusqu'à la Révolution," *Mémoires de la Société de l'Histoire de Paris* (1918), pp. 171–227.

Baptismal records for the Bath region, several areas of London with connections to Elizabeth Macie, and the parishes around Alnwick in Northumberland yield no mention of Smithson's birth. The 1773 naturalization petition, which states Smithson's age as "nine years and four months or thereabouts," would make his birthdate February 1764. This is the source used to justify 1764 as Smithson's birth year in the new *Oxford Dictionary of National Biography*. This is contradicted, however, by the Oxford record of matriculation, which states that Smithson was seventeen in May 1782. Smithson's tomb, erected by Smithson's nephew, gives no date of birth; it states only that Smithson "died at Genoa the 26th June, 1829, aged 75 years." This would place his birth in about 1754, which is clearly widely off the mark. I think it possible that he was born in the spring of 1765; such a date would make the transfer of land that Smithson's mother made to him on April 10 and 11, 1786, a celebration of his coming of age. Deeds of 9 Friar's Walk, Lewes; Add. MSS, Catalogue X, Ref. AMSX, East Sussex Record Office, Lewes.

36 John Guillemard to Richard Rush, July 4, 1837; Box 13, Rush Family Papers, Princeton. Not all of Guillemard's recollections are accurate.

37 Will of Walter Hungerford, June 26, 1754; TNA: PRO PROB 11/809. Keate v. Hungerford, 1764 and 1765; TNA: PRO C 12/1011/39 and C 12/1230/46.
38 Macie v. Hungerford, November 17, 1766; TNA: PRO C 12/1019/4.
39 Henrietta Maria Keate to Charles Yorke, January 4, 1769; BL Add MS 35639, ff. 1–4.
40 The testimony of Mr. William Harris mentioned Elizabeth Macie "putting two children" in the school that his wife ran at Hammersmith; one was probably Smithson, the other unknown. That Macie and Dickinson met in Amsterdam in April 1768 was revealed in the testimony of Dickinson's butler. Joseph Tournon; Macie v. Dickinson, 1769; London Metropolitan Archives (LMA), DL/C/277.
41 *La Liste des Personnes, qui sont venues aux Eaux Minerales de Spa l'an 1768* (Spa and Liege, 1751). "Madame Macie, Dame Angloise," was announced on List no. 10, July 12. She appears to have been traveling with a young Mademoiselle Sorenzy from The Hague and an English gentleman named Mr. Pennant. Dickinson arrived August 11, alone. He was staying at the Moulinet d'Or, which does not seem to have been a large or particularly fashionable place to stay. I am extremely grateful to Vyvyan Lyle for all her work retrieving this information.
42 Madame du Deffand in Paris was staggered at Irwin's "folles dépenses." A. I. Dasent, rev. Roger T. Stearn, "Irwin, Sir John (1728–88)," *Oxford Dictionary of National Biography* (Oxford, 2004). Massereene ended up imprisoned for debt in Paris; he remained there for eighteen or nineteen years, escaping only in 1789, shortly before the fall of the Bastille. G.E.C. [Cockayne], *The Complete Peerage*, revised by the Hon. Vicary Gibbs (London, 1932), vol. 8, pp. 546–47; see also John Goldworth Alger, *Englishmen in the French Revolution*, (London, 1889), p. 25.
43 Dickinson v. Blaake, December 6, 1768; TNA: PRO C 12/1230/23.
44 LMA, DL/C/002/001–007.
45 LMA, DL/C/002/001–007.
46 The Temple, later famous as the dungeon that held the royal family prior to their march to the guillotine (and which was as a result demolished by Napoleon, in order to prevent it becoming a pilgrimage site for royalists), was like a small city within Paris, with its own justice system and its own police. It was owned by the Knights of Malta; Conti had gained his apartments there as part of his appointment as grand-prieur de France. The Temple was a sink of dissipation, and Conti set the standard—notoriously exacting a trophy from each of his sexual conquests. Countless locks of hair and four thousand ladies' rings, each with a little label naming its owner, were said to have been found among his possessions after his death. The numbers were exaggerated, but an actual inventory after Conti's decease did reveal 492 rings of precious stones, many engraved, and some thirty of which featured scenes from the legend of Priapus. G. Capon and R. Yve-Plessis, *Paris Galant au Dix-Huitième Siècle: Vie privée du prince de Conty, Louis-François de Bourbon (1717–1776)* (Paris, 1907), pp. 112–14, 290.
47 *Mémoires de M. le duc de Lauzun* (Paris, 1822), 2 vols. Smithson Library, SIL.
48 LMA, DL/C/277. TNA: PRO C 12/56/39.
49 LMA, DL/C/56/002/001–007.
50 TNA: PRO C 12/1028/19. Rate Books, SRO D/P/Wal. SW 4/1/1, Bath Record Office.
51 Elizabeth Macie lodged her case of jactitation in the Consistory Court of London on November 25, 1769; LMA, DL/C/176 and DL/C/277. Five days later Dickinson executed an indenture of lease and release and assignment with his bankers Biddulph & Cocks for control of lease, in right of his wife, of the Queen Square house and the rents and profits of the Weston estate, and the undivided moiety of the Hungerford estates; TNA: PRO C 12/1038/11 and 1035/12. On January 10, 1770, Dickinson

launched a countersuit in the King's Bench against Macie and her lawyer Woodcock; TNA: PRO C 12/56/39. On July 2, 1770, Elizabeth Macie launched another suit against Dickinson; TNA: PRO C 12/1028/19. John Marshe Dickinson's new will was drawn up on April 18, 1770; TNA: PRO PROB 11/969.

52 Mrs. Harris, to her son James, then in Madrid, April 12, 1771; Hants RO, 9M73/G1258/18/2.

53 Description of the two lots were "inclosed in Balls of Wax of equal Size as near as might be," and an independent third party picked a ball out of a hat for each sister. TNA: PRO C 12/1261/38.

54 TNA: PRO C 12/1028/19.

55 Alex Kidson, *George Romney, 1734–1802* (London, 2002), cat. no. 31. See Heather Ewing, "A Possible Identification for Romney's Portrait of a Mother and Child, c. 1770," *Transactions of the Romney Society* (forthcoming).

56 J. Lawrence Angel, "The Skeleton of James Smithson (1765–1829)," October 15, 1973; SIA, Smithson reference file. "As he was delicate," from Greville to Hamilton, n.d. [1784]; printed in *The Hamilton and Nelson Papers* (London, 1893–4), pp. 91–2. "Penury of vital power" from William Drew to Lady Webster, n.d. [c. June–5 July, 1797]; BL Add MS 51814, ff. 37–8.

57 "Spitting up blood" from James Smithson to Sir Joseph Banks, September 18, 1808; Sutro Library, California. "Loss of hearing" from James L. Macie to Charles F. Greville, January 1, 1792; BL Add MS 41199, f. 82. "Terrible cold" from Smithson to Miss Eccles, n.d.; SIA, RU 7000, Box 1. The forensic report from Angel, "The Skeleton of James Smithson," 1973. 1805 report from "No. 9890, Smithson agent anglais sur le Rhin," F7/4641, Archives Nationales, Paris (AN). Blagden Diary, October 2, 1814; Blagden Papers, Royal Society.

58 David M. Morens, "At the Deathbed of Consumptive Art," *Emerging Infectious Diseases Journal*, vol. 8, no. 11 (2002).

59 John Marshe Dickinson's will, April 18, 1770; TNA: PRO PROB 11/969.

60 In the family genealogy that his relatives, the de la Batuts, supplied the Smithsonian in the late nineteenth century, Henry Louis Dickenson was called a son of the Duke of Northumberland. An example of the Alnwick medal of 1766 is depicted and described in Laurence Brown, *British Historical Medals* (Seaby, 1980), I, nos 106–7. I am very grateful to Peter Barber for his help on this subject; personal communication with the author, November 2004. The medal is mentioned in a list of items retained by the de la Batut family; its whereabouts today are unknown. See Labatut to the Smithsonian, February 9, 1879; SIA, RU 7000, Box 4. The inventory of Smithson's possessions made following his death included some silver plate engraved with the arms of the duke. A BBC Television *Antiques Roadshow* episode in November 2005 featured an intriguing rummer (a large drinking glass), with the Northumberland arms on one side and the initials "JS" on the other. Many thanks to Sue Palmer for drawing my attention to this.

61 The Woodcock payments can be seen in the Hoare's ledgers for the Woodcocks, the Duke of Northumberland. The payments from the duke do not correlate exactly with payouts to Mrs. Macie; as an example, the duke paid Mr. Woodcock £500 on July 5, 1777; Woodcock recorded a payment of £700 to Mrs. Macie on July 26, 1777. The Woodcock Partnership Accounts are kept at Dawson's, Lincoln's Inn Fields. They run from 1762 to 1774; Northumberland was not a client during these years. Elizabeth Macie incurred charges of £175 in 1772–3, a sum exceeded by only three other clients that year, out of a total of about 450 clients (including figures like the Earl of Bute, the Duke of Devonshire, and the Duke of Newcastle). She did not pay the firm at all that year or the next.

62 See Philadelphia and Dorothy Percy's obituary notices in the *Gentleman's Magazine* (1791), p. 1068, and (1794), pp. 1060–61. Today, all that remains connected to these two girls is a row of brick almshouses in Brighton that their mother raised to their memory in the last years of the eighteenth century; Brighton City Archives. Margaret Marriott was painted by Angelica Kauffmann, who was very close to Smithson's cousin George Keate; see Angela Rosenthal, "Kauffmann and Portraiture," in Wendy Wassyng Roworth, ed., *Angelica Kauffmann: A Continental Artist in Georgian England* (London, 1992), p. 100. Smithson's description of her is in a letter to Lord Holland, June 20, 1797; BL Add MS 51821, f. 47.

63 Davies Giddy, note of 1826, in diary entry for June 11, 1786; DG 13, CRO.

64 *Gentleman's Magazine* (1801), p. 380; *The Times*, April 14, 1801, p. 3, col. d. Many thanks to Major David Gape and also to Brian Moody of St. Albans and Hertfordshire Architectural and Archeological Society for their help.

65 House of Lords Record Office, Main Papers, May 21, 1773.

66 William A. Shaw, ed., *Letters of Denization and Acts of Naturalization for Aliens in England and Ireland, 1603–1700* (London, 1911), vol. 18 (1911), pp. iii–x.

67 Generally, attendance records for this period are scanty at best. Unless the child was a scholar—i.e., receiving funds for his education—he was often not recorded. I have checked the records of Westminster, Eton, St. Paul's, Christ's Hospital, Dulwich, Shrewsbury, and Charterhouse to no avail.

68 R. L. Arrowsmith, *A Charterhouse Miscellany* (1982), and Arrowsmith, *Charterhouse Register, 1796–1872, with appendix of non-foundationers, 1614–1769* (London, 1974). The first Charterhouse students to go up to Pembroke College, Oxford, on Dame Elizabeth Holford's Scholarship went in 1737. Many thanks to Brian Wilson for sharing his research on Pembroke's matriculations.

69 For background on Smithson's education see Robin Eagles, *Francophilia in English Society, 1748–1815* (Macmillan, 2000), and George C. Braner, Jr., *The Education of a Gentleman: Theories of Gentlemanly Education in England, 1660–1775* (New York, 1959). The description of Smithson's notes is from Walter R. Johnson, "A Memoir on the Scientific Character and Researches of James Smithson, Esq., F.R.S." (Washington, 1844).

70 Trevor I. Williams, "Wollaston, William Hyde (1766–1828)," *Oxford Dictionary of National Biography* (Oxford, 2004). Wollaston's friendship with Smithson is alluded to in Edward C. Howard to Henry Warburton, August 4, 1816, in the Wollaston Papers, Cambridge University Library, Manuscript Division, Add MSS 7736, Box 2.

71 For Adam Walker and Percy Bysshe Shelley, see James Bieri, *Percy Bysshe Shelley, A Biography* (University of Delaware Press, 2004), p. 74. Smithson's contemporary (and probable acquaintance) William Gregor's interest in chemistry was awakened by lectures by Priestley's associate John Waltire, which he heard while attending Bristol Grammar School in the late 1770s; John Ayrton Paris, *A Memoir of the Life and Scientific Labours of the late Rev. William Gregor* (London 1818), p. 17; Smithson Library, SIL.

2. Oxford: The Lure of Novelty, 1782–1784

1 Henrietta Maria Walker to the Earl of Shelburne, April 14, 1782; BL Bowood Papers, B50, ff. 7–12. See also Andrew Stockley, *Britain and France at the Birth of America* (University of Exeter, 2001).

2 Davies Giddy diary, April 10, 1785; DG12/1785, CRO. Graham Midgley has other examples of young men going up with their fathers; Midgley, *University Life in Eighteenth-Century Oxford* (London and New Haven, 1996), p. 16.

3 Christopher Hibbert, ed., *The Encyclopedia of Oxford* (London, 1988), p. 246. The tutor system was, and is, the backbone of the university system. All financial arrangements were handled between the family and the tutor, however, and the colleges today have no record of who served as tutor for which student. Elizabeth Macie made a series of regular payments in Smithson's first years at Pembroke to Edward Dupré, about £300 in total, making it very likely that Dupré served as Smithson's tutor. Biographical information on Dupré from the Jersey Heritage Trust and J. Foster, *Alumni Oxonienses* (Oxford, 1888).

4 Smithson's matriculation entry is in the Oxford University Archives, SP 14. It was also published in Samuel P. Langley, "James Smithson," in G. B. Goode, ed., *The Smithsonian Institution 1846–96, The History of Its First Half-Century* (Washington, 1897), p. 9. The Pembroke register [Pembroke College Archives (40/5/1), Oxford], which also gives this information, was compiled in 1935 by the then bursar, L. E. Salt, from a variety of sources. Although Smithson was not entitled to bear arms, someone could have petitioned for arms on Smithson's behalf. The College of Arms, however, has no record of Smithson (or Macie) ever being granted arms. I am very grateful to William Hunt, the Windsor Herald, for his help and research on this matter. Correspondence with the author, July 2004; March 2006.

5 Giddy diary, May 26, 1786; DG13/1786, CRO. Regarding his father's attendance at Oxford in the 1780s Giddy wrote: "Dr. Adams the Master more than once observed to me that I was of a sufficient Age, & sufficiently prudent to remain at Oxford alone like other young men." March 22, 1786; DG13/1786, CRO.

6 Giddy noted in his diary that he had executed the task, "but he [Egremont] did not live to receive it [the excerpt from the Oxford register]." George Wyndham, third Earl of Egremont, died in 1837, which suggests that Egremont's attention was drawn to James Smithson as the United States' claim to the Smithson bequest came to Chancery Court in late 1836. Giddy diary, May 26, 1786; DG13/1786, CRO.

7 Midgley, *University Life in Eighteenth-Century Oxford*, pp. 11–15. The commoners wore sleeveless gowns of simple black stuff, with streamers of black braids on either side of the yoke, and a cap without a tassel. The servitors wore the same gown but without the streamers, and instead of a square academic cap they wore a round hat, which was sometimes derisively called a cowpat.

8 Quoted in Hibbert, ed., *The Encyclopedia of Oxford*, p. 320.

9 Buttery Books 1782–6, Pembroke College Archives, Oxford.

10 Vicesimus Knox quoted in Midgley, *University Life in Eighteenth-Century Oxford*, p. x. Interestingly, Elizabeth Macie made several payments to "Boldero & Co. for V. Knox" and "to Mr. Knox's bill" from late 1786 to 1788; if this V. Knox is Vicesimus, perhaps she procured Knox's counsel for her second son Henry Louis Dickenson, who did not attend university; Hoare's Archives, vol. 26, ff. 5–6, and vol. 29, ff. 232–3.

11 Pembroke's Master William Adams had been a Fellow of Pembroke when Johnson arrived in 1728; he was also a cousin of Johnson's tutor William Jorden and took over Jorden's students when Jorden left Oxford in late 1729. Had Johnson not left Oxford that same week, he would have enjoyed Adams as his tutor, a bond that the two probably relished. Adams told Boswell that he (Adams) was Johnson's "nominal tutor, but he was above my mark." Aleyn Lyell Reade, *Johnsonian Gleanings: Part V* (London, 1928), pp. 6, 34. See also Douglas Macleane, *A History of Pembroke College, Oxford* (Oxford, 1897), p. 203. For Johnson at Pembroke see Boswell's *Life of Johnson*, George Birkbeck Hill, L. F. Powell, eds, 6 vols (Oxford, 1934–64), and also W. Jackson Bate, *Samuel Johnson* (New York and London, 1977), p. 588.

12 Richard Price was the author of *Observations on the Importance of the American Revolution* (1784). The "new aera in the history of mankind" quote is in Roy Porter, *Enlightenment: Britain and the Creation of the Modern World* (London, 2000), p. 402. The "amendment in human affairs" quote is from a letter to Adams, March 25, 1785, printed in W. Bernard Peach and D. O. Thomas, eds, *The Correspondence of Richard Price*, 3 vols (Duke University Press, University of Wales Press, 1991).

13 J. James, Jr. to J. James, Sr., December 12, 1781; printed in Margaret Evans, ed., *Letters of Richard Radcliffe and John James of Queen's College, Oxford, 1755–83* (Oxford, 1888), p. 177.

14 Quoted in J. A. Bennett, S. A. Johnston, and A. V. Simcock, *Solomon's House in Oxford: New Finds from the First Museum* (Oxford, 2000), p. 21. See also A. V. Simcock, *The Ashmolean Museum and Oxford Science, 1683–1983* (Oxford, 1984), pp. 7–10. And E. G. W. Bill, *Education at Christ Church Oxford, 1660–1800* (Oxford, 1988), pp. 136–7.

15 G. L'E. Turner, "The Physical Sciences," in *The History of the University of Oxford*, vol. 5: *The Eighteenth Century* (Oxford, 1986). The "Lyceum of Brittain" is from Thomas Hutchins to Joseph Black, April 10, 1784; EUL, Gen 873/II/167–68.

16 H. M. Sinclair and A. H. T. Robb-Smith, *A Short History of Anatomical Teaching in Oxford* (Oxford, 1950), pp. 37–8.

17 Chemistry had been taught at Oxford in various guises, the first teacher generally being recognized as Peter Stahl, who came to England in 1658 and gave his first course at Oxford in 1660; prior to Wall, the subject was occasionally covered by the lecturers in anatomy. Dr. John Parsons, who taught anatomy at Christ Church, gave a course of lectures in the 1760s, the syllabus of which is located at Christ Church. Turner, "The Physical Sciences," p. 660; personal communication with A. V. Simcock, 2000.

18 Nitre was potassium nitrate, or saltpeter, the primary raw material in gunpowder. Quoted in Dorothy Stansfield, *Thomas Beddoes, M.D., 1760–1808: Chemist, Physician, Democrat* (Dordrecht, Lancaster, c. 1984), p. 15.

19 Martin Wall, *Dissertations on Select Subjects in Chemistry and Medicine* (Oxford, 1783), p. vii.

20 Colin Russell, *Science and Social Change, 1700–1900* (Macmillan, 1983), pp. 13–15; Richard Yeo, "Natural Philosophy (Science)," in *An Oxford Companion to the Romantic Age: British Culture, 1776–1832* (Oxford, 1999), pp. 320–28.

21 William Drew to Lady Holland, October 27, 1798; BL Add MS 51814, ff. 62–3.

22 Smithson's friend William Thomson was a friend of Price's. Thomson sent a full report of the event up to Scotland. Wall had been tarred by virtue of his earlier promotion of Price's ingenuity; he was worried that Joseph Black would think that he supported Price's alchemical work. Both men had heard that Black had referenced the scandal in his lectures that fall at Edinburgh. Correspondence between Joseph Black and Martin Wall and William Thomson, concerning Dr. Price, November 1782; EUL Gen 873/II/19–23F. See also H. C. Cameron, *Sir Joseph Banks: The Autocrat of the Philosophers* (London, 1952), pp. 151–7.

23 Joseph Black quoted in Arthur Donovan, "British Chemistry and the Concept of Science in the Eighteenth Century," *Albion*, vol. 7, no. 2 (1975), p. 133.

24 Alexander Law, "Notes of Doctor Black's Lectures on Chemistry"; quoted in Henry Guerlac, "Joseph Black," *Dictionary of Scientific Biography* (New York, 1970).

25 Smithson, "On the Discovery of Acids in Mineral Substances," *Annals of Philosophy* (1823).

26 Quoted in Donovan, "British Chemistry," *Albion* (1975), p. 200.

27 Jan Golinski, "Chemistry," in Roy Porter, ed., *Science in the Eighteenth Century* (Cambridge, 2003), pp. 388–91.

28 Jan Golinski, *Science as Public Culture* (Cambridge, 1992), pp. 112–14.
29 Martin Wall, "An Inaugural Dissertation on the Study of Chemistry," in *Dissertations on Select Subjects in Chemistry and Medicine* (Oxford, 1783), pp. 85–7.
30 Beddoes to Black, February 23, 1788; quoted in Trevor Levere, "Dr. Thomas Beddoes at Oxford: Radical Politics in 1788–1793 and the Fate of the Regius Chair in Chemistry," *Ambix*, vol. 28, part 2 (July 1961), pp. 161–9.
31 *Letters of Richard Radcliffe and John James*, pp. 176–7.
32 Quoted in Rupert Christiansen, *Romantic Affinities: Portraits of an Age, 1780–1830* (London, 1988), p. 41.
33 Mrs. Harris to her son, February 16, 1765; printed in the Right Hon. The Earl of Malmesbury, G.C.B., ed. *A Series of Letters of the First Earl of Malmesbury, His Family and Friends, from 1745 to 1820* (London, 1870), vol. 1, p. 122.
34 J. R. Partington, *A History of Chemistry* (London, 1962), vol. 3, pp. 705–6.
35 *Letters of Richard Radcliffe and John James*, p. 177.
36 Bill, *Education at Christ Church*, p. 317.
37 Davies Gilbert, eulogy of James Smithson at the anniversary dinner of the Royal Society, November 30, 1830. Quoted in the *Philosophical Magazine* (January–June 1831), vol. ix, p. 41. This opinion of Smithson's reputation during his university years was seconded by John Guillemard, who told Richard Rush, "I know not whether he was at any School but he entered of Pembroke College Oxford about the year 1783 and took an honorary degree of M.A. on the 26th of May 1786 soon after which he left the University. He was at that time considered as distinguished for his knowledge of Chemistry, a Science which he cultivated with success during his whole life." Letter of July 4, 1837, Rush Family Papers, Princeton.
38 Others connected to Oxford, like William Thomson, the astronomer Thomas Hornsby, and the botany professor John Sibthorpe, all stepped forward to sponsor Wall, but Smithson did not. Royal Society Archives, EC/1788/06.
39 William Thomson to Joseph Black, August 28, 1784; EUL Gen 873/II/ 184–5. Martin Wall's chemistry course covered minerals in several lectures dedicated to earthy substances, metals, and salts. Lecture XIV "Of Earthy Substances," touched on the "Advantages of the chemical Mode of arranging Minerals." Martin Wall, *A Syllabus of a Course of Lectures in Chemistry* (Oxford, 1782), p. 22.
40 Theodore M. Porter, "The promotion of mining and the advancement of science: the chemical revolution and mineralogy," *Annals of Science* 38 (1981), pp. 543–70. M. D. Eddy, "Scottish chemistry, classification and the early mineralogical career of the 'ingenious' Rev. Dr John Walker (1746 to 1779)," *British Journal for the History of Science* 35 (December 2002), pp. 411–38; M. D. Eddy, "Scottish chemistry, classification and the late mineralogical career of the 'ingenious' Rev. Dr John Walker (1746 to 1779)," *British Journal for the History of Science* 37 (December 2004), pp. 373–99.
41 Rachel Laudan, *From Mineralogy to Geology: The Foundations of a Science, 1650–1830* (Chicago, 1987), p. 61. Quote (emphasis Smithson's) is from James Smithson, "On the Composition of Zeolite," *Philosophical Transactions* 101 (1811).
42 J. J. Berzelius, *The Use of the Blowpipe* . . . (London, 1822), p. 20; quoted in D. R. Oldroyd, "Edward Daniel Clarke, 1769–1822, and his role in the history of the Blowpipe," *Annals of Science*, vol. 29, no. 3 (October 1972), pp. 213–35. In 1802 Smithson asked his friend Charles Greville: "Pray are you acquainted with Cavallo? I much want to see a portable blowpipe, constructed with a bladder, which he described some years ago, to the R. Society, as it is quite impossible to stand the fatigue of blowing with one's lungs when one has a number of specimens to try at the same time." Smithson to Greville, July 16, n.y. [1802]; BL Add MS 42071, f. 166.

43 Oersted to his wife, March 5, 1832; Oersted Papers, Danish Royal Library, Copenhagen. Smithson, "Method of fixing particles on the sappare," *Annals of Philosophy* (1823).
44 Martin Welch, "The Ashmolean as Described by its Earliest Visitors," in *Tradescant's Rarities: Essays on the Foundation of the Ashmolean Museum*, Arthur MacGregor, ed., (Oxford, 1983), pp. 59–68.
45 Christopher Pegge to Mark Noble, March 29, 1784; MS. Eng. misc. d. 149, Bodleian Library, University of Oxford.
46 Sinclair and Robb-Smith, *Short History of Anatomy Teaching at Oxford*, pp. 40–41.
47 H. S. Torrens, "Thomson, William (bap. 1760, d. 1806)," *Oxford Dictionary of National Biography* (Oxford, 2004). See also G. Waterston, "William Thomson (1761–1806): a forgotten benefactor," *University of Edinburgh Journal* 22 (1965), pp. 122–34; and R. T. Gunther, "William Thomson, FRS: A Forgotten Mineralogist," *Nature* 143 (1939), pp. 667–8.
48 B. B. Woodward, rev. Jacob W. Grober, "Shaw, George (1751–1873)," *Oxford Dictionary of National Biography* (Oxford, 2004). David Philip Miller, "Gilbert (formerly Giddy) Davies (1767–1839)," *Oxford Dictionary of National Biography* (Oxford, 2004). Norman Moore, rev. Claire L. Nutt, "Austin, William (1754–93)," *Oxford Dictionary of National Biography* (Oxford, 2004). See also Alexander George Gibson, *The Radcliffe Infirmary* (Oxford, 1926), p. 96.
49 H. S. Torrens, "Sadler, James (bap. 1753, d. 1828)," *Oxford Dictionary of National Biography* (Oxford, 2004). Michael Neve, "Beddoes, Thomas (1760–1808)," *Oxford Dictionary of National Biography* (Oxford, 2004). Although Beddoes and Smithson both became best friends with their fellow Pembroke student Davies Giddy, there is no indication that Smithson and Beddoes were friendly.
50 James Smithson, "A Chemical Analysis of Some Calamines," *Philosophical Transactions* 93 (1802).
51 William Thomson to Joseph Black, November 15, 1784. EUL Gen 873/II/160–1.

3. Staffa: The Cathedral of the Sea, 1784

1 See J. E. Hodgson, *The First English Aeronaut, James Sadler, of Oxford (1753–1828)* (London, 1928). The quote is from *The Rambler's Magazine; or, The Annals of Gallantry, Glee, Pleasure, and the Bon Ton* (1784), vol. 2, p. 393.
2 Boulton and Watt sent up a balloon to which they attached a firework, intending to mimic the effects of thunder from the explosion; the tremendous shouts of the crowd, however, drowned out the sounds and the experiment was deemed a failure. Quoted in Robert E. Schofield, *The Lunar Society of Birmingham* (Oxford, 1963), p. 253.
3 The principal account of the journey is Barthélemy Faujas de St. Fond, *A Journey Through England and Scotland to the Hebrides in 1784*, 2 vols, Sir Archibald Geikie, ed. (Glasgow, 1907). Andreani's diary of the Paris and London segments of his journey survives and has been published; *Diario di Viaggio di un Gentiluomo Milanese: Parigi–Londra 1784* (Milan, 1975). Daniel Preston, "William Thornton (20 May 1759–28 Mar. 1828)," *American National Biography*, vol. 21 (New York and Oxford, 1999), pp. 609–11.
4 Blagden to Sir Joseph Banks, October 6, 1803; DTC, vol. XIV, pp. 157–9.
5 G. L. Herries Davies, *The Earth in Decay: A History of British Geomorphology, 1578–1878* (New York, 1969), p. 145.
6 James Smithson, "On a Saline Substance from Mount Vesuvius," *Philosophical Transactions* 103 (1813). Smithson apparently also owned a copy of William Hamilton's *Letters concerning the northern coast of the county of Antrim. Containing a natural history of its basaltes . . . In these letters is stated a plain and impartial view of the volcanic theory*

of the basaltes (London: G. Robinson & Co., 1786), the first detailed description of the Giant's Causeway. The book was included in the inventory of Smithson's possessions that formed a part of Henry Hungerford's Chancery suit in 1831 to claim his inheritance. The whereabouts of the book are unknown, however, as it was not inventoried as part of the Smithson collection in the United States. Inventory in TNA: PRO C 125/H/33.

7 Davis A. Young, *Mind Over Magma* (Princeton University Press, 2003), p. 25.

8 Thomas Percy in an October 11, 1765 letter to Lady Northumberland wrote, "Dr Blair [Hugh Blair, professor of rhetoric and mentor to Algernon Percy at Edinburgh] has brought the two Mr Grevilles [Charles and his brother Robert] to . . . [Algernon], and a great friendship seems to have commenced on both sides." BL Add MS 32334, f. 9, quoted in Bertram Davis, *Thomas Percy: A Scholar-Cleric in the Age of Johnson* (Philadelphia, 1989), p. 147.

9 Andreani, *Diario di Viaggio di un Gentiluomo Milanese, Parigi–Londra 1784*, pp. 82–5. Carl Gustaf Bernhard, "Berzelius as a European Traveler," in Evan Melhado and Tore Frängsmyr, eds, *Enlightenment Science in the Romantic Era* (Cambridge, 1992), p. 225. *Mémoires et Souvenirs de Auguste-Pyramus de Candolle, écrits par lui-même et publiés par son fils* (Geneva and Paris, 1862), p. 272.

10 William Thomson was the guest of a Dr. Coombe, and Smithson was the invitee of Charles Blagden; List of Visitors, November 1783–June 1788, vol. 392; JBC XXXI, 488–9, Royal Society Archives (RS).

11 Faujas, *A Journey*, vol. 1, pp. 123–4, 232.

12 Smithson's address as West Haugh, Surrey, is from the records of the Society for Promoting Natural History (SPNH), Linnean Society. Hoare's Bank records have an undated address listing for "Macie, Mrs Eliz.th at Westhall near Mortlake Sury" in addition to her in-town address. John Guillemard described Smithson's mother as "Elizabeth Macie of Eastwick Park in the County of Surrey, Widow," suggesting that she may have also rented Eastwick Manor in Great Bookham, Surrey, at some point. Guillemard to Richard Rush, July 14, 1837; Rush Family Papers, Princeton.

13 Thomson to Black, August 28, 1784; EUL Gen 873/II/184–5.

14 Records of the SPN are located in the archives of the Linnean Society in Burlington House, London. I am grateful to Hugh Torrens for alerting me to Smithson's connection with this group.

15 Smithson owned William Bray, *A Sketch of a Tour into Derbyshire and Yorkshire* (1783), which was probably purchased for this trip; Smithson marked a number of items of interest, including the china manufactory at Derby. Smithson Library, SIL.

16 Thomson to Black, November 15, 1784; EUL Gen 873/II/160–1.

17 Faujas, *A Journey*, vol. 1, pp. 125, 130.

18 Faujas, *A Journey*, vol. 1, p. 135.

19 Faujas, *A Journey*, vol. 1, p. 134.

20 Daniel Preston, "Thornton, William," *American National Biography Online* (February 2000). Discussion of America in Pembroke deduced from Adams' correspondence with Richard Price, author of *Observations on the Importance of the American Revolution*; Faujas, *A Journey*, vol. 1, p. 156.

21 *The Works of Samuel Johnson* (London, 1820). Smithson Library, SIL.

22 Rev. Theophilus Lindsey in 1770; marveled at seeing daily upwards of two hundred pairs of hands widening the river and renovating the chapel; Lindsey to Francis, tenth Earl of Huntington, September 4, 1770. *HMC Report on MMS of the late Reginald Rawdon Hastings*, vol. III, pp. 149–50. The gilded nails in the stable were noted by Alexandre de la Rochefoucauld; Norman Scarfe, *To the Highlands in 1786: The Inquisitive Journey of a Young French Aristocrat* (Woodbridge, Suffolk, 2001), pp. 88–92.

23 Louis Dutens, *Mémoires d'un voyageur qui se repose* (London, 1807), vol. 1, p. 108; Smithson Library, SIL. The duke increased the rent rolls at Alnwick sixfold. Eileen Harris, *The Interiors of Robert Adam* (2001), pp. 84–93.

24 Alnwick MSS, Northumberland Misc., Syon: Corr of 1st Duke, 1758–1785, G/1/16. The quotation of the two men landing almost as naked as the trees comes from a letter written the following day by Jeffries to a Mr. Thayer c/o Mr. Fector, Dover, a copy of which was also sent to the Duke, and is G/1/17.

25 Jan Golinski, *Science as Public Culture* (Cambridge, 1992), pp. 11–15.

26 At Oxford Martin Wall, William Thomson, and Thomas Beddoes had all studied with Black. Others were Smithson Tennant at Cambridge; Thomas Garnett, the first chemistry lecturer at the Andersonian Institution in Glasgow and then at the Royal Institution in London; and in the new world, Benjamin Rush, who founded a chemical school in Philadelphia (and whose son, Richard, half a century later, would be the one to pursue the Smithson bequest on behalf of the United States). Andrew Kent, ed., *An Eighteenth Century Lectureship in Chemistry* (Glasgow, 1950), p. 46. For Brougham's comment on Black, see J. G. Crowther, *Scientists of the Industrial Revolution* (London, 1962), pp. 48–9.

27 Louis Macie to Joseph Black, February 27, 1785; EUL Gen 873/II/252–3.

28 James Smithson, "Note to a letter from Dr. Black, describing a very sensible balance," *Annals of Philosophy* (1825), p. 52.

29 Crowther, *Scientists of the Industrial Revolution*, p. 82.

30 Faujas, *A Journey*, vol. 1, p. 223.

31 For Hazlitt see Fiona J. Stafford, "'Dangerous Success': Ossian, Wordsworth, and English Romantic Literature," in Howard Gaskill, ed., *Ossian Revisited* (Edinburgh University Press, 1991) p.49. For Napoleon, see W. Jackson Bate, *Samuel Johnson* (New York and London, 1977) p. 520. See also Paul Van Tieghem, *Ossian en France* (1917), p. 365, and Fiona J. Stafford, *Sublime Savage: A Study of James MacPherson and the Poems of Ossian* (Edinburgh University Press, 1988). And for Jefferson see Jefferson to C. McPherson, February 25, 1773; quoted in Paul J. Degategno, "'The Source of Daily and Exalted Pleasure': Jefferson reads the Poems of Ossian," in Gaskill, ed., *Ossian Revisited*, pp. 98–9.

32 Faujas, *A Journey*, vol. 1, p. 236.

33 Ian G. Lindsay and Mary Cosh, *Inveraray and the Dukes of Argyll* (Edinburgh, 1973), pp. 221–5. Thanks to Hugh Torrens for directing my attention to this reference. Faujas, *A Journey*, vol. 1, pp. 241–54.

34 Information based on a letter Smithson sent to Greville, recounting the adventure, now lost. Greville to Hamilton, n.d. [1784]; printed in *The Hamilton and Nelson Papers* (London, 1893–4), pp. 91–2.

35 Faujas, *A Journey*, vol. 1, pp. 310–11.

36 Faujas, *A Journey*, vol. 1, p. 315.

37 Charles Greville to William Hamilton, n.d. [1784].

38 Faujas, *A Journey*, vol. 2, p. 63. Most of the prominent families in the area carried the name Maclean. The one in Torloisk was Lachlan Maclean, who lived until 1799, and dined with Boswell in Edinburgh in 1775; Boswell, *Life of Johnson*, George Birkbeck Hill and V. F. Powell, eds, vol. 2, p. 308.

39 This quotation and the ones by Smithson in the following paragraphs are from W. R. Johnson, "A Memoir on the Scientific Character and Researches of James Smithson, Esq., F. R. S.," (Philadelphia, 1844). Some aspects of this story will probably remain unclear. The dating in Faujas' book is very inexact, but it seems likely that the three travelers (together or separately) arrived at Maclean's around September 21, but did not leave for Staffa until the 24th. Smithson wrote to

Greville that he had gotten ahead of the others and landed first on Staffa; he left Torloisk at 11.30 a.m. on the 24th, according to his diary. According to Faujas (who admittedly was not present), the other two left at 5.00 a.m. on the 24th, which would have meant they arrived at Staffa well before Smithson. When Smithson resolved to stay the night, he mentioned that a "Mr. Maclaire stays with me;" it is likely that this is a misreading by Johnson of Smithson's spelling of Maclaine [Maclean]; we know from Greville that Maclean's nephew accompanied Smithson to Staffa. Faujas' narrative is in *A Journey*, Vol. 2, pp. 18–25.

40 W. Daniell, *Illustrations of the Island of Staffa* (London, 1818), pp. 10–11.

41 Smithson's diary excerpt from W. R. Johnson, "A Memoir.', Faujas noted that Smithson's friend William Thomson, who had been on the island in 1782, had made "a very interesting collection of zeolites, and among others, a number of large cubic crystals clustered upon a black compact lava . . . the most considerable and the most perfect [specimen] of its kind." Faujas, *A Journey*, vol. 2, p. 60. Greville to Hamilton, n.d. [1784]. James Smithson, "On the Composition of Zeolite," *Philosophical Transactions* 101 (1811).

42 See Url Lanham, *The Bone Hunters* (Columbia University Press, 1973), p. 35. Thanks to Raymond Rye for sharing this anecdote with me.

43 Information from Nigel Bishop, Kilmadock Development Trust. Correspondence with the author, 2004.

44 Louis Macie to Joseph Black, February 27, 1785; EUL, Gen 873/II/252–3.

45 Diary excerpt from W. R. Johnson, "A Memoir." Another contemporary account of descending the mines is found in Norman Scarfe, *Innocent Espionage: The La Rochefoucauld Brothers' Tour of England in 1785* (Woodbridge, Suffolk, 1995), pp. 84–6.

46 *Cheshire Magazine*, October 1, 2002.

47 William Thornton to F. X. Swediaur, n.d. [1784], C. M. Harris, ed., *Papers of William Thornton* (Charlottesville, 1995), vol. 1, pp. 16–20.

48 Blagden to Banks, October 17, 1784; DTC, vol. 4, ff. 75–6. Banks to Blagden, October 26, 1784, Blagden Papers, BLA.b.32, Royal Society.

49 Dryander to Banks, October 21, 1784; DTC, vol. 4, p. 79.

50 Blagden to Banks, October 17, 1784; DTC, vol. 4, pp. 75–6. Curiously, Blagden is listed as the Royal Society member who took Smithson as his guest on August 12, 1784, shortly before Faujas' group departed for Staffa; he does not seem here to have any recollection of the event. He did later become one of Smithson's sponsors for membership in 1787, but they do not seem ever to have been good friends.

51 Donald B. MacCulloch, *Staffa* (Newton Abbot, 1975), especially pp. 29, 99, 157–62.

4. London: Science Like Fire, 1784–1788

1 G. Keate, *An Account of the Pelew Islands*, Karen L. Nero and Nicholas Thomas, eds (London and New York, 2002), p. 259.

2 James C. McKusick, "'That Silent Sea': Coleridge, Lee Boo, and the Exploration of the South Pacific," *The Wordsworth Circle* 24 (1993), pp. 102–6.

3 Nicholas Thomas, "'The Pelew Islands' in British Culture," in *An Account of the Pelew Islands*, pp. 27–39.

4 Fanny Burney described meeting Keate: "He is an author, comme il faut; for he is in affluent circumstances, and writes at his leisure and for his amusement." Annie Raine Ellis, ed., *The Early Diary of Frances Burney, 1768–1778* (London, 1907), vol.

1, pp. 305–7. For Keate's biography, see Haydn Mason, "Keate, George (1729–1797)," *Oxford Dictionary of National Biography* (Oxford, 2004), and Katherine Gilbert Dapp, *George Keate, esq., eighteenth-century English gentleman* (Philadelphia, 1939). For an account of the museum, see Clive Wainwright, "The 'Distressed Poet' and his architect: George Keate and Robert Adam," *Apollo* (January 1996), vol. 143, no. 407, pp. 39–44.

5 In Smithson's collection of books, the two volumes of James Anderson's *Letters to Sir Joseph Banks*, 1788 and 1789, are both inscribed from the author to Keate; Smithson Library, SIL.

6 Dapp, *George Keate*, p. 2.

7 Smithson, in one of his handwritten mineral catalogues (part of the small collection of mineralogical notes that survived the fire of 1865), described "a single mackle of the white feldspar of Dauphiné called by the French Schoerl blanc. I detached it from a large group given to me by Mr. Keate." Keate evidently presented Smithson with a large and probably very beautiful cabinet specimen; Smithson detached a single crystal, illustrative of the properties of the mineral, for his scientific cabinet. SIA, RU 7000, Box 2.

8 Davies Giddy diary, November 17, 1791, note of 1838, quoted in A. C. Todd, *Beyond the Blaze: A Biography of Davies Gilbert* (Truro, 1967), p. 207.

9 Election certificate for Sir Hugh Smithson, EC/1736/04, Royal Society Archives. See also Maurice Crosland, "Explicit Qualifications as a Criterion for Membership of the Royal Society: A Historical Review," *Notes and Records of the Royal Society* 37 (1983): 167–87.

10 Sandford's election certificate at the Royal Society Archives is Ref. No. EC/1786/02. While George Keate could very well have come to know Sandford through his young cousin Smithson, it is also likely that Mary Delany played a hand in bringing the Pembroke student to Keate's attention. Delany was Sandford's godmother and actively promoted his advancement. For biographical information see Joseph Foster, *Alumni Oxonienses: the members of the University of Oxford, 1715–1886*, 4 vols (Oxford, 1891).

11 Paolo Andreani, *Diario di Viaggio di un Gentiluomo Milanese, Parigi–Londra 1784* (Milan, 1975), pp. 82–3. Sir Joseph Banks wrote to George Leonard Staunton on February 24, 1793: "The Royal Society blackballed Count Andreani for a suspicion of republican principles which I believe was ill founded & I am verily of the opinion that if Sir Isaac Newton had held Republican Language that all the influence I have could not procure him three votes as a Fellow." RS Archives, MM XIX 120, printed in George Thomas Staunton, *Memoir of the Life and Family of Sir G. L. Staunton* (Havant, 1823), pp. 351–3.

12 Roy Porter, *Enlightenment: Britain and the Creation of the Modern World* (London, 2000), pp. 34–8. See also David Barnett, *London, Hub of the Industrial Revolution, A Revisionist History 1775–1825* (London and New York, 1998).

13 Richard Altick, *The Shows of London* (Cambridge, MA, and London, 1978), pp. 82, 121–4.

14 Weeks' Museum, *A Description of the Temples* (London, 18—). William Bullock, *A Descriptive Catalogue of the Exhibition, entitled Ancient and Modern Mexico . . .* (London, 1824). "*Murder Most Foul,*" *Trial of Charles Squire & Hannah his wife, at Stafford Lent Assizes, 1799 . . .* (1799). Smithson Library, SIL.

15 J. L. Macie to James Hutton, January 17, 1788; Packet J (J7), Perceval Bequest, Fitzwilliam Museum, Cambridge University.

16 Smithson's bank ledgers are at Hoare's. Payments from Charles Vere, a banker and "chinaman" who died in 1789, appear to relate to property in Exhall; an abstract

to the title is found in the Coventry Archives, PA 171/14/13. Smithson was also receiving regular payments from Apsley Pellatt, related to his ownership of the mortgage of Pellatt's property in Lewes, which his mother had purchased in 1776 and assigned to him in 1786; East Sussex Record Office, Add MS, Catalogue X, Ref. AMSX.

17 Lottery tickets were returnable, like today's savings bonds, with the added benefit of the chance of a prize. The odds of winning were close to 25 per cent. Geoffrey Grant, *English State Lotteries 1964–1826: a history and collector's guide to the tickets and shares* (London, 2001), pp. 8, 19.

18 The only evidence of Smithson living here is the letter he wrote to Joseph Black of February 27, 1785, written from No. 18 Portland Place; Macie to Black, February 27, 1785; EUL, Gen 873/II/252–3. Although it does not conclusively prove that Smithson was living there at the time he was pleased to boast of an affiliation with the address. 1785 is before the city directories really come into their own; rate books, too, yield owner rather than tenant, so it is difficult to confirm Smithson's association with this particular address.

19 Z. [Anonymous], "James Smithson," *Biographie Universelle Ancienne et Moderne* 39 (Bad Feilnbach, 1998; facsimile of 1854–6 edition), pp. 488–9.

20 Louis Simond, *An American in Regency England: The Journal of a Tour in 1810–1811*, Christopher Hibbert, ed. (London, 1968), p. 32.

21 "An Abstract of such Resolutions and Precedents as relate to the constitution of the Philosophical Society," March 14, 1788; Wedgwood-Mosley MSS 1109, Keele University. I'm very grateful to Hugh Torrens for sharing this document.

22 Peter Clark, *British Clubs and Societies, 1580–1800: The Origins of an Associational World* (Oxford, 2000), p. 246–251.

23 Peter Clark, *British Clubs*, pp. 108–9.

24 Records of the SPNH, Linnean Society.

25 William Withering, "Experiments and Observations on the Terra Ponderosa," *Philosophical Transactions* 74 (1784), pp. 293–311. Adair Crawford's work quoted in Larry Stewart, "Putting on Airs," in Trevor Levere and Gerard L'E. Turner, eds, *Discussing Chemistry and Steam: The Minutes of a Coffee House Philosophical Society, 1780–87* (Oxford, 2002), p. 233. William Thomson to Joseph Black, November 15, 1784; EUL, Gen 873/II/160–1. In February 1785 Smithson wrote to Black: "I was not as successful in my expedition to Leadhills as I expected to have been. Mr [St?]enting was not there, the weather was extremely bad, &c &c, so that I got but very few things, & them but mideling [sic], but the principal aim of my journey thither had been to procure some of the peculiar *Terra Ponderosa Aerata* and Phosphorated Lead, which you had mentioned to me, of the first I got none, and of the latter but one very bad specimen." Louis Macie to Joseph Black, February 27, 1785; EUL Gen 873/II/252–53.

26 Martin Klaproth, *Observations relative to the mineralogical and chemical history of the fossils of Cornwall* (London, 1787). Smithson wrote in the front flap: "From the translator." Smithson Library, SIL.

27 Black to Smithson, September 18, 1790; printed in *Annals of Philosophy* (1825) reprinted in the *Technical Repository* (1826).

28 Buttery Books, Pembroke College Archives, Oxford.

29 *Jackson's Oxford Journal* 1690, iii (85:253e).

30 Larry Stewart, "Putting on Airs," in *Discussing Chemistry and Steam*, p. 230.

31 E. G. W. Bill, *Education at Christ Church Oxford, 1660–1800* (Oxford, 1988), p. 318.

32 John Davy, *Memoirs of the Life of Sir Humphry Davy, Bart.*, vol. 1 (London, 1836),

p. 222; quoted in Christa Jungnickel and Russell McCormmach, *Cavendish: The Experimental Life* (Lewisburg, PA, 1999), p. 511.

33 March 9, 1786; Minute Book of Royal Society Club, p. 8; Royal Society Archives. Sir Archibald Geikie, *Annals of the Royal Society Club: The Record of a London Dining-Club in the Eighteenth & Nineteenth Centuries* (London, 1917), p. 71.

34 E. L. Scott, "Kirwan, Richard (1733–1812)," *Oxford Dictionary of National Biography* (Oxford, 2004). M. Donovan, "Biographical Account of the late Richard Kirwan," *Proceedings of the Royal Irish Academy* 4 (1847–50), pp. 81–118.

35 *Discussing Chemistry and Steam*, p. 157. For discussion of the CHPS see essays by Jan Golinski and Larry Stewart in *The Minutes of a Coffee House Philosophical Society, 1780–87* and also the chapter "Priestley and the English Enlightenment" in Golinski's *Science as Public Culture: Chemistry and Enlightenment in Britain, 1760–1820* (Cambridge, 1992), pp. 50–90.

36 Golinski, "Conversations on Chemistry: Talk about Phlogiston in the Coffee House Society, 1780–87," in *Discussing Chemistry and Steam* (2002), especially pp. 192, 198.

37 Magellan was also very interested in mineralogy, and in the 1780s he was producing a new two-volume English edition of Cronstedt's *Essay on Mineralogy*. Smithson kept both Mendes da Costa's 1770 edition and Magellan's 1788 edition in his library, each heavily annotated. Interestingly, Smithson's copy of Magellan's Cronstedt is inscribed "James Smithson, 1788." He was of course James Louis Macie in 1788; this backdating may have been done to show that he had purchased it immediately upon publication, or it could possibly be an early example of him toying with the idea of changing his name. Smithson Library, SIL.

38 Benjamin Franklin to Magellan, January 24, 1786; B F58X Franklin Miscellaneous Collection (APS). Thanks to Rob Cox for his assistance with this query.

39 Bryant Lillywhite, *London Coffee Houses* (London, 1963), pp. 106–7.

40 Quotes from the minutes of the meetings April 14, April 28, and May 12, 1786; *Discussing Chemistry and Steam*, pp. 160–64.

41 The April 1786 meeting was held at Greenwood's in Leicester Square. Soon after, that group—which was struggling to maintain a quorum at meetings—moved again to Leicester House, the commanding house at the head of the square, which had once served as the home of George II and now housed Ashton Lever and his vast museum of curiosities, the Holophusikon. Eventually the SPNH gained its own dedicated quarters on Golden Square. SPNH files, Linnean Society.

42 See Pembroke College Buttery Books for evidence of when a student was in residence. Smithson received his M.A. during convocation at the end of May. Encaenia, the official graduation ceremony, was held the following month on June 28, 1786; University Archives, Bodleian Library, Oxford. It appears from the battel books at Pembroke that Smithson returned to Oxford for Encaenia as well.

43 In another example from the same letter, indicative of how Smithson spoke to Giddy, he wrote with news of the French Revolution, explaining, "You have understood, I hope, that the church is now here quite unacknowledged by the state, and is indeed allowed to exist only till they have leisure to give it the final death-stroke." Smithson to Giddy, 9 May, 1792; Collection of the Smithsonian Institution Libraries. Davies Giddy Diary entry for May 26, 1786 (probably written in c. 1826), CRO. For weather conditions I am grateful to archivist Kate Strachan for compiling information from Private Weather Diaries at the Met Office.

44 Timothy Mowl, *William Beckford: Composing for Mozart* (London, 1998), pp. 103–4. Davies Giddy diary, March 6, 1788; DG14/1787–1790, CRO. Smithson's portrait has been attributed to James Roberts, who also painted Master Adams in 1784 and executed a sketch of Johnson for Adams' daughters Sarah at that time, by Jacob

Simon of the National Portrait Gallery, London. See correspondence with the Smithsonian National Portrait Gallery, November 14, 1997.

45 Barbara English and John Saville, *Strict Settlement: A Guide for Historians* (Hull, 1983), p. 33.

46 His mother, perhaps in an effort to compensate for this, assigned the mortgage (worth £2,000) on the Friar's Estate (9 Friar's Walk) in Lewes, which she had bought from Apsley Pellatt ten years earlier, to Smithson on April 10 and 11, 1786. This property remained a steady source of income for Smithson for many years, until the property was sold by the Pellatts to George Verrall of Lewes in 1804, when Smithson was in Hanau. At that time Smithson transferred legal rights to his solicitor Thomas Graham, who received the £2,000 on his behalf. Deeds of 9 Friar's Walk; East Sussex Record Office, Add MS, Catalogue X, Ref. AMSX.

47 *Gentlemen's Magazine* 56 (1786), no. 1, pp. 529–30.

48 Cavendish took Smithson as his guest to the Royal Society Club dinner on March 9 and December 14, 1786; Minute book of the Royal Society Club, RS Archives. He was Kirwan's guest at the meetings of the Royal Society on December 7 and 21, 1786, and January 11, 1787; List of Visitors, November 1783–June 1788; RS MS vol. 392. Smithson's election certificate in RS Archives, EC/1787/03.

49 Smithson was not by any means the youngest member ever elected, though that claim has often been made. One only has to look as far as Smithson's father, the Duke of Northumberland, to find one who was elected at a younger age; Hugh Smithson was about twenty-one when he was elected in 1736. Christopher Wren was only eighteen when he became a member in 1693, and Charles Somerset, fourth Marquis of Worcester, was a mere thirteen years old when he was elected in 1673. From a survey of members current in 1787, it seems that Smithson was the youngest of them. But it was not a claim that Smithson held onto for very long, apparently. In early 1788 Erasmus Darwin's son Robert, the future father of Charles Darwin, became a member at age twenty-two, knocking Smithson off his "youngest member" pedestal after only a year. I am grateful to Clara Anderson at the Royal Society for her work on this problem. Personal communication with the author, summer 2004.

50 Gadolin arrived in London with recommendation letters from the German chemist Lorenz von Crell and was embraced by Kirwan, Blagden, Adair Crawford, and others—all people who formed part of what might be called Smithson's circle at the Royal Society. Blagden to Crell, March 20, 1787; Blagden Letterbook, MS Osborn fc 15, James Marshall and Marie-Louise Osborn Collection, Beinecke Rare Book and Manuscript Library, Yale University. See also List of Visitors, Journal Book Copy (JBC) 32, RS Archives; and Blagden to Watt, June 7, 1787; Blagden Papers 7.62, RS. Thanks to Marjut Hjelt for checking the Gadolin Papers at the Helsinki University Library for evidence of Smithson, and especially to Dr. Peter B. Dean for his investigation of the Gadolinian Library, University of Åbo.

51 Sniadecki was carrying letters of introduction from the botanist and physician Jan Ingen-Housz, a favorite of the court at Vienna. He was a frequent presence at the Royal Society meetings—the guest of Smithson, Blagden, and others. Michala Balinskiego, *Jan Sniadecki: Dziela Jana Sniadeckiego* (Warsaw, 1839). No correspondence between Sniadecki and Smithson has been found among his papers; personal communication with Ewa Bakowska, Biblioteka Jagiellonska, 2002. See List of Visitors, JBC 32 and 33, RS Archives.

52 Crell to Sir Joseph Banks, November 1790. BL Add MS 8097, f. 302. For background on Crell and the German chemical community, see Karl Hufbauer, *The Formation of the German Chemical Community, 1720–1795* (Berkeley and London, c. 1982).

53 In his paper Cavendish wrote that he "desired some of the Gentlemen most conversant with these subjects to be present at putting the materials together, and at the examination of the produce." Henry Cavendish, "On the Conversion of a Mixture of dephlogisticated and phlogisticated air into nitrous acid, by the electric spark," *Philosophical Transactions* 78 (1788), pp. 261–76. For a description of the experiment see Jungnickel and McCormmach, *Cavendish: The Experimental Life*, pp. 366–8. In 1790 Cavendish invited Smithson to breakfast and spend the day with him south of the river at Clapham, where he had fitted up his large Georgian house on the Common with an extensive laboratory. Sir Charles Blagden and Adair Crawford, a physician at St. Thomas' Hospital and a chemistry professor at Woolwich Arsenal, were the other participants. Lack of surviving archives means this is the only documented instance of Smithson's attendance at Cavendish's laboratory; but it may have been a relatively common event—one that has led to the story (unproven) that Smithson was a laboratory assistant to Cavendish. Blagden Letters, 7: 702, Royal Society Archives; published in Jungnickel and McCormmach, p. 679. The theory about Smithson being Cavendish's laboratory assistant was put forward in J. C. Long's notoriously error-ridden chapters on Smithson in Leonard Carmichael and J. C. Long, *James Smithson and the Smithsonian Story* (New York, 1965); it was repeated, with caution, in Jungnickel and McCormmach.

54 Smithson owned a copy of the *Monthly Review* of May 1783 (which he inscribed "Mr. Macie/Pembroke"), which featured a front-page review of Kirwan's 1782 *Philosophical Transactions* paper entitled "Continuation and Observations on the specific gravities, and attractive powers, of various saline substances." Smithson Library, SIL.

55 Cavendish to Blagden, draft letter, September 16, 1787; quoted in Golinski, *Science as Public Culture*, p. 149. See Golinski's entire discussion of this debate, pp. 129–52.

56 Maurice Crosland, "Research Schools of Chemistry from Lavoisier to Wurtz," *British Journal for the History of Science* (2003), p. 338.

57 Joseph Priestley, "Considerations on the Doctrine of Phlogiston, and the Decomposition of Water" (Philadelphia, 1796).

58 Smithson seems to have been fully engaged over the matter; the title page verso of his original 1630 copy of the *Essays de Jean Rey*—a prescient seventeenth-century drafting of Lavoisier's ideas—is marked with a stamp "BRITISH MUSEUM/SALE DUPLICATE/1787," which suggests that he might have purchased the book around this time. Smithson Library, SIL.

5. Science and Revolution, 1788–1791

1 Rhoda Rappaport, "Jean-Louis Giraud Soulavie," *Dictionary of Scientific Biography*, vol. 12, pp. 549–50 (*DSB*).

2 In 1787 the Royal Society established new rules for the admission of foreign members. The number was to be limited to one hundred, and each certificate had to be signed by six members (foreign or domestic) and presented some time between Easter 1787 and the end of November, the ballot to take place the Easter following. This vote before Easter 1788 was the first election of foreign members under the new rules. Charles Blagden draft letter to Claude Louis Berthollet, April 27, 1787, Blagden Letterbook, MS Osborn fc 15, James Marshall and Marie-Louise Osborn Collection, Beinecke Rare Book and Manuscript Library, Yale University. Soulavie's certificate and rejection can be found in the Royal Society Archives, Ref. No. EC/1787/24.

3 Joseph Banks to Antoine Lavoisier, April 8, 1788; Papiers Lavoisier, Archives du Comte de Chabrol, Archives de l'Académie des Sciences, Paris; published in Michelle

Goupil and Henri Kagan, *Oeuvres de Lavoisier, Correspondance*, vol. V, *1787–1788* (Paris, 1993), p. 153.

4 William K. Wimsatt, Jr., and Frederick A. Pottle, eds, *Boswell for the Defence, 1769–1774* (Melbourne, 1960), p. 274.

5 Smithson's trip to Paris is discerned from his bank ledgers at Hoare's, vol. 32 (1788–9), f. 76, and from passport control information in Paris: the "Etat des Etrangers qui ont loger à Paris en Chambres Garnier, Dans les Hotels ou auberges depuis le 2 Juillet 1788 Jusqu'au 4 Inclus," Archives du Ministère des Affaires Etrangères, Controle des Etrangers, Registre 91. I am grateful to Anne Eschapasse for her tip to check this archive. Entry for Sir William Hamilton in John Ingamells, *A Dictionary of British and Irish Travellers in Italy, 1701–1800* (Yale University Press, 1997), pp. 456–60.

6 The emphasis is Greville's. Charles Greville to Sir Joseph Banks, n.d., BL Add MS 33982, f. 238.

7 Smithson to Greville, July 16, n.y. [1802]. BL Add MS 42071, f. 166.

8 Michael P. Cooper, "Greville, Charles Francis (1749–1809)," *Oxford Dictionary of National Biography* (Oxford 2004). See also Lawrence H. Conklin, "James Sowerby, His Publications and Collections," *Mineralogical Record* 26 (1995), pp. 85–105.

9 J. Andrews, *Letters to a Young Gentleman on his setting out for France* (1784), p. 2.

10 Davies Giddy diary, note of 1831, in the entry of June 23, 1791; DG15/1791–95, CRO.

11 Archives du Ministère des Affaires Etrangères, Controle des Etrangers, Registre 91 and Vol. 67. The registers at Spa give no notice of Smithson appearing in Spa; *Liste des Seigneurs et Dames Venus aux Eaux Minérales de Spa, L'An 1788*. Many thanks to Vyvyan Lyle for her work on this.

12 Arthur Young, *Travels in France during the years 1787, 1788 & 1789*, Constantia Maxwell, ed. (Cambridge, 1950), p. 374.

13 Entry for Friday September 19, 1788; Archives du Ministère des Affaires Etrangères, Surveillance des Etrangers en France, September, October 1788, vol. 70. In Switzerland they might have picked up another companion, a Baron Cogels, member of an ancient Antwerp banking family, as the other passport control register (vol. 91), listing place of abode in Paris, gives Macie and Greville and a Milord Cogels, "Gentilhomme D'Anvers," together at the Hôtel du Moscovie on rue des Petits Augustins.

14 Katherine Gilbert Dapp, *George Keate, esq., eighteenth-century English gentleman* (Philadelphia, 1939), p. 30.

15 The Earl of Ilchester, ed., *The Journal of Lady Elizabeth Holland (1791–1811)* (London, 1908), vol. 1, p. 67.

16 Lydie Touret, "Charles-François Exchaquet (1746–1792) et les Plans en Relief du Mont-Blanc," *Annals of Science* 46 (1989), pp. 1–20. See G. R. de Beer, *Early Travellers in the Alps* (London, 1930), p. 181. Smithson's copy of *Instructions pour les voyageurs* (Berne, 1787) is in the Smithson Library, SIL.

17 Horace-Bénédict de Saussure, *Voyages dans les Alpes: précédés d'un essai sur l'histoire naturelle des environs de Genève*, 4 vols (Neuchâtel, 1779–96). De Saussure offered a reward to the first person who scaled Mont Blanc; it was claimed in 1786, the year before de Saussure managed his own ascent. In the summer of 1788, around the time of Smithson's visit, de Saussure spent sixteen days making observations on the Col de Géant. Blagden to Banks, August 9, 1788, printed in G. R. de Beer, "Some Letters of Sir Charles Blagden," *Notes and Records of the Royal Society* (1951), p. 254.

18 See A. E. Sayous, "La haute bourgeoisie de Genève et ses travaux scientifiques," *Zeitschrift für Schweizerische Geschichte* 20 (2), pp. 195–227.

19 Douglas William Freshfield, *The Life of Horace Bénédict de Saussure* (London, 1920), pp. 161–2.

20 De Beer, *Early Travellers in the Alps*, p. 179.

21 Christopher Hibbert, *The Days of the French Revolution* (New York, 1980), p. 40.

22 Smithson's Hoare's ledgers show a payment of £40 to Perregaux & Co. on September 27, 1788. See also "Jean-Frédéric Perregaux et le Comité des Banquiers et des Agents de Change," in Jean Bouchary, *Les Manieurs d'Argent à Paris à la fin du XVIIIe Siècle*, 3 vols (Paris, 1939–43). Mary Berry quoted in Geoffrey de Bellaigue, "Jean-Frédéric Perregaux: The Englishman's Best Friend," *Antologia di Belle Arti* (1986), pp. 80–90.

23 *Etat Actuel de Paris; ou Le Provincial à Paris, ouvrage indispensable à ceux qui veulent connoitre & parcourir Paris sans faire aucune question*, 4 vols (1788), pp. 122–7.

24 C. C. Gillispie, *Science and Polity in France at the End of the Old Regime* (Princeton, 1980), p. 191.

25 Harold B. Carter, *Sir Joseph Banks, 1743–1820* (London, 1988), p. 222.

26 Quoted in V. A. Eyles, "The Evolution of a Chemist, Sir James Hall, Bt., F.R.S., P.R.S.E." *Annals of Science* 19 (1963), pp. 167–8. See also Arthur Donovan, *Antoine Lavoisier: Science, Administration, and Revolution* (Oxford, 1993), pp. 175–6.

27 Arthur Young, *Travels in France during the years 1787, 1788 & 1789* (Cambridge, 1950), pp. 82–3.

28 R. Hahn, "Scientific Careers in Eighteenth-century France," in Maurice P. Crosland, ed., *The Emergence of Science in Western Europe* (New York, 1976), pp. 132–4.

29 *Etat Actuel de Paris* (1788).

30 R. Hookyaas, "René-Just Haüy," *DSB*, pp. 178–83. Smithson frequently mentioned Haüy in his papers, and his library contains several of Haüy's publications, most inscribed "A Monsieur Smitson [sic], hommage de l'auteur." Smithson Library, SIL.

31 Jan Golinski, *Science as Public Culture* (Cambridge, 1992), pp. 273–4. See also D. C. Goodman, "William Hyde Wollaston," *DSB*, pp. 486–94. Romé de l'Isle was the other chief architect of crystallography, and his extensive cabinet of crystallography, located near the Palais Royal, was justly renowned in Paris as one of a kind. He guided visitors through the collection, engagingly illustrating the structure of crystals first with large-scale wooden models he had crafted before leading visitors to the actual specimens. Smithson owned and referred constantly to de l'Isle's *Crystallographie* of 1783, which he might have acquired here in Paris on this trip. In a letter to Fabbroni in Florence in 1794 Smithson mentions having checked Fabbroni's specimens against the figures in de l'Isle—an indication probably that he was traveling with his own marked-up copy. Smithson Library, SIL.

32 William Thomson to Ottaviano Targioni-Tozzetti, July 23, 1793. Ottaviano Targioni-Tozzetti Papers 75, vol. 4, Biblioteca Nationale Centrale di Firenze (BNCF).

33 Macie to Fabbroni, December 23, 1793; B F113 APS Fabbroni Papers. In 1804 he wrote to another friend, "You remember perhaps that my cabinet is almost wholly confined to small good crystals separated from their matrix or rock." Smithson to unknown [Ricca or Santi], September 4, 1804; Autografi Porri: 36/15, Biblioteca Comunale degli Intronati, Siena.

34 William Thomson to John Hawkins, December 14, 1789. Hawkins Papers, J3/2/34, CRO. I am grateful to Hugh Torrens for bringing this letter to my attention.

35 *Bulletin of the Proceedings of the National Institute*, July 12, 1841; SIA, RU 7078, Box 11.

36 RS Archives, Ref. No. EC/1788/13.

37 Wilcke does not appear to have been someone Smithson knew personally; he seems to have signed the certificate on the basis of his knowledge of Wilcke's publications; RS Archives, Ref. No. EC/1788/22. There is no evidence in the archives of the

Royal Swedish Academy of Sciences in Stockholm that Smithson ever corresponded with Wilcke. Nor does he appear to have visited Stockholm to attend a seance of the Academy. Correspondence with the Academy of Sciences, November 2001.

38 Duke of Dorset to Lord Carmarthen, quoted in John Goldworth Alger, *Englishmen in the French Revolution* (London, 1889), p. 25.

39 James L. Macie to Charles Greville, January 1, 1792; BL Add MS 41199, f. 82.

40 *Papers of Thomas Jefferson*, vol. 14, pp. 420–22 (January 8, 1789), quoted in Peter Burley, *Witness to the Revolution: British and American Despatches from France, 1788–94* (London, 1989), p. 21.

41 Quoted in Peter M. Jones, "Living the Enlightenment and the French Revolution: James Watt, Matthew Boulton, and Their Sons," *The Historical Journal* 42 (1999), p. 181.

42 Davies Giddy diary, DG 15 (1791–5), CRO.

43 Burke quotes from the excellent Maurice Crosland, "The Image of Science as a Threat: Burke versus Priestley and the 'Philosophic Revolution,'" *British Journal for the History of Science* 20 (1987), pp. 277–307 (in particular pp. 284, 288).

44 Quoted in Simon Schaffer, "Natural Philosophy and Public Spectacle in the Eighteenth Century," *History of Science* xxi (1983), p. 25.

45 "Library and laboratory" in Blagden to Kirwan, March 20, 1790; Blagden Papers 7.322, RS. Chevenix story in *The Life and Letters of Maria Edgeworth*, A. J. C. Hare, ed. (London, 1895), vol. 1, p. 70.

46 The only reference to Smithson's continuation of Fourcroy's work is an illegible mention in a draft of a letter Blagden wrote to Kirwan, March 20, 1790; Blagden Papers 7.322, Royal Society. Fourcroy's experiments on liver, part of his study of the changes animal matter underwent in putrefaction, were spurred by his being witness to the exhumation of over a thousand corpses from an abandoned cemetery, and the discovery—well-known to grave-diggers but a shock to scientists—that muscles and fat converted to a greasy spermaceti-like substance. See W. A. Smeaton, *Fourcroy, Chemist and Revolutionary (1755–1809)* (Cambridge, 1962), pp. 141–2.

47 James L. Macie to Charles Greville, October 6, n.y. [1790 or 1791]; BL Add MS 42071, ff. 164–5.

48 "An Account of the Tabasheer, in a letter from Patrick Russell, M.D. F.R.S. to Sir Joseph Banks, Bart. P.R.S.," *Philosophical Transactions of the Royal Society of London* 80 (1790), pp. 273–83. Blagden to Berthollet, September 3, 1790; Blagden Papers 7.442, RS.

49 James Macie, "An Account of Some Chemical Experiments on Tabasheer," *Philosophical Transactions* 81 (1791).

50 Blagden to Kirwan, July 25, 1791, and Blagden to Berthollet, July 22, 1791; Blagden Papers 7.546 and 7.543, RS.

51 A copy of *Breve Notizia di un Viaggiatore*, inscribed "from Dr. Thomson", mentions Smithson on p. 16; Smithson Library, SIL. The book, though undated, was published at Naples in October 1795 according to the *Bibliothèque Britannique*, which published it in its first issue (*BB*, vol. 1, no. 1 (January 1796), pp. 65–88) with an introduction by Pictet; it was also printed in the Naples journal *Giornale Letterario* vol. 41 (December 15, 1795), pp. 39–51, Crell abstracted it in his *Annalen*, and it also appeared in the *Annales de Chimie*. For Jameson, see "Jameson's Approach to the Wernerian Theory of the Earth, 1796" in *Annals of Science* 23 (1967), pp. 81–95. William Batt, resident in Genoa, occupied the first chair in chemistry at the university in Genoa; Sandro Doldi, *Scienza e Tecnica in Liguria* (Genoa, 1984), p. 46. For the reference to the chemical Macie, see Batt to Sir Joseph Banks, February 7, 1803; Banks Collection, Sutro Library, California. Humphry Davy mentioned Macie in Lecture 7; Robert

Siegfried and Robert H. Dott, Jr., eds, *Humphry Davy on Geology: The 1805 Lectures for the General Audience* (University of Wisconsin Press, 1980), p. 93.

52 In response Black sent a long letter describing his home-made balance, which Smithson published in 1825. Joseph Black to James Louis Macie, September 18, 1790; EUL Gen 873/II/158–9. The letter begins, "I had the pleasure to receive your letter of the 9th. The apparatus I use for weighing very small masses such as the globules of metals produced by essays with the blowpipe &c is as follows. . . ." It was published in *Annals of Philosophy*, vol. 10, no. 1 (July 1825) with a note by Smithson, and republished in the *Mechanics Magazine* 6 (1827), pp. 119–20.

53 James Louis Macie, Esq. F.R.S., "An Account of Some Chemical Experiments on Tabasheer," *Philosophical Transactions* 81 (1791), pp. 368–88. Norman Moore, "Pitcairn, William (1712–1791)," rev. Catherine Bergin, *Oxford Dictionary of National Biography* (Oxford, 2004). Pitcairn was, with Smithson, a member of the Society for Promoting Natural History; he had a five-acre botanical garden behind his house on Upper Street. Jan Ingen-Housz, the discoverer of photosynthesis, was in the audience when Smithson's paper was read out to the society. He too was evidently impressed with Smithson. His list of contacts in London included "James L. Macie, F.R.S., a good chemist, Orchard Street on Portman Square." Breda Archives. Thanks to the archivist Dr. Jan Wessels for his assistance, and thanks too to Dr. and Mrs. Beale, authors of a forthcoming biography of Ingen-Housz, for an interesting correspondence on the topic.

54 "Thomson, William (bap. 1760, d. 1806)," *Oxford Dictionary of National Biography* (Oxford, 2004). Thomson to George Paton, September 25, 1790, National Library of Scotland, Adv. MS 29.5.8 (ii), fo. 80., quoted in E.G.W. Bill, *Education at Christ Church Oxford, 1660–1800* (Oxford, 1988), p. 316. Minutes and Register of Convocation 1776–93, pp. 437–8, Oxford University Archives.

55 Anonymous, *Satan's Harvest Home: or the Present State of Whorecraft, Adultery, Fornication, Procuring, Pimping, Sodomy . . . and other Satanic Works, daily propagated in this good Protestant Kingdom* (1749), quoted in H. Montgomery Hyde, *The Love that Dared Not Speak its Name* (Boston, 1970), pp. 67–8.

56 Blagden reported the results to the Royal Society on February 16, 1775; Harold B. Carter, *Sir Joseph Banks, 1743–1820*, (London, 1988), p. 127.

57 Macie, "An Account of Some Chemical Experiments on Tabasheer," *Phil. Trans.* (1791). Smithson mineral notes from Paris May 1819 experiments; SIA, RU 7000, Box 2.

58 M. P. Crosland, "Pierre Louis Dulong (1785–1838)," *DSB*, vol. 4, pp. 238–42. Paul Dorveaux, "Bertrand Pelletier," *Revue d'Histoire de la Pharmacie* (March 1937), pp. 5–24.

59 The receipt book came into the Smithson Collection in 1914, well after the Smithsonian fire and cannot be definitively attributed to him. It is signed "Smithson" on one of the first pages. The bulk of the text is not, contrary to what has sometimes been stated, written in Smithson's hand. SIA, RU 7000, Box 2.

60 Dr. William Drew to Lady Webster, n.d. [June–July 5, 1797]; BL Add MS 51814, ff. 37–8. See also W. F. Bynum and Roy Porter, eds, "Brunonianism in Britain and Europe," *Medical History Supplement*, no. 8 (1988).

61 James Smithson to Lady Holland, May 1, n.y. [1801]. BL Add MS 51846, ff. 104–5.

62 Smithson to Greville, January 1, 1792; BL Add MS 41199, f. 82.

63 Edward Wedlake Brayley, *A Topographical and Historical Description of London and Middlesex* (London, 1820) pp. 543–4. Smithson may well have been the J.L.M. who was listed as a new subscriber (alongside William Adams, Master of Pembroke

College) to the relief of the poor in Oxford the week of January 6, 1789; *Jackson's Oxford Journal* 1863, iii (89:6b).

64 John Richardson, *Annals of London: a year-by-year record of a thousand years of history* (London, 2000), p. 226. Adam Walker to Giovanni Fabbroni, January 24, 1791; APS B F113.

65 Philadelphia Percy's obituary in *Gentleman's Magazine* (1791), part 2, p. 1068. Smithson does not appear to have arrived in Paris yet in November 1791, according to registers maintained by police, held in the archives of the Ministère des Affaires Etrangères, Paris; no records are held for after November 1791, so it is not possible to ascertain exactly when he arrived in Paris. When he finally appeared in Florence he wrote to Fabbroni (in the third person), stating, "He [Smithson] would be much obliged to him [Fabbroni] if he could lend him a volume or two of the Monthly Review, as he he [sic] has never seen this work since Nov.br 1791." This letter suggests perhaps that November 1791 was the last month that he was in England. Macie to Fabbroni, n.d. [c. 1793]; B F113 APS.

66 Will of Margaret Marriott, written April 16, 1821, was proved November 12, 1827; TNA: PRO PROB 11/1733. Personal communication with the Westminster Abbey archivist, August 2003.

6. Grand Tour, 1791–1797

1 James L. Macie to Charles F. Greville, January 1, 1792; BL Add MS 41199, f. 82.

2 James L. Macie to Davies Giddy, May 9, 1792; collection of the Smithsonian Institution Libraries (SIL); printed in *Smithsonian Annual Report of 1884*, pp. 5–6.

3 David Garrioch, "When to Wear a Red Bonnet," review of *The Politics of Appearance: The Symbolism and Representation of Dress in Revolutionary France*, by Richard Wrigley, in the *London Review of Books*, April 3, 2003, pp. 32–3. Macie to Giddy, May 9, 1792; SIL.

4 John Goldworth Alger, *Glimpses of the French Revolution: Myths, Ideals, Realities* (London, 1894), p. 70.

5 Quoted in John Fisher, *The Elysian Fields: France in Ferment, 1789–1804* (London, 1966), p. 130.

6 Macie to Giddy, May 9, 1792; SIL.

7 Quoted in George Woodcock, "The Meaning of Revolution in Britain," in Ian Small, *The French Revolution and British Culture* (Oxford, 1989), p. 5.

8 James Watt, Jr., quoted in John Goldworth Alger, *Paris in 1789–94* (London, 1902), pp. 324–5.

9 Thomas Cooper, "A Reply to Mr. Burke's Invective against Mr. Cooper and Mr. Watt, in the House of Commons, on the 30th of April, 1792" (Manchester, 1792), p. 5. John Goldworth Alger, *Englishmen in the French Revolution* (London, 1889), p. 45–6.

10 Stephen L. Newman, "Cooper, Thomas (1759–1839)," *Oxford Dictionary of National Biography* (Oxford, 2004). Dumas Malowe, *The Public Life of Thomas Cooper, 1783–1839* (Columbia, 1961).

11 Richard Price, "A Discourse on the love of our country, delivered on 4 Nov., 1789 . . .," quoted in Jenny Graham, "Revolutionary Philosopher: The Political Ideas of Joseph Priestley (1733–1804): Part II," *Enlightenment and Dissent* 9 (1990), p. 15. Macie to Greville, January 1, 1792; BL Add MS 41199, f. 82.

12 Macie to Greville, January 1, 1792; BL Add MS 41199, f. 82.

13 Gouverneur Morris to Thomas Jefferson, June 10, 1792, from the *Diary and Letters of Gouverneur Morris* (1888); quoted in William Howard Adams, *Gouverneur Morris: An Independent Life* (Yale, 2003), p. 237.

14 In June 1793 the Muséum was born; all other state-sponsored academies and societies, including the Académie des Sciences, were suppressed. See E. C. Spary, *Utopia's Garden: French Natural History from Old Regime to Revolution* (Chicago, 2000), especially pp. 10, 17–18, 162, 173, 179. Berthollet to Martinus van Marum, February 3, 1792; quoted in Michelle Sadoun-Goupil, *Le Chimiste Claude-Louis Berthollet (1748–1822): sa vie, son oeuvre* (Paris, 1977), p. 319.

15 Smithson to Giddy, May 9, 1792; SIL. Arthur Young, *Travels in France in the Years 1787, 1788, and 1789*, Constantia Maxwell, ed. (Cambridge, 1950), p. 187. Blagden movements from Gavin de Beer, "The Diary of Charles Blagden," *Notes and Records of the Royal Society of London* (London, 1951), col. 8, p.72. Donald McDonald, "Smithson Tennant, F.R.S. (1761–1815)," *Notes and Records of the Royal Society* 17 (1962), p. 82.

16 Walter Johnson, "A Memoir on the Scientific Character and Researches of James Smithson, Esq., F.R.S." (Philadelphia, 1844). Smithson to Greville, January 1, 1792; BL Add MS 41199, f. 82.

17 Fisher, *Elysian Fields*, pp. 126–7.

18 De Beer, "The Diary of Sir Charles Blagden", pp. 75–6, 81.

19 MSS journal of Mrs. Crewe, Paris, 1785–86; BL Add MS 37926, ff. 93–4.

20 De Beer, "The Diary of Sir Charles Blagden," pp. 71–2. The Earl of Ilchester, ed., *The Journal of Elizabeth Lady Holland (1791–1811)* (London, 1908), vol. 1, p. 7. Beddoes back in England wrote to Giddy of the "wonderful diversion" coming in the news from Italy. He gave elaborate instructions for how to replicate the experiment, beginning by cutting the frog in half and delicately flaying the thighs "without disturbing the nerves, which you dissect a little way down." After coating the nerve endings with lead in tin foil, one then used silver or any conductor different from the coating to connect the coating and the frog's muscles. "The half-frog will jump with considerable force." The poor flayed frog could also be made to jump out of a glass of water by hanging the coated nerves into a second nearby glass of water, dipping a finger in and swirling it around while with one's other hand holding a piece of silver one touched the frog's muscles. Beddoes to Davies Giddy, October 8, 1792, DG41/54, CRO. See also Marcello Pera, *The Ambiguous Frog: The Galvani-Volta Controversy on Animal Electricity*, trans. Jonathan Mandelbaum (Princeton, 1992).

21 Beddoes to Giddy, October 8, 1792, quoted in Larry Stewart, "Putting on Airs," in *Discussing Chemistry and Steam: The Minutes of a Coffee House Philosophical Society* (Oxford, 2002), p. 232.

22 Davy to Samuel Taylor Coleridge, November, 25 1800, Pierpont Morgan Library, MS MA 1857 no. 11; quoted in Trevor Levere, *Poetry Realized in Nature: Samuel Taylor Coleridge and Early Nineteenth-Century Science* (Cambridge, 1981), p. 32.

23 Quoted in Gavin de Beer, *Travellers in Switzerland* (Oxford, 1949), p. 94.

24 Lady Spencer to Mrs. Howe, June 1, 1792; quoted in Amanda Foreman, *Georgiana, Duchess of Devonshire* (London, 1998), p. 278.

25 Rachel Laudan, *From Mineralogy to Geology: The Foundations of a Science, 1650–1830* (University of Chicago Press, 1987), p. 194. Blagden "saw the Dolomite, milky white opaque substance," at the Duchess of Devonshire's salon in Geneva in the early fall of 1792. De Beer, "The Diary of Sir Charles Blagden," p. 81.

26 Smithson gave a half-dozen or more different specimens from this region to Father Petrini at the Collegio Nazareno; examples of "Felspato in massa grigio delle montagne di Trento fra Braunsdorf e Neumark," "Sasso argillioso Magnesiaco di Bressanano nel Tirolo," "Granulite di grani di felspato bianchi delle montagne del Tirolo fra Colmar e Braunsdorf," and "Porfido rosso di fegato con felspeti bianchi crossigni con horneblenda scura, di Bautsen nel Tirolo," are among those marked

as "Dono del Sig. Macie," in Petrini's *Catalogo Inventario di Mineralogia*, c. 1794, Collegio Nazareno, Rome. I am grateful to Tonino Caruso, Librarian at the Collegio, for permission to consult the catalogue and quote from it. The mineral collection still exists but is in a state of disarray, and it is no longer possible to collate actual specimens with those listed in the catalogue.

27 H. S. Torrens, "Thomson, William (bap. 1760, d. 1806)," *Oxford Dictionary of National Biography* (Oxford, 2004). The letters Thomson wrote to Cardinal Borgia are in the Vatican, Borg. Lat. 286, ff. 118–119v; 124–125v. Luigi Sementini wrote to Ottaviano Targioni-Tozzetti (OTT), February 19, 1803, explaining that he had made the best collection of Vesuviana for OTT that he possibly could, in light of the fact that Thomson was taking all the best specimens. OTT Papers 75, vol. 3, Biblioteca Nazionale Centrale di Firenze (BNCF).

28 Macie to Greville, January 1, 1792; BL Add MS 41199, f. 82.

29 William Thomson to Ottaviano Targioni-Tozzetti, July 23, 1793. OTT Papers 75, vol. 4, BNCF. (The enclosed letter to Smithson no longer exists.) William Thomson to Giovanni Fabbroni, July 23, 1793. APS B F113.

30 Eric Cochrane, *Florence in the Forgotten Centuries, 1527–1800: A History of Florence and the Florentines in the Age of the Grand Dukes* (Chicago and London, 1973). Diary of Henry Louis Dickenson, SIA RU 7000, Box 2.

31 Nicholas Hans, "Franklin, Jefferson, and the English Radicals at the end of the Eighteenth Century," *Proceedings of the American Philosophical Society*, vol. 98, no. 6 (1954), pp. 416–17.

32 John C. Greene, *American Science in the Age of Jefferson* (Iowa State University Press, 1984), p. 409.

33 Quoted in Cochrane, *Florence in the Forgotten Centuries*, p. 446.

34 Isaac Weld, *Travels through the States of North America and the Provinces of Upper and Lower Canada, during the years 1795, 1796, and 1797* (London, 1807), 2 vols; Smithson Library, SIL. Smithson made many notes in this book, but the marking of the entire section on the city of Washington seems uncharacteristic and may be an indication of someone subsequently trying to emphasize Smithson's interest in the capital. For more on Brant see Thomas S. Abler, "Joseph Brant," *American National Biography* (New York, 1999). Perhaps Smithson met Brant when he came to London in 1786; Smithson's half-brother commissioned a portrait of Brant from Gilbert Stuart at this time.

35 Quoted in Cochrane, *Florence in the Forgotten Centuries*, p. 446.

36 The siege began in September, Toulon having rebelled against the Convention and appealed to the English, who sailed in along with some Spanish troops and occupied the port in late August. The French eventually retook the city in December, a victory that gained Napoleon, whose family had fled to Toulon from Corsica earlier in the summer and who had proposed the successful plan to eject the British, one of his first promotions. John Udny was the British consul in Livorno; his papers are at the British Library. The correspondence of John Hervey, consul in Florence, to William Hamilton is also full of information regarding Toulon; BL Egerton MS 2638, ff. 29–105.

37 James Macie to Dr. Targioni [Ottaviano Targioni-Tozzetti], December 9, 1793; OTT 75 vol. 2, BNCF.

38 Macie to Targioni-Tozzetti, December 9, 1793; OTT 75, vol. 2, BNCF. When Smithson had been in Florence, Fabbroni had loaned him "an immense box of crystals," inviting him to select a series of its offerings for himself and to do the same for the museum's cabinet. Smithson had happily complied, telling Fabbroni he hoped "to restore it to him again very soon, tho' despoiled . . . of some very

curious specimens." When Smithson returned the box of crystals to Fabbroni, he noted he had "joined to each parcel a label referring to the plate of Delisle's book where it is figured." Macie to Fabbroni, n.d. [c. 1794], APS B F113.

39 Marcello Mellini, "Paolo Mascagni Minore: II Naturalista," in *La Scienza Illuminata: Paolo Mascagni nel suo Tempo (1755–1815)* (Siena, 1996), pp. 37–45.

40 Macie to Fabbroni, December 23, 1793, APS B F113.

41 Much of Zoëga's correspondence is at the Danish Royal Library; there is no mention of Smithson, however. Smithson did have some Danish acquaintances. At one point he wrote to Fabbroni, "Mr. Macie requests the favor of Mr. Fabbroni's [sic] company to breakfast tomorrow morning at half after eight o'clock to meet a Danish Gentleman whom he knows." Undated letter (c. 1794), APS B F113. It is possible that these contacts were coming to Smithson via his friend Thomson, as Thomson's address in Naples was "chez M. Heigelin" at the Danish consulate. R. T. Gunther, "Dr. William Thomson, F.R.S., a Forgotten English Mineralogist, 1761–c. 1806," *Nature*, no. 3625 (April 22, 1939), p. 667. On May 12, 1794, Petrini wrote to Fabbroni to introduce a "Sig[nore]. Wat," a friend of both Thomson's and Petrini's, and an "excellent Danish mineralogist." APS B F113.

42 Macie to Fabbroni, December 23, 1793. APS B F113.

43 Lord Wycombe to Lansdowne, Rome, November 8, 1794. Bowood Muniments, Microfilm 2030, Bodleian Library.

44 Macie to Fabbroni, December 23, 1793. APS B F113.

45 Macie to Fabbroni, n.d., c. 1793–4. APS B F113.

46 *Diccionario Enciclopedico Escolapio* (Salamanca, 1983), vol. 2, p. 433. Petrini made a new catalogue of the collection following Joseph II's donation: *Musei Mineralogici Descriptionem, exhibentem metallorum ex Hungaria parte maxima serieum, liberalitate Iosephi II, Romanorum Imperatoris, ad usum Collegii N. dono datorum: Romae, typ. Zempel, 1794.* Smithson also made a number of gifts to the collection, which are documented in the catalogue of the collection today at the archives of the Collegio Nazareno.

47 Lady Vassall-Webster to Fabbroni, February 27, 1796; APS B F113.

48 Petrini to Fabbroni, December 14, 1793; APS B F113.

49 William Thomson to Fabbroni, June 17, 1793; APS B F113.

50 See Blagden letters to Banks at the BL and the Blagden Papers at the Royal Society. David Philip Miller, "Blagden, Sir Charles (bap. 1748, d. 1820)," *Oxford Dictionary of National Biography* (Oxford, 2004).

51 Charles Blagden to Georgiana, Duchess of Devonshire, January 4, 1794. Devonshire MSS, Chatsworth, 5th Duke's Group, 1202. I'm grateful to Hugh Torrens for bringing this letter to my attention, and to the Duke of Devonshire and the Chatsworth Settlement Trustees for permission to quote from it.

52 Blagden to Banks, October 17, 1784; DTC, vol. 4, ff. 75–6. Georgiana's natural child Eliza Courtney, whom she called "my sweet but hidden violet" in a poem, was born in Aix-en-Provence on February 20, 1792; Earl of Bessborough, ed., *Georgiana: Extracts from the Correspondence of Georgiana, Duchess of Devonshire* (London, 1955), p. 294.

53 Petrini's original letter to the duchess is lost. We can recover what his comments on "that other part of [Macie's] character" would have been from his ecstatic letter to Fabbroni probably penned the same day (December 14). The duchess' letter to Blagden asking about Macie is also gone. The duchess was in Bath from late November 1793 to mid-January 1794, according to Bessborough, *Georgiana* (1955), p. 204. Thanks to the Archivist at Chatsworth for his assistance.

54 Archivio di Stato di Napoli, Ministero degli Affari Esteri, Legazione del Governo Inglese a Napoli; 673 covers 1789–90, and 674 covers 1795–7.

55 Dr. Drew to Lady Webster, January 25, 1794. BL Add MS 51814, f. 13.

56 Thomas Brand to Lady Webster, December 21, 1793; BL Add MS 51845, ff. 59–60.

57 Macie to Greville, January 1, 1792; BL Add MS 41199, f. 82.

58 Entry for Sir William Hamilton in John Ingamells, *A Dictionary of British and Irish Travellers in Italy, 1701–1800* (Yale University Press, 1997), pp. 456–60.

59 Smithson published his analysis in "On a Saline Substance from Mount Vesuvius," *Philosophical Transactions* 103 (1813), p. 257.

60 Smithson's mineral notes; SIA, RU 7000, Box 2. There is also one exemplar, a specimen of potassium sulfate found on Vesuvius, which Smithson gave to Haüy in Paris and forms part of the Muséum d'Histoire Naturelle's collection today. Haüy's catalogue does not clarify whether Smithson found the specimen himself, or whether it was in his collection because it had been sent to him or he had purchased it.

61 Baron Muller to John Parish, Naples, March 12, 1804; Parish Family Archives, Hamburg Staatsarchiv, microfilm copy (Z Filmes 6655) of material deposited in Prague.

62 James Smithson, "Some Observations on Mr. Penn's Theory Concerning the Formation of the Kirkdale Cave," *Annals of Philosophy* 24 (1824).

63 The Hon. H. A. Wyndham, *A Family History, 1688–1837: The Wyndhams of Somerset, Sussex and Wiltshire* (London, 1950), pp. 261–80.

64 Michael Rocke, *Forbidden Friendships: Homosexuality and Male Culture in Renaissance Florence* (Oxford, 1996), p. 3.

65 For Wycombe's comments on marriage see Wycombe to Holland, Lausanne, November 2, 1796; BL Add MS 58613, ff. 43–6. See also entry for William Frederick Wyndham in Ingamells, *A Dictionary of British and Irish Travellers in Italy*, pp. 1028–9. *The Journal of Lady Holland*, vol. 1, p. 117.

66 Earl Macartney to George L. Staunton, December 20, 1795; quoted in George T. Staunton, *Memoir of the Life and Family of Sir G. L. Staunton* (Havant, 1823), pp. 357–9. Entry for Wyndham in Ingamells, *A Dictionary of British and Irish Travellers in Italy*, pp. 1028–9. Partial letter from Lord Wycombe to Lord Holland, dated c. October 23 to November 16, 1791; BL Add MS 58613, ff. 27–8.

67 He served in this position for other English aristocrats as well, including even the powerful patron the Earl-Bishop, Lord Bristol (father of John Augustus Hervey). In July 1794 Smithson provided Bristol with an introduction to the Sienese anatomist Paolo Mascagni, an expert on the Lagoni. Macie to Mascagni, July 7, 1794; Archivio Paolo Mascagni, filza 3a, carteggio 36, Accademia dei Fisiocritici, Siena, Italy.

68 Back in London after this trip Smithson wrote to Lady Holland, "I will certainly take the first opportunity of paying my respects to you, and will, with much readiness & pleasure, give any aid in my power towards the arrangement of your collection of minerals." May 1, n.y. [1801]; BL Add MS 51846, ff. 104–5. Lord Holland's poem entitled "To L.y W: 25th March 1795 Florence" is located in Holland Papers, BL Add MS 51730, ff. 1–3, 5–7.

69 Poem of March 25, 1831, in Holland Papers, BL Add MS 51730, ff. 61–2.

70 Giovanni Fabbroni, *Di una Singolarissima Specie di Mattoni* (Florence, 1794).

71 Macie to Fabbroni, no date [c. 1794]; APS B F113.

72 Milady Vassall (Lady Webster, soon to be Lady Holland) to Giovanni Fabbroni,

March 27, 1797; APS B F113. Fabbroni to Milady Vassall, May 8, 1797. BL Add MS 51845, ff. 114–15.

73 Francis Russell, "Notes on Grand Tour portraiture," *The Burlington Magazine* 136 (July 1994), p. 443.

74 Louis Gauffier, "Portrait of a Young Gentleman, Florence, 1796," was published in the *Gazette des Beaux-Arts* (May 1926). It was listed then as part of the Prince Koudacheff collection [Sergei Vladimirovich Koudacheff, 1863–1933]; its current whereabouts are unknown. It is probably a small cabinet-size picture and thus unlikely if it is Smithson to be the large oil painting that Smithson gave Mrs. Marriot, which remains unidentified.

75 Sir William Hamilton, "An account of the late eruption of Mount Vesuvius," *Philosophical Transactions* 85 (1795), pp. 73–116.

76 Pictet printed a description of Thomson's finds in *Bibliothèque Britannique*, t. 4, no. 2 (February 1797), pp. 128–35, as a follow-up to the publication of his original article ('Notices d'un Voyageur Anglais . . .") in t. 1. Smithson lists the "Crust from the Church bells of Torre del Greco formed by the lava in 1794" in his mineral catalogue. The original list from Thomson, entitled "Sent to Mr Macie [Via] Dr. Robertson Nov.r 22[17]96" exists still among Smithson's papers. SIA, RU 7000, Box 2.

77 Massimiliano Ricca, *Discorso sopra le opere del Soldani* (Siena, 1810), pp. 14–15. I have drawn from Ricca as well as two other contemporary accounts, Ambrogio Soldani, *Sopra una pioggetta di sassi . . .* (1794) and Domenico Tata, *Memoria sulla pioggia di pietre . . .* (1794), for this discussion. I have also relied heavily on the excellent survey of the early history of meteoritics by Ursula B. Marvin, "Ernst Florens Friedrich Chladni (1756–1827) and the origins of modern meteorite research," *Meteoritics & Planetary Science* 31 (1996), pp. 545–88. I am very grateful, too, to Dr. Roy S. Clarke for his help and insights in examining Smithson's meteorite interests.

78 Drew to Lady Webster, n.d. [c. June–July 5, 1797], BL Add MS 51814, ff. 37–8. Smithson seems to have remained curious about the different theories regarding the origins of meteorites; he marked the page in his copy of La Métherie's *Leçons de Minéralogie* (1812), vol. 2, p. 554, that discusses a number of possible explanations. Smithson Library, SIL.

79 *Bulletin of the Proceedings of the National Institute*, July 12, 1841. Quoted in a typescript made for Rathbun; SIA RU 7078, Box 11.

80 From Peter Pallas, Smithson obtained a specimen of "Molybdena in Quartz from Ghutai near Salengha towards the Chinese frontiers." Mineral catalogue notes, SIA, RU 7000, Box 2.

81 Ursula B. Marvin, "The Meteorite of Ensisheim: 1492 to 1992," *Meteoritics* 27 (1992), pp. 28–72.

82 The Danish scientist Peter Christian Abildgaard wrote to Giovanni Fabbroni from Venice in July 1794, to announce his acquaintance with the "very interesting and very learned" Mr. Macie; Abildgaard to Fabbroni, July 26, 1794; APS B F113.

83 Petrini to Fabbroni, March 28, 1795; APS B F113.

84 Smithson appears to have written one paltry letter to Thomson in September 1793, two months after his arrival in Florence, but even then he neglected to supply any clear indication of his travel plans; Thomson to OTT, October 8, 1793. Thomson wrote again three weeks later asking again for news; Thomson to OTT, October 29, 1793. OTT 73, BNCF.

85 Smithson to unknown [probably Massimiliano Ricca or Giorgio Santi], September 4, 1804. Autografi Porri 36/15, Biblioteca Comunale degli Intronati, Siena. Smithson

made numerous efforts to recover his case of books. In addition to asking this correspondent to look into it, Smithson also hoped Mrs. Wyndham, if she were still in
Italy, could make inquiries. Smithson to Holland, December 3, 1801; BL Add MS
51822, ff. 54–5.

86 James J. Sheehan, "What is German History? Reflections on the Role of the *Nation*
    in German History and Histiography," *Journal of Modern History* 53 (1981), p. 1.
    David Blackbourn, *The Long Nineteenth Century: A History of Germany, 1780–1918*
    (Oxford, 1998), p. 9.

87 Milady Vassall to Fabbroni, March 27, 1797; APS B F113.

88 Richard Chenevix in Dresden to Sir Joseph Banks, June 24 [1804]; DTC, vol. 14,
    ff. 285–8.

89 Review of *Sketches and Observations made on a tour through various parts of Europe,
    1792–4* (London: 1797), printed in the *Monthly Review*, September 1797, p. 23;
    Smithson Library, SIL.

90 W. V. Farrar, "Science and the German University System, 1790–1850," in Maurice
    P. Crosland, ed., *The Emergence of Science in Western Europe* (New York, 1976),
    pp. 179–80.

91 Smithson's mineral catalogue notes are bound in J. R. McD. Irby, 1879; the slag
    from the copper works is listed on page 20. Smithson conducted experiments on
    the specimen in Paris on August 4, 1819. SIA, RU 7000, Box 2.

92 For a discussion of German science in this period see Karl Hufbauer, *The Formation
    of the German Chemical Community, 1720–1795* (Berkeley and London, c. 1982);
    see also Ernst Homburg, "Two factions, one profession: the chemical profession
    in Germany society 1780–1870," in *The Making of the Chemist: The Social History
    of Chemistry in Europe, 1789–1914*, David Knight and Helge Krath, eds (Cambridge,
    1998), pp. 39–76. There is a very extensive two-volume mineral catalogue in
    German that forms part of the Smithson Collection at the SIA; there does not
    appear to be any indication of who amassed the collection or how Smithson attained
    a copy of the catalogue. It is possible that he purchased the collection, which seems
    to be entirely a regional one, while on this trip—as part of his efforts to amass
    representative specimens of particular regions.

93 Many travelers also made a point of stopping to pay their respects to Goethe,
    installed at Weimar. Goethe's interests in mineralogy made him an especially
    appealing stop for natural philosophers. See for example, Hugh S. Torrens, "Geology
    in Peace Time: An English visit to study German mineralogy and geology (and
    visit Goethe, Werner, and Raumer) in 1816," in Bernhard Fritscher and Fergus
    Henderson, eds, *Toward a History of Mineralogy, Petrology, and Geochemistry* (Munich,
    1998), pp. 147–75. Smithson, however, does not seem to have paid a visit, as there
    is no record of his presence in the very complete archive in Weimar; correspondence
    with the Goethe-und-Schiller-Archiv, October 2001.

94 Smithson's mineral notes; SIA, RU 7000, Box 2. Many thanks to Paul Pohwat for
    his help.

95 Lady Holland to OTT, January 9, n.y. [c. 1798]; OTT 76/81, BCNF. OTT to
    Lady Holland, August 11, 1798; BL Add MS 51845, ff. 46–7.

96 Duchess of Newcastle Papers, BL Add MS 33082. Woodcock Partnership Accounts,
    Dawson's, Lincoln's Inn Fields.

97 James Louis Macie to Sir Joseph Banks, May 14, 1796. BL Add. MS 33980, f. 64.

98 James Macie to Ottaviano Targioni-Tozzetti, September 11, 1798; OTT 75, vol.
    2, BNCF.

99 Smithson's 1797 Catalogue of Fossils manuscript lists several Klaproth donations;
    SIA, RU 7000, Box 2.

100 Lord Wycombe to Lord Lansdowne, August 22 and also September 7, 1796; Bowood Muniments, Microfilm 2030, Bodleian Library. Alexander Douglas of Kelso was the person who was permitted to pass through France with his sickly wife; he reproduced the cordial exchange of letters between him and the French government in his book *Notes of a Journey from Berne to England through France made in the year 1796* by A.D. (Kelso, n.d.); printed in De Beer, *The Sciences Were Never at War* (London, 1960), pp. 69–72.

101 On September 4, 1804, Smithson wrote to an Italian friend, "I am now in this country waiting for the taking of Holland, or some other event which shall make it possible for me to return to England without going the wild and endlessly-circuitous road of Embden; equally terrible in the part which is land and the part which is sea." Biblioteca Comunale degli Intronati, Siena; Autographi Porri, 36/15. On November 22, 1805, he wrote to Lord Holland, "Having waited for the capture of Holland, to avoid the circuitous passage by the pole, I now expect to be soon at home." BL Add MS 51823, ff. 258–9. And on July 26, 1806, he told Cuvier, "Une santé faible me fait préférér d'attendre en Allemagne a m'exposer au rude et desagréable retour chez moi par la mer du Nord, auquel j'ai une fois au paravant été forcé de m'exposer." L'Institut de France, Fonds Cuvier, No. 3228, item 27.

7. London: Citizen of the World, 1797–1803

1 Milady Vassall to Fabbroni, March 27, 1797; APS B F113. When Smithson visited, the trial over her separation from Lord Webster had just been successfully concluded, and she had begun using her maiden name Vassall. The letter to Fabbroni announcing the arrival of Smithson is signed "Milady Vassall." A misreading of this name has mistakenly led to a proposed connection between Smithson and the Italian Turin-based scientist Anton Vassalli-Eandi.

2 Florence for Lady Holland was "that lovely spot, where I enjoyed a degree of happiness for a whole year that was too exquisite to be permanent." Lady Holland's Journal, vol. 1; quoted in John Ingamells, *A Dictionary of British and Irish Travellers in Italy, 1701–1800* (New Haven and London, 1997), p. 986.

3 Edward Wedlake Brayley, *A Topographical and Historical Description of London and Middlesex* (London, 1820), vol. 1, p. 565.

4 Lord Holland in Prague to Fabbroni, May 14, 1796; APS B F113.

5 Hoare's bank ledgers, vol. 51 (1794–1796), f. 340.

6 Entry for Randle Wilbraham in Ingamells, *A Dictionary of British and Irish Travellers*, p. 999.

7 Kirwan to Banks, April 9, 1797; DTC, vol. 1, pp. 119–21. Smithson had at least one mishap on the Continent, because when back in London he reclaimed £200 from Ransom & Co. "for Circular Notes lost." Hoare's, entry for May 15, 1797; vol. 51 (1794–1797), f. 340.

8 Smithson, "Catalogue of Fossils 1797," transcribed in J. R. Mc D. Irby, "Notes on Minerals and Rocks by James Smithson Esq. F.R.S. Being the whole of his manuscripts which escaped the fire at the Smithsonian Institution, 1865," 1878; SIA, RU 7000, Box 2. Abildgaard's list and Thomson's list (which is unsigned but clearly in his hand) are also in RU 7000, Box 2. Smithson met Abildgaard in Venice in July 1794; Abildgaard to Fabbroni, Venice, July 26, 1794. APS B F113.

9 James Macie to Ottaviano Targioni-Tozzetti, September 11, 1798; Ottaviano Targioni-Tozzetti Papers (OTT) 75, vol. 2; Biblioteca Nazionale Centrale Firenze (BNCF).

10 *Gentleman's Magazine* (1794), pp. 1060–61.

11 Macie to Holland, June 20, 1797; BL Add MS 51821, f. 47.

12 Margaret Marriott specified the return of these pictures to Smithson in her will, which she made in 1821; she died in 1827; TNA: PRO PROB 11/1733. The small picture might well be the 1816 Aix-la-Chapelle portrait that the Smithsonian acquired from the La Batuts in the late nineteenth century, now in the collection of the Smithsonian American Art Museum. The "very large" picture is still unidentified.

13 George Keate, *An Account of the Pelew Islands*, Karen L. Nero and Nicholas Thomas, eds (London and New York, 2002), p. 263.

14 "They [the two girls] both died of consumptions & their mother had their fortunes (w.ch were very handsome) devoted to charitable uses, after having in vain endeavoured to prevail on Lady Beverly to take y.m under her Protection & bring them forward, w.ch she declined as the Duke had never intimated any Desire on that subject, but rather kept their birth secret nor had the Duke ever allowed them to take the name of Percy in his lifetime." Alnwick MSS, vol. 57, 23/1 (Letters 1789–95).

15 Dorothy Percy's will of April 1, 1794, with October 22 codicil, proved December 8, 1794 by Margaret Marriott; TNA: PRO PROB 11/1263.

16 Smithson signed two letters, both written c. July–August 1797, from Elm Grove near Mortlake; BL Add MS 51821, f. 22, and BL Add MS 51845, f. 108.

17 The ledgers at Hoare's record a payment of £70 to Christie & Co. on May 12, 1797. A person identified as "M" made purchases totaling £69.13 in Christie's sale of May 1–2. Although "M" can not be conclusively attributed to Macie, if one factors in delivery and other charges the total and the dates make a strong case. "A Catalogue of all the Elegant Household Furniture . . . of a Gentleman, which will be Sold by Auction by Messrs. Christie, Sharp, and Harper, on the Premises, At the Entrance of Kingston upon Thames, in the county of Surry [sic], on Monday, May 1st, 1797, and following Day, at Twelve o'clock." Christie's Archives, London. Thanks to Jeremy Rex-Parkes for this information.

18 James Macie to Lady Holland, February 5 and February 22, n.y. [1799 or 1800]; BL Add MS 51845, ff. 51–2, 53–4. The identification of the names of tradesmen from Smithson's Hoare's ledgers was made with the aid of directories like the British Directory of 1793, the databases of the Centre for Metropolitan History at the Institute for Historical Research, and Celina Fox, ed., *London: World City 1800–1840* (New Haven and London, 1992).

19 Lord Holland, *Further Memoirs of the Whig Party* (London, 1905), p. 371; quoted in C. J. Wright, "Holland House and the Fashionable Pursuit of Science," *Journal of the History of Collections* 1, no. 1 (1989), pp. 97–102.

20 H.M.S., "Fox Elizabeth Vassall, Lady Holland (1770–1845)": *Dictionary of National Biography*, Leslie Stephens, ed. (London, 1885–1904).

21 James Macie to Lord Holland, June 20, 1797; BL Add MS 51821, f. 47. Lawrence S. Rowland, Alexander Moore and George C. Rogers, *The History of Beaufort County, South Carolina: Volume I, 1514–1861* (University of South Carolina Press, 1996), p. 161.

22 While Smithson was writing of "the excellence of his moral character," Joseph Allen Smith was actually in Europe, and he spent some of 1797 carousing in Ireland with Smithson's friend Lord Wycombe. Wycombe and Smith were both enamored of the Irish revolutionary cause, but they ended up devoting much of their time to conquering the dark Irish beauties; Wycombe called Smith "the Lothario of Carolina," and they both managed to get "Poxed" in the process. Wycombe to Holland, n.d. and October 20, 1797, BL Add MSS 58613, ff. 113–14, 119–20. See also George C. Rogers, Jr., *Evolution of a Federalist: William Loughton Smith of*

Charleston (1758–1812), (Columbia, 1962), pp. 338–40; R. A. McNeal, "Joseph Allen Smith, American Grand Tourist," *International Journal of the Classical Tradition,* vol. 4, no. 1, pp. 64–91; and E. P. Richardson, "Allen Smith, Collector and Benefactor," *American Art Journal* (Fall 1969), vol. 1, no. 2.

23 Sabine, *Loyalists of the American Revolution*; quoted in George Gordon Byron, *English Bards and Scotch Reviewers* (Philadelphia, 1870), p. 76.

24 Quoted in Isaac Kramnick, "Eighteenth-Century Science and Radical Social Theory: The Case of Joseph Priestley's Scientific Liberalism," *Journal of British Studies* 25 (January 1986), pp. 1–30.

25 Quoted in Dumas Malone, *Jefferson and the Rights of Man* (Boston, 1951), p. 85; see also Isaac Kramnick, *Republicanism and Bourgeois Radicalism: Political Ideology in Late Eighteenth-Century England and America* (Cornell, 1990), p. 69.

26 For George Washington's Farewell Address as published in *The Independent Chronicle,* September 26, 1796, see http://www.earlyamerica.com/earlyamerica/milestones/farewell.

27 Royal Institution of Great Britain, *The Archives of the Royal Institution of Great Britain in Facsimile: Minutes of Managers' Meetings, 1799–1900* (Yorkshire, Scholar Press, 1979), vol. 1, p. 1. For analysis of the early Royal Institution I have relied on Morris Berman, *Social Change and Scientific Organization: The Royal Institution, 1799–1844* (Ithaca, New York, 1978) and Jan Golinski, *Science as Public Culture: Chemistry and Enlightenment in Britain, 1760–1820* (Cambridge, 1992).

28 Thomas Webster to Thomas Garnett, n.d. [August or September 1800], printed in Nicholas Edwards, "Some Correspondence of Thomas Webster (circa 1772–1844), Concerning the Royal Institution," *Annals of Science* 28 (February 1972), pp. 51–53.

29 J. Davy, ed., *The Collected Works of Sir Humphry Davy Bart.* (London, 1839–40), vol. 2, pp. 211–13; Golinski, *Science as Public Culture,* p. 202.

30 Royal Society Archives, Journal Book Copy 37. See also RS Council Minutes 1782–1810, vol. 7, Copy.

31 *The Times,* April 3, 1802, p. 3, col. c.

32 Obituary for Albany Wallis, *Gentleman's Magazine,* September 1800, pp. 908–9. The lawsuit, Smithson v. Bayley, is at TNA: PRO C 13/23/67. It was lodged November 24, 1802, and on December 9 Wallis' heir paid £4,000 into Hoare's via his agent Hugh Smith. Smithson wrote to his bankers on February 17, 1803: "I am in daily expectation of Col. B. Wallis paying £4000 into your house. I beg, when he does so, to have it laid out in Exchequer bills or India bonds as you think best, if you consider this as the best way, as a temporary one, of disposing of this money." Hoare's Bank Archives, File Box B from Tin Box 27, envelope 10. The rest of the money came in £200 payments, the last one finally in late 1809. Albany Wallis was appointed by the House of Commons as a solicitor to the prosecution for one of the great political trials in British history, the impeachment trial of Warren Hastings, the first Governor-General of British India. The prosecution of Hastings for colonial misdeeds ended in April 1795 with acquittal—a failure for Wallis. When Smithson loaned Wallis the money, Wallis and his partner were unsuccessfully petitioning the House of Commons for the nearly £30,000 they felt they were still owed for their services. BL Add MS 37890, ff. 351–2. Albany Wallis had a son around Smithson's age, who drowned in the Thames as a Westminster schoolboy in 1776; I imagined that a connection between Smithson and Albany Wallis' son, who was with a number of Westminster scholars at the time of his death, might have been the reason Smithson was friendly with Wallis or would have agreed to loan him the astonishing sum of £8,000 in 1795. However, the records of Westminster School do not show that Smithson matriculated there. Like most schools of the period, though, they do not

hold complete accounts of their students, especially if the students did not board. Personal communication with Westminster School archivist, 2003.

33 *Bath Chronicle*, Thursday May 29, 1800, p. 3, col. 2. *The Sussex Weekly Advertiser or Lewes Journal*, Monday June 2, 1800, vol. 52, no. 2805. Thanks to Hugh Torrens for this information.

34 Smithson to Lord Malmesbury, February 28, 1802; Hants RO, 9M73/G2215.

35 The name change is noted on June 18, 1800, in Hoare's Bank Ledger vol. 68 (1800–1801).

36 Blagden diary, October 2, 1814; Royal Society Blagden Papers. William Thomson spread the word in Italy, informing one colleague that Smithson "ora ha mutato nome, e si chiama <u>Smithson</u>." William Thomson to Ottaviano Targioni-Tozzetti, December 6, 1803; OTT 75, vol. 4, BNCF.

37 Georgiana Henderson (née Keate), MSS diary, 1802; collection of Susan Bennett. I am extremely grateful to Susan Bennett for sharing her research on Georgiana and the Hungerford family with me.

38 Georgiana's husband John Henderson was the one who wrote to Keate about the naming of the child, according to Farington's diary; Diary of Joseph Farington, entries for April 14 and June 1, 1797; *The Diary of Joseph Farington*, Kenneth Garlick and Angus Macintyre, eds (Londond and New Haven, 1979), vol. 3. Although Georgiana was disinherited by her father, the executors of the will seem to have felt that Keate had been unjust in his treatment of her and did not fulfill all the terms of his bequests. In her diary Georgiana mentions being involved in the sale of her father's collections, helping to move them to the auction house. Personal communication with Susan Bennett, May 2006.

39 At the end of 1788, for example, Smithson gave A. Raby, a banker with associations to Lunar Society members such as Josiah Wedgwood, the large sum of £2,500, followed by another £500 a few months later; perhaps this was related to some kind of speculative undertaking. Over the course of the next few years Smithson received a few installments of £75 from Raby, but there is no evidence of any real restitution of the £3,000. Hoare's Bank Archives.

40 Charles Hadfield, *British Canals: An Illustrated History* (Newton Abbott, 1969), pp. 115–120.

41 A copy of the inventory of possessions at time of Smithson's death is in SIA, RU 7000, Box 1.

42 *London World City*, pp. 317–18; Hadfield, *British Canals*, p. 122.

43 Hoare's ledgers show payments such as "To Martin & Co for Tunnel under the Thames," from early January 1799 through August 1803. See also John Richardson, *The Annals of London: a year-by-year record of a thousand years of history* (London, 2000), p. 249.

44 JS mineral catalogue, SIA, RU 7000, Box 2. A number of Smithson's colleagues were making such trips; Humphry Davy, for example, spent some of the summer of 1801 in Cornwall, where he met up with George B. Greenough, and the summer of 1802 in Derbyshire and North Wales with Samuel Purkis. David Knight, *Humphry Davy: Science and Power* (Cambridge University Press, 1996), p. 55.

45 Smithson, "A Chemical Analysis of Some Calamines," *Philosophical Transactions* (1802). I am indebted to Steven Turner for his explanations of this work (personal communication with the author, 2006), and to Daniel Kelm for the opportunity to witness a re-creation of a part of this experiment. See also John Sampson White, "Calamine and James Smithson," *Matrix: A Journal of the History of Minerals*, vol. 2, no. 2 (March–April 1991), pp. 17–19. A specimen of hydrozincite, which Smithson presented to Haüy, was given to the Smithsonian in the 1970s by the Muséum d'Histoire

Naturelle. Although the Smithsonian in its first decades held Smithson's immense collections of minerals, today this sliver of hydrozincite is the only specimen in the Smithsonian that was once owned by Smithson. The Muséum still retains four other gifts from Smithson. Thanks to Gian-Carlo Parodi of the Muséum for his assistance.

46 Smithson, "A Chemical Analysis of Some Calamines," *Philosophical Transactions* (1802).

47 James Smithson, "On the Composition of the Compound Sulphuret from Huel Boys, and an Account of its Crystals," *Philosophical Transactions* (1808).

48 A review of Humphry Davy's *Elements of Chemical Philosophy* explained the recent progress in chemical theory, in particular the establishment of a law of definite proportions: "the science is principally indebted after Mr. [William] Higgins, to Dalton, Gay Lussac, Smithson, and Wollaston." *Quarterly Review*, vol. VIII (1812), p. 77.

49 Smithson to Lady Holland, November 10, 1801; BL Add MS 51846, ff. 163-4.

50 Georgiana Henderson (née Keate), MSS diary, 1802; collection of Susan Bennett. Smithson to Lady Holland, November 10, 1801; BL Add MS 51846, ff. 163-4. Several years later, on the Continent in 1806, he recalled for the esteemed French scientist Georges Cuvier the details of one of his fossil finds in the Sussex chalk; Smithson to Cuvier, July 26, 1806; L'Institut de France, Fonds Cuvier, No. 3228, item 27.

51 Smithson to Lord Holland, December 3, 1801; BL Add MS 51822, ff. 54-5.

52 The statue of Isis is mentioned in "An Examination of Some Egyptian Colors," *Annals of Philosophy* (1824). Dickenson's army career is reconstructed from records in TNA: PRO, WO 25/745. His diary detailing his trip home to England is in the SIA, RU 7000, Box 2. See also correspondence in the Long Collection at the SIA, Accession # T90020.

53 Horace Walpole to Richard Gough, Monday August 24, 1789; *Walpole Correspondence* 42, pp. 259-60. Gough, *Sepulchral Monuments in Great Britain* (London, 1786-96), vol. 2, pp. 186-91. The Hungerfords erected two chantries in Salisbury Cathedral in the 1400s. By the eighteenth century they were in a ruinous state. The Iron Chapel, or Walter Lord Hungerford's Chapel, was removed in 1779 by Earl Radnor to make way for a pew for his family, though the monuments were preserved in a different part of the Cathedral. Only traces of the brass effigies on the tombs of Walter Lord Hungerford and his wife were still visible in the 1780s, having been vandalized, probably during the Civil War. The architect James Wyatt demolished the other chapel, the Robert Hungerford chapel, during renovations in 1789.

54 On April 19, 1803, Smithson's bank account reveals that he acquired £100 in Hammersley's notes, the eighteenth-century equivalent of traveler's checks. Hoare's Bank Archives, vol. 77 (1802-3), ff. 88-9. Three days later—after what one might fairly presume was a trouble-free passage across the Channel—his passport was signed in Paris on April 22. The passport, which indicates that Smithson was given a laissez-passer to enter France for himself "avec son Domestique, ses Hardes, et ses Baggages," can be found in F7/6461, Archives Nationales, Paris. The servant might well have been Joseph Fitall, who was in Smithson's pay at this time. If Fitall endured the years of incarceration that followed during the Napoleonic Wars with Smithson, it might explain why he was especially remembered in Smithson's will. Fitall also owned the portrait of Smithson as an Oxford student, given to him perhaps at the end of his service to Smithson. The Smithsonian purchased this painting from Fitall's widow in 1850; it survived the fire of 1865 because it was on display in the library in the unscathed west wing of the building.

8. The Hurricane of War, 1803–1807

1 Christophe Léribault, *Les Anglais à Paris au 19e Siècle* (Paris, 1994), p. 14. Diary of Henry Louis Dickenson; SIA, RU 7000, Box 2.

2 Smithson to Lord Holland, December 3, 1801; BL Add MS 51822, ff. 54–5.

3 James Smithson, "Seigneur Anglais" in Hanau near Frankfurt to an unidentified Italian [probably Giorgio Santi in Pisa or Massimiliano Ricca in Siena], September 4, 1804; Biblioteca Comunale degli Intronati, Siena, Autografi Porri: 36/15.

4 Michael Lewis, *Napoleon and His British Captives* (London, 1962), p. 69.

5 Smithson to Cuvier, July 26, 1806; L'Institut de France, Fonds Cuvier, No. 3228, item 27.

6 John Goldworth Alger, *Englishmen in the French Revolution* (London, 1889), p. 262.

7 J. P. T. Bury, and J. C. Barry, eds, *An Englishman in Paris, 1803: The Journal of Bertie Greatheed* (London, 1953), quoted in Tom Pocock, *The Terror Before Trafalgar: Nelson, Napoleon and the Secret War* (New York, 2003), p. 76.

8 The following comments are drawn from Smithson's annotations in A. G. Camus, *Voyage dans les départemens nouvellement réunis . . . à la fin de l'an X [1802]*, 2 vols (Paris, 1803); *Description de la Ville de Bruxelles* (Brussels, 1794); and C. M. Dubois-Maisonneuve, *Nouveau voyage de France*, 2 vols (Paris, 1806). Smithson Library, SIL.

9 Dubois-Maisonneuve, *Nouveau voyage*, vol. 1, p. 333.

10 Camus, *Voyage*, vol. 1, pp. 125–8.

11 Smithson, "Some Observations on Mr. Penn's Theory Concerning the Formation of the Kirkdale Cave," *Annals of Philosophy* (1824).

12 *Essai sur Cassel et ses Environs* (Cassel, 1798), especially pp. 63–79, 182. Smithson bought "terra luminia" from an apothecary in Kassel in 1804; SIA, RU 7000, Box 2. Chenevix's presence in Kassel is revealed in Charles Blagden to Sir Joseph Banks, October 6, 1803; DTC, vol. 14, ff. 457–9. I am grateful to Dr Gerhard Menk at the Staatsarchiv Marburg for his search for evidence of Smithson's stay at Kassel.

13 Smithson to Cuvier, July 26, 1806; L'Institut de France, Fonds Cuvier, No. 3228, item 27.

14 William Wordsworth, *The Prelude, Book Eleventh: France*, lines 363–4 in *The Complete Poetical Works* (London, 1888).

15 Smithson to Lord Holland, November 22, 1805; BL Add MS 51823, ff. 258–9.

16 "Secondly, [I write] to recall to you a certain wager, which, if I mistake not much, is come to its termination both according to the spirit and the letter of it, monarchy being reestablished in France, as I always maintained that it would. . . . I hope that you have not forgotten that we have a second wager, that I gave you a second guinea to receive an other hundred when a Bourbon is King of France, as I think the period not now remote when that wager too will be mine." Smithson to Lord Holland, November 22, 1805; BL Add MS 51823, ff. 258–9.

17 Smithson mineral catalogue notes; SIA, RU 7000, Box 2.

18 Smithson's police file is F7/6461, subtitled no. 9890, "Smithson agent anglais sur le Rhin," in the Archives Nationales, Paris. This account is the only indication that Smithson spoke German. All his correspondence with German friends so far identified was conducted in French.

19 Mengaud described Smithson as being "cinq pieds, cinq pouces" (five feet and five thumbs or inches, the French foot, based on *le pied du Roi*, being about 1.07 feet); F7/6461, Archives Nationales. Charles C. Gillispie gives an account of French

measurements in the preface to his *The Montgolfier Brothers and the Invention of Aviation, 1783–84* (Princeton, 1983), p. ix.

20 Mengaud to Talleyrand, S.E. le ministre des Relations Extérieures, Francfort 22 Mess.or an 13 [July 11, 1805]; F7/6461, Archives Nationales.

21 Count Rumford to Lady Palmerston, October 14, 1795; quoted in Brian Connell, *Portrait of a Whig Peer* (London, 1957), p. 330.

22 Smithson to Sir Joseph Banks, September 18, 1808; Banks Collection, Sutro Library, California. Published in A. Grove Day, "James Smithson in Durance: Letter from James Smithson to Sir Joseph Banks, from Hamburg, September 1808, as a Prisoner of War," *Pacific Historical Review* (1943). Copy in SIA, RU 7000, Box 6.

23 Smithson to Lord Holland, June 13, 1806; BL Add MS 51823, ff. 32–3.

24 Smithson to Lord Holland, November 22, 1805; BL Add MS 51823, ff. 258–9.

25 "Having waited for the capture of Holland, to avoid the circuitous passage by the pole, I now expect to be soon at home." Smithson to Lord Holland, November 22, 1805; BL Add MS 51823, ff. 258–9.

26 Smithson to unknown [Ricca or Santi], September 4, 1804; Biblioteca Comunale degli Intronati, Siena, Autgrafi Porri: 36/15.

27 Ralph Heathcote to his mother, May 7, 1806; *Letters of A Young Diplomatist and Soldier during the time of Napoleon* (London, 1907), p. 79.

28 Claire Harman, *Fanny Burney* (New York, 2001), pp. 288–9.

29 Royal Institution of Great Britain, *The Archives of the Royal Institution of Great Britain in Facsimile: Minutes of Managers' Meetings, 1799–1900* (Yorkshire, Scholar Press, 1979, vol. IV, p. 74. Copley was permitted to exchange the ticket for a new one, despite the fact that "Mr. Macie Smithson is now on the Continent, and his address not known."

30 Smithson to unknown [Ricca or Santi], September 4, 1804; Biblioteca Comunale degli Intronati, Siena, Autgrafi Porri: 36/15.

31 Letter of William Artaud to his father, quoted in Ingamells, *Dictionary of British and Irish Travellers in Italy*, p. 28.

32 "Gian-Vicenzo Petrini (1725–1814)," *Diccionario Enciclopedico Escolapio* (Vol. II) (Salamanca, 1983), p. 433. Petrini to Fabbroni, n.d. [c. 1802]; Fabbroni Papers, APS F B 113.

33 Laura Vigni, "Il 'Perfido Insinuatore d'Iniquità,'" in *La Scienza Illuminata: Paolo Mascagni nel suo Tempo* (Siena, 1996), pp. 69–83.

34 H. S. Torrens, "Thomson, William (bap. 1760, d. 1806)," *Oxford Dictionary of National Biography* (Oxford, 2004).

35 Smithson to Lord Holland, June 13, 1806; BL Add MS 51823, ff. 32–3. Brook Taylor had been the focus of diplomatic jousting among France, Hesse, and England; Napoleon was convinced Taylor had been among those plotting the Emperor's death and demanded that the Elector refuse to receive Taylor, else Napoleon would have to assume a tacit alliance between England and Hesse. Despite a polite request from the Elector, George III declined to send a different representative in Taylor's stead. When Taylor finally appeared at Kassel, the French minister in Kassel, Baron Louis Pierre Edouard Bignon, had stalked off from the city until the matter was resolved—which it was, finally, by Taylor slipping away with Ralph Heathcote in the midst of the dancing at a masked ball he was hosting. Smithson, once again passionately taking the side of the English, told Lord Holland that Taylor had been "driven away with indignity." Countess Louisa E. C. von der Groeben, *Ralph Heathcote: Letters of a Young Diplomatist and Soldier During the Time of Napoleon, giving an account of the dispute between the Emperor and the Elector of Hesse* (London, 1907), p. 58.

36 I am indebted to Steve Turner for his interpretation of his experiment; Steven Turner, "Draft document, commenting on Smithson's investigation of a mineral sample, 1806," April 2006. James Smithson, "Account of a Discovery of Native Minium," *Philosophical Transactions* 96 (1806).

37 Smithson to Cuvier, July 26, 1806; L'Institut de France, Fonds Cuvier, No. 3228, item 27. In a letter to Lord Holland, he announced he was soon going to Pyrmont; and, probably still thinking about his box of books in Milan, he offered to be of assistance in helping others retrieve their possessions: "There is a picture of the late L.d Bristol's at one of the inns of this town. And I am told effects of his at Pyrmont where I am going soon. If I can be of any use in sending these things to England, or selling them, it will be with great readiness." Smithson to Holland, June 13, 1806; BL Add MS 51823, ff. 32–3.

38 Niall Ferguson, *House of Rothschild: Money's Prophets (1798–1848)*, (London, 2000), p. 64.

39 Smithson to Lord Holland, June 13, 1806; BL Add MS 51823, ff. 32–3.

40 Over the course of eight months in Germany, Denon sent more than 250 cases of artworks—pictures, statues, and other fine objects—to Paris. *Dominique-Vivant Denon: L'Oeil de Napoleon* (Louvre, 1999), pp. 172, 503–4.

41 *Lettre à Madame la Comtesse F ___ de B ___ [Fanny de Beauharnais]; contenant un récit des événements qui se sont passés à Lubeck dans la journée du jeudi 6 novembre 1806, et les suivantes* (Amsterdam, 1807). Smithson made no markings in the booklet. Smithson Library, SIL.

9. Vibrating between Existence and the Tomb, 1807–1810

1 Silvia Marzagalli, *Les Boulevards de la Fraude: le négoce maritime et le Blocus continental, 1806–1813* (Paris, 1999), pp. 155–6. Klaus Rybiczka, "Tönning während der Blockade Anfang des 19 Jahrhunderts," *Gesellschaft für Tönninger Stadtgeschichte e.V. Mitteilungsblatt* (1994), pp. 25–43.

2 *The London Gazette Extraordinary*, September 16 and 17, 1807; copies in 302 Dept. of Foreign Affairs, Topografisk henlagte sager, England 1807 May–December, Lb. nr. 1989, Rigsarkivet, Copenhagen.

3 Information on Tönning during the Blockade, and the holding of the English in the town, from the Tönning City Archive. Correspondence between the Gesellschaft für Tönninger Stadtgeschichte e.V. and the author, November 2001.

4 The "hurricane of war" comes from Smithson to Lord Holland, November 22, 1805; BL Add MS 51823, ff. 258–9. The comment about the climate of Schleswig-Holstein is from Smithson to Sir Joseph Banks, September 18, 1808; Banks Collection, Sutro Library, California. This letter is the central source for Smithson's thoughts and activities during this time and is frequently quoted in this chapter.

5 *The London Gazette Extraordinary*, September 16 and 17, 1807; Rigsarkivet, Copenhagen.

6 Francis James Jackson to George Canning, September 7, 1807; TNA: PRO FO 22/54. See also J. A. van Houtte, "The Low Countries and Scandinavia," in *War and Peace in an Age of Upheaval, 1793–1830* (New York, 1965), p. 486.

7 Smithson to Sir Joseph Banks, September 18, 1808; Banks Collection, Sutro Library, California.

8 George Harward file, August 16, 1809; TNA: PRO FO 33/42, ff. 26, 28A.

9 Reuben Smith was running a large merchant ship on the River Eider from Frederikstadt to the U.S. He had received permission from the Danish to pass an unlimited number of men through the territory and he used this freedom to his

advantage. He cunningly offered to furnish the English with 1,000–1,500 men fit for service, dropping them at Tönning in parties of three hundred at a time, for which he would charge seven guineas a man; he also offered to convey the men all the way to England if necessary, for a fee to be negotiated. The French intercepted one of his letters (April 17, 1804), which sits today in the Archives Nationales (AN), F7/6451. The account of his arrest is in the Rigsarkivet in Copenhagen. The despatches of J. M. Forbes, U.S. consul at Hamburg, to Secretary of States James Madison are filled with accounts of his efforts to maintain U.S. commerce in the region; Forbes made a trip to Tönning in October or early November 1807 but his letters to Madison do not specifically mention Smith's case. National Archives and Records Administration (NARA), Microfilm T211, Roll T-1.

10 Jas. Thomson for the Danish Consul's Office, Leith, to His Excellency Count Weddel Jarlsberg, September 25, 1807; Rigsarkivet.

11 Js. Lavine Wade, Königsberg, to the King, March 1, 1808; Rigsarkivet.

12 Mrs. Harward writing on behalf of herself and her two girls, from "Sleswick" on August 20, 1807. Her husband, the former FO official, was imprisoned at Tönning like Smithson, and her other children were at "Lortmark & Ludwigsburg." Rigsarkivet.

13 Smithson to Banks, September 18, 1808; Sutro.

14 Smithson's petition was sent with a physician's report confirming his poor condition; the actual petition is missing from the files, but the covering documentation written by the government is extant. From Tönning Smithson's petition traveled to the Schleswig-Holstein chancel in Copenhagen, the first of many steps in the Danish bureaucracy. Finally on January 19, 1808, five months into Smithson's imprisonment, it was forwarded on for a final reckoning at the Superior Court at Gottorf. No records concerning Smithson have been found in the Tönning City Archives. Papers relating to his case, given the number 663, are located at the Rigsarkivet in Copenhagen and at the Landesarchiv in Kiel, but there is no evidence that the petition was ever reviewed at the Superior Court in Gottorf (the papers of which are also located at Kiel). I am indebted to Helmut Wrunsch at Tönning for all his help in this matter, including the laborious transcription of the antique German into modern typescript; to Peter Buntzen at the Rigsarkivet for all his help; to Hans-Henning Freitag at the Landeshauptstadt Kiel; and especially to Judd Stitziel for the translation of the documents.

15 Smithson to Banks, September 18, 1808; Sutro.

16 There are no extant letters from Smithson to Greville dating from this period. Many years later, in 1819, Smithson wrote of his experiments on sulphurets in a letter to Berzelius. Smithson to Berzelius, June 16, 1819; Archives of the Royal Swedish Academy of Sciences, Stockholm.

17 John Thornton to Smithson, April 19, 1808. PWI: 39, Banks Collection, Sutro Library, California. I am grateful to Hugh Torrens for sharing his discovery of this letter with me.

18 Kiel Weekly Journal for the Best of the Poor, May 11, 1808; Landeshauptstadt Kiel.

19 In Rhees' biography (Rhees, James Smithson and his Bequest, p. 17) the Thorvaldsen bust is recorded as having been "presented to Mr. Smithson at Copenhagen by Dr. Brandis, physician to the King of Denmark." It is not known when or where Smithson and Brandis became friends, but Smithson does not seem to have visited Copenhagen, especially not after 1810, the year when Brandis assumed his post as physician to the Queen (not King) of Denmark. It is conceivable the two men met in Germany in the mid-1790s, but a connection forged in Schleswig-Holstein seems to make the most sense. For biographical information on Brandis see the

Dansk biografisk Lexikon (Copenhagen, 1887–1905). No image of the Thorvaldsen sculpture that Brandis presented to Smithson, which was lost in the Smithsonian fire, survives. It was identified in early Smithsonian guidebooks as "a marble head of Saint Cecilia." The Thorvaldsens Museum in Copenhagen, however, has no record of the bust, or of Thorvaldsen ever executing such a design. (It is difficult to imagine how St. Cecilia, the patron saint of music and usually depicted playing an instrument, would have been identified in a bust.) I am grateful to Dr. Margarethe Floryan for her assistance.

20 Ralph Heathcote to his mother, May 2, 1806. *Letters of A Young Diplomatist and Soldier During the Time of Napoleon* (London, 1907), pp. 77–9.

21 Ralph Heathcote to his mother, April 30, 1806. *Letters of A Young Diplomatist*, pp. 75–9.

22 Archives Nationale, AF iv, 1494. See also E. d'Hauterive, *La Police Secrète du Premier Empire* (Paris, 1908), vol. 1, pp. 194, 484, 505.

23 Monsieur Bourrienne, Minister at Hamburg to the Ministry at Paris, October 26, 1808. Letter 130, Microfilm at the Archives of the Ministry of Foreign Affairs, Paris.

24 A. Raffalovich, "John Parish, Banquier et negociant a Hambourg," *Journal des Economistes*, vol. VII (1905), pp. 199–208; J. Walters and Raymond Walters, "The American Career of David Parish," *Journal of Economic History*, vol. 4, no. 2 (1944), pp. 149–66. When Smithson met Richard Parish, Parish's brother David had recently left the family's commercial house in Antwerp for an opportunistic posting as the American agent of the fantastically lucrative Spanish colonial bullion trade; while there he immediately began buying up property in northern New York with the idea of developing the St. Lawrence River as a trade route. The Parish family history was assiduously maintained by its descendants; family papers are located today in Hamburg Staatsarchiv, in Prague, at the New-York Historical Society, and at St. Lawrence University in New York. I have found no mention of Smithson; thanks to Mark McMurray at St. Lawrence for his assistance.

25 Smithson to Banks, September 18, 1808; Sutro.

26 Hoare's Bank. Payments began January 4, 1809; vol. 100 (1807–8), f. 117. Smithson appears also to have been getting help from a prominent Göteborg merchant, Martin Holtermann & Co., who had offices in Hamburg and Paris. Large sums of money were drawn, totaling some £850, beginning in April 1808 and continuing through August 12, 1809. Many thanks to my friend Patrik Ohlson for his help ferreting out information about Holtermann.

27 Banks to William Hamilton, November 8, 1799; DTC, vol. 11, ff. 313–15; quoted in Gavin de Beer, *The Sciences Were Never at War* (London, 1960), p. 83. Dolomieu, a Knight of Malta, was threatened with criminal charges by the Neapolitans at Taranto on account of his supposed assistance in Napoleon's taking of Malta. Banks was unsuccessful in his efforts to secure Dolomieu's release, but did manage to have the conditions of his confinement improved. Dolomieu was eventually released in late March 1801, one of the first conditions specified by Napoleon for an armistice. De Beer, pp. 81–104. To the devastation of his colleagues, Dolomieu died later that year, his health having been severely compromised by his captivity.

28 Delambre, "Eloge de Lagrange," *Les Mémoires de l'Institut* (1812), p. 14; quoted in Jean-Pierre Poirier, *Lavoisier: Chemist, Biologist, Economist* (Philadelphia, 1996), p. 382.

29 De Beer, *The Sciences Were Never at War*, pp. 31–2; see also Douglas McKie, "Antoine-Laurent Lavoisier, F.R.S, 1743–1794," *Notes and Records of the Royal Society* 7 (December 1949), pp. 1–41. De Beer posits that the intended recipient of the Copley Medal for 1793 was Lavoisier, and that the Royal Society withheld the medal that year precisely in order to prevent fueling any persecution of him.

30 Quoted in de Beer, *The Sciences Were Never at War*, p. 197. Faujas de St. Fond, *A Journey Through England and Scotland to the Hebrides in 1784*, edited by Sir Archibald Geikie (Glasgow, 1907), vol. 1, p. 53.

31 Smithson to Cuvier, April 2, 1806; MS 627, fo. 101, Fonds Cuvier, Muséum d'Histoire Naturelle, Paris. Translation from the Smithsonian; SIA, RU 7000, Box 1.

32 Draft of a letter from Charles Blagden to Delambre, August 2, 1808; Blagden Papers, BLA.d21.a, Royal Society Library.

33 Draft of a letter from Sir Joseph Banks to Delambre, n.d. [c. late 1808/early 1809]. Delambre to Comte d'Hunebourg, April 16, 1809. Printed in translation by David Eugene Smith, *Delambre and Smithson* (New York, 1934). See also *Procès Verbaux de l'Académie des Sciences*, March 20 and June 19, 1809, vol. 4, p. 179 and pp. 220–21.

34 Smithson was highly skeptical of many of Pinkney's observations. "Folly!," he wrote in one margin. "Indeed she was AWFUL pretty," he wrote in another, concerning the French wife of one of the secretaries in the consulate, whose "perfect beauty" excited in Pinkney "such a mixed emotion of wonder, awe, and pleasure." Pinkney, *Travels through the South of France in 1807 and 1808 by a route never before performed, made by permission of the French government*. (London, 1814), pp. 148, 343. Smithson Library, SIL.

35 Paul R. Sweet, *Wilhelm von Humboldt: A Biography* (Columbus, 1980), vol. 2, pp. 14–15.

36 Between 2000 and 2003 the Berlin-Brandenburg Academy of Science (BBAW) hosted an interdisciplinary thematic study devoted to Classical Berlin; details at www.berliner-klassik.de.

37 Laurence Brockliss, "Humboldt's Rift," *The Times Literary Supplement*, June 10, 2005. Sweet, *Wilhelm von Humboldt: A Biography*, vol. 2, p. 57.

38 Humboldt to Dohna, March 25, 1809, *Gesammelte Schriften*, 10, pp. 31–2, printed in Sweet, p. 56.

39 That Holland House had continental servants is mentioned in Derek Hudson, *Holland House in Kensington* (London, 1967), p. 85. Beckford's servant is in Timothy Mowl, *William Beckford: Composing for Mozart* (London, 1998), p. 203. Bill Richmond is discussed in Pierce Egan, *Boxiana; or, Sketches of antient & modern Pugilism* (London, 1818), pp. 440–49. Information on Henri Honoré Sailly is from Smithson's bank account at Hoare's and from his will (TNA: PRO PROB 11/1763).

40 William Allen (1770–1843) is discussed in Ian Inkster, "Science and Society in the Metropolis: A preliminary examination of the social and institutional context of the Askesian Society of London, 1796–1807," *Annals of Science* 34 (1977), pp. 1–32. See also E. C. Cripps, *Plough Court: The story of a notable pharmacy, 1715–1927* (Allen and Hanbury, 1927).

41 Smithson's mineral notes; SIA, RU 7000, Box 2.

42 Hoare's, vol. 9, f. 91.

43 Minutes of May 10, 1810, and June 7, 1810, pp. 544, 546–50. RS Archives.

44 For biographical information see Jungnickel and McCormmach, *Cavendish: The Experimental Life* (Lewisburg, PA, 1999), pp. 366–7, 453, 462–3, 673–4, 694.

10. London: A New Race of Chemists, 1810–1814

1 Smithson gave his address as St. James's Place in the byline of his "On the Composition of Zeolite," *Philosophical Transactions* (1811); *Boyle's Court Guide* indicates that the exact address was No. 3. In 1841 Alexander Dallas Bache in the United States wrote to Faraday asking for any information on Smithson and the Royal Institution.

Faraday replied that he had only the address "3 Stanhope Place" to supply; Faraday to Bache, November 12, 1841; Letter 1371 in Frank A. J. L. James, *The Correspondence of Michael Faraday* (London, 1996), vol. 3. There is no known Stanhope Place, according to English Heritage research. Presumably this was in fact the St. James's Place address. After the Smithsonian was established, Faraday in correspondence with the Secretary Joseph Henry stated: "I did not know Mr Smithson though I think I used to hear his name I was then of no consequence." Faraday to Henry, July 23, 1851; Letter 2448 in *Correspondence of Michael Faraday* (London, 1999), vol. 4. Smithson moved in 1812 to 19 Crawford Street, according to *Boyle's Court Guide*.

2 PRO TS 11 documents reveal that Henry James Hungerford (Enrico de la Batut in Italy) was born in Pondicherry. His passport documents, at the SIA in RU 7000, show that he was twenty-one in 1829, indicating that he was probably born in 1808. His father, Henry Louis Dickenson, referred in his will to Mary Ann as "going by my name and the mother of my Son." It is not clear that they were ever married. Her last name is given as Coates in the will; in the French archives recording the decease of Dickenson she is listed as Marianne Corson. Archives de Paris, DQ8/644/fo. 71.

3 Royal Society Club minutes, August 23, 1810; RS Archives. Sir Alexander Johnston, Smithson's neighbor in St. James's, was the only other guest that evening.

4 For example, Alexander Marcet, "A Chemical Account of Various Dropsical Fluids," inscribed "From the Author"; Smithson Library, SIL. Smithson was also distributing copies of his own works. As "James Smithson, Esqr. M.R.I." he gave two copies of his Ulmin paper to the Royal Institution in 1813; RI, Managers' Minutes, vol. V, p. 362, item 4. The copy of that same paper that he gave Sir Joseph Banks, inscribed "Sir Joseph Banks From the Author," is located now at the BL, shelfmark 8896.i.11.

5 Thomas Thomson, *A History of the Royal Society from its institution to the end of the eighteenth century* (London, 1812), p. 485.

6 Davy dreaming of greatness and utility is quoted in the foreword by Sir John Meurig Thomas to E. A. Davis, ed., *Science in the Making: Scientific Development as Chronicled by Historic Papers in the Philosophical Magazine—with commentaries and illustrations*, vol. 1: *1798–1850* (London, 1995), p. xiii. For Carlyle see, George A. Foote, "Sir Humphry Davy and his audience at the Royal Institution," *Isis* 43 (1952), p. 7; quoted in Jan Golinski, *Science as Public Culture* (Cambridge, 1992), p. 194.

7 The squall at the opera comment is from Bostock to Marcet, March 16, 1811; quoted in Gilbert Papers, University of London archives, Box 4, file 1, folder B. Refining and exalting quote from John Davy, *Memoirs of the Life of Sir Humphry Davy* (London, 1836), p. 210.

8 *Memoirs of the Life of Sir Humphry Davy*, pp. 164, 217. Golinski, "The Literature of the New Sciences," in James Chandler, ed., *The New Cambridge History of English Literature: The Romantic Period* (Cambridge, forthcoming). Available at http: //www.unh.edu/history/golinski/paper7.htm.

9 Maurice Berman, *Social Change and Scientific Organization: The Royal Institution, 1799–1844* (London, 1978), p. 98.

10 Golinski, *Science as Public Culture*, p. 193.

11 Thomas Kelly, *A History of Adult Education in Great Britain* (Liverpool, 1962), quoted and discussed in Berman, pp. 94–5.

12 William L. Bird, Jr., "A Suggestion Concerning James Smithson's Concept of 'Increase and Diffusion,'" *Technology and Culture* (April 1983), pp. 246–55, 248 especially.

13　F. Kurzer, "A History of the Surrey Institution," *Annals of Science* 57, no. 2 (April 2000), pp. 109–41.

14　Golinski, *Science as Public Culture*, pp. 221–2.

15　Thomas Thomson, "On the Daltonian Theory of Definite Proportions in Chemical Combinations," *Annals of Philosophy* (1813); quoted in David M. Knight, ed., *Classical Scientific Papers: Chemistry* (New York, 1968).

16　J. Davy, ed. *The Collected Works of Sir Humphry Davy, Bart.* (London, 1839–40), vol. 1, pp. 382–84.

17　Quoted in David Knight, *Humphry Davy: Science and Power* (Cambridge, 1996), p. 39.

18　Recollection by Augustin Pyramus de Candolle, quoted in C.W.P. MacArthur, "Davy's Differences with Gay-Lussac and Thenard: New Light on Events in Paris and on the Transmission and Translation of Davy's Papers in 1810," *Notes and Records of the Royal Society* (1985), p. 216.

19　Golinski, *Science as Public Culture*, p. 254; Knight, *Humphry Davy*, p. 68.

20　Roy Porter, *The Making of Geology: Earth Science in Britain, 1660–1815* (Cambridge, 1977), p. 202. Humphry Davy, Royal Institution 1805 lectures; quote about Newton from Davy's unpublished 1811 lectures, Royal Institution Archives. I am grateful to David Haas for his research into Smithson at the Royal Institution.

21　Smithson mineral notes; SIA, RU 7000, Box 2. H. S. Torrens, "Thomson, William (1760–1806)," *Oxford Dictionary of National Biography* (Oxford, 2004).

22　James Smithson, "On a Saline Substance from Mount Vesuvius," *Philosophical Transactions* 103 (1813). Smithson explained that the "present saline substance was sent to me from Naples to Florence, where I was, in May 1794, with a request to ascertain its nature. . . . I was informed by letter, that it had 'flowed out liquid from a small aperture in the cone of Vesuvius,' and which I apprehend to have happened in 1792 or 1793." In the Smithsonian Archives is a list of specimens in William Thomson's handwriting, "sent to Mr. Macie via Dr. Robertson Nov.r 22 [17]96." Number 7 on this list is "Vitriolated tartar, probably with copper, spewed out liquid f[ro]m a small aperture in the cone of Vesuvius." Thomson described obtaining these specimens in his *Breve Notizia di un Viaggiatore sulle incrostazioni silicee termali d'Italia, e specialmente di quelle dei Campi Flegrei nel regno di Napoli* [1795], p. 25; Smithson marked this paragraph in his copy. Smithson Library, SIL.

23　Membership records of the Geological Society, Burlington House, London. Smithson referenced Smithson Tennant's article on the volcanic productions of the Lipari islands, published in the *Transactions of the Geological Society* in his paper "On a Saline Substance from Mount Vesuvius," *Philosophical Transactions* (1813).

24　Smithson's transfers from his Hoare's account to a new Drummonds account began September 19, 1811, with a transfer of £854.9.10 and continued throughout the next three years. Hoare's Bank Archives. Drummonds account begins in September 1811; 1811 P–S, DR/427/228, f.541, Royal Bank of Scotland Archives. Drummonds as part of their war effort pulped most of their archive, retaining only one year a decade beginning in 1815, so of James Smithson's final years we have only 1815 and 1825. Many thanks to Philip Winterbottom for his assistance.

25　Journal Book Copy (JBC) 40; Royal Society Archives (RS).

26　Berzelius Archives, Center for History of Science, Royal Swedish Academy of Sciences. There are four letters from Smithson there, all dated 1818–19, suggesting that Smithson first met Berzelius when they were both in Paris at that time. Dinner Books for Holland House in the Holland Papers at BL.

27　Papers related to Greville's collection and its purchase in BL Add MS 40716, ff. 12, 56, 73, 150, 164.

28　D. L. Meyer, *A Method of Making Useful Mineral Collections, to which are added some experiments on a Deliquescent Calcareous Earth, or Native fixed Sal Ammoniac* (London, 1775), p. 6; Smithson Library, SIL.

29 Fitton presented a description of the mineralogy of the Dublin area to the Geological Society in 1811, and he inscribed a copy of the subsequent publication to Smithson. William Fitton, *Notes on the Mineralogy of Part of the Vicinity of Dublin*, based on the work of the late Rev. Walter Stephens (London, 1812). It is inscribed "For James Smithson Esq.," Smithson Library, SIL.

30 Johnston became F.R.S. in 1811, and was, along with Smithson, the only other guest at the Royal Society Club dinner in July 1810. Johnston gave Smithson some specimens for his mineral cabinet; see Smithson mineral notes, SIA, RU 7000, Box 2.

31 Edward Howard, "Experiments and observations on certain stony substances, which at different times are said to have fallen on the Earth; also on various kinds of nature now," *Philosophical Transactions* 92 (1802). Smithson made a payment to him in 1813 of £30.18. He also made a payment that year of £10.12 to an R. Molyneux, which was the name of Howard's maternal family. Drummonds 1813 P–S, DR/427/240 ff. 545, 544. The two apparently stayed in fairly close contact, even after Smithson went abroad in 1814. "Pray also tell Wollaston to enquire about Smithson in his travels. I have not heard from him for months. He was then at Aix la Chapelle under the care of Mons.r Schlosser Banker." Howard to Henry Warburton, August 4, 1816, Wollaston Papers, Add MSS 7736, Box 2, Cambridge University Library.

32 Smithson, "On the detection of very minute quantities of arsenic and mercury," *Annals of Philosophy* (1822).

33 Trevor Levere, *Poetry Realized in Nature: Samuel Taylor Coleridge and Early Nineteenth-Century Science* (Cambridge, 1981) especially pp. 1–2, 87, 185. Golinski, *Science as Public Culture*, pp. 203–35, esp. pp. 218–19. J. Davy, ed., *The Collected Works*, vol. 8, p. 271; quoted in June Z. Fullmer, "Humphry Davy: Fund Raiser," in *The Development of the Laboratory: Essays on the Place of Experiment in Industrial Civilization*, Frank A. J. L. James, ed. (New York, 1989).

11. Paris: Private Vices, Publick Benefits, 1814–1825

1 François Arago, "Eloge for Ampère," translated for the Smithsonian and published in the *Annual Report of 1872*, pp. 124–5. Samuel P. Langley learned that the "distinguished foreigner" referred to by Arago in the *éloge* was in fact James Smithson from the American astronomer Benjamin Apthorp Gould, who was a friend of Arago's. Memorandum by Secretary S. P. Langley, September 14, 1894; SIA, RU 7000, Box 5.

2 *Annual Register for 1814*, pp. 29–32. Edward Wedlake Brayley, *A Topographical Description of London and Middlesex* (London, 1820), vol. 3, pp. 89–92.

3 Drummonds 1814 P–S, DR/427/246, f. 577; Royal Bank of Scotland Archives.

4 Quoted in Edward Stanley, *Before and After Waterloo* (London, 1907), p. 291. See also Margery Elkington, *Les Relations de Société entre l'Angleterre et la France sous la Restauration (1814–1830)* (Paris, 1929), p. 12.

5 See Philip Mansel, *Paris Between Empires: Monarchy and Revolution, 1814–1852* (New York, 2003), p. 53. Smithson owned a guidebook to the Louvre pictures; Smithson Library Collection, SIL. The "vampyre" quote is from *Galignani's Messenger*, Saturday, July 2, 1814.

6 Smithson to Lord Holland, 22 November, 1805; BL Add MS 51823, ff. 258–9.

7 The illumination was done by the Englishman F. A. Windsor; see Mansel, p. 143.

Smithson owned his pamphlet on the use of hydrogen gas for illumination (Paris, 1816), on which Windsor had proudly scrawled, "This is the only copy I have left of 1000 given away." Smithson Library, SIL.

8 Humboldt to Pictet, May 26, 1808; quoted in Karl Bruhns, ed., *Life of Alexander von Humboldt* (London, 1873), vol. 2, p. 10.

9 J. Erik Jorpes, *Jac. Berzelius, His Life and Work*, translated by Barbara Steele (Stockholm, 1970), p. 82. Smithson was scouring the city's dealers for interesting and unusual specimens soon after he arrived, and must have promptly established a place where he could conduct experiments. "Small green polished stone bought at Paris. August 1814," he wrote in the notes he maintained on his collection. "This readily marked by a knife, yet it is scarcely possible to break it on the anvil with a hammer." Smithson notes; SIA, RU 7000, Box 2.

10 See Maurice Crosland, *The Society of Arcueil* (London, 1967). Berzelius' "cooking muck" comment is in Carl Gustaf Bernhard, "Berzelius as a European Traveler," in Evan Melhado and Tore Frängsmyr, *Enlightenment Science in the Romantic Era: The Chemistry of Berzelius and its Cultural Setting* (Cambridge, 1992) p. 228. Smithson's friendships with this younger generation are evidenced by the calling cards and signatures from his time in Paris, located in SIA, RU 7000, Box 2.

11 "Smithson Tennant, F.R.S. (1761–1815)," *Notes and Records of the Royal Society* 17 (1962), p. 92.

12 Blagden diary, October 2, 1814, Royal Society Archives. I am very grateful to Dr. Wales, whose father wrote a biography of Smithson Tennant, for directing my attention to this reference.

13 Crosland, *Society of Arcueil*, p. 244. Smithson shared this fascination with Egypt and later published "An Examination of Some Egyptian Colours," *Annals of Philosophy* (1824).

14 Blagden diary, October 9, 1814, and September 29, 1814; RS Archives.

15 Blagden diary, September 29, 1814; RS Archives.

16 Smithson, "On Native Hydrous Aluminate of Lead, or Plumb Gomme," *Annals of Philosophy* (1819).

17 Blagden diary, February 5, 1815, RS Archives. Smithson's Drummonds bank ledger contains a £100 payment to "Smithson Tennant," on January 25, 1815; 1815 P-S, DR/427/252 f. 577.

18 Alexander Marcet to Jacob Berzelius, March 29, 1815; H. G. Soderbaum, *Jac. Berzelius Bref*, vol. 3 (Uppsala, 1913), p. 119.

19 Count Las Cases, *Journal of the Private Life and Conversations of the Emperor Napoleon at Saint Helena* (London, 1824), quoted in Crosland, *Society of Arcueil*, pp. 278, 396–7.

20 Quoted in Mansel, *Paris Between 1814 and 1852*, p. 71. *Galignani's Messenger*, April 18, 1815, reported that "Verdun, and imprisonment for life, immediately haunted the imagination of every Englishman—and many a gallant Officer who had boldly met the French in the field, now fled towards the coast with the utmost precipitation."

21 June 5, 1815. Royal Institution, General Minutes, Vol. II, p. 79.

22 Smithson's Drummonds bank ledgers list several large payments—£100 and £200 at a time, totaling some £1,300—beginning in December 1814 and continuing through the end of March 1815; one entry gives "for the French attestation," as explanation, but it is otherwise not clear what these payments were for. 1814 P-S, DR/427/246, f. 577; 1815 P-S, DR/427/252, f. 577.

23 SIA, RU 7000, Box 2. Alfred Marquiset, *Jeux et Joueurs d'autrefois, 1789–1837* (Paris, 1917). Entry for George Galway Mills (1765–1828), *The History of Parliament: The House of Commons, 1790–1820*, R. G. Thorne, ed. (London, 1986), vol. 4, pp. 591–3.

24 William Parson to Charles Blagden in Paris, February 20, 1818; BLA. p. 10, RS Archives.
25 Davies Gilbert, undated diary entry [1826]. DG 14, CRO. Reprinted in *Smithsonian Annual Report for 1884*, p. 4.
26 Archives de Paris, DQ8/644/fo. 71. Dickenson died in Paris on May 22, 1820; his will was probated by Smithson in London on September 6, 1820; TNA: PRO PROB 11/1634; and TS/11/623/2012.
27 Smithson lived at one point at rue Montmartre, no. 121 (calling card at SI); in 1818 and 1819 he was at rue du Helder (letters to Berzelius of 1818 and 1819, located in the Royal Swedish Academy of Science), and in 1820 on the rue de la Chaussée d' Antin, no. 37 (letter to Smithson, undated [1820] in the Crewe Papers, held privately; I am very grateful to Mary, Duchess of Roxburghe, for supplying me with a copy.
28 Both Gay-Lussac and Cordier inscribed pamphlets to "Monsieur de Smithson" in 1814, 1815, and 1816; Smithson Library, SIL. Smithson signed himself as such in an undated [November 1814] letter to the chemist Louis Augustin d'Hombre-Firmas; at the Staatsbibliotek zu Berlin, and also in an undated [c. 1819, according to notes at L'Institut] letter to Cordier; L'Institut de France, Fonds Cordier, 2724, item 246.
29 *Galignani's Traveller's Guide through Holland and Belgium* (Paris, 1822), Smithson Library, SIL.
30 Margaret Marriott bequeathed to Smithson "two portraits of himself painted in Oil Colours one very large and one smaller." She wrote her will in 1821 and died in 1827. The Smithsonian retrieved the Aix-la-Chapelle picture from the descendants of Henry Dickenson's wife in the late nineteenth century; the whereabouts (and the appearance) of the other "very large" portrait remain unknown today. TNA: PRO PRO B 11/1733.
31 This medallion is sometimes referred to as having been done by the famous Italian sculptor Antonio Canova. The mark, however, is that of Pierre Joseph Tiolier. Many thanks to Rick Stamm for his work on this.
32 Joseph Henry related Wheatstone's story in a letter to General John Henry Lefroy, February 12, 1878. Henry had spent a day with Wheatstone in London in 1870; Henry to Caroline Henry, July 1, 1870; Joseph Henry Papers. I am grateful to Kathy Dorman for her assistance in this matter.
33 L. Agassiz, "Letter on the Smithsonian Institution," *Science*, March 28, 1919, p. 301; quoted in H. S. Torrens, "Smithson, James Lewis (1764–1829)," *Oxford Dictionary of National Biography* (Oxford, 2004).
34 Smithson, "Expériences sur l'Ulmine," *Journal de Physique* (April 1814), pp. 311–15 (trans. M. Vogel). Smithson, "Mémoire sur la Composition de la Zéolite," *Journal de Physique*, August 1814, pp. 144–9 (trans. Smithson). The extensive list of errata for the April 1814 article, which Smithson annotated in his own copy, was published in the August issue, on pp. 150–51; Smithson Library, SIL.
35 James Smithson, "On Some Compounds of Fluorine," *Annals of Philosophy* (1824).
36 James Smithson, "A Discovery of Chloride of Potassium in the Earth," *Annals of Philosophy* (1823).
37 B. A. Gould, *Putnam's Monthly Magazine* (January–June 1853), p. 105. Gould was friends with Arago and received his information on Smithson's gambling from the French astronomer. Memorandum by Secretary S. P. Langley, September 14, 1894; SIA, RU 7000, Box 5.
38 Smithson to Berzelius, December 30, 1818; Royal Swedish Academy of Sciences, Archives.

39 Arago, "Eloge for Ampère," *Annual Report of 1872*, pp. 124–5.

40 "I know of no other habit in which he indulged which was at all eccentric." John Guillemard to Richard Rush, July 4, 1837; Box 13, Rush Family Papers, Princeton.

41 "Plain dinner" invitation from Smithson to Berzelius, December 30, 1818; Archives, Royal Swedish Academy of Sciences. Becquerel note to Smithson, undated, from a nineteenth-century translation; SIA, RU 7000, Box 2. James Smithson, "On Some Capillary Metallic Tin," *Annals of Philosophy* (1821).

42 Hans-Christian Oersted to his wife, March 5, 1823; Oersted Papers, Danish Royal Library. Thanks to Else Mogeson at Eriksen Translations, Inc., for the English translation.

43 "Great beauty" quote in James Smithson, "Method of Fixing Particles on the Sappare," *Annals of Philosophy* (1823). "Little more than visible," in Smithson, "On a Native Compound of Sulphuret of Lead and Arsenic," *Annals of Philosophy* (1819).

44 Mention of Cuvier and Lavoisier parties are in Carl Gustaf Bernhard, *Through France with Berzelius: Live Scholars and Dead Volcanoes* (Oxford, 1989), p. 40. Replies to Smithson's invitations are in SIA, RU 7000, Box 2.

45 Hans-Christian Oersted to his wife, February 23, 1823; Oersted Papers, Danish Royal Library. Translation by Mogeson.

46 J. C. F. Hoefer, *Nouvelle Biographie Générale* (Paris, 1852) and Marcel Roche, *Le Philanthrope Charles de Lasteyrie, Importateur de la Lithographie en France* (Brive, 1896). Lasteyrie du Saillant could have been the source of a pamphlet Smithson owned on French industry and might have also gotten Smithson interested in the school run by the reformed church in Paris, which provided free education and vocational training for Protestant boys and girls deprived of other education. *Du Développement à Donner à quelques Parties Principales et Essentielles de notre Industrie Intérieure, et de l'Affermissements de nos Rapports Commerciaux avec les Pays Etrangers* (Paris, 1819) and Eglises Réformées de France, *Rapport sur l'état de l'Ecole [d'enseignement mutual] au 31 décembre 1818* (Paris, 1819). Smithson Library, SIL.

47 Jens Wolff, *Runakefli: Le Runic Rim-Stock, ou Calendrier Runique* (Paris, 1820). Smithson Library, SIL. R. Composto, "Airoldi, Cesare," *Dizionario Biografico degli Italiani* (Rome, 1960). Salvatore Carbone, *Fonti per la Storia del Risorgimento Italiano negli Archivi Nazionale di Parigi* (Rome, 1962), pp. 145–6.

48 Baume biographical information from Roger Cooter's research in the Baume Collection, Manx Museum. Smithson's Spanish stock—thirteen certificates, equalling "350 piastres rente d'Espagne," listed in the inventory made after his death—yielded some 24,127 francs in 1829. SIA, RU 7000, Box 1.

49 Personal communication with Roger Cooter.

50 "If unhappily this depressing Doctrine (which is that of Smithson and of so many others who appear to me superior men) cannot be successfully contest[ed] by men . . . oh well! . . . I wouldn't lose heart because of that, I would think that the genie for good had been put on earth to do constant battle with the genie for evil; to prevent him making Progress and push him back to proper boundaries; I would be happy to be officially appointed in charge of this good work!" Dreams book (November 1824), p. 18; Baume Papers, Manx Museum. Thanks to Roger Cooter.

51 Lester D. Stephens, *Science, Race, and Religion in the American South: John Bachman and the Charleston Circle of Naturalists, 1815–1895* (Chapel Hill, 2000). I am grateful to Professor Stephens for sharing his thoughts and suggestions with me; correspondence with the author, June 2004. Thanks also to Stephen Mackessy for information on early venom studies.

52 It is possible that this work may be another indication of his attention to scientific discourse in the United States; in 1822, the same year Smithson's arsenic paper was published, the *Technical Repository* reprinted Benjamin Silliman's article from the *American Journal of Science and Arts* (vol. 3), entitled "On the Tests for Arsenic." It opens, "It is a question very interesting to Medical jurisprudence, whether there is any test for arsenic, which can be implicitly relied on, to such an extent as to justify, on that ground alone, the condemnation of an accused person." The article discusses the tests of a Dr. T. D. Porter, who was a faculty member of the University of South Carolina and once a pupil of Silliman's. His "experiments appear, then, to throw still greater suspicion on the infallibility of tests for arsenic, and, are worthy of being repeated." Perhaps Smithson took this as an invitation. *Technical Repository*, vol. 1, no. 82.

53 Smithson's published papers are collected in William J. Rhees, ed., "The Scientific Writings of James Smithson," *Smithsonian Miscellaneous Collections* 21 (Washington, 1881).

54 Nicolaas Rupke, *The Great Chain of History: William Buckland and the English School of Geology* (Oxford, 1983), pp. 42–63.

55 John C. Thackray, ed., *To See the Fellows Fight: Eye Witness Accounts of the Meetings of the Geological Society of London and its Club, 1822–1868* (British Society for the History of Science monograph no. 12, 2003), p. 2.

56 Rupke, *The Great Chain of History*, pp. 44–9.

57 Smithson, "Some Observations on Mr. Penn's Theory Concerning the Formation of the Kirkdale Cave," *Annals of Philosophy* (1824).

58 Smithson, "An Account of an Examination of Some Egyptian Colors," *Annals of Philosophy* (1824).

59 Honoré de Balzac, *Peau de Chagrin* (tr. *The Wild Ass's Skin* by Herbert Hunt (Penguin, 1977)), p. 41.

60 Smithson to Lord Holland, November 22, 1805; BL Add MS 51823, ff. 258–9.

61 Balzac, *The Wild Ass's Skin*, p. 42. One of Smithson Tennant's friends, for whom he was the executor and beneficiary, enclosed a passage from Pindar's *Odes* in with his will: "In the paths of dangerous fame / Trembling cowards never tread; / Yet since all of mortal frame / Must be numbered with the dead, / Who in dark inglorious shade / Would his useless life consume / And with deedless years decay'd / Sink unhonour'd to the tomb? / I that shameful lot disdain / I this doubtful list will prove."

62 Dickenson wrote his will at Paris on July 17, 1819; he died May 22, 1820. Smithson probated the will on September 16, 1820; TNA: PRO PROB 11/1634. The freezing of the Seine is mentioned in a letter Chaptal wrote to Bentham, on January 12, 1820; a precis of the letter, listed in a sale catalogue, is found in the Chaptal dossier at the Archives de l'Académie des Sciences, Paris.

63 Louis Jebb searched for Dickenson's tomb at Père Lachaise in August 2003, but the tombs in the area were so deteriorated as to be unidentifiable. Charles Read, "La sepulture des protestants étrangers," *Bulletin de la Société du Protestantisme Français* (1887), t. xxxv.

64 A list was made of eight letters written by Smithson which were presented in the 1831 court case. Among them were letters from Smithson to Henry James Dickenson on July 4, 1822, and to Henry James Hungerford on n.d. [postmark October 1825], March 22 and September 16, 1826; TNA: PRO TS/11/623/2012. Smithson's friend John Guillemard confirmed that it was Smithson who had ordered the nephew to adopt the name Hungerford; Guillemard to Richard Rush, July 1, 1837; Rush Family Papers, Princeton.

12. London: The Will, 1825–1829

1 William Buckland to Georges Cuvier, March 26, 1825; Fonds Cuvier, 3247, item 3, Institut de France.

2 Victor Hugo told the story of the duke renting the main house on the square across from the Cathedral for the extraordinary sum of 30,000 francs for three days, when the house had been put up for sale before the announcement of the coronation at 10,000 francs. See chapter one, "Reims," in *The Memoirs of Victor Hugo* (New York, 2006). See also "Percy, Hugh (1785–1847)," *Dictionary of National Biography* (London, 1895).

3 Smithson to Jöns Jakob Berzelius, June 6, 1819; Archives of the Royal Swedish Academy of Sciences.

4 Royal Society Club record book, RS Archives. Staunton's villa was Leigh Park, near Portsmouth; the Staunton Papers at Duke University include a list of guests between 1820 and 1858, but it does not feature Smithson. Richard Rush was invited to come for a few weeks in the summer of 1837, when he was in England pursuing the Smithson bequest in the Court of Chancery; the reference to "bachelor's villa" is George Thomas Staunton to Rush, May 25, 1837; Rush Family Papers, Princeton.

5 Smithson's copies of the Egyptian Hall exhibition pamphlet and the Heuland auction catalogue are both in the Smithson Library, SIL.

6 The first sale by "Smithson," on October 15, 1825, was "An Historical painting" by an unknown painter, which sold for £0.5; the second sale on December 14, 1825, was "A Lady reading a letter," by "Hamilton." This last was bought in by the house, for £1.1. Getty Provenance Index Sale Catalogs Database.

7 Dr/427/258, ff. 635 and 639; Royal Bank of Scotland Archives, London. When Richard Rush was in London, 1836–8, pursuing the Smithson bequest at Chancery Court, the solicitors consulted Smithson's accounts at Drummonds "to ascertain whether any drafts had been drawn upon them by the testator, which would tally with the claim brought forward by Mrs. Batut, but found it was the testator's habit to draw only for large sums, and his account proved nothing." Bill of Costs submitted by Clarke, Fynmore & Fladgate, quoted in Rhees, *Documents*, p. 89.

8 James Smithson, "A Method of Fixing Crayon Colors," *Annals of Philosophy* (1825).

9 "When the sole view . . ." is from Smithson's "Some Improvements of Lamps," *Annals of Philosophy* (1822). "In all cases means of economy . . ." is from "An Improved Method of Making Coffee," *Annals of Philosophy* (1823).

10 Colin Russell, *Science and Social Change, 1700–1900* (Macmillan, 1983), pp. 138–46, 155–61. D. S. L. Cardwell, *The Organisation of Science in England* (London, 1972), p. 41.

11 Brougham, *Preliminary Treatise on the Objects, Advantages, and Pleasures of Science* (1826?), quoted in F. A. Cavenagh, "Lord Brougham and the Society for the Diffusion of Useful Knowledge," *The Journal of Adult Education* 4, no. 1 (October 1929), pp. 3–37. See also the excellent article, William L. Bird, Jr., "A Suggestion Concerning James Smithson's Concept of 'Increase and Diffusion,'" *Technology and Culture*, vol. 24, no. 2 (April 1983), pp. 246–55.

12 Ian Britain, "Education," in *An Oxford Companion to the Romantic Age, British Culture 1776–1832*, Ian McCalman, ed. (Oxford, 1999), p. 165.

13 Morris Berman, *Social Change and Scientific Organisation: The Royal Institution, 1799–1844* (Ithaca, NY, 1978), p. 111. Warburton's friendship with Smithson is

indicated in Warburton to Howard, August 4, 1816, Wollaston Papers, Cambridge University Library, Add MS 7736, Box 2.

14 John C. Greene, *American Science in the Age of Jefferson* (Iowa State University Press, 1984), p. 12.

15 William Stanton, "Banks and New World Science," in *Sir Joseph Banks: A Global Perspective*, eds R. E. R. Banks and others (Royal Botanic Gardens, Kew, 1994), pp. 149–50.

16 Tait's *Edinburgh Magazine* (1832), p. 234; quoted in Rhees, *James Smithson and His Bequest*, p. 22.

17 See E. M. Butler, ed., *A Regency Visitor: The English Tour of Prince Meckler-Muskau 1826–28* (London, 1957), quoted in Celina Fox, ed., *London: World City, 1800–1840* (London and New Haven, 1992), p. 20.

18 Quoted in Merrill D. Peterson, *The Jefferson Image in the American Mind* (New York and Oxford, 1960), p. 6.

19 Quoted in Peterson, *The Jefferson Image in the American Mind*, pp. 5–6. I am grateful to David Shayt for his inspiration and conversation on this subject.

20 J. F. C. Harrison, *Quest for the New Moral World: Robert Owen and the Owenites in Britain and America* (New York, 1969). For Goethe see Karl Arndt, ed., *Harmony on the Wabash in Transition* (Worcester, MA, 1982), pp. 795–6. Owen's quote from Gregory Claeys, *Selected Works of Robert Owen* (London, 1997), vol. 4, p. 209. For Maclure and Thomson see H. S. Torrens, "The Geological Work of Gregory Watt, his travels with William Maclure in Italy 1801–02 and Watt's 'proto-Geological' map of Italy of 1804," in *The Origins of Geology in Italy* (Geological Society of America, 2006). Baume biographical material, from the Manx Museum, courtesy of Roger Cooter.

21 Davy to his wife Lady Jane, quoted in David Knight, *Humphry Davy: Science and Power* (Cambridge, 1996), p. 161.

22 Sir Henry Lyons, ed., *The Record of the Royal Society of London* (London, 1940), p. 142. Charles Lyell was not so critical as Davy; he told his sister: "He [Wollaston] has left £2000 to the Royal Society, and £1,000 to the Geological Society, a bequest, as Fitton says, which although of great consequence in itself, will do us more good as showing the deliberate approbation of such a mind." Charles Lyell to his sister Marianne, Rome, January 21, 1829; printed in *Life, Letters and Journals of Sir Charles Lyell, Bart.* (1881). Wollaston's obituary in the *Gentleman's Magazine* asserted that his platinum production alone yielded some £30,000, but some have argued this is much exaggerated, and that his profits were more like £15,000. L. F. Gilbert, "W. H. Wollaston Mss. at Cambridge," *Notes and Records of the Royal Society* 9 (1951–2), pp. 326.

23 Davy's will was published in *The Times*, December 4, 1829, p. 2. Paris, *Life of Davy*. See also John Ayrton Paris, *The Life of Sir Humphry Davy* (London, 1831), 2 vols.

24 Blagden suggested in his diary that Davy had hoped for some bequest: "Davy said, Mr. C. has at least remembered one man of science [i.e. Blagden], in a tone of voice which expressed much." Blagden diary for 1810, Royal Society; quoted in Christa Jungnickel and Russell McCormmach, *Cavendish: The Experimental Life* (Bucknell University Press, 1999); see pp. 493, 502, 504.

25 George E. Ellis, *Memoir of Sir Benjamin Thompson, Count Rumford, with Notices of his Daughter* (Boston, 1871), p. 635.

26 A. H. B., "Francis Douce (1757–1834)," *Dictionary of National Biography* (Oxford, 1973 reprint), vol. 5, p. 1161.

27 Correspondence with Barbara English, author of *Strict Settlement*, spring 2000.

28 Will of Hugh Percy, first Duke of Northumberland, July 4, 1786; TNA: PRO PROB 11/1144.

29 *Plain Advice to the Public, to Facilitate the Making of Their Own Wills* (London, 1826); SIA, RU 7000, Box 2.

30 John Guillemard to Richard Rush, July 4, 1837; Box 13, Rush Family Papers, Princeton.

31 I am very grateful to Roger Cooter for sharing his research on Baume from the Baume papers in the Manx Museum, Isle of Man.

32 A "bond for 20,000 francs dated 8th July 1828 due by Sailly and Soeur of Paris" and also a bill for 2000 francs dated February 8, 1822 are listed in "An Inventory of the Effects left at Genoa by the late James Smithson Esqr with a valuation thereof transmitted by the British consul," undated [1829]; SIA, RU 7000, Box 1.

33 An inventory of Smithson's possessions was made at the time of his death in Genoa by the British consul; SIA, RU 7000, Box 1. Another inventory was made of the belongings in Paris/London, which was submitted as part of the suit Henry James Hungerford pursued to claim his inheritance after Smithson's death. Richard Rush, the American agent who was sent to England to collect the bequest, annotated this second inventory prior to sailing to America with everything in 1838; this list was published in Rhees, *Documents*, vol. 1, pp. 98–9. The inventory does not appear to have been completely accurate, however. The list of Smithson memorabilia on display in the Patent Office in 1855, as part of the National Institute, includes a riding whip, "a sword belt and plume," portable chemistry set, silver plate with the coat of arms of the Northumberland family, and other objects which were not detailed in any previous Smithson inventory; Alfred Hunter's "Popular Catalogue of the Extraordinary Curiosities in the National Institute" (1855), quoted in Rhees, *James Smithson and His Bequest* (1880), pp. 16–17.

34 Entry for May 14, 1824; Paula R. Feldman and Diana Scott-Kilvert, eds, *The Journals of Mary Shelley, 1814–1844* (Oxford, 1987), vol. 2, p. 476.

35 For a detailed discussion of Smithson's connections with Genoa, see Francesca Boschieri, "James Smithson: il mecenate dimenticato," in *Viaggio In Liguria*, vol. 2, no. 1 (Fondazione Regionale Cristoforo Colombo, 2004). Smithson made notes on Genoa in C. M. Dubois-Maisonneuve, *Nouveau voyage de France* (1806), vol. 2, pp. 82–3. Smithson Library, SIL. A guidebook of 1830 explained: "Genoa is generally healthy, but the winter is severe, and the neighbouring mountains are covered with snow for a long period. It is by no means a place for an individual threatened with pulmonary or cutaneous complaints, or for an invalid; indeed it has few or no inducements as a place of long residence for any one who visits Italy either for health or pleasure." William Cathcart Boyd, M.D., *A Guide and Pocket Companion Through Italy* (London, 1830), pp. 279–80.

36 Sandro Doldi, *Scienza e Technica in Liguria dal Settecento all'Ottocento* (Genoa, 1984), p. 46. Batt in a letter to Sir Joseph Banks referred to "the chemical Mr. Macie (who analysed the Tabaschir)." February 7, 1803; Sutro Library, California.

37 Quoted in Robert Perceval Graves, *Life of Sir William Rowan Hamilton* (Dublin, 1882), vol. 1, p. 381.

38 Thomas Thomson, *History of Chemistry* (London, 1831), vol. 2, p. 151; quoted in Pierre Lemay and Ralph Oesper, "Claude Louis Berthollet (1748–1822)," *Journal of Chemical Education* (May 1946), p. 235.

39 Report of "J.B." to the Superintendent of the Consular Service and Report of the Consulate to the Attorney General of Genoa, quoted in Long and Carmichael, *Smithson and the Smithsonian Story* (New York, 1964), pp. 141–2.

40 *Philosophical Magazine* (1830), vol. vii, p. 42.

41 *Gentleman's Magazine* (1830), pp. 275–6. Smithson's will was probated on December 4, 1829; TNA: PRO PROB 11/1763.
42 *Gentleman's Magazine* (1830), p. 541.

13. America: The Finger of Providence

1 Henry James Hungerford's passport is located in SIA, RU 7000, oversized box.
2 For information about Monsieur Pierre-Claude Aubouin, the master of a pension for young men in Bourg-la-Reine where Henry James Hungerford was lodged, see Charles Oudiette, *Dictionnaire Topographique des Environs de Paris* (Paris, 1817), p. 93. Rhees, *Documents*, vol. 1, p. 8. A calling card for "Henry de la Batut" [n. d.], in the SIA, gives his address as the "Hotel Britannique, rue Louis le Grand, 20." His last address in Paris, according to his passport, was at "Boulevard des Capuchins [sic], no. 15." In Italy Baron Henri de la Batut became Baron Enrico de la Batut. At some point in the nineteenth century, perhaps even at the time of the court case in the late 1830s, some hapless soul misread Enrico as "Eunice." The nephew has been tarred with the name Baron Eunice de la Batut ever since. TNA: PRO TS 11/623/2012.
3 TNA: PRO C 125/V/4. Henry de la Batut or Baron Enrico de la Batut traveled with his servant Auguste Lefevre. He presented himself to the English consul on May 27 and died on June 5. Richard Rush detailed the financial situation of the nephew at the time of his death. Rush Family Papers, Princeton.
4 Clàrke, Fynmore & Fladgate to Aaron Vail, July 21, 1835; printed in Rhees, *Documents*, p. 3.
5 This story is told much more fully in Madge E. Pickard, "Government and Science in the United States: Historical Backgrounds," *Journal of the History of Medicine* (April 1946), pp. 446–81. I have also referred to Margaret C. S. Christman, *1846: Portrait of the Nation* (Smithsonian Institution Press, 1996), pp. 11–24.
6 Aaron Vail to John Forsyth, July 28, 1835; vol. 957A, RG 59, National Archive and Records Administration.
7 Rhees, *Documents*, p. 150.
8 Records of the 24th Congress, April 30, 1836; quoted in Rhees, *Documents*, p. 138.
9 John Claiborne to Martin van Buren, July 27, 1836; Library of Congress; SIA, RU 7000, Box 4.
10 John Forsyth to Richard Rush, July 11, 1836; printed in Rhees, *Documents*, pp. 6–7.
11 See Bradford Perkins, "Richard Rush," *American National Biography Online* (February 2000), and J. H. Powell, *Richard Rush: Republican Diplomat, 1780–1859* (Philadelphia, 1942).
12 In the case at Chancery, Theodore and Mary Ann de la Batut alleged "that the said Testator James Smithson had given them to understand and believe that the sum of £240 per Annum was the half of the Income of the property of the said Henry Lewis Dickinson to which she was entitled under his said Will." TNA: PRO C 38/1714. Rush's statement of the case, made October 1, 1836, and the subsequent opinion of counsel, given November 2, 1836, are printed in Rhees, *Documents*, pp. 10–12.
13 Prince Pückler-Muskau, diary, February 28, 1828; quoted in Celina Fox, ed., *London: World City, 1800–1840* (London and New Haven, 1992), p. 20.
14 Charles Dickens, *Bleak House* (Random House Modern Library edition, 2002), p. 54.
15 Quoted in J. H. Powell's *Richard Rush*, p. 238.

16 I am very grateful to Ronald Graham for all his help with this subject. Richard Rush, "Smithsonian Trust," vol. 1, pp. 46–7; Rush Family Papers, Princeton. In a way, the English government had already taken their cut of the Smithson money. In 1831, during the nephew's case against Drummonds to claim the estate after Smithson's death, it was determined that although Henry James Hungerford was said to be the testator's nephew, the court in fact believed him to be "a Stranger in Blood" to Smithson and thus subjected the estate to a ten-percent legacy duty. Henry James Hungerford v. Charles Drummond, July 9, 1831; TNA: PRO C 33/813, 99909.

17 Richard Rush to Secretary of State John Forsyth, June 9 and June 24, 1837. Quoted in Rhees, Documents, pp. 29–30, 31–3. See also William J. Rhees for the record, February 17, 1892. SIA, RU 7000, Box 4, f. 6.

18 Richard Rush to Secretary of State John Forsyth, April 28, 1837. Quoted in Rhees, Documents, p. 26.

19 General J. D. Evereux to Richard Rush, May 27, 1838; Box 30, Rush Family Papers, Princeton.

20 Richard Rush to Secretary of State John Forsyth, April 24, 1838. Quoted in Rhees, Documents, p. 50.

21 Richard Rush to Colonel Aspinwall, June 16, 1838; SIA, RU 7000, Box 4. Secretary of State John Forsyth, June 13, 1838. Quoted in Rhees, Documents, pp. 61–2.

22 The inventory is undated; it may have been prepared as part of the Chancery Court case that the nephew brought after Smithson's death. Clarke, Fynmore & Fladgate to Richard Rush, July 13, 1838. Quoted in Rhees, Documents, pp. 92–3.

23 For modern equivalents of UK pounds, see Lawrence H. Officer, "What is its relative value in UK pounds?" Economic History Services, October 30, 2004; http://eh.net/hmit/ukcompare. This source also suggests that the equivalent in US dollars would be over $10,500,000, using the consumer price index, or $220,000,000, using the nominal per-capita GDP. Memorandum regarding the Smithson bequest, Edie Hedlin to Jim Hobbins, November 1, 1999; Budget Reference File, Institutional History Division, SIA. The total was later augmented by the repayment of certain charges for freight, insurance, etc., that had been incurred during the prosecution of the claim, so that the trust in the end equaled £106,374, 9s. 7d., or $515.169. Proceedings of Board of Regents, February 1, 1867, printed in Rhees Documents, pp. 130–31; Rhees, "Founding of the Institution," in Goode, ed., History of the Smithsonian Institution (1897), p. 31.

24 Madge Pickard, "Government and Science in the United States," p. 454. Rhees, Documents, pp. 146–63, 336–7.

25 Samuel Gilman Brown, The Works of Rufus Choate, with a memoir of his life (Boston, 1862), vol. 1, p. 101.

26 Rhees, Documents, p. 362. Trevor Levere and Gerald L. E. Turner, eds, Discussing Chemistry and Steam: The Minutes of a Coffeehouse Philosophical Society (Oxford, 2002), p. 22. Seymour S. Cohen, "Thomas Cooper," American National Biography Online (2002).

27 John Quincy Adams was wary of Cooper, whom he called "a man whose very breath is pestilential to every good purpose." Madge Pickard, "Government and Science," p. 454.

28 Consideration in the Senate of Bill S292, February 29, 1839. Rhees, Documents, p. 176.

29 Marc Rothenberg, ed., The Papers of Joseph Henry (Washington, 1992), vol. 6, p. xxvi.

30 Sally Kohlstedt, "A Step toward Scientific Self-Identity in the United States: the Failure of the National Institute, 1844," *Isis*, vol. 62, part 3, no. 213, pp. 339–62.

31 Under the auspices of the National Institute, Francis Markoe and James Dwight Dana looked at the mineral collection. W. R. Johnson examined the papers for his 1844 article on Smithson, which was written with an eye towards making a case for the National Institute as the natural repository of the Smithson monies. Walter R. Johnson, "A Memoir on the Scientific Character and Researches of James Smithson, Esq., F.R.S." (Philadelphia, 1844).

32 George Ord of the Academy of Natural Sciences in Philadelphia to Titian Ramsey Peale, March 16, 1843; Peale MSS, Historical Society of Pennsylvania; quoted in Kohlstedt, "A Step toward Scientific Self-Identity," p. 347.

33 Entries of October 26, 1839, and April 14, 1841; Charles Francis Adams, ed., *Memoirs of John Quincy Adams* (Philadelphia, 1876), vol. 10, pp. 139, 462. This problem was not resolved until the act for the Smithsonian was finally passed, at which time it was agreed that the Smithson fund was to be lent to the Treasury, at a 6 percent annual interest dating from September 1, 1838. The resulting interest, which amounted to some $242,129 was allocated for the construction of the building and other expenses of the Smithsonian, and the 6 percent interest was to be paid out from then on for the Smithsonian's operating budget. Act of Congress passed August 10, 1846 (9 Stat. 102; 20 U.S.C. 41, 50 61).

34 Quoted in Madge Pickard, "Government and Science," p. 468. See also Rhees, *Documents*, pp. 276–319.

35 Rhees, *Documents*, pp. 335–49.

36 Robert Owen, *Millennial Gazette* (London, May 15, 1856), pp. 21–3; copy in SIA, RU 7000, Box 4.

37 Rhees, *Documents*, p. 428.

38 August 10, 1846, diary entry, quoted in Wilcomb E. Washburn, *The Great Design: Two Lectures on the Smithson Bequest by John Quincy Adams* (Smithsonian Institution Press, 1965), p. 28.

39 The account of the first years of the Smithsonian is superbly told in the introductions to *The Papers of Joseph Henry*, vols 6 and 7. I am very grateful to Kathy Dorman and Marc Rothenberg of the Henry Papers for their discussions with me.

40 Henry to Alexander Dallas Bache, September 5, 1846; *The Papers of Joseph Henry*, vol. 6, p. 494.

41 His close friend and advocate Alexander Dallas Bache, on the board of regents, assured him that the position of secretary would be "most favorable for carrying out your great designs in regard to American science. . . . Come you must for your country's sake." Bache to Henry, December 4, 1846; *Papers of Joseph Henry*, vol. 6, pp. 587–8.

42 *Smithsonian Annual Report of 1872*, p. 8.

43 Pamela M. Henson, "A National Science and a National Museum," *Proceedings of the California Academy of Sciences*, vol. 55, supplement 1, no. 3, pp. 45–6.

44 Robert H. Bremmer, *American Philanthropy* (Chicago, 1988), pp. 49–51.

45 Levi Woodbury, "The Remedies for Certain Defects in American Education," in *The Writings of Levi Woodbury* (Boston, 1852), vol. 3, p. 73.

46 Details on the residual legacy are contained in Rhees, *James Smithson & His Bequest*, p. 24; Rhees, *Documents*, pp. 126–7. The U.S. consul in Genoa, looking over the history of the Smithson bequest in 1904, wrote to Smithsonian Secretary Samuel P. Langley: "Have you happened to notice, by the way . . . what a good thing the Smithsonian chanced to make out of the trust sum . . .? Thus the La Batuts

have not been an unmixed evil." William Henry Bishop to Langley, July 16, 1904. SIA, RU 7000, Box 6.

47 Emma Kerby de la Batut to General Noyes, U.S. minister in Paris, February 28, 1881; SIA, RU 7000, Box 6. The translations of this and other La Batut letters were done at the Smithsonian in the nineteenth century.

48 Thomas Donaldson to Langley, April 16, 1893. SIA, RU 7000, Box 4.

49 La Batut's letter to the Smithsonian was dated February 9, 1879; it and other La Batut material, including nineteenth-century English translations, are located in SIA RU 7000, Box 4.

50 Melville Bell Grosvenor, "How James Smithson came to rest in the institution he never knew," *Smithsonian Magazine* (January 1976), pp. 30–35.

51 Robert V. Bruce, *Bell: Alexander Graham Bell and the Conquest of Solitude* (Cornell University Press, 1990), pp. 362, 376–7. Alexander Graham Bell to Edwin A. Grosvenor, February 1, 1904; Container 285, Bell Papers, Manuscript Division, Library of Congress (LC).

52 Copies of the editorial are located in SIA, RU 7000, Box 7.

53 Bell notes on Eden Palace Hotel, Genoa, paper, December 30, 1903; LC, Bell Papers, Container 287.

54 SIA, RU 7000, Box 6.

55 Bell recounted all the difficulties to Langley, February 10, 1904; a copy of the letter is in SIA, RU 7000, Box 7. Regarding the removal of the tomb itself, see Bell to J. B. Henderson, July 27, 1904; and other letters in RU 7000, Box 7.

56 William Henry Bishop to Alexander Graham Bell, February 17, 1904; LC, Bell Papers, Container 285.

57 Bell diary, December 31, 1903; LC, Bell Papers, Container 287.

58 The *Princess Irene* was met by the U.S. dispatch boat *Dolphin* as it was coming into harbor at Hoboken, New Jersey; Smithson's remains carried on to Washington on the Navy ship, accompanied by Bell (Mrs. Bell had debarked in New Jersey and made her way home overground). Melville Bell Grosvenor, "How James Smithson came to rest in the institution he never knew," *Smithsonian Magazine* (January 1976), pp. 30–35.

59 Richard E. Stamm, "Smithson's Personal Effects, Proposed Memorials, and Crypt," unpublished paper, 1995.

Epilogue 1832

1 George A. Foote, "The Place of Science in the British Reform Movement, 1830–1850," *Isis* 42 (1951), pp. 192–208.

2 Hungerford's half-brother, Georges Henri de la Batut, who gave the Smithsonian a number of items of Smithson memorabilia in the late nineteenth century, wrote that he was also "sending a passport made out in the name of my half brother, of whom I have only a few sketch books." The whereabouts of the sketchbooks now are unknown. G. H. La Batut to Pres. Dir. of the Smithsonian, December 12, 1877; SIA, RU 7000, Box 4.

3 Smithson in fact died on June 27, and his age was approximately sixty-four, not seventy-five.

4 When Langley got home he wrote a memorandum: "What is completely lacking, however, is that evidence of continued care which should be found about the last resting place of any one whose memory is honored, and whose grave is not forgotten by the living. . . . There is nothing whatever about the tomb to indicate that he is the founder of the Smithsonian Institution . . ." September 14, 1891; SIA, RU

7000, Box 6. Langley commissioned a young American artist William Ordway Partridge to design a panel commemorating Smithson's legacy. Three copies were made: one for the church in Genoa, one for the gravesite, and one to be placed in Pembroke College, Oxford. The Italian ones were stolen shortly after their installation, the Pembroke one can still be seen in the main courtyard of the college. Richard E. Stamm, "Smithson's Personal Effects, Italian Grave Site, Proposed Memorials, and Crypt Designs," unpublished manuscript, April 1995.

5 *New-York American*, January 26, 1830.

6 Lt. Col. Pinkney, of the North American Native Rangers, *Travels through the South of France in 1807 and 1808 by a route never before performed, made by permission of the French government* (London, 1814), p. 69, Smithson Library SIL.

7 Smithson to Lord Holland, November 22, 1805, BL Add MS 51823, ff. 258–9.

Picture Credits

Illustrations in the Text

The great hall of the Smithsonian building, c. 1867. (*Courtesy of the Smithsonian Institution Archives, Record Unit 95, Photograph Collection, 1850s– , Neg. # MAH-60144A*)

The regents' room, c. 1857. (*Courtesy of the Smithsonian Institution Archives, Record Unit 95, Photograph Collection, 1850s– , Neg. # 2005-10436*)

Weston, near Bath, by Samuel Hieronymus Grimm, 1789. (*Copyright © The British Library, all rights reserved, Add MS 15547, f. 115*)

Engraving of the first Duke of Northumberland, after a pastel by Hugh Douglas Hamilton. (*Courtesy of the Smithsonian Institution Archives, Record Unit 95, Photograph Collection, 1850s– , Neg. # 91-6951*)

Doctor Johnson at Pembroke College, Oxford, 1784, by James Roberts. (*This image forms part of a research program coordinated by the University of Oxford and has been supplied under license by Isis Innovation Ltd. © Isis Innovation Limited 2006*)

Fingal's Cave, Staffa, from Faujas de St. Fond's *A Journey through England and Scotland to the Hebrides in 1784*. (*Courtesy of Smithsonian Institution Libraries, Washington, D.C.*)

Faujas' tour stops at a Druidical circle, from Faujas' *A Journey . . . to the Hebrides in 1784*. (*Courtesy of Smithsonian Institution Libraries, Washington, D.C.*)

Prince Lee Boo, engraving by T. Kirk. (*Courtesy of Southwark Local Studies Library*)

The meeting room of the Royal Society at Somerset House. (© *The Royal Society*)

"The Manner of Passing Mount Cenis," by George Keate, 1755. (© *Copyright the Trustees of the British Museum*)

Joseph Priestley as "Dr. Phlogiston." (© *Copyright the Trustees of the British Museum*)

Luigi Galvani's "animal electricity" experiments. (*Science Museum / Science and Society Picture Library*)

Gillray caricature of C. J. Fox, 1795. (*National Portrait Gallery, London*)

Members of the Society of the Dilettanti, 1777, mezzotint engraving by William Say, after a painting by Sir Joshua Reynolds. (*National Portrait Gallery, London*)

Frontispiece from A. J. Garnerin's *Air Balloon and Parachute*, 1802. (*Courtesy of Smithsonian Institution Libraries, Washington D.C.*)

The Hungerford chapel at Salisbury Cathedral, by J. C. Schnebbelie, 1788. (*Reproduced by permission of Wiltshire Archaeological and Natural History Society*)

Vivant Denon in Kassel, 1807, by Benjamin Zix. (*Réunion des musées nationaux / Art Resource, NY*)

The harbor at Tönning, 1805. (*Courtesy of Gesellschaft für Tönninger Stadtgeschichte e.V.*)

William Buckland entering Kirkdale Cave. (*Oxford University Museum of Natural History*)

Frontispiece from William Bullock's *Descriptive Catalogue of the Exhibition entitled Ancient and Modern Mexico*, 1824. (*Courtesy of Smithsonian Institution Libraries, Washington D.C.*)

Henry James Hungerford. (*James Smithson Collection, Division of Politics & Reform, National Museum of American History, Smithsonian Institution. Courtesy of Smithsonian Institution Archives, Record Unit 95, Photograph Collection, 1850s– , Neg. # 2002-12209*)

"Distinguished Men of Science Living in 1807–08." (© *The Royal Society*)

"A Chancery Suit!" Anon., 1828. (© *Copyright the Trustees of the British Museum*)

William Henry Bishop at Smithson's exhumation, photographed by Mrs. Alexander Graham Bell, 1903. (*Courtesy of Smithsonian Institution Archives, Record Unit 95, Photograph Collection, 1850s- , Neg. # 71-57-2*)

Design for a Mausoleum for Smithson, 1904, by Henry Bacon. (*Courtesy of Smithsonian Institution Archives, Record Unit 92, Prints and Drawings, 1840- , Neg. # 90-16191*)

Smithson's Tomb in Genoa, engraving. (*Courtesy of Smithsonian Institution Archives, Record Unit 95, Photograph Collection, 1850s- , Neg. # 82-3202*)

Plate Section

Portrait of a Mother and Child, by George Romney. (*Private collection*)

London, a View of Northumberland House, looking eastward, by Canaletto. (*Collection of the Duke of Northumberland, Alnwick Castle*)

Hugh Percy, the first Duke of Northumberland, by James Barry. (*Collection of the Duke of Northumberland, Syon House*)

Margaret Marriott, by Angelica Kauffman. (*Courtesy of the Royal Pavilion, Libraries & Museums, Brighton & Hove*)

Portrait of Hugh, Lord Warkworth, later second Duke of Northumberland, and the Rev. Jonathan Lippyat, his tutor, by Nathaniel Dance. (*Collection of the Duke of Northumberland, Syon House*)

Portrait of Lord Algernon Percy, later first Earl of Beverley, by Pompeo Batoni. (*Collection of the Duke of Northumberland, Alnwick Castle*)

James Louis Macie, 1786, by James Roberts [Smithson in his Oxford robes]. (*National Portrait Gallery, Smithsonian Institution*)

Henry Louis Dickenson, 1805, by Jacob Spornberg. (*James Smithson Collection, Division of Politics & Reform, National Museum of American History, Smithsonian Institution. Courtesy of Smithsonian Institution Archives, Record Unit 95, Photograph Collection, 1850s- , Neg. # 82-3147*)

Paolo Andreani's balloon ascent, 1784, by Francesco Battaglioli. (*Courtesy of the Museo della Società, Gallarate*)

MacNab's Hut, from Faujas' *A Journey . . . to the Hebrides in 1784*. (*Courtesy of Smithsonian Institution Libraries, Washington, D.C.*)

A salt mine in Cheshire, 1814, a colored aquatint engraving by J. Bluck, after an original work by R. H. Marten. (*Science Museum/ Science and Society Picture Library*)

Portrait of a Young Man in Florence, by Louis Gauffier, 1796. (© *Private Collection/Giraudon/The Bridgeman Art Library*)

Elizabeth, Lady Webster, in Naples, by Robert Fagan, 1793. (*Private Collection*)

The Vesuvius eruption of 1794, by Giovanni Battista Lusieri. (*Copyright © The British Library, all rights reserved, Tab.435.a.15.(1)*)

"Scientific Researches! New Discoveries in Pneumakicks! Or An Experimental Lecture on the Powers of Air," by James Gillray, 1802. (*Copyright © the Trustees of the British Museum*)

The fire of 1865 at the Smithsonian, January 24, photographed and retouched by Alexander Gardner. (*Courtesy of the Smithsonian Institution Archives, Record Unit 95, Photograph Collection, 1850s- , Neg. # 37082*)

James Smithson, by Henri Johns, 1816. (*National Portrait Gallery, Smithsonian Institution*)

Endpapers

The will of James Smithson. (*The National Archives of the UK, PROB 10/5127*)

Acknowledgments

The path to Smithson all but vanished long ago. It was not clear at the outset where even to start, and I am grateful to many friends and colleagues and family for their help and encouragement. Pam Henson, head of Institutional History at the Smithsonian, whose idea this book was, has helped in countless ways, reading the manuscript at different stages and assisting with grant applications, documents, and illustrations. Hugh Torrens generously shared all that he had gathered on Smithson, much of which I would not have found on my own. Judd Stitziel was the best reader one could ever wish for, and he also translated endless amounts of German for me. Steven Turner deciphered the secrets of Smithson's laboratory world and patiently explained them in layman's terms. Roy S. Clarke, Jr., did the same for the world of meteorites, as well as commenting on the entire manuscript, and his enthusiasm and support for this project have made all the difference. Vyvyan Lyle poured her brilliant energy into exploring many of the enduring mysteries of Smithson's family story. Louis Jebb took me tomb-hunting for Hungerfords and did so much more besides, searching for Henry Louis Dickenson at Père Lachaise and bringing his editorial skills to bear on an unwieldy draft of chapter one. And without Will Palin this would have been a much more lugubrious book.

I am grateful especially to the friends and colleagues who read and commented on all or parts of the book, especially William St. Clair, Elizabeth Kostova, Peter Clasen, Nadja Durbach, Cynthia Field, Paul Pohwat, Jenny Allen, David Clasen, and Laura Wexler. And thanks especially to Rodolph de Salis for his help fact-checking footnotes, tracking down elusive sources, and researching Hungerfordiana.

At the Smithsonian, I owe many people thanks for their help and support, especially Kelly Crawford, Leslie Overstreet and Daria Wingreen, Rick Stamm, Marc Pachter, Laura Brouse-Long, Tom Crouch, David Shayt, Ellen Miles, Larry Bird, Kathy Dorman, Marc Rothenberg, and Cesare Marino.

Thanks also to Peter Barber, Simon Werrett, John Detloff, David Aubin, and Eliza Byard, for many stimulating conversations; Susan Bennett, for sharing her work on Georgiana Keate Henderson with me; Christopher Woodward, for talk of Holland House and sons with chips on their shoulders; Ronnie Graham, for all his help interpreting the case in chancery; Lady Caroline Percy, who showed me Syon; Major David Gape and his daughter; Brian Wilson, for all his help with Pembroke matriculations; Roger Cooter for generously sharing his work on Baume; and Sue Palmer, for many wonderful discoveries.

It will be clear from the notes how much I owe to the archivists and librarians who have assisted me in my research. I have thanked many directly in the relevant citation but extend special thanks to all the staff at the Smithsonian Archives; Neil Chambers and the Joseph Banks Archive Project at the Natural History Museum, London; Jane Cunningham of the Photographic Survey at the Courtauld Institute of Art; Arnold Hunt and Matthew Shaw at the British Library; Joanna Corden and staff at the Royal Society; Frank James at the Royal Institution; the archivists at Pembroke College, Oxford; Clare Baxter at Alnwick Castle; Roy Goodman and Rob Cox at the American Philosophical Society; Sarah Millard at the Bank of England; and Tonino Caruso at the Collegio Nazareno in Rome.

Thanks to the Piegaya brothers at the Royal Victoria in Pisa, who took such good care of me, as they do their guest registers filled with the signatures of Queen Victoria, Charles Dickens, Virginia Woolf, and other latter-day Grand Tourists. Thanks to Helmut Wrunsch of the Gesellschaft für Tönninger Stadtgeschichte e.V. for his generous help investigating Smithson in Tönning. Thanks to my friend Patrik Ohlson for his help tracking down the Holtermann connection in Sweden, to Massimo Pellegrini for his research on Smithson's seal, and to Francesca Boschieri for all her work on Smithson in Genoa. Thanks to Alex Kidson for his help with research on the Romney portrait. Many thanks to Luda Smikovskaya for her efforts to help me find the original Gauffier painting, and to Lucia Tonini in Florence, Anna Ottani Cavina in Bologna, John Lloyd in London, and Amy Ballard and her legion of St. Petersburg contacts for the same. Special thanks too to the graphologist JoNeal Scully, who generously analyzed a Smithson letter in her own time, and whose insights into Smithson gave me confidence to rely on my own.

James Smithson's story could not really have been told if it were not for the scholarship in the history of science and the culture of the English Enlightenment that has been advanced in the last generation. I am indebted to the work of Jan Golinski, Isaac Kramnick, Trevor Levere, Maurice Crosland, the late Roy Porter, Hugh Torrens, Matthew Eddy, David Knight, Brian Dolan, and others. My woeful science literacy, while a pretty standard product of a liberal arts education in late twentieth-century America, has hardly been up to some of the challenges Smithson's life story poses, and I take full responsibility for the shortcomings of the book in that regard. I find some consolation in the fact that Smithson has not much caught the attention of historians of science (the *Dictionary of Scientific Biography* characterized his contributions as "minimal"), but I hope that by excavating Smithson's story he might now be drawn back into the narrative of the late English Enlightenment and his experiments enjoy the scrutiny of those scholars concerned with the birth of mineralogy and modern chemistry.

I am very grateful for grants and fellowships from the following institutions, which enabled me to carry out the research for this book, and to George L. Hersey, John Newman, and Steven Parissien for supporting my applications: the British Academy for a Visiting Fellowship; the Map Library of the British Library for the Helen Wallis Fellowship; the Max Planck Institut für Wissenschaftgeschichte in Berlin and Dr. Ursula Klein's group in particular for a working environment I shall probably spend my entire life trying to replicate; the Center of American Overseas Research Centers and the American Academy in Rome for a CAORC Multi-Country Fellowship; the American Philosophical Society for a Franklin Library Fellowship; the Trustees of the London Library for assistance with membership; the Institute for Historical Research's Center for Metropolitan History for granting me Honorary Fellow status for the summer of 2002; the Smithsonian's Office of Fellowships and Grants for a Short-Term Visitor's Fellowship; and the Smithsonian Archives' Institutional History Division, for according me research associate status, logistical support, and several honoraria.

I would need another ten pages to thank all the people who have housed and fed and otherwise sustained me during the *anni di vagabondaggio* that comprised the search for Smithson. I am especially grateful to my family, and to all the Whittingtons, Elliot, Viva, Denise, Walter and Ray, Dino and Clare, the Kostovi, Jessica, Kate, Melanie, the Zukerbergs, the Davids, Jamie, Dan and Theresa, Julian and Cheryl, Juliet, Keith, Lucy and Mark, Rosetta and Gael, Esther, Laurie O., Niccolò and Piccarda, Joan, Polly, Sarah Meschutt and the much missed David, Michael Goldman, and Nicholas Scheetz.

Lastly, I owe many thanks to Bonnie Nadell and Mary Clemmey, who did so much to find this book the perfect home at Bloomsbury. Bill Swainson was my ideal editor, and I am grateful too to Emily Sweet for her outstanding editorial work, to Reginald Piggott for the beautiful maps and to Leslie Robinson for solving so well the challenge of depicting Smithson's family tree. Many thanks too to Colin Dickerman, Miles Doyle, Sarah Marcus, Sarah Morris, Richard Collins, Sarah Barlow, David Atkinson, and others at Bloomsbury who shepherded the manuscript through production.

Index

INDEX

A NOTE ON THE AUTHOR

Heather Ewing is a graduate of Yale University and the Courtauld Institute of Art. An architectural historian, she has worked for the Smithsonian Museum and the Ringling Museum of Art. *The Lost World of James Smithson* is her first book. She lives in New York.